D1712228

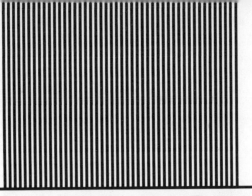

NUTRITION
MANAGEMENT IN
REHABILITATION

Edited by

Deon J. Gines, RD, PhD, LDN

Associate Professor of Nutrition and Dietetics
Louisiana Tech University
Ruston, Louisiana

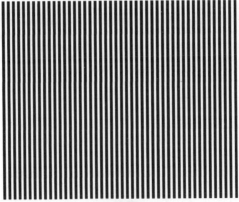

AN ASPEN PUBLICATION®
Aspen Publishers, Inc.
Rockville, Maryland
1990

Library of Congress Cataloging-in-Publication Data

Nutrition management in rehabilitation / edited by Deon J. Gines.
p. cm.
"An Aspen publication."
Includes bibliographical reference.
ISBN: 0-8342-0133-X
1. Dietetics. 2. Diet in disease. 3. Rehabilitation. I. Gines, Deon J.
[DNLM: 1. Dietetics. 2. Rehabilitation. WB 320 N976]
RM217.N76 1990
362. 1'76—dc20
DNLM/DLC
for Library of Congress
89-18526
CIP

The authors have made every effort to ensure the accuracy of the information herein, particularly with regard to drug selection and dose. However, appropriate information sources should be consulted, especially for new or unfamiliar drugs or procedures. It is the responsibility of every practitioner to evaluate the appropriateness of a particular opinion in the context of actual clinical situations and with due consideration to new developments. Authors, editors, and the publisher cannot be held responsible for any typographical or other errors found in this book.

Editorial Services: Ruth Bloom

Library of Congress Catalog Card Number: 89-18526
ISBN: 0-8342-0133-X

Printed in the United States of America

1 2 3 4 5

Table of Contents

Contributors

Norma F. Berry, PhD, RD
Associate Professor of Nutrition and
  Dietetics
College of Human Ecology
Louisiana Tech University
Ruston, Louisiana

Fredda Blanchard-Fields, PhD
Associate Professor of Psychology
Louisiana State University
Baton Rouge, Louisiana

Maria Ferraco, RD
Consultant Nutritionist
Verona, Pennsylvania

Donna L. Frankel, MD, RD
Clinical Assistant Professor
Department of Rehabilitation Medicine
School of Medicine
University of Washington
Seattle, Washington

Deon J. Gines, RD, PhD, LDN
Associate Professor of Nutrition and
  Dietetics
Louisiana Tech University
Ruston, Louisiana

Carolyn Gleason, MS, RD
Seattle-King County Department of Public
  Health
WIC Administration
Seattle, Washington

William Drew Gouvier, PhD
Assistant Professor of Psychology
Louisiana State University
Baton Rouge, Louisiana

Margaret Howison, BS
Occupational Therapist
Feeding Program
The Pennsylvania State University
Elizabethtown Hospital and Rehabilitation
  Center
Elizabethtown, Pennsylvania

Daniel H. Ingram, MEd
Developmental Psychologist
Milton S. Hershey Medical Center
The Pennsylvania State University
Department of Psychiatry
Hershey, Pennsylvania

Carol Kaltreider, RN
Feeding Program
The Pennsylvania State University
Elizabethtown, Pennsylvania
Feeding Resource Person
Lancaster Cleft Palate Clinic
Lancaster, Pennsylvania

Betty Whittle Kozlowski, PhD
Chief of Nutrition and Associate Professor
The Nisonger Center for Mental
  Retardation and Developmental
  Disabilities
Department of Human Nutrition and Food
  Management
The Ohio State University
Columbus, Ohio

Phyllis Ann Mandella, RD
Director of Nutritional Services
Rehabilitation Institute of Pittsburgh
Pittsburgh, Pennsylvania

Margaret J. Morris, RD
Director of Nutritional Care
Feeding Program
The Pennsylvania State University
Elizabethtown Hospital and Rehabilitation
Center
Elizabethtown, Pennsylvania

Charles A. Nichter, MD
Director of Pediatric Rehabilitation
Assistant Professor
Department of Pediatrics
Hershey Medical Center
The Pennsylvania State University
Hershey, Pennsylvania

Randi Yarmeisch O'Brien, RD
Institutional Sales Representative
Bristol Myers Institutional Products
Evansville, Indiana

Lynda Suhrer Roussel, MS
Department of Psychology
Louisiana State University
Baton Rouge, Louisiana

Janel Schmitz, LRD
Clinical Dietitian
Medcenter One Nutrition Services
Bismarck, North Dakota

John R. Schweitzer, PhD
Senior Rehabilitation Technologist
Center for Rehabilitation Science
 and Biomedical Engineering
Louisiana Tech University
Ruston, Louisiana

Madeline Uddo-Crane, MS
Psychology Intern
Lousiana State University
Baton Rouge, Louisiana

Patricia Giblin Wolman, EdD, RD
Associate Professor of Human Nutrition
Winthrop College
Rock Hill, South Carolina

Kathleen Wreford, RD
Clinical Dietitian
Dietetics Department
Rehabilitation Institute of Detroit
Detroit, Michigan

Sharon Yankelson, RD, LD
Chief Clinical Dietitian
Healthcare Rehabilitation Center
Austin, Texas

Preface

As the editor of this book, I had the challenge and pleasure of defining, planning, and participating in writing the first book about the place of nutrition in rehabilitation settings. Because of the rehabilitation experience of each of the contributors, they shared the knowledge that there is a real, immediate need to have this work available for dietetic practitioners, educators, and other professionals.

Nutrition Management in Rehabilitation is designed around these needs. It is the only book that provides background information and applications specific to nutrition and dietetics about a diverse set of diseases and related problems in rehabilitation. Dietetic and other rehabilitation practitioners, students, and educators will find it to be an invaluable tool.

Nutrition plays a strong part in rehabilitation services. Because of the philosophy of rehabilitation—regaining abilities, slowing degeneration, avoiding complications—nutrition is vital. Nutrition assessment, planning for provision of appropriate foods and textures, counseling and education, long-term follow-up and evaluation, and integration with community services are all important.

AUDIENCES

Rehabilitation is the newest and most rapidly expanding area of practice in dietetics. Dietetic practitioners are responsible for nutrition services in a large and increasing number of institution-based rehabilitation units, as well as free-standing rehabilitation centers. Dietetic educators are incorporating information about rehabilitation in coursework and in practice settings. The American Dietetic Association has identified rehabilitation as being part of the role of the entry-level dietitian and has included it in requirements for approval of education programs.

Rehabilitation practice is necessarily team-oriented. Whereas other medical areas may use a team approach, in rehabilitation teams are a must. Skills and training overlap among team members; sharing, negotiation, and mutual support are important. The physician (physiatrist), nurse, occupational therapist, physical therapist, recreational therapist, psychologist, and social worker need adequate nutrition training, too.

CONTENT

More than any other area of practice, rehabilitation is extremely diverse—in its client characteristics as well as in the multitude of types of diseases which it encompasses. Rehabilitation serves persons with traumatic injury such as spinal cord or head injury; it addresses individuals with muscular dystrophy, cerebral palsy, and multiple sclerosis; persons with chronic diseases such as arthritis and stroke are also part of this fascinating field. Clients are young and old, men and women, students and retirees.

Nutrition Management in Rehabilitation covers selected topics, chosen because of their prevalence or close link with nutrition and dietetics. No one book can cover rehabilitation in a completely comprehensive manner.

Finding and utilizing current information about all the different aspects of nutrition and rehabilitation are challenging, even for the full-time rehabilitation specialist. For an educator or practitioner with responsibilities for several courses or medical units, it may become impossible. This book provides the foundation for work and study in the area.

Each chapter includes background information and literature review including an excellent bibliography. In addition, each topic is considered from the perspective of current practice. As the authors are primarily registered dietitians and working team members, the application to nutrition practice is strong.

For the practitioner, the chapters can be utilized individually to gain insight about a particular topic. For an educator, the chapters can also be organized in various sequences to provide the foundation for a course of study in nutrition and rehabilitation.

Deon J. Gines

Acknowledgments

I would like to thank each of the contributors for sharing their experience, knowledge, and judgment with the readers. Present and future rehabilitation efforts have a positive impact on individuals and our society as a whole. This book will assist in expanding that positive outcome.

Chapter 1

Introduction to Nutrition and Rehabilitation

Deon J. Gines

Rehabilitation is a unique and relatively new area of practice in dietetics. Free-standing rehabilitation centers are appearing all over the country, and many hospitals and clinics are also opening units that specialize in rehabilitation. Rehabilitation specialists help persons gain, or regain physical, mental, and/or social capabilities. The primary focus of efforts in rehabilitation is on improved function of the individual client, in contrast to a cure. Independent living for each client is the objective.

Injuries or diseases in the rehabilitation arena are manageable: the client is stabilized after a traumatic head or spinal cord injury; there are treatments to slow the progress of a degenerative disease; there are no cures. Rehabilitation encompasses traumatic injuries such as head injury and spinal cord injury, as well as genetic/congenital diseases such as Prader-Willi syndrome and muscular dystrophy and chronic diseases such as arthritis and stroke.

In rehabilitation the major goal is for the client to reach and maintain an optimal level of functioning. The next goal is to prevent the development of any complications. Complications, such as urinary tract infection in a person with a spinal cord injury, may cause the client to lose the ability to function and may lead to death.

The clients who are seen in the rehabilitation setting have more diverse backgrounds than in most other areas of dietetics specialization. Persons with these impairments are of all ages, races, sexes, and levels of physiological functioning. Management is complicated since all aspects of the client's life have to be considered in evaluation and treatment of the problem.

Current and future economic resources must be considered in setting goals since the conditions last a lifetime and are probably expensive and difficult to treat. Social supports and resources are also critical to increase the independence of a disabled person.

Because of the diversity and complexity of care, a team approach is essential. The team includes the physician, nurse, speech therapist, dietitian, and physical therapist, as well as social workers, psychologists, occupational and recreational therapists, medical librarian, and rehabilitation counselor.

The receiver of services is always a client (rather than a patient), with the implication that he or she plays an active role in the entire process of rehabilitation. The client helps with setting realistic objectives, decides which options are viable, and participates as fully as possible in implementing the decisions and reaching goals.

The goals for the client are based on input from all members of the team. They must be realistic for each individual. Involvement of the family and other caregivers is crucial to success. Because of the long-term nature and complexity of many of these types of impairments, family members and others frequently have a role in providing care and must be part of an effective planning, implementation, and evaluation process.

Dietitians play a major role in assessment, planning, treatment, and evaluation of care in rehabilitation settings because of their expertise in nutrition. The incidence of malnutrition, in various forms, in the rehabilitation setting has been well documented. It is generally agreed that more than 70% of clients seen have some form of malnutrition. Malnutrition may result from medical complications prior to transfer to the rehabilitation setting, anorexia, nausea, epigastric distress, malabsorption, altered nutritional requirements, poverty and social isolation, alcoholism and drug abuse, maladaptive behavior, depression, altered mental status, motor and perceptual deficits, ignorance, and/or dysphagia.

DEFINITIONS: IMPAIRMENT, DISABILITY, HANDICAP

The terminology of rehabilitation is evolving toward new definitions and usage that help both the client and the provider think of their relationships in more creative ways. The *International Classification of Impairments, Disabilities, and Handicaps* of the World Health Organization (WHO) provides assistance in creating a common understanding of the terms *impairment, disability,* and *handicap:*

- An *impairment* is any permanent or temporary disturbance of the normal structure and/or functioning of the body, including the mind.
- A *disability* is the loss or reduction of functional ability in everyday life and activity, as a result of an impairment.
- A *handicap* is the disadvantage (social or environmental) experienced

as a result of impairment or disability. A handicap reflects the difference between a person's performance and social or personal expectations of behavior.

The WHO concept is that a disease or disorder *may* lead to an impairment, which *may* lead to a disability, which *may* become a handicap. A physical condition or disease is not always a disability. For example, most of us have colds with varying degrees of severity and frequency. We have learned to treat them in a myriad of ways. Usually a cold is not thought of as a disability because it does not generally interfere with our ability to live our lives. Consider vision impairment that requires correction with glasses. Poor vision can restrict driving, reading, and food preparation, among other activities. Many persons wear glasses to correct vision problems without being, or thinking of themselves as being, disabled. The technology of glasses is readily available and inexpensive in most of Western society.

It seems simple to classify persons as to whether or not they have a disease. One either has diabetes mellitus, or one does not. But who has a disability? All persons have some degree of impairment, although they are not necessarily disabled. It is easy to see whether a person is in a wheelchair. But there is a very wide continuum of disabilities ranging from slight vision impairment correctable with ordinary glasses to reduced cardiovascular performance due to obesity to a C5 spinal cord injury resulting in quadriplegia.

At what point does a gradual loss of bone mass result in osteoporosis and then become a disability in terms of everyday functioning or finally a handicap? A person with a high spinal cord injury may be able to attend college if a special wheelchair, eating devices, or other technology is available. Some of the required technology is expensive and may have to be custom designed and produced. Additional costs are incurred with services required for activities of daily living such as dressing, bathing, and transportation.

To know if an impairment will become a disability or handicap, the following questions must be answered:

- How does the person adapt to the condition?
- How effective and costly is the technological support?
- What environmental barriers exist to normal functioning?

If the person with a disability learns to adapt in a positive manner, can afford the technological support that is available, and has few environmental barriers, then a handicap may not exist. On the other hand, if the person is depressed about a spinal cord injury, is not in a position to purchase a modified van to allow for transportation to work, and lives in a city without ramp access to sidewalks and stores, he or she may become handicapped.

In traditional health care settings, professionals tend to think of identifying and meeting needs of individual clients. In rehabilitation settings, many of the clients' needs are outside the control of any one professional. Dimensions of handicaps include degree of physical independence (in activities of everyday living); mobility; occupation (work, school, retirement activities); social integration, including hobbies, clubs, and recreation; and economic self-sufficiency, particularly considering the extra expenses attributable to the disability.

In rehabilitation settings, the health care team is responsible not only for arranging appropriate medical treatment but also for ensuring that the client is helped to overcome related social barriers. Social policy and support are frequently inadequate and lag behind need. Communities provide access to facilities and formulate attitudes regarding employment and social opportunities of persons with disabilities. Work through professional and lay organizations with the objective of impacting on the community as a whole has tremendous potential to remove barriers and reduce or eliminate handicapping conditions that exist in the community. Health promotion and prevention of impairments are part of the overall effort to control disablement.

Community awareness regarding barriers will become more acute. As the population ages and health concerns turn increasingly to chronic diseases, the loss of personal and social potential due to disability will become more and more unacceptable. In an age of scarce resources, the ability of each person to be functional is more and more important. Policy regarding urban design, educational and employment opportunities, transportation, and programs to impact on public attitudes will minimize handicaps.

INFORMATION

The field of rehabilitation has experienced an information explosion during the past decade. Much work is being done to cope with information overload. However, since rehabilitation is so diverse, information is found in many different journals, textbooks, monographs, and clearinghouses and may not be readily identifiable or accessible by the novice. Finding research support for protocols, special adaptive equipment, and even basic descriptions of rare diseases is a professional challenge and requires sophisticated searching. Many professional and lay organizations strive to meet these needs (see Appendix A).

Much of the research is new and has not been repeated with large numbers of subjects. It becomes difficult to apply the information to other groups. As examples, there are no growth standards for persons with traumatic head or spinal cord injuries. There is limited information about what would be considered to be normal laboratory values. Anthropometric techniques frequently do not fit for persons who have unusual body conformation, contractures, or cannot stand.

There is a rich potential for research in nutrition care for the various population groups served in rehabilitation settings. There is a need for development and testing of techniques and protocols for nutrition services in rehabilitation. Data from which to draw norms for standards must be compiled. Research methods to test procedures over long time periods must be devised and applied.

THE ROLE OF THE REGISTERED DIETITIAN IN REHABILITATION

Services in rehabilitation areas are provided over a longer term and may be required during the entire lifetime of the client. Follow-up, monitoring, and evaluation are essential. Selected roles of the registered dietitian include the following:

- comprehensive initial nutrition assessment (dietary, anthropometric, clinical, and physical) and reassessment at appropriate intervals
- prescription of appropriate nutrient intake to meet the individual needs of the client during the initial period of rehabilitation, over the long term, and during periods of acute problems
- feeding assessment and prescription of assistive devices or other technologies to aid in obtaining, preparing, serving, self-feeding, or other food-related tasks
- conferences with the occupational therapist concerning food purchasing, preparation, service, and sanitation needs of the client
- textural and other modifications of foods to meet individual needs, such as in the case of dysphagia
- referrals to, and communication with, home health care agencies, vocational rehabilitation agencies, public health, and other community services
- nutrition education and counseling of both the individual client and family members or other caretakers

- participation in organizations that have as their objective changing social policies and attitudes regarding disability so that the barriers that are not under the control of the individual client can be addressed by the community

BIBLIOGRAPHY

Arego DE, Koch S. Malnutrition in the rehabilitation setting. *Nutr Today.* 1985; 21:28–32.

Frankel DL. Nutrition care of the rehabilitation patient: Comments on activity and needs. *Network.* 1987; 6:5.

Gines DJ, Holliday ME, Erwin K. Nutrition assessment during rehabilitation of the spinal cord injury patient. *Top Clin Nutr.* 1987; 2:39–46.

Gines DJ. Long-term nutrition care for the client with spinal cord injury. *Top Clin Nutr.* 1988; 3:61–69.

Goodwill CJ, Chamberlain MA, eds. *Rehabilitation of the Physically Disabled Adult.* London, England: Croom Helm Sheridan Medical Books; 1988.

World Health Organization. *The International Classification of Impairments, Disabilities, and Handicaps—A Manual of Classification Relating to the Consequences of Disease.* Geneva, Switzerland: World Health Organization; 1980.

Chapter 2

Cerebral Palsy

Betty Whittle Kozlowski

GENERAL DESCRIPTION

Definition, Etiologies, Prevalence

The term *cerebral palsy* is a general designation for disorders of motor control and posture that result from permanent, nonprogressive brain abnormalities originating during prenatal, perinatal, or early childhood phases of development.[1-4] While a multitude of etiologic factors have been identified, the pathogenesis of cerebral palsy continues to be incompletely understood. Events occurring later than the perinatal period, including trauma, infections, toxins, and anoxia, have been estimated to account for approximately 10% of the cases.[4] Commonly described etiologic factors in the prenatal and perinatal periods include prematurity, intracranial hemorrhage, anoxia, toxemia of pregnancy and other maternal conditions, multiple pregnancy, central nervous system malformations, other congenital abnormalities, hereditary/genetic conditions, hyperbilirubinemia, and infections.[1,2] Approximately one third of the cases appear to occur in association with low birth weight.[4] Advances in prenatal and perinatal care have been credited with lowering the incidence of cerebral palsy in developed countries in recent decades. However, survival rates have increased among very low birth weight infants, and varying reports have appeared concerning the rates of severe impairment among that group. Gortmaker and Sappenfield estimated the overall prevalence of cerebral palsy in the United States in 1980 as 2.5 per 1000 persons birth to 20 years of age, placing it seventh in rank among chronic diseases and conditions in children.[5,6] While available data are sketchy regarding life expectancy, it can be expected to vary with the nature and severity of the condition and the quality of services received. Today, most persons with cerebral palsy live to adulthood, and Healy comments that "average longevity" can be expected if comprehensive evaluation, care, and treatment are provided.[3]

Clinical Classifications

Disorders encompassed by the designation *cerebral palsy* vary widely in severity, predominating muscle tone pattern, and distribution of the motor dysfunction throughout the body. The nature and magnitude of the manifestations are influenced by the location, severity, and timing of the insult, with certain types of insults being associated with certain types of cerebral palsy.

The most commonly used clinical classifications of cerebral palsy are based on distribution of the tone and movement disorder. Detailed descriptions of this classification system can be found in many references.[1,2,7] Spasticity, which Healy[3] estimated to be present in about 60% of all cases of cerebral palsy, is characterized by hypertonicity and by stereotyped and limited patterns of movement. Primary topographic distribution patterns include hemiplegia, affecting only one side of the body; diplegia, affecting the total body but with greater involvement in the trunk and lower extremities than in the upper extremities; and quadriplegia, affecting the whole body. Involvement may be mild, moderate, or severe. Dyskinesia refers to involuntary extraneous motor activity. The activity increases with stress or exertion. Athetosis, choreoathetosis, and dystonia are all forms of dyskinesia, with athetosis being the most common. Dystonia often occurs in combination with spasticity. Ataxia, like dystonia, occurs most often in combination with other types of cerebral palsy. It is characterized by wide-based stance and gait, poor walking and standing balance, and uncoordinated movement. Fluctuating muscle tone may prevent patterns of movement from being classified specifically into any one distinct clinical category. Hypotonia, or decreased muscle tone, often appears in infants and young children who later develop spasticity, athetosis, or ataxia. Although the brain abnormalities per se that result in cerebral palsy are nonprogressive, the manifestations often change as persons age. These changes and the occurrence of mixed types of cerebral palsy in many persons complicate diagnosis, assessment, and clinical classification.[1-3,7]

Associated Disorders

Many other disorders or problems frequently appear along with the motor deviations of cerebral palsy. Just as the motor problems vary in magnitude and nature, so, too, do the problems in other areas of functioning. Problems commonly seen include seizures, impairments of vision and hearing, oral-dental disorders, speech problems, sensory impairments, perceptual motor deficits, learning disabilities, and behavior disorders.[1-3,7] Mental retardation appears to be present in approximately 50% or more of persons with cerebral palsy.[3,8]

NUTRITIONAL IMPLICATIONS

Nutritional implications of cerebral palsy are as varied as are other aspects of this group of disorders. For the person with very mild motor deviations and no apparent associated disorders, nutritional needs and risks may be no different than are those of the general population. At the other end of the spectrum is the person with severe motor dysfunction and multiple severe concomitant disorders, for whom the greatest threat to survival may be posed by inadequate nutritional support. As a group, persons with cerebral palsy are at increased risk for nutrition-related problems owing to many complex and interrelated physical, environmental, and psychosocial factors, which can best be addressed through ongoing interdisciplinary assessment and intervention.[9-11]

NUTRITIONAL RISK FACTORS AND COMPLICATIONS

Nutritional risk factors and complications of this population are outlined in Table 2-1. These are described below, beginning with factors related to food availability, continuing with factors related to food intake, and ending with factors related to energy and nutrient needs.

Table 2-1 Nutritional Risk Factors and Complications

- Financial constraints
- Feeding dependence and caregiver characteristics
- Feeding problems
    Oral-sensory-motor
    Behavioral
    Oral-facial
    Nonoral feeding
- Gastrointestinal factors
    Gastroesophageal reflux
    Constipation
- Medical effects
- Difficulties in evaluating growth, physical size, and energy and nutrient needs
    Altered physical size characteristics
    Altered energy needs for activity

Financial Constraints

High health care costs and other constraints on available income may limit resources available for purchasing food or special dietary formulas, feeding equipment, or needed nutrition-related services. Public and private sources of assistance are available, but major gaps in coverage continue to exist. Persons and families likely to be particularly hard hit are those whose incomes are low but in excess of Medicaid limits and those who do not have private insurance coverage.[9,12,13]

Feeding Dependence and Caregiver Characteristics

Dependence on others for feeding is frequently increased by cerebral palsy. Some persons need assistance only with obtaining and/or preparing food, while others are partially or totally dependent on caregivers for all aspects of the feeding process. Oral-motor deviations, difficulty in getting food or feeding equipment to the mouth, difficulty attaining or maintaining body positions needed for mature eating, impaired ambulation, impaired communication skills, and impaired learning are all factors that can contribute to dependence on caregivers to meet nutritional needs. Clues of hunger, thirst, satiety, and food likes and dislikes of the person with cerebral palsy may be misinterpreted or unnoticed by caregivers. Caregivers sometimes become physically or emotionally overwhelmed and become unable to make adequate and appropriate decisions related to diet and feeding, and some lack the knowledge needed to make sound choices. Caregivers may be reluctant to set appropriate limits on diet and feeding behaviors, or their expectations of the person with a handicapping condition may be inconsistent and inappropriate for the person's abilities or developmental potential. The combination of factors may result in diet and feeding practices that are neither nutritionally nor developmentally appropriate, and the feeding situation may become very emotionally charged for all parties involved.[9–11,14,15]

Feeding Problems

Feeding problems may result directly or indirectly from the neuromotor deviations of cerebral palsy, other factors associated with the disorder, or characteristics of the caregiving environment. The high incidence of feeding problems is one of the major factors contributing to the high nutritional risk of this population. Negative nutritional and social consequences of feeding problems range from minimal to profound and may lead to compromises in health, development, and overall performance when early identification and effective intervention do not occur. Potential problems can sometimes be prevented, and some problems can be easily remediated when screening, anticipatory guidance, and appropriate management occur. Other problems require very complex ongoing management strategies. Feeding development and feeding problems have been extensively described by many authors.[14-19]

Oral-Sensory-Motor

Delays or deviations in neuromotor development may alter the feeding process from birth, or they may not become apparent until later. Manifestations such as choking, vomiting, weak suckling response, and extremely long feeding times in early infancy sometimes are the earliest clues that neuromotor deficits are present.[20] In other infants, the effects become apparent as attempts to progress from a liquid diet to semisolids and then to solid foods are fraught with increasing difficulty. Abnormalities may be present in tone, reflex development, and/or responses to sensory stimulation. As indicated previously, these abnormalities may alter the ability of the person to assume or maintain positioning needed for eating, take food to the mouth, or ingest food that is provided. Achieving adequate fluid intake may be complicated by problems with drinking from a nipple, cup, or straw. Tongue thrust or poor lip closure may result in food loss from the mouth. Acceptance of hot or cold items of various textures may be altered by hypersensitivity. Problems with biting, chewing, or swallowing may also result from abnormal oral-motor patterns. Texture progression typically is delayed by these problems. In some persons, food does not move normally through the oral, pharyngeal, and nasopharyngeal areas, and aspiration of food or liquids may result. Any combination of these problems may cause the feeding–eating process to be slow and laborious. Both the feeder and the eater may tire before adequate intake has occurred. Without careful planning, dietary patterns may emerge that are inadequate or excessive in energy and nutrient density, imbalanced in nutrient distribution, and inadequate in fluid and fiber.

Behavioral

Delays or deviations in the behavioral aspects of eating and feeding also may be manifested, and their potential for impacting negatively on nutritional status should not be underestimated. Very narrow ranges of food acceptance, for example, may result in entire food groups being excluded from the diet. Rumination and vomiting may occur as maladaptive behaviors; however, swallowed food also may come back up into the mouth as the result of nonvolitional gastroesophageal reflux. Other behavioral considerations include skill attainment for self-feeding. In some persons, behavioral aspects of feeding deviations may be difficult to differentiate from neuromotor dysfunction. While the immediate nutritional consequences may be the same, the differentiation may have important implications relative to the development of appropriate intervention.

Oral-Facial

Neuromotor and behavioral characteristics that interfere with feeding also may interfere with oral hygiene practices. When inadequate professional dental care and inadequate oral hygiene are accompanied by frequent, prolonged feeding of soft foods and the lack of oral stimulation that is normally provided by hard crunchy foods, tooth decay and periodontal diseases are likely to ensue. These, in turn, may further impede food acceptance and eating ability.

Feeding may be adversely affected by structural and iatrogenic conditions of the oral area. Structural characteristics such as malocclusion or high-arched palate may complicate drinking, chewing, and swallowing. Gingival hyperplasia is a common side effect of phenytoin, an anticonvulsant medication taken by many persons with cerebral palsy. The hyperplasia may lead to functional chewing problems.[21]

Nonoral Feeding: A Consequence of Nutritional Risk

In some persons with cerebral palsy, adjuncts or alternatives to oral feeding are necessary. These nonoral feeding approaches are treatments brought about by nutritional risk or problems but may also be linked to the occurrence of secondary problems. Sometimes enteral feeding is contraindicated entirely and parenteral nutrition is instituted. More often, the gastrointestinal tract is functional but adequate intake cannot be achieved because of feeding impairment. Placement of feeding tubes may occur in conjunction with a health crisis such as surgery or a severe illness, or it may occur following failed, and often very prolonged, attempts to establish oral feeding. Transnasal tubes may be placed initially or when tube feedings are expected to be of short duration. The gastrostomy or, less commonly, enterostomy tube is generally placed when longer periods of enteral alimentation are anticipated.[22] Unless oral feeding is contraindicated by factors such as aspiration associated with dysphagia, tube and oral feedings may be used adjunctively. With improved nutritional status brought about by tube feedings, appetite and energy level for oral feeding sometimes improve to the point that tube feedings can be discontinued.[23]

With early identification and systematic intervention, many feeding difficulties can be ameliorated or compensated so that nutritional needs can be met via oral feeding. Social and emotional benefits from feeding interactions may be derived for caregivers and persons being fed, particularly when adequate intake is achieved with reasonable amounts of effort. In addition, oral-motor therapy is often considered important for the development of prelanguage skills as well as for improving feeding. Oral feeding is generally considered to be consistent with the concept of normalization and is promoted as long as health and safety are not jeopardized or unreasonable amounts of effort are not expended in the process. However, with some persons, literally hours of time are devoted every day to attempts at oral feeding while evidence of chronic malnutrition intensifies. In the past few years, several groups of investigators have presented evidence of weight gain and, to a lesser extent, of linear growth improvement following the establishment of tube feeding in persons with severe feeding impairments.[23-26] In addition, improved diagnostic techniques and increased attention to the problem are leading to increasing recognition of gastroesophageal reflux, dysphagia, and aspiration.[27-29] With these reports, many questions are being raised regarding when tube feeding should be initiated.[30] The issue is seldom clear-cut, and much more carefully controlled exploration of the topic is needed. Weight gain and/or maintenance patterns, nutrient and energy intake reasonably achieved by oral means, efficiency of feeding, attitudes of caregivers and/or the person with the impairments, risks associated with tube versus oral feeding, and overall health status of the person are all important considerations for the health care team, the person with the feeding problem, and the parents or guardians.

When prolonged periods of hyperalimentation or tube feeding occur before oral feeding is established (eg, high-risk infant) or when satisfactory oral feeding is interrupted for a prolonged period (eg, illness, surgery), strong resistance from the person may be encountered when the transition to oral feeding is attempted. This problem is being reported in many children who have experienced stormy courses during the first 1 or 2 years of life, including many with cerebral palsy. Various causes and courses of treatment for these problems have been proposed. With any treatment approach, careful monitoring is needed to ensure that a satisfactory level of nutrition is maintained during the transition period to oral feeding.[31,32]

Gastrointestinal Factors

Gastroesophageal Reflux

Gastroesophageal reflux is increasingly being recognized as a common and frequently very serious problem among persons with severe cerebral palsy. Use of esophageal pH monitoring is resulting in improved detection of the condition and increased information concerning responsible mechanisms. The pathogenesis of gastroesophageal reflux continues to be an area of active investigation. Potential components may include altered lower esophageal sphincter functioning, irritation of the esophageal mucosa by refluxed material, impaired esophageal clearing of refluxed material, and delayed gastric emptying.[33-36] Prevalence rates as high as 27% have been reported in groups of children with severe cerebral palsy.[27] Jolley and co-workers reported that 72% of a group of children with feeding problems (multiple diagnoses) who were referred to them for placement of feeding gastrostomies had gastroesophageal reflux prior to placement of the gastrostromies and six of the remaining nine developed gastroesophageal reflux after the feeding gastrostomies were placed.[37] The development of gastroesophageal reflux following placement of feeding gastrostomies is recognized as a significant complication.[24,37] Some evidence exists of relatively late age at onset of symptoms of gastroesophageal reflux in persons with neurologic compromise compared with neurologically normal children, and the incidence appears to be increased among persons with scoliosis.[28] In addition to emesis, which may or may not be present, reported manifestations include heartburn, extreme irritability, feeding difficulty, failure to thrive, anemia secondary to chronic blood loss from esophageal bleeding, esophageal stricture, recurrent pneumonia, and possibly the development of chronic lung disease.[28,35,38] Sixteen of 19 children with severe spastic cerebral palsy and gastroesophageal reflux who were studied by Rubin and associates were found to have active esophagitis. They suggested that the incidence of gastroesophageal reflux in this population may be higher than currently recognized and urged that an approach be developed to enhance early detection and prompt and effective management of the condition.[27] Intervention may include dietary compositional changes and changes in feeding volumes and positioning (see Nutrition Intervention), pharmacotherapy, and/or surgical intervention with Nissen fundoplication or some other procedure. Limitations in the effectiveness of the current interventions have been recognized.[34-37,39,40]

Chronic Constipation

Chronic constipation occurs commonly in persons with cerebral palsy and appears to be more prevalent among persons who are nonambulatory than among those with less severe neuromotor dysfunction. It has been attributed to numerous factors, including inadequate intake of fluid and fiber, decreased physical activity, decreased muscle tone in the intestinal wall, decreased response to physical signs to defecate, failure to establish a bowel routine, and effects of anticonvulsant medications. Diazepam, which may be taken as a muscle relaxant by persons with severe hypertonia, and antacids, which may be taken by persons with gastroesophageal reflux, also may have constipating effects.[41,42] Laxative dependence, including regular use of mineral oil, is not an unusual finding.

Medication Effects

For many persons with cerebral palsy, medication use begins in the neonatal period and continues throughout life. Medications used include anticonvulsants, laxatives, muscle relaxants, stimulants, and medications administered to persons with gastroesophageal reflux. Nutritional risk implications are summarized in Table 2-2. The long-term use of medication generally increases the likelihood that clinically significant adverse effects on nutrient intake, utilization, or need will result. If nutritional status is precarious owing to low nutrient intake or stresses of disease or surgery, little additional stress may have to be imposed by a medication in order for nutritional deficiency to result.[41]

Anticonvulsants

Anticonvulsants are the most commonly prescribed medications for persons with cerebral palsy. Reynolds has commented that it is doubtful that any other category of drugs presents a more serious problem of chronic nutritional side effects.[43]

Folic Acid. Adverse effects of anticonvulsant medications on folic acid status have been linked with the use of phenytoin, phenobarbital, primidone, and carbamazepine and have been found in short-term and long-term users of single drugs and drug combinations. Use of the drugs may lead to reduced folic acid levels in serum, red blood cells, and cerebrospinal fluid; to the development of macrocytosis; and, ultimately, to the development of megaloblastic anemia. Whereas megaloblastic anemia apparently occurs less than 1% of the time, Reynolds estimated that mild to moderate deficiency of the vitamin may be detectable in approximately 55% of the nonanemic users of the drugs.[43] Widely varying frequency figures for these effects may be found in the literature.[41,44,45]

Table 2-2 Medication Effects with Nutritional Implications

Medications	Effects
Anticonvulsants	
Phenytoin, phenobarbital, primidone, carbamazepine	Decreased concentration of folic acid in serum, red blood cells, cerebrospinal fluid; may result in megaloblastic anemia
Phenytoin, phenobarbital, others	Reduced vitamin D status; may result in rickets or osteomalacia
Carbamazepine, primidone	Reduced biotin status
Phenytoin	Gingival hyperplasia; may alter eating ability
General	Nausea, vomiting, gastric distress, altered appetite, diarrhea, or constipation
Laxatives (Chronic Use)	Loss of fat-soluble vitamins (mineral oil), malabsorption, depletion of phosphate and potassium
Muscle Relaxants	
Diazepam	Nausea, constipation, salivary changes, drowsiness, increased appetite, and weight gain
Dantrolene	Drowsiness, fatigue, changes in taste sensation, loss of appetite, diarrhea
Stimulants	
Methylphenidate, dextroamphetamine, pemoline	Reduced appetite, reduced weight gain
Medications Taken by Persons with Gastroesophageal Reflux	
Aluminum hydroxide	Phosphate depletion, increased calcium excretion, bone demineralization, constipation
Sodium bicarbonate	Reduced folic acid absorption, constipation
Cimetidine	Impaired vitamin B_{12} absorption, diarrhea

The administration of folic acid to alleviate the deficiency induced by anticonvulsant medications has been reported by some investigators to result in increased seizure activity[46-48]; other investigators have seen little or no evidence of that effect[49-51]; and still others have reported improvement in seizure control with the supplementation.[52] Some evidence has been presented that the administration of folic acid results in lowering of anticonvulsant levels in blood and cerebrospinal fluid.[41] Neubauer reported increased seizure activity when folic acid alone was supplemented but a reduction in seizures and improvement in mental condition when supplementation with folic acid and vitamin B_{12} occurred.[53] Low vitamin B_{12} levels have been reported in some clients with megaloblastic anemia associated with anticonvulsant medication use,[54,55] but, according to Roe, reduced vitamin B_{12} status has not been found in most studies of anticonvulsant drug users.[41] Some authors have warned that increased hematopoietic activity in association with repletion of folic acid could exhaust low vitamin B$_{12}$ levels,[56,57] and others have reported that vitamin B$_{12}$ levels fell with folic acid supplementation even when stores of vitamin B$_{12}$ probably were not depleted.[56] Folic acid supplementation with anticonvulsant drug therapy is discussed further in the sections on nutritional assessment and intervention.

Vitamin D. Impairment of vitamin D status in persons receiving anticonvulsant medications also has been extensively documented. Phenytoin and phenobarbital have been cited most often, but vitamin D–associated effects have been reported with several other anticonvulsants. While many cases of rickets and osteomalacia have been reported in users of these drugs, more subtle aberrations in vitamin D and calcium status usually appear that can be detected only through biochemical tests or photon absorptiometry. From his review of the literature, Hahn reported the incidence of hypocalcemia to range from 4% to 70% and the incidence of significant elevations in serum alkaline phosphatase to range from 24% to 40%. Serum concentrations of 25-hydroxyvitamin D$_3$ appear to be reduced 40% to 70%, and bone mass reductions of 10% to 30% have been revealed by photon absorptiometry.[58] Severity of the effects generally has been reported to increase with increasing drug dosage and duration of use and to be increased by use of multiple drugs. The effects are exacerbated by inactivity, particularly lack of ambulation; by lack of exposure to sunlight; by dark skin coloring; and by low intakes of vitamin D and calcium.[41,44,45,58] The mechanisms of the effects are not fully understood but may involve direct inhibition of bone mineral metabolism.[41] Monitoring of vitamin D and calcium status and issues related to prophylactic and therapeutic supplementation are discussed later in the chapter (see Nutritional Assessment and Intervention).

Biotin. Biotin transport in the human intestine has been reported to be inhibited by the anticonvulsant drugs carbamazepine and primidone.[59] The drugs appear to act as competitive inhibitors of transport of the vitamin in intestinal tract border membrane vesicles. Impaired biotin status has been observed in persons receiving long-term treatment with anticonvulsant drugs,[44,60] and Said and associates have suggested that the impairment may relate to the altered transport of the vitamin. These investigators also speculated that reduced biotin status could be the cause of dermatitis and ataxia, observed with anticonvulsant therapy in humans, and of reduced brain aspartate levels, observed with anticonvulsant drug administration in rats.[59] Kraus and co-workers hypothesized that alterations in carboxylase activity, as a result of reduced biotin status, could not only reduce levels of the excitation neurotransmitter aspartic acid but also elevate the inhibition neurotransmitter glycine.[44] While these possibilities await further exploration, biotin status of persons receiving long-term anticonvulsant drug therapy, particularly with carbamazepine and primidone, should not be overlooked.

Other. Anticonvulsant medications have been reported to alter status of persons with respect to many other nutrients, but neither the effects nor their physiological or clinical significance have yet been well defined. Undoubtedly, other effects will be identified in the future.[41,44,61]

More generalized effects of the anticonvulsant medications also have nutritional implications. Nausea and vomiting, gastric distress, increased or decreased appetite, and diarrhea or constipation may result from their use.[41–43,62] Gingival hyperplasia is a major side effect of the use of phenytoin. While the primary effect and secondary inflammatory changes in the gum tissue can be minimized by good oral hygiene and appropriate professional dental care, surgical removal of gingival tissue sometimes becomes necessary. Inflammation and overgrowth of the tissue can reduce a person's interest in eating and alter chewing ability. Dietary modification may be necessary to ensure adequate nutrition until appropriate professional oral care occurs.[21,41,45]

Laxatives

Chronic laxative use is widely recognized to have the potential of impairing nutritional status. In addition to the frequently referenced adverse effects of mineral oil on absorption of fat-soluble vitamins, abuse of laxatives may result in severe malabsorption syndromes, protein-losing enteropathy, and depletion of phosphate and potassium.[41,42,62]

Muscle Relaxants

Muscle relaxants used in the treatment of spasticity include diazepam and dantrolene. Diazepam has been reported to cause nausea, constipation, salivary changes, drowsiness, and fatigue, any of which could alter appetite and food intake. However, increased appetite and increased weight gain also are reported side effects. Dantrolene has been reported to cause drowsiness, fatigue, changes in taste sensation, loss of appetite, and diarrhea.[3,42,62]

Stimulants

Stimulant medications are used in conjunction with behavioral measures for treatment of attention deficit disorder. Methylphenidate, dextroamphetamine, and pemoline are used for this purpose. Reduced appetite is a common side effect of these drugs and is believed to be an important factor in the slowing of growth that also is common with their use. The drug effect requires approximately 30 minutes to be manifested clinically and is usually minimal 4 to 6 hours after administration. Lucas and Sells have suggested that food offerings be planned accordingly to take advantage of least drug effect and greatest appetite.[63] Growth patterns and energy and nutrient intakes of children receiving these drugs should be closely monitored.[63,64]

Medications Taken by Persons with Gastroesophageal Reflux

Medications used by persons who have gastroesophageal reflux that may have nutritional risk implications include antacids, alginic acid in combination with sodium bicarbonate, and cimetidine. Aluminum hydroxide, a common antacid, may combine with phosphates in the intestine and lead to increased excretion of phosphate in the feces. Abuse of this antacid can result in phosphate depletion, increased calcium excretion, and bone demineralization and possibly lead to osteomalacia or rickets. Sodium bicarbonate may reduce the absorption of folic acid. These effects may be of particular significance in persons taking anticonvulsant medications, which also may affect vitamin D status, bone mineralization, and folic status. Cimetidine, an H_2-receptor antagonist, is administered to reduce acid toxicity of reflux. According to Roe, this drug impairs the absorption of protein-bound vitamin B_{12} from the protein binder. Vitamin B_{12} deficiency may occur if gastric secretion is continuously suppressed by the drug, if it is taken within 1 hour of mealtime, or if body stores are otherwise depleted. When the medication is taken at bedtime, vitamin B_{12} status does not appear to be jeopardized.[41] Diarrhea is sometimes reported as a side effect of cimetidine, whereas constipation may result from the antacids.[33,34,41,42,62]

Difficulties in Evaluating Growth, Physical Size, and Energy and Nutrient Needs

Since disorders of motor control and posture characterize cerebral palsy, it logically follows that energy and nutrient needs would be altered in line with alterations in levels and patterns of activity. A major dilemma continues to exist, however, concerning how best to determine when the energy and nutrient needs are being met, particularly in persons with severe impairment. Body size and composition, together with patterns of change in those variables, serve as key indicators of nutritional status in the general population, and they are affected by nutritional status in persons with cerebral palsy also. However, the variability in growth and development among persons with cerebral palsy is much greater and the factors contributing to the variability are less well defined than with the general population. Such factors as paresis or reduced weight bearing may lead to alterations in muscular and skeletal development, with or without dietary modulation. Low weight and short stature may be of nonnutritional origin in one person with spastic quadriplegia and may indicate that the person has reduced nutritional needs, owing to reduced potential for physical development, whereas identical physical dimensions and body composition in another person with the same diagnosis may be indicative of chronic or acute malnutrition. The dilemma is compounded by the fact that recognized risk factors for altered growth and body composition, including malnutrition, and for altered energy and nutrient needs tend to cluster within the same subgroups of this population. For example, feeding problems and dependence on caregivers for feeding are most common among persons with major deviations in neuromotor functions and in other areas of performance. Persons in this same group are most likely to experience the effects of long-term anticonvulsant medication use, the physical stress of repeated illnesses and/or operations, and the financial stress of high medical expense.

Alterations in Body Size and Composition

Differences between physical size characteristics of persons with cerebral palsy and their general population peers have been reported by many authors. Yet, qualitative, quantitative, and etiologic aspects of the deviations remain poorly defined. Children have been the subjects in most reports, and recent reports in particular have focused on those with severe impairment.[23-25,65] Little information concerning physical size characteristics is available regarding children with mild dysfunction or adults with any degree of impairment. It also should be recognized that many of the frequently cited reports in this area were published at least 20 years ago[66-72] and most of those were based on institutionalized subjects.[67,69,70,72] In the intervening years, changes have occurred in the incidences of various causative factors of cerebral palsy and, consequently, in frequencies of various patterns of motor dysfunction. Approaches to feeding, physical activity, health care, and other aspects of care also have changed. Since any of these factors could affect physical size, it is reasonable to expect that differences may exist between the physical size characteristics of groups included in the earlier reports and conditions today. However, from the recent reports that are available and from clinical observation, trends, if not absolute amounts of difference, in physical size characteristics of this population continue to appear similar to earlier descriptions.

Available data consistently reflect increased incidences of short stature and low weight for age, relative to general population reference data, among children with cerebral palsy.[67–69,71–73] Delays in skeletal maturation also have been reported.[67,69] The proportion of children with lower heights and weights and the magnitude of the reductions appear to increase with increasing severity of motor deviation,[68,71,72] and several authors have reported height and/or weight reductions to be greater in persons with athetoid than in those with spastic forms of cerebral palsy.[66,68,69] When weight has been evaluated in relation to height, fewer values have fallen into lower percentile ranking than when it has been evaluated in relation to chronologic age; however, disproportionately high numbers of children, particularly among those with severe motor dysfunction, fall into lower percentile rankings of weight for stature as well as weight for age.[24,25,65,73] Excessive weight gain is mentioned in conjunction with spasticity, particularly in the teen years and later, but the relative frequency of excessive weight versus weight deficit is not clear.[66,68,69,71]

Information regarding body composition is extremely useful in further characterization of body development. However, little information is available regarding body composition of this population.

Using isotope dilution techniques with ^{42}K and tritiated water, Berg and Isaksson estimated body cell mass, extracellular and total body water, and body fat of 23 subjects with cerebral palsy, aged 7 to 21 years. They considered the subjects to be short for age but to show a general tendency to be heavy for their heights. These investigators reported that average body cell mass of the subjects was only 86% of the value predicted on the basis of normal children, whereas average total body water was 116% of that predicted. They concluded that the ratio of extracellular to intracellular water in the subjects was increased and suggested that the picture was similar to that presented by children with severe malnutrition. They also reported that estimated body fat was reduced in all of the subjects with dyskinesia and approximately half of those with spasticity but increased in the other subjects with spasticity despite what the authors considered to be a low caloric intake.[74] From intervention trials of physical training, dietary change, or a combination of diet change and physical training, Berg reported that body cell mass did not change with any of the approaches, body fat increased and extracellular water decreased when only physical training was emphasized, and extracellular water decreased when physical training and diet were changed. No significant changes were detected when diet alone was altered.[75]

In a study of triceps and subscapular skin folds of 95 children with cerebral palsy, Spender and co-workers found that triceps fat was reduced without comparable reduction of subscapular fat. They reported that truncal fat distribution has been found in chronically malnourished children without cerebral palsy and proposed that the truncal distribution of fat of their subjects with cerebral palsy could be related to a high prevalence of undernutrition.[76] Dietz suggested that subcutaneous fat distribution over paralyzed limbs may be increased. He presented data for 35 children with cerebral palsy, showing none to have high weight for stature but 17% to have triceps skin folds that exceeded the eighty-fifth percentile of general population data.[73] However, Spender and co-workers found the fat distribution to be more truncal when the triceps fat measurement was taken on a paralyzed area than when the measured arm was not affected, and they suggested that triceps fat depletion may be related to arm muscle wasting.[76]

These data reinforce the need for much more research concerning factors affecting body size and composition of this population. They also lend support to the accuracy of what logic would suggest, namely, that the proportions and distributions of fat and lean body mass represented by a given weight-for-stature ratio are likely to be influenced by the presence of cerebral palsy in a person and by the type and topographical distribution of the disorder. A given weight-for-stature ratio may reflect a desirable amount of body fat in one person whose muscle mass is within general population normal limits but excessive fat in another whose muscle mass is greatly reduced. Differentiation between these two situations can be facilitated by monitoring triceps and subscapular skin folds and mid upper arm circumference, together with weight for age, stature for age, and weight for stature. This is discussed further in the section on nutritional assessment.

Investigators and clinicians over the years have acknowledged the coexistence of subaverage physical size, feeding problems, and low food intake among persons with cerebral palsy.[67–69] Clinicians who work with this population cite examples of linear growth and/or weight gain having occurred in clients following dietary intervention. However, few data are available from intervention trials in this area. Recently, several reports have appeared concerning growth changes following nutrition intervention in persons with severe neuromotor involvement. Weinstein and associates reported that over half of a group of 16 children with quadriplegic cerebral palsy demonstrated weight gains of 5% or more within 1 year of receiving outpatient nutritional counseling.[77] Other recent reports have focused on growth outcomes following the initiation of gastrostomy feeding. These reports have been in general agreement in documenting increases in weight gain and linear growth but not total correction of the growth deviation. Reported increases in weight gain have exceeded increases in linear growth, and many of the children have remained below the fifth percentile of general population reference data for length even after extended periods of gastrostomy feeding. For example, Rempel and colleagues reported that

75% of a group of 57 children followed in their clinic remained below the fifth percentile of general population reference data for length, 70% remained below the fifth percentile for weight, but only 14% remained below the fifth percentile of weight for length. Of the 35 children for whom data were available, length of 91%, weight of 94%, and weight for length of 49% were below the fifth percentiles of reference data prior to gastrostomy feeding. These authors reported that linear growth increases were only apparent after a year or more of gastrostomy feeding and, even then, were seen in only one fourth of the children.[24] Shapiro and co-workers reported that weight for length increased in 16 of 19 children in their program following the establishment of gastrostomy feeding, whereas length for age apparently increased in only 11. Unlike Rempel and colleagues, these investigators did not find evidence of relationships between acceleration of linear growth and length of follow-up.[25] Rempel and colleagues reported that weight for length of 21% of their subjects with gastrostomies exceeded the seventy-fifth percentiles of weight for length, whereas only 6% had exceeded that level prior to the gastrostomy feeding.[24] Others have described the shift in weight for stature from below the fifth to above the ninety-fifth percentiles of reference data within periods of 5 to 25 months of introducing the feedings with calorie prescriptions of 150% to 175% of basal metabolic rate.[78] Information about body compositional changes of subjects would be useful in evaluating the changes in nutritional status that occurred with the tube feedings, as would information regarding nutrient and energy intakes of subjects prior to and following the introduction of tube feedings and changes in biochemical indices of nutritional status. These reports are important in documenting increased, although not "normalized," growth with increased intake among persons with very severe impairments. Much more work remains to be done to define the contributions of nutrition among the interrelated factors that affect physical size and performance of persons of varying ages and levels of disability.

Alterations in Energy Needs

Attempts to define effects of cerebral palsy on energy needs have been complicated by the many types and levels of severity of conditions represented. When the implications are considered of superimposing the variability of cerebral palsy on the variability of energy requirements of persons in the general population, the necessity of evaluating energy requirements on a person-to-person basis becomes readily apparent.

The report of Culley and Middleton is often cited in consideration of energy needs of this population. From a study of 52 institutionalized children with moderate to profound mental retardation, aged 5 to 12 years, they reported mean energy intakes of 14.7 kcal/cm of height by those who were ambulatory and had no motor dysfunction, 13.9 kcal/cm of height (not significantly different from the first group) by those who were ambulatory but had motor dysfunction, and 11.1 kcal/cm of height (significantly lower than the other two groups) by those who were nonambulatory. Culley and Middleton considered the children to have desirable weight for stature and, therefore, to have appropriate energy intakes. They reported that apparent caloric needs per centimeter of height were not affected by type, location, or severity of motor dysfunction as long as the children were ambulatory. The apparent energy needs also were not found to differ by age or gender.[72]

While the Recommended Dietary Allowances (RDA)[79] for energy are not expressed in relation to stature, values can be calculated using the heights reported for the reference individuals in the respective age groups. That approach yields values of 11.6 to 25 kcal/cm and median values of 15.2 and 18.5 kcal/cm, respectively, for the two age ranges corresponding to the subjects in the study by Culley and Middleton. The absolute RDA values are 1300 to 2300 kcal (median, 1700) for children aged 4 to 6 years and 1650 to 3300 kcal (median, 2400) for the 7- to 10-year age group. Thus, the value given by Culley and Middleton for the ambulatory children was within the RDA range while that for the nonambulatory children was below. From the values reported for their individual subjects, it appears that absolute energy intakes of all except one of the nonambulatory children and approximately one half of the ambulatory children were below current RDA ranges.

The approach of relating energy needs to stature is often useful when working with groups whose needs may differ from those of the general population, and many professionals have found the figures given by Culley and Middleton to be useful reference points when beginning to plan or evaluate intakes of children with cerebral palsy. It should be kept in mind, however, that the sample included in the study of Culley and Middleton was small. It also should be kept in mind that chronic or acute malnutrition can contribute to the occurrence of reduced linear growth in childhood. Carefully monitored trials of increased intake for several months are often needed to rule out inadequate nutrition as a contributing factor to poor growth and/or low weight. The values reported by Culley and Middleton were based on children who presumably had been receiving adequate nutrition, so that nutrient and energy needs to support catch-up growth were not an issue. Dietz suggests that energy intakes may need to be greater than 150% of maintenance to support catch-up growth. He has also estimated that energy expenditure per unit of lean body mass may be substantially increased with either spasticity or athetosis.[73]

Other authors have emphasized that absolute caloric needs of persons with athetosis are substantially higher than those of persons with spasticity.[66,69,71] Mechanical efficiency is likely to be reduced and the energy costs of task performance per unit of time may be higher with either athetosis or spasticity than in normal persons.[80,81] However, this may be offset by reduced time spent in strenuous activity. Campbell and Bell found in a study of children with spastic diplegia, aged 5 to 15 years, that rate of energy expenditure for walking was greater than that of general population children of the same age walking at comparable speeds. They also reported that the rate of energy expenditure for walking decreased with age in the normal children but increased in the children with cerebral palsy. These authors commented that older children with spastic diplegia might prefer to walk less or use a wheelchair because of the greater physical exertion associated with walking as their body weight increased with age.[82] This observation may have relevance to the reports that persons with spasticity have increased tendency toward obesity as they reach the teen-age years and beyond.

Much research continues to be needed concerning energy needs of this population. Energy needs during rest, for example, have not been extensively studied. The energy and other nutritional consequences of recurrent aspiration pneumonia and other frequent illnesses also have not been extensively evaluated with this population, although infections are known to bring about metabolic alterations and increase energy requirements. While some authors have suggested that basal metabolic rates may be lower in persons with spasticity, it is not clear that evaluations have taken needs per unit of lean body mass into account.

Specific nutrient requirements have received even less research attention with this population. Some nutrient requirements are related to energy requirements, and low absolute energy requirements may reduce the levels needed of those nutrients. However, this has not been established with this population, and any potential reduction in requirement due to lower energy needs may be offset by other factors. Professional judgment has to be applied in interpreting data from all aspects of the nutritional assessment in determining satisfactory nutrient and energy intake levels for individual clients. When calorie needs are low, intakes of high nutrient density are necessary if RDAs for nutrients are to be met.

NUTRITIONAL ASSESSMENT

Nutritional assessment of persons with cerebral palsy, as with the general population, necessitates the integration of information gained through subjective and objective appraisal of biological and psychosocial characteristics of individuals and their environments. Components of the assessment should be influenced by characteristics of the individual client and undoubtedly will be influenced by available resources. The assessment is best accomplished as an interdisciplinary activity that includes consideration of health, social, and developmental histories; clinical, biochemical, anthropometric, and dietary variables; feeding performance; and characteristics of the support system or caregiving environment. Depending on the nature and complexity of problems of the individual client, the expertise of many different combinations of professionals may be beneficial. In addition to the nutritionist/dietitian, these may include the physical therapist, occupational therapist, speech pathologist, psychologist, primary care physician and a variety of physician specialists, nurse, dentist, dental hygienist, and social worker. For clients with mild cerebral palsy and no evidence of impaired feeding, nutritional assessment may differ little from that of persons without the disorder and generally can be accomplished in the primary, generic health care setting. Resources for assessment of more complex disorders are found in specialty clinics or tertiary care settings. Coordination between tertiary care and community-based services is critical to ensure referral to the specialty setting when needed and to promote continuity of care in the community of residence.

The heterogeneity of conditions associated with cerebral palsy precludes the development of highly specific standards and guidelines for anthropometric, dietary, biochemical, or other areas of assessment that could appropriately be applied across this diagnostic grouping. The more severe the neuromotor dysfunction and other disorders, the less applicable are general population reference data and the more complex are the processes of collecting and interpreting the data needed for nutritional assessment and intervention planning. Serial observations are critical for evaluating the appropriateness and the effectiveness of proposed treatments. Proficiency in nutritional assessment of the general population and thorough knowledge of principles underlying the assessment process should be prerequisite to attempting assessment of persons with cerebral palsy. That background prepares the professional to apply information that is more specific to problems associated with cerebral palsy and tailor the assessment to the needs of the individual client. This includes recognizing factors that place the client at increased risk for selected nutritional problems, recognizing factors that cause guidelines used with the general population to be inappropriate, identifying alternative assessment approaches when traditional approaches cannot or should not be applied, and recognizing indicators that various specialty areas need to be included in the assessment.

Health, Social, and Developmental Histories

Information concerning a person's health, social, and developmental histories provides a cornerstone for interpreting his or her current physical size characteristics, feeding practices, and nutritional status and for planning nutrition and feeding interventions. A combined approach of record review, interview with the client and/or primary caregivers, and discussions with other service providers may be needed to develop a comprehensive profile of significant data related to the areas of nutrition and feeding. Information should be elicited regarding family history of disease; history of health, educational, vocational, and social services received by the client; medical or social complications experienced, their timing, interventions, and current status; developmental history, including feeding development; history of nutrition and/or feeding problems and use of extraordinary feeding measures; history of medication use; heights and weights at various ages; availability of resources for purchasing food and feeding equipment and accessing health and nutrition services; availability of assistance with food preparation and feeding (if needed); services currently being used; and current sources of stress to the client and/or primary caregivers. Many persons with cerebral palsy present very complex histories and are likely to have received services from many professionals in many different locations. Identifying and accessing relevant background information can be tedious but can make an invaluable contribution to the assessment and is essential for care coordination. By building assessments and interventions on what has gone on before and what is currently in place, duplication of tests and services can be avoided and continuity of care can be promoted.

Clinical Assessment

Medical evaluations often need to be much more extensive in conjunction with nutritional assessment of persons with cerebral palsy, particularly in those with moderate to severe levels of impairment, than is usually indicated with the general population. Since clinical signs typically do not appear until late in the development of malnutrition, information gained through other aspects of the assessment may provide a preclinical indication of nutritional risk, even when a picture of satisfactory health, free of clinical signs of malnutrition or other evidence of medical problems, is presented. When evidence of medical problems or unsatisfactory health status is revealed by the examination, two major issues are raised relative to nutrition: (1) what is the contribution of nutritional factors to the occurrence of the problem(s), and (2) what are the implications of the problem(s) with respect to dietary and feeding recommendations? The expertise of a variety of medical specialists may be required for this aspect of assessment. All members of the health care team should be aware of signs that referrals for specialized, in-depth assessments are indicated.

The physical examination should include consideration of possible clinical signs of malnutrition, which have been described extensively.[83] In persons who are dependent on caregivers to provide food and fluid, have limited communication skills, have difficulty eating and drinking, and/or are being fed highly concentrated (high osmolality) formulas, attention should be paid to possible physical signs of dehydration. Skin, hair, gastrointestinal, and physical size characteristics consistent with protein and/or energy malnutrition also should be recognized, as should signs consistent with deficiencies and excesses of various vitamins and minerals. Particular attention should be paid to possible signs of deficiency of folic acid, vitamin B_{12}, vitamin D, calcium, and biotin in persons taking anticonvulsant medications. Information from the medical history and from biochemical and dietary aspects of the assessment is needed for differentiating between nutritional and non-nutritional causes of some physical manifestations and between various nutritional factors that may be associated with some manifestations.

Radiographs and photon absorptiometry may be used to evaluate skeletal maturity and bone quality, respectively. Information gained from these determinations is useful in evaluating effects of anticonvulsant medications[41] and also may reveal characteristics consistent with malnutrition from other causes.[84] Bone age provides a better indication of biologic maturity than does chronologic age, and evaluation of stature in relation to this variable may be useful in monitoring growth during nutrition intervention trials in children whose size is outside general population normal limits for chronologic age.[85]

The oral-facial area should be examined for structural aberrations or disease characteristics that could interfere with food acceptance or eating ability. Evaluation should also be performed for clinical signs of malnutrition in the oral area and for gingival hyperplasia. Swollen, bleeding gums may result from poor oral hygiene or from nutritional factors, including deficiency of vitamin C. Nursing bottle mouth may be seen in the client who receives a bottle for prolonged periods. Damage to the teeth may also result from failure to clear the mouth due to ineffective swallow, behaviorally based holding of food in the mouth, or gastroesophageal reflux.

Evaluations for swallowing disorders, aspiration, esophagitis, and/or gastroesophageal reflux may be indicated with this population, especially persons with severe neuromotor dysfunction. Recurrent pneumonia, frequent coughing or croup, excessive crying, unexplained changes in weight (loss in adults, reduced rate of gain in children), vomiting or spitting up, heartburn, or other evidence of discomfort during or after eating may provide clues that evaluation for these conditions needs to be considered.[27,28,35,37,40] Particular attention should be paid to possible signs of discomfort during or following feeding in persons with impaired communication.

Elimination patterns also need to be evaluated. Constipation is the most commonly reported problem in this area, although diarrhea or fluctuation between constipation and diarrhea also occur. Considerations should include dietary factors possibly contributing to the occurrence of the problems; nutritional implications of past, current, and proposed treatments; and possible dietary treatment measures.

Anthropometric Assessment

Anthropometric measures are an invaluable component of nutritional assessment of persons with cerebral palsy. Serial profiles of body size, proportions, and composition, based on accurate and reliable data, provide an objective means of comparing persons with reference populations and with themselves over time. Together with information gained from the physical examination, health and dietary histories, and other examination components, these profiles provide clues to the timing of nutritional and non-nutritional insults, the need for nutrition intervention, and effects of nutrition and other interventions.

The use of high-quality, appropriately maintained equipment is essential. Some equipment needs with this population differ slightly from those with the general population. Standard beam–balance platform scales are satisfactory for use with subjects who can stand without support, and models with posts or bars for subjects to grasp for stability are also available. The pan scale is appropriate for use with infants who can lie on the pan or for young children who have adequate sitting balance to support themselves. Chair scales are desirable for use with the older child or adult who cannot stand unsupported. Bed scales may be useful with severely disabled adults. Stadiometers are commercially available, or satisfactory devices for measuring stature can be improvised, but the moveable rods attached to platform scales are not recommended for use. Length rather than stature must be measured for many adults and older children with cerebral palsy. A measuring table with fixed perpendicular headboard and sliding footboard that is parallel to the headboard, rather than the standard 100-cm infant length measuring board, may be useful. Insertion tapes used in measuring head circumference, locating upper arm midpoint, and measuring normal arm circumferences of older children and adults are not flexible enough to use for measuring circumferences of very thin arms. Narrow flexible steel tapes are preferred for measuring small arm circumferences and are useful for measuring lengths and circumferences of other body areas as well. A special caliper available for measuring knee height may be useful in facilities providing service to nonambulatory elderly persons.

Measurements should be performed as nearly in accordance with techniques recommended for use with the general population as characteristics of the individual client allow.[85,86] However, physical and/or behavioral characteristics of some persons complicate the measurement process and may preclude the performance of some measurements. Any deviations from standard techniques should be recorded, as should any difficulty encountered in performing the measurement. Measurements should be performed at least two times, preferably by different examiners. If reasonable agreement between the two sets of measurements is not achieved, the process should be repeated. Differences of no more than 1 cm for stature or length, 2 mm for skin folds, 0.2 cm for arm circumference, and 0.2 kg or 0.5 lb for weight are desirable. If reasonable agreement is not achieved in the second set of trials, little benefit is likely to be derived from attempting to repeat the measurement at that time. Either defeat should be acknowledged, the mean of the four trials accepted and the difficulty noted, or measurement attempted again later during the examination period. In some instances an alternative measurement can be performed. On some clients, some measurements just cannot be satisfactorily performed, no matter how useful the information might be. Inaccurate data can lead to false conclusions about the client's condition and can be worse than missing data. Uncertainty and anxiety of the examiner can be conveyed to the client and, particularly with children, can reduce the likelihood of obtaining a satisfactory measure. As indicated previously, proficiency should be achieved by examiners in performing measurements with the general population before they attempt to measure the client with cerebral palsy.

Weight of most clients with cerebral palsy can be accurately determined, but adaptations of general population techniques sometimes are necessary. Care must be taken to ensure that the subject does not alter the measure by grasping the scale or some other item for support. As indicated above, many scale designs are available to accommodate various client characteristics. The client who is light enough to be held and either cannot stand or is noncompliant sometimes can be weighed while being held by an adult, whose weight is then subtracted. Braces should be removed when feasible. Otherwise, attempts should be made to determine the weight of the brace, and the weight should be recorded for routine subtraction from the weight of the client wearing it. When a client is scheduled to receive a cast, particularly if it is to be worn for an extended time, arrangements sometimes can be made for weight to be measured immediately prior to and following the procedure. Otherwise, weight of the cast can be estimated or "weight with cast" can be monitored while it is being worn. Casting often occurs following surgery and that may be a particularly important time to monitor weight. The combination of physical and emotional stress may affect food acceptance and nutritional needs of the client. When persons with cerebral palsy are being weighed, they should be clothed according to the guidelines recommended for the general population. Infants should be weighed unclothed, the young child should be dressed in undergarments, and older children, adolescents, and adults should be dressed in lightweight indoor clothing without shoes. Weights of diapers should always be subtracted.

Length or stature frequently is the most difficult anthropometric measurement to perform on persons with cerebral palsy. If satisfactory positioning can be achieved, length of the child should be measured through age 2 years and stature measured thereafter. When satisfactory positioning of the person older than 2 years of age cannot be achieved for measuring stature, measurement of length should be considered. Measures taken with the subject in a recumbent position will generally be 1 to 2 cm greater than when the subject is positioned upright. If one side of the body is longer than the other, either the length of each side should be recorded or the asymmetry noted and the same side of the body measured at each reevaluation. If total length measurement cannot be satisfactorily accomplished but curvature of the spine is not present, sitting height or the recumbent counterpart, crown–rump length, offers alternative means of obtaining some indication of linear dimension.[85] Arm span measure offers another alternative to length or stature measurement if upper extremity contractures are not present and the subject can be appropriately positioned.[86,87] Knee height measurement has considerable appeal, but reference data currently are readily available only for elderly persons.[88]

Contractures commonly obstruct length measurement with this population, but physical or occupational therapists sometimes are able to position the person satisfactorily to accommodate measurement. For example, one leg of some children with mild lower extremity contractures can be extended by holding the leg above the knee but below the thigh muscle belly with one hand and at the ankle with the other hand, while leaving the other leg in a flexed position. Three examiners may be needed to establish and maintain anatomical alignment through the subject's trunk, pelvis, and lower extremities. Therapists or physicians should be consulted if any uncertainty exists regarding positioning that can safely be attempted with individual clients. Questions should be asked about the presence of dislocated hips or any other conditions with which any measuring techniques might be contraindicated. Some professionals use a segment-by-segment measuring approach for arriving at an estimate of total body length of clients who have contractures. However, neither accuracy nor reliability is easily achieved using this technique, even in persons without contractures or spinal curvature. When spinal curvature and upper and lower extremity contractures are present, any linear measure is subject to question. Techniques employed when measures are recorded under those circumstances should be carefully documented, and the potential error should be taken into account in any interpretation that is attempted of the data.

Skin fold measures can be particularly useful in nutritional assessment of this population since a given weight-for-stature ratio may not represent the same fat-to-muscle proportions as in the general population.[76] In addition, since stature or length sometimes cannot be satisfactorily measured, weight for stature cannot always be evaluated. Triceps and subscapular sites are the most commonly measured skin folds in the general population and are appropriate for most clients with cerebral palsy. An exception might be the client with substantially different upper body and lower body involvement for whom measurements taken on the thigh or calf might be useful adjuncts to upper body measures. However, lower extremity skin folds are more difficult to measure than are triceps skin folds. Since triceps and subscapular fat may not be comparably altered in cerebral palsy, both measures provide a more complete picture of the client's body fat than does either measure by itself. Difficulty may be experienced in differentiating between fat and muscle in the hypotonic subject. If hemiplegia is present, both sides of the body should be measured. Otherwise, either side may be measured but the side selected should be noted and consistently measured. Commonly used reference data have been derived from right side measurements. Upright positioning of the client has been most widely used for performing skin fold measurements, but techniques have now been described for performing the measurements with the subject in a recumbent position. The anatomical sites of measurement are the same with either position. It is recommended that clients not be positioned in wheelchairs while measurements are being performed.[87,89]

Mid upper arm circumference provides an indication of muscle and fat combined or, when considered in conjunction with triceps skin fold measures, an indication of muscle in the upper arm. The same considerations relative to side of body to measure apply as with the triceps skin fold. Care must be taken not to leave gaps between the measuring tape and the subject's arm when performing this measurement on very thin subjects. The tape should be snug but not tight enough to indent the arm.

Head circumference is usually measured to age 6 years for children with developmental delays or disabilities. Cerebral palsy should not affect the procedure used for this measurement.

Anthropometric data obtained for the client with cerebral palsy may be compared with general population reference data, particularly for evaluating patterns of difference and change. While acknowledging that some persons with cerebral palsy will not attain size or growth rate that is within general population normal limits, reasons for values falling outside those limits should be sought and attempts should be made to rule out suboptimal nutrition as a contributing factor. Measurements repeated over time are more meaningful than are a single set, and a composite profile that includes skin fold measures as well as weight and length or stature is more meaningful than is any one of the measures by itself.

Growth charts from the National Center for Health Statistics are widely available for use in plotting weight and length or stature for chronologic age of persons from birth to 18 years; weight for length or stature from birth to puberty; triceps and subscapular skin folds, mid upper arm circumference, and increments in weight and stature from 2 to 18 years.[90–92] Corrections for gestational age should be made for at least the first 1 to 2 years when evaluating anthropometric data from children born prematurely.[87]

Data published by the Metropolitan Life Insurance Company are the most widely used for evaluating weight for stature of adults. However, the value of those data for use in assessing nutritional status has been questioned.[93] Data derived from the National Health and Nutrition Examination Surveys (NHANES) I and II also are available.[94,95] Reference data published by Frisancho are widely used for assessing skin fold thickness, upper arm circumference, and estimated upper arm muscle circumference.[95,96]

Dietary and Feeding Assessments

Diet and feeding are inexorably linked, and neither of the areas should be ignored in assessment of the other. When deviations from normal feeding performance are present, assessment is best accomplished through integration of the expertise of professionals from other disciplines with that of the nutritionist. Some physical therapists, occupational therapists, and speech pathologists have expertise in assessment of neuromotor aspects of feeding, whereas psychologists may provide in-depth assessment of behavioral aspects of the process. Approaches in which professionals collectively are present for dietary interviews and feeding assessments, including demonstration by the client and primary caregivers, offer benefits for the client, the caregivers, and the professionals.

Information regarding diet and feeding practices should be obtained from the primary client to the extent possible. With some clients this may involve the use of alternative communication approaches. Frequently, one or more assistants serve as informants with or for the client with cerebral palsy. Clients may consume food in a variety of settings with assistance from many persons over the course of even one day, and assistants may change from one day to another. Therefore, it commonly occurs that no one person has knowledge of the client's total diet or knows whether feeding practices or the client's responses are consistent across feeders or locations.

When the client is unable to serve as primary informant, communication with persons in all settings in which he or she regularly spends time is often necessary to obtain an accurate picture of diet and feeding. Very different reports of intake and feeding performance by the client may be obtained from different caregivers.[97] Parents, having established satisfactory feeding approaches at home, may assume that the school lunch menu provides an accurate account of what the child eats at school, whereas communication with the teacher may reveal that the child consumes only small quantities of food at school. Or the therapist who is adept at feeding may not realize that the techniques she has introduced that enable the adolescent to successfully feed himself at school have not been accepted by the parents for use at home and that the adolescent has stopped eating at home altogether. Parents may feel personal failure when they are unable to feed a child and may be reluctant to acknowledge that they are experiencing any difficulty. Not only may problems be more accurately defined, but solutions are sometimes revealed when information is collected from all persons who have primary contact with the client. A combination of interview, record-keeping by client and/or caregivers, and observation is useful.

Careful probing and attention to subtle clues are important in collecting dietary and feeding information needed to calculate nutrient, energy, and fluid intake and to evaluate dietary and feeding practices. Changes from standard product dilutions or addition or deletion of ingredients may not be reported unless specific questions are asked. Terms such as "milk shake" or "pudding" often have different meanings in relation to the diets of persons with cerebral palsy than for the general population. Care must be taken to determine whether reported food portions reflect amounts served, amounts that left the dish, or amounts actually consumed. Plate and bib waste and losses from vomiting or gastrostomy tube leakage should be taken into account, although they are difficult to quantify. Questions should be asked about the use of nutrient and energy supplements or any special products and about any dietary restrictions that are practiced. Reasons for any reported dietary restrictions should be asked. When food allergies or intolerances are reported, the informant should be asked to describe evidence. Information regarding textures, consistencies, and temperatures of foods consumed assists the therapist in determining sensory characteristics of the client and is needed by the therapist and nutritionist when planning dietary changes. That information as well as information regarding intake schedules; durations of intake periods; characteristics of the environment in which feeding and eating occur; major determinants of quantity, variety, and timing of intake; and presence of maladaptive or noncompliant feeding-related behaviors can be elicited in conjunction with the diet history.

It is important to determine how the diet of the primary client compares with that of other family members, who makes the primary decisions regarding diet and feeding of the client, who is responsible for food preparation and feeding of the client at home and in other settings, and how adequate the primary client and/or caregivers perceive the client's diet and feeding practices to be. Other important considerations include adequacy of the knowledge level of the client and/or caregivers with respect to diet and feeding practices and the adequacy of resources for obtaining needed food and feeding equipment.

Observation of feeding/eating is a critical aspect of the assessment. Assessment teams often prefer to observe the client feeding independently or with assistance, as "typically" practiced, and then to use various assessment techniques to further evaluate motor, sensory, oral-motor, and behavioral characteristics. During the feeding observation, information may be gained regarding behaviors of both the primary client and the caregivers, including their interactions and their respective responses to the feeding task and to other factors in the environment. Positioning of the client for feeding is evaluated from several perspectives. The physical position of the head, trunk, and upper and lower extremities can have a major impact on motor functioning and, therefore, on ability to eat. Comfort and head and trunk stability of the client and the positioning of the feeder in relation to the client also are considered. The positioning in relation to environmental stimuli may affect oral-motor skills as well as ability to attend to the task of eating. Formally and informally, therapists evaluate the ability of the client to take food and feeding equipment to the mouth and the response of the client to foods of various temperatures, consistencies, and textures. General body tone and movement, reflex activity, and oral-facial structures are evaluated. Jaw, lip, and tongue control and the oral-motor patterns needed for sucking, biting, chewing, and swallowing also are examined. Videofluoroscopy is sometimes used for evaluation of the swallow.[17,19,98]

Biochemical Assessment

The components of biochemical assessment are frequently determined by findings from other components of the nutritional assessment. A nutritional screen may include complete blood cell count and routine urinalysis. When generalized malnutrition or deficiencies or excessive intakes of specific nutrients are suspected on the basis of the physical examination, anthropometric, and/or dietary data, laboratory tests should be requested accordingly.[97] Serum total protein and albumin and serum electrolyte values are useful in evaluating protein status, and more sensitive indicators of protein status may also be needed. These include transferrin, thyroxin-binding prealbumin, and retinol-binding protein. These parameters may be affected by factors other than protein status and must be interpreted with caution. Assessment of immune status may provide an additional indication of the severity of malnutrition.[99] Review of a client's medical records may reveal recent laboratory data that obviate the need for tests to be performed specifically in conjunction with a nutritional assessment. However, when problems are suspected, serial laboratory data may be needed to evaluate responses of the client to intervention trials.

In persons receiving anticonvulsant medications, monitoring of status with respect to folic acid, vitamin B_{12}, and vitamin D warrants particular consideration. Roe has recommended that serum and red blood cell folic acid levels, serum vitamin B_{12} levels, and hematologic profiles be evaluated prior to the initiation of anticonvulsant drug therapy and regularly thereafter.[41] Laboratory data, including plasma calcium, phosphorus, and alkaline phosphatase levels, may be useful with radiographic evidence in identifying vitamin D deficiency states. However, obtaining normal laboratory values for these parameters does not rule out the possibility that vitamin D status is stressed. Evaluation of 25-hydroxyvitamin D_3 levels may provide an additional indication of vitamin D status.[41,44,100]

INTERVENTION

Variability in characteristics of persons with cerebral palsy has been emphasized throughout this chapter and must be considered in planning for nutrition intervention. Most persons with the disorder reside in the community, and some require only primary health care. Those with more complex problems, and most likely to have complex nutrition problems, may receive services from multiple providers associated with many different agencies and institutions. Fragmentation of services creates complications for clients, their families, and the service providers. Nutrition and feeding recommendations may be received from many different sources and may be confusing, contradictory, and overwhelming. Community-based, co-ordinated, interdisciplinary services systems and integrated service plans reduce gaps and duplications in services, while promoting and facilitating the acquisition of needed services in a timely and consistent manner. This necessitates coordination and collaboration among disciplines and agencies both within and among primary, secondary, and tertiary levels of care, including health, educational, habilitation, social, and family resources. Linkages are necessary among tertiary care centers, specialty clinics, primary care physicians, hospitals, Special Supplemental Food Program for Women, Infants, and Children (WIC), public health departments, neighborhood health centers, early intervention programs, school programs, state programs for children with special health care needs, state developmental disabilities programs, vocational programs, private therapists, therapy programs, social services, residential programs, and all other agencies, programs, and persons from whom clients or client families receive services. Establishing the linkages can be time-consuming and awkward for professionals, but it becomes less difficult as community-based, coordinated service systems evolve. The initial investment of time and energy can result in improved services for the client and more effective use of time and expertise of the service provider. For some clients, a care coordinator or "case manager" will have been identified and that person can facilitate the coordination. In other situations, the nutritionist or another member of the nutritional assessment team will need to assume leadership in coordinating nutrition services for the client. Federal and state regulations have increasingly ensured the right of persons and their families or guardians to actively participate with professionals in the development of service plans.[9,10,97,101–103]

When no problems are suspected on the basis of the assessment, strengths of current health practices should be reinforced, guidance should be provided in the prevention of nutrition-related problems, and a plan for periodic monitoring should be developed. When problems are revealed or suspected, an integrated plan for intervention should be developed by the team in partnership with the client, parents, and/or guardian and in consultation and collaboration with other agencies, programs, and professionals and/or the care coordinator, as indicated. Recommendations should be prioritized and, when multiple agencies or professionals are involved, the roles and responsibilities of each in implementing the recommendations should be delineated. The recommendations should be clearly stated since many parties may be involved in their implementation. A plan for follow-up should be included.

The nutrition intervention plan for persons with cerebral palsy may include recommendations for surgical or other medical intervention, dental treatment, counseling for parents or other caregivers, behavioral interventions, changes in positioning during feeding, changes in equipment used for eating/feeding, changes in feeding techniques for oral-motor facilitation, changes in feeding schedules, and changes in diet/nutrient intake. Recommended dietary changes may relate to texture, temperature, variety and/or quantity of foods, formulas, or supplements. Financial constraints may impede the implementation of recommendations, and identification of resources should be considered in the development of intervention plans. Education, counseling, or technical assistance for the client, primary caregivers, and/or community service providers may be needed in behavior management techniques, oral-motor facilitation or other feeding considerations, dental hygiene techniques, and/or dietary selection and preparation techniques. Consistent application of appropriate techniques and practices across situations increases the likelihood that success will be achieved. Therefore, it is essential that all parties involved in a particular activity know how to implement the recommendations. Means of providing or obtaining this support should be included in intervention planning. Monitoring and follow-up are additional critical areas for inclusion in the plans.

Dietary recommendations should be based on findings from all aspects of the assessment and should be developed by the nutritionist/dietitian in concert with other team members. Working within the context of feeding goals arrived at by the assessment team, the client, family, other primary caregivers, and/or guardian, the diet should be planned to promote nutritional habilitation and optimize functioning of the client. Client food preferences, family dietary patterns, and available resources should be considered in developing the recommendations.

For the large majority of persons with cerebral palsy, feeding is accomplished through oral intake. In considering problems that may be encountered, it is important not to lose sight of the fact that not all persons with cerebral palsy have feeding problems. Nutritional problems of the general population, to which persons with cerebral palsy also are vulnerable, should not be overlooked. If feeding problems are present, therapist(s) generally determine consistencies, textures, temperatures, and volumes of intake appropriate for the client, and dietary recommendations are developed accordingly. When eating is slow and laborious, frequent feedings of shorter duration are preferable to long feeding sessions in which both the client and caregiver tire. Six to eight feedings per day, with nutrient- and energy-dense intakes at every feeding, are indicated for some clients. For others, lower calorie feedings may be indicated but the frequent feedings may still be needed to meet nutrient and fluid needs. Still other clients may be able to consume regular portions and meet their nutritional needs through more typical meal schedules. Fluid needs, fiber intake, nutrient amounts and proportions to one another, and the distribution of calories from carbohydrate, fat, and protein should be taken into account. By selecting high-nutrient and/or energy-dense food, and modifying textures and consistencies as indicated, the use of special products frequently becomes unnecessary. The addition of dehydrated infant foods, nonfat dry milk solids, dry cereals, wheat germ, margarine, or cheese is sometimes useful. Amounts should be specified. Commercially available fortified puddings or liquid supplements are indicated for some clients. Osmolality as well as nutrient distribution of the products should be taken into account.

Although requirements for specific nutrients are not known to be increased by cerebral palsy per se, questions frequently arise regarding the advisability of nutrient supplementation. The need should be evaluated individually in relation to dietary intake, medication use, apparent health status, and laboratory data. Roe has stated that the administration of small amounts of folic acid to correct folic acid deficiency in persons taking anticonvulsant drugs is warranted, despite the risk of lowering cerebrospinal fluid concentrations of anticonvulsants by administering large doses of the vitamin. Severe folic acid deficiency itself may cause neurologic deficits. She has suggested that the folacin requirement of children and adults on phenobarbital, phenytoin, and primidone is 400 to 1000 µg/d and has emphasized that effects of folic acid supplementation, which is likely to be necessary to meet those levels, should be carefully monitored hematologically and biochemically.[41] Some authors have suggested prophylactic vitamin D supplementation of patients receiving anticonvulsant medications, but vitamin D intoxication can occur.[58] Not in relation to users of anticonvulsant medications but in regard to vitamin D intakes in general, DeLuca has indicated that prophylactic doses of vitamin D greater than 1000 IU/d are not advisable. He recommends that amounts greater than 1000 IU/d be taken only by physician prescription, with serum calcium or fasting urinary calcium levels monitored once every month. According to him, serum calcium levels should not be allowed to go above 12 mg/dL.[100]

Chronic constipation frequently can be alleviated through dietary measures or through a combination of diet and exercise. Increasing fluid and fiber intake of the person often is helpful. Prunes and prune juice have a laxative effect for many persons, and other fruit juices are reported to promote defecation by some. Careful instruction may be necessary to ensure that, in the attempt to increase fluid and fiber intake of persons with feeding problems, intake of energy and nutrients does not decline. If other measures fail and laxatives are determined by the physician to be the method of choice for treating the constipation, consideration should be given to the time of administration to minimize potential adverse nutritional effects.

Several dietary measures have been recommended for clients with gastroesophageal reflux. Chocolate, alcohol, and foods high in fat are reported to reduce lower esophageal sphincter pressure, and, therefore, it has been suggested that they be avoided. Tomato and citrus products and coffee are considered to have a direct irritating effect on the esophagus and, therefore, to be avoided. Small, frequent feedings have been recommended in order to reduce gastric volume, and the thickening of feedings for infants on liquid diets has been recommended. Blount comments that the recommendations are based on very little data from controlled trials but are low risk and supported by empiric use and anecdotal records.[35] Elevation of the head is also considered to be an effective therapy.[34,35]

If the client is tube fed, the same considerations apply in selection of the formulas as with the general population. Age and size of the client, apparent fluid and nutrient requirements, osmolality of the formula, gastrointestinal function, and tolerance by the client are important considerations.[22,104] Formulas are now commercially available for infants, children, and adults. Dilutions necessary for the individual client, total volume consumed per 24 hours, and other food consumed with the formula will influence whether nutrient levels will be adequate, will be excessive, or will need to be supplemented. According to Roe, the levels of vitamin B_6 and folic acid in some commercial formulas interfere with the absorption of phenytoin and can reduce the therapeutic efficiency of the anticonvulsant in persons receiving continuous nasogastric feedings. She suggests that the feeding tube be flushed and clamped 2 hours before the medication is administered and flushed 2 hours after the medication before the formula is started again.[105] Schedules of feeding as well as formula selection should be arrived at in consultation with the physician. If oral feeding is to be continued along with tube feeding or initiated with a client who has been exclusively tube fed, it may be advantageous to space the tube feedings so as to allow the client some opportunity to experience hunger. If tube feeding occurs every 2 hours throughout the day, for example, the client may have little reason to be interested in oral feeding. The continuation of some form of oral stimulation is generally recommended whether oral feeding is to be continued or not. Therapists can make recommendations in that regard.

In considering changes in diet or feeding methods, professionals, clients, and primary caregivers should weigh potential short-term and long-term benefits and risks. While changes in food-related behaviors or feeding techniques may offer long-term benefits, attempts to implement change in diet or feeding techniques may be met with resistance from the person and result in temporary reductions in intake. Periods of nutritional habilitation need to precede the introduction of behaviorally based interventions or oral-motor facilitation techniques with some clients.

Monitoring and follow-up evaluations are critical, regardless of interventions proposed. Nutrient and energy recommendations or feeding recommendations, made with the best of professional judgment and all of the data available at the time of the evaluation, may prove to be inappropriate. Recommendations may be appropriately formulated but misunderstood, or implementation may not occur. Clients and circumstances change and, with any degree of success, recommendations are "outgrown." Through early identification of problems, intervention based on comprehensive assessment, monitoring, and periodic re-evaluations, optimal functioning is supported and the chances are minimized that the health and functioning of the person with cerebral palsy will be jeopardized by malnutrition.

REFERENCES

1. Schangenbacher KE. Diagnostic problems in pediatrics. In: Clark PN, Allen AS, eds. *Occupational Therapy for Children.* St. Louis, Mo: CV Mosby Co; 1985:94–95.

2. Wilson JM. Cerebral palsy. In: Campbell SK, ed. *Pediatric Neurologic Physical Therapy.* New York, NY: Churchill Livingstone; 1984:353–356.

3. Healy A. Cerebral palsy. In: Blackman JA, ed. *Medical Aspects of Developmental Disabilities in Children Birth to Three.* Iowa City, Iowa: Division of Developmental Disabilities, University of Iowa; 1983:31–38.

4. Holm VA. The causes of cerebral palsy: A contemporary perspective. *JAMA.* 1982; 247:1473–1477.

5. Gortmaker SL, Sappenfield W. Chronic childhood disorders: Prevalence and impact. *Pediatr Clin North Am.* 1984; 31:3–18.

6. Gortmaker SL. Chronic childhood disorders: Prevalence and impact on planning services, now and in the future. In: Dwyer J, Egan MC, eds. *The Right to Grow.* Boston, Mass: Frances Stern Nutrition Center, New England Medical Center; 1986:37–41.

7. Powell NJ. Children with cerebral palsy: Scope of the problem. In: Clark PN, Allen AS, eds. *Occupational Therapy for Children.* St. Louis, Mo: CV Mosby Co; 1985:312–314.

8. Hardman ML, Drew CJ. The physically handicapped retarded individual: A review. *Mental Retardation.* 1977; 15:43–48.

9. Kozlowski BW, Powell J. The position of the American Dietetic Association: Nutrition services for children with special health care needs. *J Am Diet Assoc.* 1989; 89:1133–1137.

10. Blyler E, Lucas B. Position of the American Dietetic Association: Nutrition in comprehensive program planning for persons with developmental disabilities. *J Am Diet Assoc.* 1987; 87:1068–1074.

11. Wodarski LA. Nutrition intervention in developmental disabilities: An interdisciplinary approach. *J Am Diet Assoc.* 1985; 85:218–221.

12. Newacheck PW, McManus MA. Financing health care for disabled children. *Pediatrics.* 1988; 81:385–394.

13. Perrin JM, Ireys HT. The organization of services for chronically ill children and their families. *Pediatr Clin North Am.* 1984; 31:235–257.

14. Kozlowski BW, et al. *Nutrition and Feeding Problems of Children with Developmental Disabilities.* Columbus, Ohio: Nisonger Center Videotape Production, Ohio State University; 1989.

15. Pipes PL, Glass RP. Nutrition and feeding of children with developmental delays and related problems. In: Pipes PL, ed. *Nutrition in Infancy and Childhood*. St. Louis, Mo: Times Mirror/Mosby; 1989:361–386.

16. Coley IL, Procter SA. Self-maintenance activities. In: Clark PN, Allen AS, eds. *Occupational Therapy for Children*. St. Louis, Mo: CV Mosby Co; 1985:218–235.

17. Lane SJ, Cloud HH. Feeding problems and intervention: An interdisciplinary approach. *Topics Clin Nutr*. 1988; 3:23–32.

18. Morris SE, Klein MD. *Pre-Feeding Skills*. Tucson, Ariz: Therapy Skill Builders; 1987.

19. Smith MAH, et al. *Feeding Management of Child with a Handicap: A Guide for Professionals*. Memphis, Tenn: Child Development Center, University of Tennessee Center for the Health Sciences; 1982.

20. Ogg HL. Oral-pharyngeal development and evaluation. *Physical Therapy*. 1975; 55:235–241.

21. Chambers DW. Patient motivation and education. In: Stewart RE, et al, eds. *Pediatric Dentistry: Scientific Foundations and Clinical Practice*. St. Louis, Mo: CV Mosby Co; 1982:630–631.

22. Wilson SE, Dietz WH, Grand RJ. An algorithm for pediatric enteral alimentation. *Pediatr Ann*. 1987; 16:233–240.

23. Patrick J, et al. Rapid correction of wasting in children with cerebral palsy. *Dev Med Child Neurol*. 1986; 28:734–739.

24. Rempel GR, Colwell SO, Nelson RP. Growth in children with cerebral palsy fed via gastrostomy. *Pediatrics*. 1988; 82:857–862.

25. Shapiro BK, et al. Growth of severely impaired children: Neurological versus nutritional factors. *Dev Med Child Neurol*. 1986; 28:729–733.

26. Davis A, Fennell K, McLaughlin J. Feeding children with cerebral palsy: Experience with supplemental gastrostomy. *Dev Med Child Neurol Abstr*. 1987; 29 (suppl 55):11.

27. Rubin L, Snyder J, Staub R. Esophagitis in children with severe cerebral palsy. *Dev Med Child Neurol Abstr*. 1987; 29 (suppl 55):10.

28. Sondheimer JM, Morris BA. Gastroesophageal reflux among severely retarded children. *J Pediatr*. 1979; 94:710–714.

29. Logemann JA. The role of the speech language pathologist in the management of dysphagia. *Otolaryngol Clin North Am*. 1988; 21:783–788.

30. Gisel EG, Patrick J. Identification of children with cerebral palsy unable to maintain a normal nutritional state. *Lancet*. 1988; 1:283–285.

31. Geertsma MA, et al. Feeding resistance after parenteral hyperalimentation. *Am J Dis Child*. 1985; 139:255–256.

32. Blackman JA, Nelson CLA. Rapid introduction of oral feedings to tube-fed patients. *J Dev Behav Pediatr*. 1987; 8:63–67.

33. Sondheimer JM. Gastroesophageal reflux: Update on pathogenesis and diagnosis. *Pediatr Clin North Am*. 1988; 35:103–116.

34. Richter JE, Castell DO. Drugs, foods, and other substances in the cause and treatment of reflux esophagitis. *Med Clin North Am*. 1981; 65:1223–1234.

35. Blount BW. Gastroesophageal reflux in children. *Am Fam Physician*. 1988; 37:201–216.

36. Johnson LF. New concepts and methods in the study and treatment of gastroesophageal reflux disease. *Med Clin North Am*. 1981; 65:1195–1221.

37. Jolley SG, Smith EI, Tunell WP. Protective antireflux operation with feeding gastrostomy: Experience with children. *Ann Surg.* 1985; 201:736–740.

38. Nussbaum E, et al. Association of lipid–laden alveolar macrophages and gastroesophageal reflux in children. *J Pediatr.* 1987; 110:190–194.

39. Staub RU, Rubin L. Nissen fundal plication for children with cerebral palsy: Long-term follow-up. *Dev Med Child Neurol Abstr.* 1987; 29(suppl. 55):10.

40. Jolley SG, et al. Surgery in children with gastroesophageal reflux and respiratory symptoms. *J Pediatr.* 1980; 96:194–198.

41. Roe DA. *Drug-Induced Nutritional Deficiencies.* Westport, Conn: AVI Publishing Co; 1985.

42. Roe DA. *Handbook: Interactions of Selected Drugs and Nutrients in Patients.* Chicago, Ill: American Dietetic Association; 1982.

43. Reynolds EH. Iatrogenic nutritional effects of anticonvulsants: Symposium on interaction of drugs and nutrition. *Proc Nutr Soc.* 1974; 33:225–229.

44. Kraus K-H, et al. Effect of long-term treatment with antiepileptic drugs on the vitamin status. *Drug–Nutrient Interactions.* 1988; 5:317–343.

45. Kozlowski BW, Wenner BB. *Nutritional Implications of Selected Medications Received by Children with Developmental Disabilities.* Columbus, Ohio: Nisonger Center for Mental Retardation and Developmental Disabilities, Ohio State University; 1982.

46. Reynolds EH. Diphenylhydantoin: Hematologic aspects of toxicity. In: Woodbury DM, Penry JK, Schmidt RP, eds. *Antiepileptic Drugs.* New York, NY: Raven Press; 1972:247–262.

47. Chanarin I, et al. Megaloblastic anaemia due to phenobarbitone: The convulsant action of therapeutic doses of folic acid. *Br Med J.* 1960; 1:1099–1102.

48. Reynolds EH, Chanarin I, Matthews DM. Neuropsychiatric aspects of anticonvulsant megaloblastic anaemia. *Lancet.* 1968; 1:394–397.

49. Eastman RD, Jancar J, Cameron JD. Red cell folate and macrocytosis during long-term anticonvulsant therapy in non-anaemic mentally retarded epileptics. *Br J Psychiatry.* 1975; 126:263–265.

50. Bowe JC, Cornish EJ, Dawson M. Evaluation of folic acid supplements in children taking phenytoin. *Dev Med Child Neurol.* 1971; 13:343–354.

51. Mattson RH, et al. Folate therapy in epilepsy: A controlled study. *Arch Neurol.* 1973; 19:78–81.

52. Hawkins CF, Meynell MJ. Macrocytosis and macrocytic anemia caused by anticonvulsant drugs. *Q J Med.* 1958; 27:45–63.

53. Neubauer C. Mental deterioration in epilepsy due to folate deficiency. *Br Med J.* 1970; 2:759–761.

54. Melpas JS, Spray GH, Witts LJ. Serum folic acid and vitamin B_{12} levels in anticonvulsant therapy. *Br Med J.* 1966; 1:955–957.

55. Reynolds EH, et al. Anticonvulsant therapy, folic acid and vitamin B_{12} metabolism and mental symptoms. *Epilepsia.* 1966; 7:261–270.

56. Hunter R, Barnes J, Matthews DM. Effect of folic-acid supplement on serum vitamin B_{12} levels in patients on anticonvulsants. *Lancet.* 1969; 2:666–667.

57. Reynolds EH, et al. Anticonvulsant therapy, megaloblastic haematopoiesis and folic acid metabolism. *Q J Med.* 1966; 35:521–537.

58. Hahn TJ. Drug-induced disorders in vitamin D and mineral metabolism. *Clin Endocrinol Metab.* 1980; 9:107–117.

59. Said HM, Redha R, Nylander W. Biotin transport in the human intestine: Inhibition by anticonvulsant drugs. *Am J Clin Nutr.* 1989; 49:127–131.

60. Krause K-H, et al. Biotin status of epileptics. *Ann NY Acad Sci.* 1985; 447:297–313.

61. Kozlowski BW, et al. Anticonvulsant medication use and circulating levels of total thyroxine, retinol binding protein, and vitamin A in children with delayed cognitive development. *Am J Clin Nutr.* 1987; 46:360–368.

62. Barnhart ER, pub. *Physicians' Desk Reference.* Oradell, NJ: Medical Economics Co, Inc.; 1989.

63. Lucas B, Sells CJ. Nutrient intake and stimulant drugs in hyperactive children. *J Am Diet Assoc.* 1977; 70:373–377.

64. Lucas B. Diet and behavior. In: Pipes PL, ed. *Nutrition in Infancy and Childhood.* St. Louis, Mo: Times Mirror/Mosby; 1989:390–392.

65. Krick J, Van Duyn MAS. The relationship between oral-motor involvement and growth: A pilot study in a pediatric population with cerebral palsy. *J Am Diet Assoc.* 1984; 84:555–559.

66. Phelps WM: Dietary requirements in cerebral palsy. *J Am Diet Assoc.* 1951; 27:869–870.

67. Leamy CM. A study of the food intake of a group of children with cerebral palsy in the Lakeville Sanatorium. *Am J Public Health.* 1953; 43:1310–1317.

68. Sterling HM. Height and weight of children with cerebral palsy and acquired brain damage. *Arch Phys Med Rehabil.* 1960; 41:131–135.

69. Ruby DO, Matheny WD. Comments on growth of cerebral palsied children. *J Am Diet Assoc.* 1962; 40:525–527.

70. Eddy TP, Nicholson AL, Wheeler EF. Energy expenditures and dietary intakes in cerebral palsy. *Dev Med Child Neurol.* 1965; 7:377–386.

71. Hammond MI, Lewis MN, Johnson EW. A nutritional study of cerebral palsied children. *J Am Diet Assoc.* 1966; 49:196–201.

72. Culley WJ, Middleton TO. Caloric requirements of mentally retarded children with or without motor dysfunction. *J Pediatr.* 1969; 75:380–384.

73. Dietz WH, Jr. Nutritional requirements and feeding of the handicapped child. In: Grande RJ, Sutphen JL, Dietz WH, Jr., eds. *Pediatric Nutrition Theory and Practice.* Boston, Mass: Butterworths Publishing, Inc; 1987:387–392.

74. Berg K, Isaksson B. Body composition and nutrition of school children with cerebral palsy. *Acta Paediatr Scand Suppl.* 1970; 204:41–52.

75. Berg K. Effect of physical activation and of improved nutrition on the body composition of school children with cerebral palsy. *Acta Paediatr Scand Suppl.* 1970; 204:53–69.

76. Spender QW, Cronk CE, Stallings VA. Fat distribution in children with cerebral palsy. *Ann Hum Biol.* 1988; 15:191–196.

77. Weinstein ML, Trahd-Morris G, Schultz L. Non-invasive means of obtaining marked improvement in growth of children with severe cerebral palsy. *Dev Med Child Neurol Abstr.* 1988; 30(suppl 57):6.

78. Brizee L, et al. Obesity of tube-fed children with cerebral palsy. *Dev Med Child Neurol Abstr.* 1987; 29(suppl 55):10.

79. Committee on Dietary Allowances, Food and Nutrition Board. *Recommended Dietary Allowances.* Washington, DC: National Academy of Sciences; 1980:23.

80. Lundberg A. Oxygen consumption in relation to work load in students with cerebral palsy. *J Appl Physiol.* 1976; 40:873–875.

81. Rose J, Medeiros JM, Parker R. Energy cost index as an estimate of energy expenditure of cerebral-palsied children during assisted ambulation. *Dev Med Child Neurol.* 1985; 27:485–490.

82. Campbell J, Bell J. Energetics of walking in cerebral palsy. *Orthop Clin North Am.* 1978; 9:374–376.

83. McLaren DS. Clinical manifestations of nutritional disorders. In: Shils ME, Young VR, eds. *Modern Nutrition in Health and Disease.* Philadelphia, Pa: Lea & Febiger; 1988:733–745.

84. Watson RC, Grossman H, Meyers MA. Radiologic findings in nutritional disturbances. In: Shils ME, Young VR, eds. *Modern Nutrition in Health and Disease.* Philadelphia, Pa: Lea & Febiger; 1988:906–928.

85. Roche AF. Growth assessment in handicapped children. *Diet Curr.* 1979; 6(5).

86. Belt-Niedbala BJ, et al. Linear growth measurement: A comparison of single arm-lengths and arm-span. *Dev Med Child Neurol.* 1986; 28:319–324.

87. Chumlea WC. Assessing growth and nutritional status of children who are chronically ill or handicapped. In: Ekvall SM, Stevens F, eds. *Nutritional Needs of the Handicapped/ Chronically Ill Child, Manual 3.* Cincinnati, Ohio: University Affiliated Cincinnati Center for Developmental Disorders; 1989:11–23.

88. Chumlea WC, Roche AF, Steinbaugh ML. Estimating stature from knee height for persons 60 to 90 years of age. *J Am Geriatr Soc.* 1985; 33:116–120.

89. Chumlea WC, Roche AF. Nutritional anthropometric assessment of non-ambulatory persons using recumbent techniques. *Am J Phys Anthropol.* 1984; 63:1.

90. Hamill PVV, et al. NCHS growth curves for children birth—18 years. *Vital Health Stat.* 1977; 11(165).

91. Roche AF, Himes HJ. Incremental growth charts. *Am J Clin Nutr.* 1980; 33:2041–2052.

92. Johnson CL, et al. Basic data on anthropometric measurements and angular measurements of the hip and knee joints for selected age groups 1–74 years of age. *Vital Health Stat.* 1981; 11(219).

93. Frisancho AR. Nutritional anthropometry. *J Am Diet Assoc.* 1988; 88:553–555.

94. Frisancho AR. *Anthropometric Standards for the Assessment of Growth and Nutritional Status.* Ann Arbor, Mich: Health Products; 1988.

95. Frisancho AR. New standards of weight and body composition by frame size and height for assessment of nutritional status of adults and the elderly. *Am J Clin Nutr.* 1984; 40:808–819.

96. Frisancho AR. New norms of upper limb fat and muscle areas for assessment of nutritional status. *Am J Clin Nutr.* 1981; 34:2540–2545.

97. Cloud HH. Nutrition assessment of the individual with developmental disabilities. *Topics Clin Nutr.* 1987; 2:53–62.

98. Sayler KL. Evaluation and management of pediatric feeding disorders. *Nutrition M.D.* 1989; 15(6):1–2.

99. MacLean WC. Protein–energy malnutrition. In: Grande RJ, Sutphen JL, Dietz WH Jr., eds. *Pediatric Nutrition: Theory and Practice.* Boston, Mass: Butterworths Publishing, Inc; 1987:421–431.

100. De Luca HF. Vitamin D and its metabolites. In: Shils ME, Young VR, eds. *Modern Nutrition in Health and Disease.* Philadelphia, Pa: Lea & Febiger; 1988:313–327.

101. Lucas B. Children with developmental disorders: Nutrition issues. *Dietitians Pediatr Practice Newsletter* 1988; 11(2):1–2.

102. Baer MT. *Nutrition Services for Children with Handicaps: A Manual for State Title V Programs.* Los Angeles, Calif: University Affiliated Training Program, Center for Child Development and Developmental Disorders; 1982.

103. Gittler J. Community-based service systems for children with special health care needs and their families. In: *The Intent and Spirit of P.L. 99–457.* Washington, DC: National Center for Clinical Infant Programs; 1989.

104. Rombeau JL, Caldwell MD. *Clinical Nutrition, Volume 1, Enteral Nutrition and Tube Feeding.* Philadelphia, Pa: WB Saunders Co; 1983.

105. Roe DA. *Diet and Drug Interactions.* New York, NY: AVI Publishing Co; 1989:52.

BIBLIOGRAPHY

Adamow CL, Glassman MS, Grant J. *Nutritional Assessment of the Handicapped Child.* American Society for Parenteral and Enteral Nutrition; 1983.

Ekvall SM, Stevens F, eds. *Nutritional Needs of the Handicapped/Chronically Ill Child. Manual 3.* Cincinnati, Ohio: University Affiliated Cincinnati Center for Developmental Disorders; 1989.

Garn SM, Weir HF. Assessing the nutritional status of the mentally retarded. *Am J Clin Nutr.* 1971; 24:853–854.

Powers DE, Moore AO. *Food–Medication Interactions.* Tempe, Ariz: F–MI Publishing; 1983.

Smith MAH, ed. *Guides for Nutritional Assessment of the Mentally Retarded and the Developmentally Disabled.* Memphis, Tenn: Child Development Center, University of Tennessee Center for the Health Sciences; 1976.

Chapter 3

Prader-Willi Syndrome

Phyllis Ann Mandella and Maria Ferraco

Prader-Willi syndrome, a complex multisystemic disorder, was first reported by Prader, Labhart, and Willi in 1956.[1] The hyperphagia and obesity associated with the syndrome present a difficult challenge for the families, educators, and health care providers working with clients with Prader-Willi syndrome. In this chapter the aspects of Prader-Willi syndrome related to obesity are reviewed, a plan is suggested for nutritional intervention, and a short-term rehabilitation program that has been successful in treating persons with Prader-Willi syndrome is described.

CLINICAL DESCRIPTION

Prader-Willi syndrome occurs once in 10,000 to 25,000 live births in all races.[2] Table 3-1 contains a list of the characteristic features of Prader-Willi syndrome.

Infancy

The hypotonia seen in infancy may present as sucking problems, in some cases necessitating the use of special nipples or tube feedings. These feeding problems are the probable cause of failure to thrive with weights generally below the 50th percentile and often below the 3rd percentile until 6 months of age.[3]

Studies done by Nugent and Holm reveal normal linear growth until about 12 months of age. Most children fall below the 50th percentile by age 36 months. Later in childhood, growth runs parallel but below the normal growth percentile curves.[3,4]

Table 3-1 Clinical Features of Prader-Willi Syndrome

Prenatal
Decreased fetal movement
Abnormal position at delivery

Infancy
Hypotonia*
Feeding problems*
Failure to thrive
Genital hypoplasia/cryptorchidism
Mild dysmorphism*
Delayed motor development*

Childhood and Adulthood
Obesity/hyperphagia*
Speech delay/poor articulation
Intellectual impairment/school problems*
Behavioral abnormalities
Small hands and feet
Strabismus/myopia
Skin picking/decreased pain sensitivity
Inability to vomit
Scoliosis
Mild short stature
Abnormal pubertal development/hypogonadism*

*Features considered essential for the diagnosis.

Source: Reprinted with permission from "Prader-Willi Syndrome" by SB Cassidy, *Current Problems in Pediatrics* (1984; 14[1]:7), Copyright © 1984, Year Book Medical Publishers.

Butler and Meaney suggest that skin fold measurements particularly over the triceps may indicate a predisposition to excess fat development before it is observed by physical examination.[5]

Childhood and Adolescence

Between the ages of 2 and 4 children with Prader-Willi syndrome develop a voracious appetite and appear to never reach a satiety point.[6] This characteristic remains throughout their life. Parents report food stealing, foraging, hoarding, gorging, and the consumption of non-normal food items (ie, dog food, unthawed frozen foods, garbage). In order to control the hyperphagia, parents have found it necessary to lock food in car trunks, place locks on refrigerators, and lock kitchens at night.

In controlled studies conducted by Zipf and Bernston, children with Prader-Willi syndrome reached a satiety level at a much slower rate than normal obese children.[7] However, contrary to earlier reports, Taylor and Caldwell state these children do have food preferences and when given a choice of volume or preference, they choose the preferred foods.[8] If adolescents and adults (16–25 years of age) are permitted to eat ad lib they can consume as much as 4600 to 5600 calories per day.[4]

Metabolic studies indicate normal uptake of fat into adipose tissue, normal regulation of mobilization of fat from adipose tissue and normal lipogenesis.[9] Fat cell numbers are similar to those of normal persons, but the cell size is significantly increased.[10,11] Serum cholesterol and triglyceride levels are normal.[12]

The energy needs of children with Prader-Willi syndrome are significantly reduced from the normal population. Schoeller and colleagues indicate the small free fat mass in persons with Prader-Willi syndrome and their reduced physical activity are the causes of the reduced energy needs, not an altered energy efficiency at the cellular level. They further suggest that body compositions calculated from total body water indicate subjects who were at near normal weight for their height still had 30% to 40% body fat. The fat distribution in Prader-Willi syndrome is atypical, with a large amount being deposited in the trunk, buttocks, and thighs. Because of this the usual skin fold standards are not reliable in the older child and adult with this disorder.[13]

Adolescents with Prader-Willi syndrome do not experience the normal adolescent growth spurt and remain short. Average adult height is 154.7 cm in males and 145 cm in females.[14] The experimental use of growth hormone in this population is limited. Lee and co-workers report linear growth in four children with the administration of growth hormone.[15] Further studies are indicated with particular monitoring of the possible side effects of growth hormone administration.

Temper tantrums that in childhood usually involve food issues escalate during adolescence. These temper tantrums make it extremely difficult for families, caregivers, and educators to withhold food.

Skin picking can lead to scarring or infection and suggests the need for adequate zinc consumption for wound healing. An increased incidence of dental caries is noted in 44% of the population. Thick, sticky, foamy saliva may be a contributing factor. Malocclusion is common (40%).[2]

Adulthood

The health of persons with Prader-Willi syndrome is compromised by obesity and its consequences. Cardiopulmonary problems (hypoventilation, hypercapnia, hypoxia, right-sided heart failure) result from the massive obesity. Type II diabetes mellitus occurs in 7% of persons with Prader-Willi syndrome, and in some cases it resolves with weight loss. Hypertension may also occur due to obesity.[2]

Greenswag surveyed the families of 232 persons with Prader-Willi syndrome 16 to 64 years of age.[14] She reported that 75% of these adults received special education and functioned at or below the sixth grade level in reading and at or below the third grade level in mathematics. The following characteristics were noted in adults with the disorder who were extremely obese:

- Families rated them as lazy, sleepy, slow moving, and antisocial with family members.
- Those who lived at home were heavier than those who lived away from their families.
- Those living alone (five persons) had weights significantly higher than those more closely supervised.
- There was a higher incidence of diabetes mellitus type I and type II.

Goldman reviewed the case histories of two women 54 and 69 years of age with Prader-Willi syndrome who were undiagnosed until age 54 and 67, respectively. Both exhibited difficult-to-control obesity even when placed on 1000- to 1500-calorie diets, short stature, temper tantrums, obsession with food, poor social skills with peers, and their physical appearance indicated premature aging beginning in middle age.[16]

The recurrence rate of Prader-Willi syndrome in families appears to be less than 1:1000.[17] In the 232 cases reviewed by Greenswag, none of the persons produced offspring.

NUTRITIONAL INTERVENTION

The treatment of Prader-Willi syndrome requires the involvement of a multidisciplinary team. The success of a weight management program for this population is dependent on whether the caregivers receive assistance with behavior management and on physical exercise regimens. A model for this interdisciplinary approach has been described by Wodarski and co-workers.[18]

Infancy

In contrast to later life the nutritional intervention indicated in infancy is one of obtaining adequate nutritional consumption. Infants are breast or bottle fed for the first 6 months. Special nipples (ie, enlarged holes, those designed for premature infants), short frequent feedings, more calorie-dense formulas, and short-term nasogastric feedings may be indicated for the hypotonic infant with Prader-Willi syndrome. Strained foods are introduced after 5 to 6 months. Caloric intake is adjusted to promote growth within the 50th to 75th percentile weight for height during the first 2 years.[19] Close monitoring of growth and weight is indicated.

Childhood and Adolescence

As the child's feeding skills develop and approach a normal pattern, weight gain is closely monitored. In 1976, Holm and Pipes defined the caloric requirements for Prader-Willi syndrome to be 7 kcal/cm of height for slow weight loss and 8 to 11 kcal/cm of height for weight maintenance.[20] Stadler's review of the literature finds these figures to be accurate today.[21]

Approximately 25% of the calories in the diet should be from high biologic protein, 50% from complex carbohydrate, and 25% from fat derived from those found naturally in foods.[21] To obtain the recommended dietary allowance for vitamins and minerals,[22] supplementation is necessary.

The Prader-Willi syndrome growth curves (Figures 3-1 and 3-2) can be used to monitor adequate growth on the low-calorie level diets dictated by the syndrome.[23]

Adulthood

The diet prescription described previously is also valid during the adult phase of the syndrome. However, diabetes mellitus and hypertension may require additional restrictions to the diet. Osteoporosis has been identified in the Prader-Willi syndrome population, and marginal calcium intakes due to the diet restrictions may be a contributing factor. Calcium intake levels of 1000 to 1200 mg/d are recommended.[24]

DIET COUNSELING

Several weight loss regimens have been reported that were unsuccessful in obtaining or maintaining weight loss in Prader-Willi syndrome. Fonkalsrud and Bray reported an initial satisfactory weight loss in a 17-year-old client after a vagotomy, but his weight had almost returned to

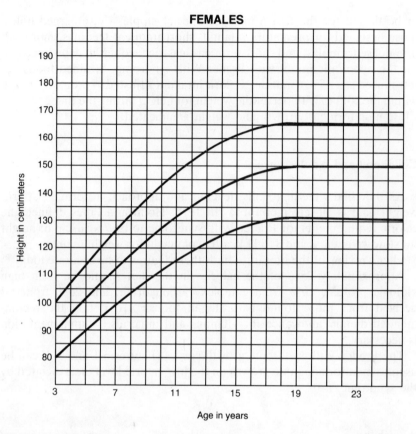

Figure 3-1 Prader-Willi syndrome growth chart: Females 3 years to early adulthood. *Source:* Reprinted from *Management of Prader-Willi Syndrome* (p 239) by LR Greenswag and RC Alexander (Eds) with permission of the Prader-Willi Syndrome Association, © 1988.

normal 11 months after surgery.[25] The use of a protein-sparing modified fast with four persons produced successful weight loss and maintenance in one case and limited weight maintenance in two cases and was unsuccessful in weight loss in the other case.[26] Naloxone[7] and naltrexone[27] (appetite suppressant drugs) appear to have no effect on appetite suppression in Prader-Willi syndrome.

In 1973, Pipes and Holm described a diet counseling program that includes the following[28]:

- careful ongoing education of the primary caregiver about the prescribed diet

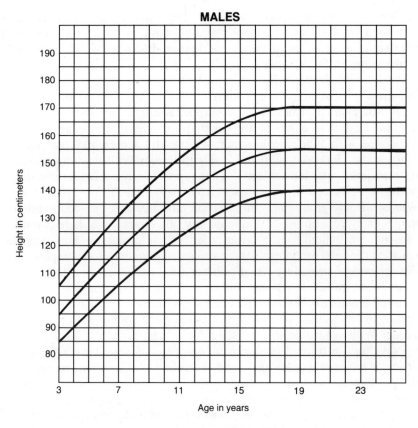

Figure 3-2 Prader-Willi syndrome growth chart: Males 3 years to early adulthood. *Source:* Reprinted from *Management of Prader-Willi Syndrome* (p 239) by LR Greenswag and RC Alexander (Eds) with permission of the Prader-Willi Syndrome Association, © 1988.

- involvement of the immediate and extended family in adherence to the diet
- environmental controls that may include locking the refrigerator and the kitchen
- education of teachers and employees about the syndrome and the necessity to control the access to food
- frequent monitoring of the child's growth and weight with diet adjustments as indicated
- education of the child in the necessary low calorie life style.

These principles have been used successfully in two outpatient programs described by Stadler[21] and Coplin and co-workers[29] and in a short-term rehabilitation program at the Rehabilitation Institute of Pittsburgh (described later in this chapter).

Persons with Prader-Willi syndrome have some intellectual and cognitive impairments that affect diet counseling strategies. One of the essential diagnostic characteristics of the syndrome is intellectual impairment (see Table 3-1), but researchers are beginning to identify learning problems associated with Prader-Willi syndrome that IQ scores may not predict. Warren and Hart compared children with Prader-Willi syndrome and undifferentiated retarded subjects.[30] They reported more short-term memory problems and more information lost from memory over time in the Prader-Willi syndrome group. This information indicates that diet counseling requires many repetitions of simple dietary objectives since there is limited capacity for building on previously learned information. For example, teaching the food exchanges for casserole dishes may be too complex without repeatedly providing visual cues for food exchanges and the components of the casserole. Grabel and co-workers noted deficits in tasks that involved auditory information processing.[31] Visual cues such as food models, scales, and measuring utensils are indicated when counseling a person with Prader-Willi syndrome.

Providing nutritional management for persons with Prader-Willi syndrome is extremely challenging and rewarding. An excellent resource for the professional and the caregiver is the National Prader-Willi Syndrome Association.* This active group of parents and professionals sponsors an annual conference, publishes six newsletters annually, and serves as a resource for researchers, practitioners, and caregivers worldwide.

The Rehabilitation Institute of Pittsburgh has been identified by the Prader-Willi Syndrome Association as a crisis center for families with a child with the disorder. Persons with life-threatening medical complications or unmanageable behavior problems may be referred for short-term inpatient treatment. A description of the services provided by the Rehabilitation Institute of Pittsburgh follows.

EXAMPLE OF A REHABILITATION PROGRAM

Philosophy and Objectives

A rehabilitation program for Prader-Willi syndrome was designed at the Rehabilitation Institute of Pittsburgh to address the unique needs of these

---

*6490 Excelsior Boulevard #102, St. Louis Park, Minnesota 55426.

children and young adults in a group setting. The plan and organization of activities and curriculum were developed to create peer interaction and provide support in dealing with weight control, physical fitness, and social adaptability.

The major objectives of the Prader-Willi program are to (1) develop nutritional awareness through the red–yellow–green color-coded system of weight control, (2) improve physical fitness with exercise, and (3) increase social adaptability through social skills and language training and through participation in a very structured environment. These three areas were chosen as focus for the program because they are the most debilitating features of the syndrome. In addition, these areas respond best to educational and behavioral intervention.[32]

Client Population

The population of persons with Prader-Willi syndrome at the Rehabilitation Institute of Pittsburgh range in age from 4 years to middle-aged adults. The program has in 8 years provided services to more than 100 clients from all over the United States. Summer sessions average 26 days of intense and condensed programming. Fall, winter, and spring sessions average 3 to 6 months and are individualized based on the person's needs. Within each session clients are grouped by IQ and social function.

Treatment Environment

The Rehabilitation Institute of Pittsburgh is licensed by the state of Pennsylvania as a specialty hospital. It is also accredited by the Joint Commission on Accreditation of Healthcare Organizations, the Commission on Accreditation of Rehabilitation Facilities, and the Pennsylvania Department of Education. The Institute is located in a residential section of the city of Pittsburgh and provides individualized comprehensive rehabilitation services.

Interdisciplinary Team

Prader-Willi syndrome presents a constellation of symptoms that require the expertise of many disciplines for management. The interdisciplinary team comprises a program coordinator, pediatrician, social worker, psychologist, psychiatrist, speech and language therapist, physical therapist, occupational therapist, registered dietitian, exercise physiologist, vocational career services developer, child development nursing unit team leader, and health care workers. Ancillary services include computer training, library sciences, music, and art.

Program Components

Psychology

Behavior management is individualized based on the Prader-Willi syndrome person's needs. The behaviors most often identified are rigidity, perseverative questioning, verbal intrusions, physical aggression and temper tantrums, poor social skills, and stubbornness. Caregivers are supplied with strategies to deal with these behaviors in the community setting. Severe behaviors may warrant small doses of psychotropic medications prescribed by the program's consulting psychiatrist.

The entire program revolves around a point system designed by the psychologist and the team leader of the nursing unit. The main focus of the system is for the client to participate in unit activities, exercise programs, therapies, activities of daily living, and an individualized behavior program. The individualized behavior program focuses on adhering to the diet, staying calm, compliance to staff requests, self-help skills, appropriate social interactions, and nonintrusive behavior with staff and/or peers. Earned points are reviewed frequently by unit staff and the client for positive reinforcement. Points are deducted for dangerous behaviors (ie, hitting others or throwing objects), destruction of property and being "off limits" (ie, not being in area/activity that is designated on the schedule). The points earned are converted into money bimonthly for shopping trips in the local community. The client may earn a maximum of $3 a week if all points are obtained in every therapy and living unit activity. Positive reinforcement for persons with Prader-Willi syndrome is effective when realistic expectations are clearly understood and consistency is maintained.

Nutrition

The initial nutritional assessment includes anthropometric measurements, review of the medical chart, and a diet history. Because clients with Prader-Willi syndrome are short, weight is correlated with height rather than age. Using the National Center for Health Statistics (NCHS) Physical Growth Percentiles,[19] it is possible to plot the height of the client at the 50th percentile and the corresponding weight (at that 50th percentile) is determined to be the ideal body weight. For extremely obese clients, 15 to 20 pounds is added to this ideal body weight to determine a realistic and achievable goal weight. The medical chart is reviewed for medications (ie, diabetic, hypertensive, psychotropic) and laboratory values (ie, abnormal blood glucose, cholesterol, triglycerides, hematocrit, and hemoglobin). Food and drug interactions are checked. A diet history is obtained from family members for previous low calorie diet instructions, past or present significant weight loss, food allergies, and typical meals or snacks at home, work, or school.

The above information is used to develop a nutritional treatment plan for the client. A client placed on a diet of less than 1000 calories is ordered a vitamin and mineral supplement.

The nutritional treatment plan goals are to

- educate the patients and parents in the red–yellow–green system of weight control, including meal patterns
- modify recipes to prepare low calorie snacks and meals
- provide follow-up after discharge from the program

Red–Yellow–Green System of Weight Control. The red–yellow–green system of weight control* involves the use of a stoplight in reference to food categories (Table 3-2).[33] Green "go" foods are low in calories (20 kcal or less per serving), and they are permitted in liberal amounts. Yellow "caution" foods are higher in calories, are rich in nutrients, and must be eaten in limited amounts (weighed or measured). Red "stop" foods are high in calories, are high in fats and/or sugars, and have limited nutrient value. Red foods are only permitted *once a month*. A red "stop" food provides diet relief and an incentive to carry on with the low calorie regimen of daily living.

Because of the low calorie level of the diet (usually 600 or 800 calories), it is essential for each client to know what breakfast, lunch, dinner, and snack include. This goal is readily accomplished within 24 to 28 hours of admission. Persons with Prader-Willi syndrome do not want to be cheated when food is involved.

Dry and liquid measurements are taught with the use of scale, measuring cups, and spoons. Portion sizes are discussed frequently in reference to calorie limits. Learning activities are designed to incorporate movement (caloric expenditure) when possible. Examples of nutrition activities include a label-reading game using empty cans or containers placed throughout the room and a meal-search game using food pictures to construct meal patterns.

---

*This system was adapted from L.H. Epstein, PhD grant 12520 from the National Institute of Child Health and Human Development *Family Based Weight Control Program and Manual.*

Table 3-2 Sample Food Lists and Serving Sizes from the Red–Yellow–Green System of Weight Control

Green "Go" Foods	Yellow "Caution" Foods	Red "Stop" Foods
Liberal amounts of the following:	*Meat Group*	*Meat Group*
Asparagus	1 oz beef roast	1 fried chicken leg
Broccoli	1 oz chicken	1 serving BBQ
Celery	1 oz ham	spareribs
Tomato juice	*Bread & Cereal Group*	*Bread & Cereal Group*
Diet beverages	1 biscuit	1 c. French fries
Sugar-free gelatin	1 dinner roll	1 c. sugar-coated
Lettuce	1 slice bread	cereal
	5 pretzels	1 donut
	1/2 c. noodles	1 slice pie
	1/2 c. beets	
	Milk & Dairy Group	*Milk & Dairy Group*
	1 c. skim milk	1 c. chocolate milk
	1 c. low calorie cocoa	1 ice cream
	1/2 c. low fat cottage	sandwich
	cheese	1 c. fruit-flavored
		yogurt
	Fruit Group	*Fruit Group*
	1/2 c. unsweetened juice	1/2 c. canned fruit in
	1/2 c. fresh pineapple	heavy syrup
	1 small apple	

A lunch and dinner training table based on the red–yellow–green system provides meal service to persons with Prader-Willi syndrome for more learning reinforcement. Green "go" foods are located on a self-service salad bar. Desserts (fruits, diet gelatin, frozen juices) are preportioned. Milk selections include skimmed milk in 4- or 8-ounce portions. The remaining yellow "caution" foods are served by a food service worker. Clients are able to select their food and build a meal within their own meal pattern design (Table 3-3).

Recipe Modification and Food Preparation. Clients are taught to lower fats in recipes by substituting bouillon or low calorie butter flavorings. They also experiment with adding sugar substitutes and herbs and spices for flavoring. Using this information, participants plan and prepare a meal from appetizer to dessert. They also prepare a low calorie snack weekly.

Table 3–3 600- and 800-Calorie Meal Patterns

600—Calorie Servings				Food Group	800—Calorie Servings			
Breakfast	Lunch	Dinner	Snack	"Caution"	Breakfast	Lunch	Dinner	Snack
Liberal	Liberal	Liberal	Liberal	Green "Go"	Liberal	Liberal	Liberal	Liberal
	1	1		Yellow "Caution" Meat		1	2	
1	1/2	1/2		Bread & Cereal	1	1	1	
1/2	1/2	1/2		Milk & Dairy	1/2	1/2	1/2	
1		1	1	Fruit	1	1	1	1

Follow-up. Prior to discharge, clients receive a set of picture and word cards that are laminated, color coded, and pocket size. Each card denotes one serving from each food group (green "go," yellow "caution" meat, yellow "caution" bread and starch, etc.). Each set contains the correct number of food group choices for the day based on the person's discharge diet meal pattern. Parents and/or caregivers are encouraged to collect the appropriate card(s) as foods are selected at meal and snack time. The cards are returned to the person each morning and reused daily for red–yellow–green system reinforcement.

At discharge it is also recommended that the client and parent mark the calendar date for the once-a-month red food choice. This prevents problems around special events throughout the month that may involve an abundance of the "stop" foods. However, special holiday meals are recognized as important "feast" days; a heaping tablespoon of each food served, including desserts, is permitted that day, at that meal. The other two meals of that day must follow the regular low calorie meal pattern.

At discharge parents or caregivers are also given a set of 12 stamped, addressed postcards. The client and family members are requested to return a card monthly stating the person's weight and a note to the dietitian. A quarterly newsletter is also mailed to clients and parents containing riddles, games, and recipes, all with the red–yellow–green theme.

Exercise Physiology

General goals for exercise physiology include

- increasing cardiopulmonary capacity through walking, climbing stairs, swimming, and floor exercises
- decreasing current body weight
- decreasing the percentage of body fat
- improving balance training
- improving locomotion awareness by learning the primary patterns of hopping and jumping

These exercises are a vital part of the program and are included two to three times within the daily routine.

Occupational Therapy and Physical Therapy

Occupational therapists and physical therapists are significant members of the interdisciplinary team. Their roles are interrelated and their program goals are to improve gross and fine motor development, bilateral hand usage, and visual perceptual skills. These therapists promote optimal health and work potential by assisting persons with Prader-Willi syndrome in mastering independence in daily living skills. These daily living skills include self-care activities (eg, dressing, bathing) and functional skills (eg, riding the bus, sorting clothes for the laundry).

Social Service

Social service provides persons with Prader-Willi syndrome with an understanding of their disability and help in handling its symptoms. Misconceptions of Prader-Willi syndrome are clarified and clients acquire knowledge to cope with their own behaviors and feelings.

Speech and Language Therapy

Communication development is necessary for the client for social acceptability in the community. Vocabulary, receptive and expressive language, decision making, and problem solving all are practiced through card and board games, group projects such as quilt making and "game show" performances, and group discussions of each day's events.

Vocational Career Services

Vocational career services are offered for the young adult with Prader-Willi syndrome who has completed formal education. The clients are assisted in identifying realistic occupations and also work on the following goals needed in any work setting: (1) following simple directions and tasks, (2) interacting appropriately with peers and staff, and (3) developing stamina for a 60-minute job.

At present, sheltered workshops are the most realistic work placements. The competitive work setting is usually not realistic for persons with Prader-Willi syndrome because of their emotional instability.

Ancillary Services

Social skills are practiced during ancillary services programming time. In computer training persons use a variety of group games to practice computer skills, cooperation among peers, information-sharing techniques, and expressive language through the use of questions and answers. Bibliotherapy is the integration of library and related materials to promote communication. During library programming time, persons actively participate in creative dramatics, library skills development activities, and demonstrations such as humane education (eg, pet care) and horticulture (eg, planting seeds). Art provides a medium for self-expression, problem solving, increased self-esteem through project completion, and eye–hand coordination practice. Music enables persons with Prader-Willi syndrome to improve their self-image and acquire rhythmic skills through the use of folk and square dancing, greeting songs, and musical instruments and games.

CONCLUSION

The person with Prader-Willi syndrome requires nutritional intervention throughout life. Nutrition professionals who assist in the management of Prader-Willi syndrome obesity need to understand the uniqueness of the syndrome. They also need the expertise of an interdisciplinary team to aid the caregiver with the behaviors centered around food accessibility. Adequate nutritional intake in infancy and, starting in childhood, well-balanced low calorie diets and environmental controls around food are the intervention techniques for effective nutritional management of this complex syndrome.

REFERENCES

1. Prader A, Labhart A, Willi H. Ein Syndrom von Adipositas Kleinwuchs, Kryptorchismus und Oligophrenie nach Myotonicartigem Zustand in Neugeborenalter. *Schweiz Med Wochenschr.* 1956; 86:1260–1261.

2. Cassidy SB. Prader-Willi syndrome characteristics, management, and etiology. *Ala J Med Sci.* 1981; 24:169.

3. Nugent JK, Holm VA. Physical growth in Prader-Willi syndrome. In: Holm VA, Sulzbacher S, eds. *Prader-Willi Syndrome.* Baltimore, Md: University Park Press; 1981:269–280.

4. Bray GA, et al. The Prader-Willi syndrome: A study of 40 patients and a review of the literature. *Medicine.* 1983; 62:59–80.

5. Butler M, Meaney FJ. An anthropometric study of 38 individuals with Prader-Labhart-Willi syndrome. *Am J Med Genet.* 1987; 26:445–455.

6. Cassidy SB. Prader-Willi syndrome. *Curr Prob Pediatr.* 1984; 14:18.

7. Zipf WB, Bernston GG. Characteristics of abnormal food-intake patterns in children with Prader-Willi syndrome and study of effects of naloxone. *Am J Clin Nutr.* 1987;46:277–281.

8. Taylor RL, Caldwell ML. Type and strength of food preferences of individuals with Prader-Willi syndrome. *J Ment Defic Res.* 1965; 29:109–112.

9. Bier DM, Kaplan SL, Havel RJ. The Prader-Willi syndrome regulation of fat transport. *Diabetes.* 1977; 26:874–880.

10. Ginsberg-Fellner F. Growth of adipose tissue in infants, children and adolescents: Variations in growth disorders. *Int J Obesity.* 1981; 5:605–611.

11. Gurr MI, et al. Adipose tissue cellularity in man: The relationship between fat cell size and number, the mass and distribution of body fat and the history of weight gain and loss. *Int J Obesity.* 1982; 6:419–436.

12. Nelson RA, et al. Nutrition, metabolism, body composition and response to the ketogenic diet in Prader-Willi syndrome. In: Holm VA, Sulzbacher S, Pipes PL, eds. *Prader-Willi Syndrome.* Baltimore, Md: University Park Press; 1981:105–120.

13. Schoeller DA, et al. Energy expenditure and body composition in Prader-Willi syndrome. *Metabolism.* 1988; 31:115–120.

14. Greenswag LR. Adults with Prader-Willi syndrome: A survey of 232 cases. *Dev Med Child Neurol.* 1987; 29:145–152.

15. Lee PDK, et al. Linear growth response to exogenous growth hormone in Prader-Willi syndrome. *Am J Med Genet.* 1987; 28:865–871.

16. Goldman JJ. Prader-Willi syndrome in two institutionalized older adults. *Ment Retard.* 1988; 26:97–102.

17. Cassidy SB. Letter to the editor: Recurrence risk in Prader-Willi syndrome. *Am J Med Genet.* 1987; 28:59–60.

18. Wodarski LA, Bundschuh E, Forbus WR. Interdisciplinary case management: A model for intervention. *J Am Diet Assoc.* 1988; 88:332–335.

19. Hamill P, et al. Physical growth: NCHS percentiles. *Am J Clin Nutr.* 1979; 32:607–629.

20. Holm VA, Pipes PL. Food and children with Prader-Willi syndrome. *Am J Dis Child.* 1976; 130:1063–1067.

21. Stadler DD. Nutritional management. In: Greenswag LR, Alexander RC, eds. *Management of Prader-Willi Syndrome.* New York, NY: Springer-Verlag; 1988:76–98.

22. Committee on Dietary Allowances Food and Nutrition Board. *Recommended Dietary Allowances—Ninth Revised Edition.* Washington, DC: National Academy of Sciences; 1980.

23. Holm VA, Nugent JK. Growth in the Prader-Willi syndrome. *Birth Defects.* 1982; 18:93–100.

24. Rubin K, Cassidy SB. Hypogonadism and osteoporosis. In: Greenswag LR, Alexander RC, eds. *Management of Prader-Willi Syndrome.* New York, NY: Springer-Verlag; 1988:31.

25. Fonkalsrud EW, Bray G. Vagotomy for treatment of obesity in childhood due to Prader-Willi syndrome. *J Pediatr Surg.* 1981; 16:888–889.

26. Bistrian BR, Blackburn GL, Stanburg JB. Metabolic aspects of a protein-sparing modified fast in the dietary management of Prader-Willi obesity. *N Engl J Med.* 1977; 296:774–779.

27. Zlotlan SH, Fettes IM, Stallings VA. The effects of naltrexone, an oral β-endorphin antagonist in children with Prader-Willi syndrome. *J Clin Endocrinol Metab.* 1986; 63:1229–1232.

28. Pipes PL, Holm VA. Weight control of children with Prader-Willi syndrome. *J Am Diet Assoc.* 1973; 63:520–524.

29. Coplin SS, Hine J, Gormician A. Outpatient management in the Prader-Willi syndrome. *J Am Diet Assoc.* 1976; 68:330–334.

30. Warren JL, Hart E. Cognitive processing in children with Prader-Willi syndrome. In: Holm VA, Sulzbacher S, eds. *Prader-Willi Syndrome.* Baltimore, Md: University Park Press; 1981:161–177.

31. Gabel S, et al. Neuropsychological capacity of Prader-Willi children: General and specific aspects of impairment. *Appl Res Ment Retard.* 1986; 7:459–466.

32. Vogl B. *The Effect of a Special Rehabilitation Group Program for Children with Prader-Willi Syndrome on Selected Measures of Weight, Physical Fitness, Social Adaptability and Personality Factors.* Pittsburgh, Pa: University of Pittsburgh; 1983. Thesis.

33. Akers M, Mandella P. *Red, Yellow, Green System of Weight Control.* Pittsburgh, Pa: Rehabilitation Institute of Pittsburgh; 1984.

Chapter 4

Muscular Dystrophy

Carolyn Gleason

Muscular dystrophy is a term applied to a group of hereditary disorders involving progressive degeneration of skeletal muscle and resulting weakness. The several forms of muscular dystrophy are classified according to genetic inheritance. Duchenne (also termed *pseudohypertrophic* or *childhood progressive*) muscular dystrophy and Becker's muscular dystrophy are sex-linked recessive genetic disorders, differing primarily in severity. Limb-girdle and congenital muscular dystrophy are autosomal recessive disorders. Facioscapulohumeral muscular dystrophy is inherited as an autosomal dominant trait.[1]

DUCHENNE MUSCULAR DYSTROPHY

Duchenne muscular dystrophy (DMD) is the most common and most severe form of muscular dystrophy. Progressive and severe muscle degeneration begins very early in life and leads to death by the second or third decade. In addition to the classic muscle involvement, cardiac and respiratory abnormalities are evident. Levels of several serum enzymes involved in energy metabolism are elevated. Numerous cellular and biochemical abnormalities are found in muscle, nerve, red blood cells, and fibroblastic cells of patients. Because of its X-linked inheritance, DMD is usually transmitted through unaffected female carriers who have a 50% probability of bearing an affected son. Spontaneous mutations, with a noncarrier mother, account for 30% of cases.[2] Incidence in the United States is one in every 3,000 boys, or three per 100,000 general population.[3,4]

No serious theories or studies indicate that nutritional or dietary factors directly cause or contribute to a cure of muscular dystrophy. However, the biochemical, physical, and psychosocial features of the disease have a tremendous impact on the client's growth, dietary intake, and nutritional status. Additionally, the person's diet and nutritional status play a significant role in treatment and management of the disease.

Clinical Features

The child with DMD appears normal at birth.[4] Infants may initially seem "floppy" but reach early motor milestones appropriately. Independent ambulation may be late, and toddlers with DMD tend to walk with toes to the ground, heel slightly elevated.[1] Clinical symptoms become apparent at 2 to 5 years of age; standing and walking are increasingly clumsy, with frequent falls, broad gait, and slight waddling.[4] Calf muscle enlargement (pseudohypertrophy) is one of the first physical features seen. The clinically enlarged but weakened muscles have a hard, rubbery texture caused by infiltration by fat and fibrous tissue. Muscle biopsy shows fibrosis and degenerating muscle fibers. As the disease progresses, these fibers are replaced by connective tissue and fat.[1] This phenomenon is believed to be an exaggeration of the condition in all of the person's muscle tissues.[5] Progressive weakness of muscles supporting and motivating the pelvic girdle leads to the lack of agility and to impaired stair climbing.[6] Lordosis gradually increases, leading to swayback in the ambulatory years. Typically, the heels are slightly off the ground in walking.[4]

The child's early years are characterized by an increasing inability to keep up with peers. Between 7 and 13 years of age, loss of ambulation is imminent but in some cases can be postponed by bracing and orthopedic surgery.[7] Quality of life can be improved by maintaining the ability to stand and walk for as long as possible. Once walking is not feasible, a wheelchair can be used as long as significant scoliosis does not develop.[1] Once the child begins using a wheelchair, calf muscles shorten and stretch reflexes disappear. The feet begin to turn downward and inward, resulting in equinovarus.[6] Contractures develop initially at ankles, knees, and hips and later at elbows, shoulders, and wrists.[6] Shoulder muscles become extremely weak, then all upper extremities weaken, and eventually use of the arms is lost. Hand muscles retain some strength longer than those of the arms, but dexterity is limited.[1]

There is no known neurologic involvement in DMD, and sensation is normal. IQ is usually about 20 points below the mean but does not deteriorate with progression of the disease.[8] In many cases, weakness of facial muscles limits facial expression, which may give the impression of intellectual dullness.[1]

As the disease progresses in the older person with DMD, scoliosis usually develops and hinders an already weak respiratory system. Vital capacity is reduced as continuing weakness and poor respiration lead to severe complications from simple colds or infections. Cardiomyopathy develops and may become severe. Ultimate involvement of face and neck muscles causes a lolling head, tongue enlargement, and slack mouth. Death usually occurs between 15 and 26 years of age. Pneumonia, ventilatory failure, or cardiac arrhythmia is usually the terminal event.[4,6]

Biochemical Features

Muscle Protein Metabolism

A common feature in DMD is loss of muscle protein. In normal muscle, protein balance results from a steady-state of synthesis and degradation.[9] In DMD, muscle protein synthesis is reduced. Protein degradation is not elevated, as evidenced by the low creatinine excretion; it may even slow in response to the decreased synthesis.[10] Apparently the fall in the rate of protein synthesis is a dominant characteristic and immediate cause of muscle wasting in DMD.[9]

Muscle Cell Membrane Defect

Studies suggest that the basic biochemical defect in DMD is an increase in muscle membrane permeability.[11-13] One widely held belief is that this permeability allows for a large influx of calcium into the muscle cell, contributing to the destruction of affected muscles and leading to many of the other abnormalities of DMD.[3,11] Muscle sodium concentration is not significantly altered. Magnesium and potassium levels are decreased, although the ratio of magnesium to potassium is normal. These findings suggest that the membrane permeability defect may be relatively specific in allowing an influx of calcium but not other extracellular components, or that there is a specific loss of some intracellular components from the cell.[13]

The earliest detectable abnormality in DMD is an increase in serum creatine kinase, which occurs before any measurable muscle degeneration. This is believed to be the result of leakage from muscle cells.[3] Normally, adult muscles use creatine in energy reactions and excrete creatinine as a waste product. In DMD, muscle wastage causes impaired creatine utilization; unused creatine "leaks" through the cell membrane and accumulates in blood and urine.[14] Serum levels of creatine kinase and myoglobin fluctuate from day to day, correlating with physical activity and suggesting the possibility of abnormal fatty acid metabolism.

The permeability of muscle cells also leads to leakage of other muscle enzymes into the blood. Creatine phosphokinase (CPK), which normally metabolizes creatine, is markedly elevated in the blood of DMD patients and carriers. CPK is now used as a diagnostic and evaluative measure. As DMD progresses and more muscles waste, serum enzyme levels tend to fall, apparently because fewer muscle cells are available to leak their enzymes.[14]

Finally, insulin resistance may characterize DMD, since some investigators report defective glucose utilization after parenteral administration of glucose and insulin. The cause of the insulin resistance might lie in a genetically induced alteration in the cell membrane involving the insulin receptor.[12]

Emotional and Psychosocial Considerations

Emotional, psychological, and social factors have a major impact on the child and the family. As noted previously, a slightly low IQ is somewhat common in DMD.[15] Passivity and social withdrawal are often observed. Heavy reliance on others often accentuates the child's stress to the family.[14] The child often develops a dispassionate acceptance of setbacks once the full impact of the disease occurs. One researcher found that 25% of persons with DMD studied believed that their problems resulted from their own incompetence.[16] Another author identified four personality traits common to children with DMD: (1) feelings of physical inadequacy, (2) immaturity, (3) body anxiety, and (4) insecurity.[17]

The most common family coping mechanisms for dealing with DMD are denial, magical thinking, and overprotection.[17] Common behaviors are socially isolating the child; seeking private education; excessive monetary indulgence; lack of discipline; and exceedingly high expectations from caregivers.[16] As the disease progresses, hopelessness and frustrations may be expressed as denial, guilt, depression, indifference, and/or hostility.[14] The mother may be especially prone to psychosocial stress, since she may shoulder excessive guilt as the carrier of the "bad gene" and she is most prone to the chronic sorrow of dealing with terminal childhood disease. She may exhibit overprotection or rejection. Anticipatory grief may help in coping with impending death as she gradually relinquishes emotional attachment to the child, but this may occur prematurely.[18]

Treatment and Management

The muscle degeneration in DMD is not reversible or even subject to remission or slowing.[14] The prognosis of early death leads to emotional upheaval for the person and the family from the time of diagnosis. Major objectives in therapy are predicting and preventing secondary complications, active physical and occupational therapy, medical monitoring, and family support.[19] Any discovery of effective treatment will only arrest the disease at that current stage; thus the person should maintain optimum possible health status in anticipation of that discovery.[20] The nutritional goal is to prevent nutrition-related complications and maintain the best nutritional status possible considering the impact of the disease.

Clinical Management

The major goal in early treatment of DMD is to maintain functional ambulation as long as possible. Stretching and night bracing are used in younger persons. Prevention of contractures of the lower extremities is stressed. Once ambulation ceases, severe contractions and scoliosis are difficult to prevent and manage and pulmonary function deteriorates. To delay the transition to a wheelchair, surgical intervention may be tried when bracing no longer works. This usually consists of incisions to release contractures of the hip and ankle. Thinner children require more simplified procedures, have greatly reduced postoperative discomfort, and require hastened postoperative mobilization. After surgery, leg casts, then continued bracing, are necessary. An additional 2 to 3 years of ambulation may be possible from surgical intervention.[1] By age 12 or 13, however, muscle weakness is so great that walking is not possible and the child is wheelchair bound. Spinal deformity becomes a threat. Severe scoliosis can lead to the inability to sit and steady decreases in pulmonary function. Many surgeons thus recommend spinal fusion for the entire thoracolumbar spine.[1]

Drug Therapy

Since the exact biochemical processes of DMD are not delineated, drug therapy is not clearly defined. However, the desperate nature of the disease has led to studies of agents with potential for modifying the synthesis or degradation of muscle protein. Leucine, branched-chain ketoacids, calcium antagonists such as nifedipine and diltiazem, allopurinol, penicillamine, and protease inhibitors have been tried, with variable results.[8,13]

One proposed therapeutic strategy of interest to nutritionists involves the use of growth inhibitors. The rationale is a theory that clinical symptoms of DMD are caused by a progressively severe imbalance of growth rate between bones and muscles. Thus symptoms could be alleviated if growth, including bone growth, could be arrested. Proponents of this strategy point out that the severity of DMD symptoms seems to correlate with height and weight. Also, heavier and taller patients appear to have poorer performance than shorter and lighter peers. Finally, a negative correlation between height and weight versus serum enzymes has been found. The theory is also supported by a report describing a person with hypopituitarism who had an unusually benign course of DMD.[7] A twin study using the growth inhibitor mazindol showed some beneficial effects of the drug.[21] Mazindol is an appetite suppressant as well, and investigators anticipate a side benefit in diminishing the effects of obesity. Another growth inhibitor, somatostatin, blocks potassium flux from cells and reduces calcium flux into cells. Since buildup of calcium in muscle cells is a major pathologic finding in DMD, one might speculate that growth hormone inhibition could serve to counteract this abnormality.[7] These theories are currently being investigated, and impact on nutritional management should be monitored. A particular nutritional challenge for boys on growth inhibitors would be providing adequate nutrients despite lowered caloric needs.

In contrast, other investigators have found that corticosteroid hormone (prednisone) therapy favorably altered the course of DMD, slowing the progression of muscle weakness and prolonging ambulation in some cases.[22] The biologic basis for the effects of corticosteroids on DMD is not understood, and they clearly do not offer a cure for the disease. Corticosteroids may have a stabilizing effect on cell membranes, thus limiting damage in the muscle cells. It is also possible that the anti-inflammatory action of corticosteroids may somehow limit the destructive processes of the disease. The side effects of prednisone therapy may render it intolerable in many already compromised persons. Cushingoid appearance almost always occurs, and increased appetite with rapid weight gain is common. Other possible effects are hyperactivity, gastritis, and hypertension.[22]

For any person, the decision for or against therapeutic intervention depends on the balance between the benefits of prolonged muscular function, ambulation, and wellness versus the inconvenience and consequences of side effects.

NUTRITIONAL ASSESSMENT

Growth

Factors Affecting Growth

Growth abnormalities, especially short stature, obesity, and underweight, are known characteristics of DMD. Younger affected children are often wasted and thin while some of the older wheelchair users are markedly overweight.[23] Many factors may play a role in growth deviations and should be considered. Unexplained failure to thrive may be present during the first year, suggesting that inadequate growth may be an early sign of DMD.[24] It is not known if growth deviations in DMD are related to the underlying molecular defect or if the deviations are nonspecific and secondary to the effects of the disease. The effects of dietary factors on growth in boys with DMD have not been extensively studied.

Alterations in protein metabolism are known to inflict characteristic changes in muscle tissue and possibly in fat mass, thus affecting the growth process.[14,25] The rate of changes accelerates with age, and different muscles are affected at different rates.[6,26] The phenomenon of "pseudohypertrophy," fatty and fibrous infiltration of degenerated muscle tissue, may give false impressions of muscle bulk in some persons.[27] Although the relentless decline in muscle and strength is linear with age, the exact age at clinical onset of symptoms and the rate of muscle deterioration varies, resulting in a spectrum of severity at any one age.[28] One longitudinal study showed that 50% loss in muscle strength could occur as early as 6.6 years or as late as 16.6 years.[29] Clinical manifestations, most notably ambulation status, also vary among persons.[30] Overall, however, the clinical course of DMD is predictable, with identifiable milestones as previously described.[31]

Other factors of DMD may influence growth and body composition. Sexual development is usually normal but puberty may be delayed.[32] Hormonal responses, especially to estrogen and human growth hormone, may be abnormal.[33] Disuse osteopenia, concentric atrophy, and reduced diameter have been noted in bones of the extremities.[14,23,27] Linear bone growth is not known to be significantly affected, because it is not dependent on normal muscle function as is circumferential growth.[27] Feeding problems are not considered a feature of DMD until later phases when weakness progresses distally so hand function, head control, and chewing become difficult.[26,34] Dental problems are common, with frequent malocclusion and macroglossia.[27] Cardiomyopathy and pulmonary complications are very common and are known causes of poor growth in normal persons.[27,32,35]

Assessment of Growth and Nutritional Status

Clinical and metabolic manifestations of the disease obviously impose unique stress on growth, and assessment of nutritional status becomes a particular challenge. Initially, fat and connective tissue may cause true enlargement of the calf and other areas, and muscle tissue does not immediately decrease. As the disease progresses, however, more fat and fibrous tissue accumulate and muscle tissue fails to grow normally. Eventually, true wasting occurs and muscle tissue declines.[23] Thus, usual estimates of body size and growth, such as weight, height, and skin fold measurements, may overestimate muscle early in the disease and then underestimate adiposity when muscle wasting becomes severe and primarily fat tissue remains.[21]

In one study of body composition in boys with DMD, total body potassium and water values were lower than normal; discrepancies increased with age, height, and advanced disability. Relatively low total body water values despite normal or low body weights reflected excess body fat. These findings indicate that simple weight and height comparisons such as Quetelet's index (weight/height^2) may be deceptive; boys with low or normal weight for height may have body fat mass values as high as 28% to 48%.[36]

Another study of body composition in boys with DMD indicates that they show a progressive increase in exchangeable sodium relative to potassium. This finding suggests that extracellular fluid space increases with age in affected boys, becoming more and more unrelated to lean tissue mass.[36] Also, fat and connective tissue content of muscle biopsies may range from 26% to 66%. Thus, loss of fat-free mass due to muscle wasting and fatty infiltration of muscle tissue may mask excessive gain of body fat. It is important to recognize this "hidden" obesity and its management implications, especially if the burden on weakened muscles is to be decreased.[36]

Weight Abnormalities

Probably the most proclaimed growth and nutritional problem in DMD, yet the least understood, is that of weight status. Most reviews of clinical course, management, and treatment in DMD mention obesity as a common complication.[27,28,30-32] Conversely, several authors note that some persons become generally wasted as the disease progresses. These cases are described as "atrophic" types.[32,37] Allsop found that two thirds of his younger clients had slow weight gain without a plateau in height. The thin boys were described as appearing moderately cachectic.[28] Most of the authors simply cite obesity and thinness as complications of DMD. Thorough investigation of incidence, patterns, factors, consequences, and prognosis have not been attempted.

Underweight

Currently there is limited discussion in the literature concerning relative dangers or merits of thinness in boys with DMD. Apparently the relatively few "atrophic" boys have not presented remarkable treatment or management problems related to their body size. On the contrary, moderate thinness may somehow slow the progression of the disease, facilitate surgical procedures, and require less muscle strength in daily functioning. On the other hand, cachexia due to nutrient deficiencies such as protein and/ or calorie malnutrition will compromise ability to fight infection, physical and mental performance, and general well-being.[38] However, thin affected boys seem to maintain at least a moderate degree of body fat; caloric deficiency is therefore not apparent. These findings suggest the need to further investigate the causes of thinness and the related clinical outcomes for these persons.

Obesity

Obesity is apparently a common problem in boys with DMD, with significant impact on care and management. Studies establish the existence of at least moderate obesity in many boys with DMD. Affected subjects showed high deposition and storage of fat in relation to muscle mass and total body size. Some of these subjects exhibited the "hidden obesity" that is a characteristic of persons with markedly decreased activity. Body fat content is maintained or increased despite normal or even decreased body weight[38] The role of DMD in this phenomenon is obvious: muscle mass is degenerating while fat tissue seems to continue to grow; thus the effect of any increase in fat on relative body composition is magnified.

The significant health and social consequences of obesity are well known. Oxygen availability to tissues is decreased; physical performance and work efficiency are compromised; the energy cost of any degree of physical activity is increased; increased demands are placed on the cardiovascular and respiratory systems and joints; the body's ability to mobilize and use fat metabolites is decreased; body image and self-esteem may be adversely affected; and other psychosocial problems may be initiated or exacerbated.[39,40] The double stigma of obesity and developmental disabilities can lead to social withdrawal and selection of sedentary activities. Parents and caregivers may also offer food as compensation for disabilities. Often overlooked is the fact that short stature and lowered muscle mass decrease a child's caloric needs compared with other children the same age.

Weight Management

Problems of obesity have an obvious potential for impact on the course and management of boys affected with DMD. One report by Edwards and co-workers has shown successful weight management in two obese adolescent boys with DMD.[41] Significant weight losses with concurrent linear growth were achieved. Potassium and water measurements indicated that the weight loss was primarily fatty tissue and that lean body mass was maintained. Both boys experienced improvements in mobility and self-esteem. The authors concluded that controlled weight reduction in obese children with DMD could be beneficial. However, individualization is im-

perative; the authors have compiled a guide to estimating the target weight
for any person. Weight centiles for zero muscle mass are given. The person's
muscle weight is calculated from a 24-hour creatinine excretion measurement and added to the "zero muscle mass weight" to identify the ideal
weight goal. Adjustments for linear growth are also given. Edwards and
co-workers suggest standard treatment strategies for weight maintenance
in DMD once a target weight has been identified. One challenge to the
nutritionist is that parents may find it difficult to accept the "cachectic"
appearance that results when a child with little muscle bulk maintains a
normal percentage of body weight as fat.[41]

Growth Assessment Protocols

In order to appropriately manage growth and nutritional stresses and prevent related complications, assessment protocols and baseline data are
needed. Recognizing the limited availability of appropriate growth data
for boys with DMD, the assessment and monitoring of physical status and
growth must take into account the physiological characteristics of the disease. Protocols should be established for reliable anthropometric measurements. Reasonable measurements, with consistent technique, can provide useful information for clients if taken over time.

Stature Estimation

Height measurement, an essential element in health assessment, correlates particularly well with growth, nutritional status, and vital capacity.[42]
However, accurate measurement of height is difficult in persons with musculoskeletal deformities. This is especially true in older boys with muscular
dystrophy, owing to progressive contractures and physical deformities. Few
researchers have addressed this problem. In practice and some studies,
clinicians ignore or make arbitrary adjustments for effects of deformities
on stature. Yet any assessment measurement using height produces an
error that is not constant but that increases with degrees of deformity.[43]
Therefore a measure is needed that either predicts (estimates) nonde-
formed height or that itself normally correlates with the parameter of
interest (eg, growth, nutritional status). This measure must be unaffected
by the disease process.[43] Crown–rump length or sitting height may be used
when legs are deformed.[43] However, no standard protocol exists for stature
estimation when a patient's trunk or torso is affected as in DMD. One
investigator found an empirical relationship between cross-sectional area
of the femur and stature and used this value as an index of height.[23] This
index is not promising for clinical and nutritional assessment since it requires computed tomography for femur measurements.

Tibial length is a promising measurement for boys with both upper and lower body deformities. The bone length can be reasonably measured with a modified anthropometer. A linear regression equation for estimating stature from tibial length has been developed.[44] However, the sample population was limited to boys aged 6 to 15 and a high standard error was found. The high standard error may be attributed to the dynamics of relative tibial lengths during growth, especially during adolescence.

Linear Growth

In one study using tibial length measurements in boys with DMD, some stunting in linear growth, at least of the tibial bone, was already present in younger boys (6- to 8-year olds) with DMD. Stunting was increasingly evident in the older boys studied (up to 16 years of age). A logical question regarding these results is whether the apparent stunting in DMD may be caused by disproportionately reduced tibial growth or overall reduced stature. Since different muscles are disproportionately affected in DMD, bone growth could also be selectively affected. However, the stature estimation study showed that the younger boys with DMD had a "normal" tibial length versus height relationship. Because stunting has already occurred in these younger boys with normal tibial lengths, it can be assumed that delayed growth in the older age groups is probably due to generalized stunting.

The true effect of bone atrophy on linear growth has not been defined. If linear bone growth is progressively delayed in proportion to muscle degeneration, the degree of linear stunting would parallel the severity of disease. Thus the older affected boys are relatively shorter than their younger peers, as indicated by their lower percentile rankings.

Other possible factors in linear growth should be considered. Any influence on endocrine gland function will have a primary affect on growth rate.[45] Since puberty is sometimes delayed in DMD, hormonal influence on growth is possible.[32] Acute or subacute illness or chronic nutritional deficiencies may lower height-for-age values[46] Finally, genetic factors play a significant role in stature growth, and any person may coincidentally have "shorter than usual" parents.[45]

Weight Measurements

Weight alone, or weight for age, is not an adequate indicator of growth or nutritional status.[46] However, sudden or large changes in weight may warn a clinician of nutritional problems. The relative contributions of fat, muscle mass, and other body tissues should also be assessed to provide any useful indication of growth or nutritional status.

In a study of weight and height status of boys with DMD, affected boys 8 to 10 years old tended to increase in weight percentiles with a corresponding decrease in height percentiles compared with National Center for Health Statistics (NCHS) standards.[47] However, there was a large intragroup variability, indicating the need to consider each case in assessing growth status. Boys in their later teens appeared "atrophic."[44]

Evaluation of Body Composition

An important consideration in evaluating body composition for nutritional assessment is that boys with DMD are known to have drastic reduction in muscle tissue, especially in the older age groups. Reference data for the simplest and most common indicator of body fat in boys, Quetelet's index (weight/height^2), assume normal proportions of muscle and fat. Therefore, any weight/height^2 value in boys with DMD would actually underestimate their total body fat. Skin fold measurements, which account for relative contribution of muscle mass, are therefore preferred over simpler weight and height relationships in body fat assessment of boys with DMD. Even these more sophisticated measurements will not account for fat and fiber infiltration of muscle tissue, however. These variables should be considered in the interpretation of results.

Triceps Skin Fold Measurements. Many authors consider triceps skin fold measurements good clinical indicators of relative body fat or the body's energy reserves.[48,49] In Roche's study of correlates of body fatness, triceps skin fold measurements had the best correlation with percent body fat in boys.[49] The technique for measuring triceps skin fold is not particularly compromised by the disease process of DMD.

Interpretation of the results is more complicated. In normal boys, triceps fat folds are "stable" at 6 to 8 years of age, then gradually increase to a peak just before puberty. Then, as muscle tissue growth usually increases faster than adipose growth during adolescence, the skin fold measurements actually decrease at 12 to 16 years of age.[46] One study showed that, generally, skin folds of boys with DMD did not follow the usual pattern. Younger boys with DMD, aged 6 to 8 years, generally had normal triceps skin fold values compared with reference data. However, percentile rankings for affected boys 9 to 11 years increased slightly. For boys aged 12 to 16 years mean triceps skin fold measurements increased drastically, compared with the normal pattern of slight decrease in this parameter.[44]

The higher triceps skin fold values in older boys with DMD did not correspond with higher weight/height^2 values, even in the boys who appeared extremely thin. Apparently, these boys experienced normal or increased fat deposition, with the expected muscle degeneration. The corresponding fatty infiltration of remaining muscle mass further compounds the assessment of fatness in older boys with DMD. Even the boys who appeared cachectic retained at least moderate fat content in relation to muscle mass.[44]

Mid-Arm Fat Area. Mid-arm fat area is calculated from triceps skin fold and mid-arm circumference.[50] This value is considered a better estimator of body fat content than weight/height^2 or triceps skin fold values because it accounts for the effect of large or small muscle mass on the fat layer. More fat is necessary to cover a larger limb with a given thickness of subcutaneous fat than to cover a smaller limb with comparable thickness.

In a study of mid-arm fat area values for boys with DMD, older boys tended toward extremes for apparent body fat content. Most had relatively high values, a few (the oldest) had low values, and only 1 in 11 had "normal" values compared with reference data.[44] In evaluating mid-arm fat area value results, several factors must be considered. The calculations are only approximations, based on the assumptions that the upper arm is cylindrical in form and that the humeral bone and the triceps muscle diameters increase proportionately. Both of these factors are known to be decreased in boys with DMD, but the proportionality of these decreases in the upper arm is not known. Also, the extent of fatty infiltration of muscle tissue in persons is unknown and would significantly influence both muscle area calculations and, consequently, the mid-arm fat area values. More research and disease-specific standards are needed.

Mid-Arm Muscle Area. The mid-arm muscle area index adjusts the mid-arm circumference measurement for effects of subcutaneous fat. In normal subjects it correlates with total body muscle, which serves as the body's major protein reserve.[48] The limitations described for fat area estimations are identical for muscle area approximations. Shape of the arm (cylindrical or not), humeral diameter, and skin compressability can significantly affect these indices of body composition.[50] In normal boys, mid-arm muscle area shows steady increase in muscle area with age, sharply increasing in older adolescent boys as they undergo the well-known increase in muscle mass during the adolescent growth spurt. In the above study, the mid-arm muscle area values for boys with DMD differed drastically from normal values. Loss of muscle mass is a major manifestation of DMD, and these results reflect that loss. The mean percentile ranking for younger boys with DMD was moderately low compared with reference standards. The sharp decline in mean mid-arm muscle area percentiles during the 9- to 11-year age range possibly indicates rapid muscle loss during these ages. The mean mid-arm muscle area values increased somewhat for the boys aged 12 to 16, since they apparently experienced some normal muscle growth and paradoxical muscle loss from the disease.

Individual mid-arm muscle area values vary more widely in successive age groups, with some older subjects showing increased values while others have values significantly lower than their younger peers.[44] These results indicate wide variations in the muscle growth, wasting, and the combined effects of these two opposing forces.

The wide spectrum of severity of DMD at any one age probably influences assessments that are based on age rather than disease condition for each person.[28] Variations in muscle mass are expected, probably influenced by pseudohypertrophy in some persons that could give false impression of retained muscle mass.[27] To adjust for these variables, the nutritional assessment that includes muscle composition should include evaluation of muscle strength, which would provide an indication of functional muscle mass as opposed to the fatty and fibrous tissue that might have replaced lost muscle mass in some persons. The "atrophic" or wasted subjects quite possibly may have similar amounts of functional muscle tissue as their heavier peers but without fatty and fibrous accumulation.

NUTRITIONAL NEEDS OF BOYS WITH DUCHENNE MUSCULAR DYSTROPHY

The unique trends in growth and body composition in boys with DMD are apparently disease-related. However, these types of conditions are also known to be affected by nutrition-related factors. Nutrient intake, activity, and psychological, social, and economic conditions are known to impact the nutritional status of any person. On the other hand, growth and body composition abnormalities may directly influence nutritional factors. For example, energy requirements may be altered by short stature or obesity may increase awareness of body image, thus heighten social withdrawal and overeating out of frustration. Finally, the stresses of dealing with a progressively debilitating and terminal disease have a major impact on the life style and health-related behavior of affected persons and their families.

For boys with DMD, many of these problems, such as growth abnormalities, obesity, psychological disturbances, social withdrawal, and stressed family interactions, have been described. Appropriate nutritional management strategies are unlikely without an understanding of these relationships in the person with DMD. Dietary intake, food habits, and related factors must be investigated and interpreted in relation to other variables in the disease process.

Energy Needs

Probably the most significant factor in the dietary needs of boys with DMD is altered caloric demands, most often related to activity, motor impairment, and metabolic abnormality. "Normal" indicators of energy requirements, such as sex, age, and weight and growth status, do not apply to children with short stature.[51] Appearance, body structure, and degree of ambulation are more reliable indicators. Many conditions characterized by low physical activity show overweight or obesity with normal caloric intakes.[52-56] Loss of ambulation can decrease caloric needs by up to 25%.[57] The condition of hypokinesia or severely restricted activity has been described: total body fat is increased; metabolic activity of adipose tissue is decreased; and the ability of muscles to use fat metabolites for energy is reduced.[39] Even on lowered caloric input, persons with reduced activity may show increased fat content despite normal or even reduced body weight. The consequences of this condition are altered lipid metabolism and lowered aerobic capacity, often leading to pathogenic stress.

Short stature is a well-known determinant of caloric needs; yet recommended intakes are often based on age and weight only. In addition, some metabolic abnormalities may decrease the overall energy cost of activity; basal energy expenditure can be as low as 50% that of healthy persons of the same weight.[58] Any delay in maturity may delay the usual increase in nutritional needs for growth.

The effects of DMD logically decrease the energy requirements of affected boys. Progressive weakness, loss of ambulation, and ultimate immobilization cause a gradual although severe restriction in physical activity. The muscle degeneration and abnormal protein and fat metabolism, plus hypokinesia, may further affect body composition. Short stature and delayed puberty will lower expected calorie needs.

Nutrient Intake

The specific psychosocial and emotional tendencies noted in boys with DMD will affect dietary intake. Low IQ, passivity, lack of motivation, and social withdrawal may hinder nutritional management strategies, especially if body weight abnormalities are severe.[35] Body anxiety and insecurity may impact the importance of nutrition. The search for magical cures may lead to unrealistic reliance or experimentation with nutrient supplementation.[16] Mothers, most often under the full psychological stresses of dealing with DMD, may exhibit overprotection, guilt, frustration, indifference, or hostility.[14,16] Their usual role of primary caregiver, which determines nutrient availability to their affected sons, may be influenced by these stresses.

The effects of DMD and its many factors on dietary intake of persons have not been studied. The need for further investigations of interrelationships among growth, body composition, nutrient intake, and related psychosocial factors is apparent.

CONCLUSION

The logical question concerning nutritional status and dietary habits of the person with DMD becomes a matter of degree of importance. Poor nutrition compromises the body's immune defenses and general health. An inadequate diet can lead to inadequate daily functioning, slower pace in activities, loss of energy and innovativeness, and a moderate departure from well-being. For the child with DMD, stresses of growth, disease, and emotional upheaval may potentiate poor nutritional habits. These factors, added to progressively decreased activity, often lead to obesity. In turn, obesity may shorten the duration of ambulation, aggravate scoliosis, and contribute to respiratory and cardiac insufficiency.[59] Scott and co-workers stress that once a person has lost 50% of muscle strength, every small physical factor is critical in precipitating the transition from independent ambulation to a wheelchair or braces.[60] This "critical stage" means a drastic decrease in physical activity, imposing even greater risk of obesity. As the child loses strength and independence, any excess weight affects the care required. Body image may be important for self-concept and for others' attitudes toward the person.

However, the emotional and psychosocial factors discussed previously must be considered. The person and his or her family must deal consistently with a devastating and fatal disease. The interrelationships between growth, nutrition, and DMD must be well understood. Ideally, nutritional assessment and monitoring should be a routine component of the child's health care, even in the absence of overt nutritional problems such as abnormal weight status. Any tendency to develop nutritional problems can then be identified early. With early, sensible, and relatively minor changes in diet, major problems can be averted and impact on the already stressed person and family can be avoided. Ultimately, nutrition and diet should be placed in perspective with the overall structure of unique growth trends and nutritional needs, attitudes, desires, and resources of persons and their families.

REFERENCES

1. Green NE. The orthopaedic care of children with muscular dystrophy. *Am Acad Orthop Surg.* 1987;36:267–274.

2. Ogg E. *Milestones in Muscle Disease Research.* New York, NY: Muscular Dystrophy Association of America; 1971.

3. Fingerman E, Campisi J, Pardee AB. Defective Ca^{2+} metabolism in Duchenne muscular dystrophy: Effects on cellular and viral growth. *Proc Natl Acad Sci.* 1984;81:7617–7621.

4. Brooke MH. *A Clinician's View of Neuromuscular Diseases.* Baltimore, Md: Williams & Wilkins Co; 1977.

5. Stanbury JB, Wyngaarden J, Fredrickson DS. *The Metabolic Basis of Inherited Disease.* New York, NY: McGraw-Hill Book Co; 1978.

6. Bonsett CA. *Studies of Pseudohypertrophic Muscular Dystrophy.* Springfield, Ill: Charles C Thomas; 1969.

7. Zatz M. Benign Duchenne muscular dystrophy in a patient with growth hormone deficiency: A five-year follow-up. *Am J Med Genet.* 1986;24:567–572.

8. Bertorini TE, Palmieri GMA, Griffin J, et al. Chronic allopurinol and adenine therapy in Duchenne muscular dystrophy: Effects on muscle function, nucleotide degradation, and muscle ATP and ADP content. *Neurology.* 1985;35:61–65.

9. Rennie MJ, Edwards RHT, Emery PW, Halliday D, Lundholm K, Millward DJ. Depressed protein synthesis is the dominant characteristic of muscle wasting and cachexia. *Clin Physiol.* 1983;3:387–398.

10. Griggs RC, Rennie MJ. Muscle wasting in muscular dystrophy: Decreased protein synthesis or increased degradation? *Ann Neurol.* 1983;13:125–132.

11. Mone J, Lefkowitz SS. The differential effects of calcium starvation on Duchenne muscular dystrophy fibroblasts. *Proc Soc Exp Biol Med.* 1988;187:267–272.

12. Freidenberg GR, Olefsky JM. Dissociation of insulin resistance and decreased insulin receptor binding in Duchenne muscular dystrophy. *J Clin Endocrinol Metab.* 1985;60:320–327.

13. Jackson MJ, Jones DA, Dewards RHT. Measurements of calcium and other elements in muscle biopsy samples from patients with Duchenne muscular dystrophy. *Clin Chim Acta.* 1985;147:215–221.

14. Scott OM, Goddard C, Dubowitz V. Quantitation of muscle function in children: A prospective study in Duchenne muscular dystrophy. *Muscle Nerve.* 1982;5:291.

15. Ziter FA, Allsop KG. The value of orthoses for patients with Duchenne muscular dystrophy. *Phys Ther.* 1979;59:1361.

16. Buchanan DC, La Barbera CJ, Roelofs R, Olson W. Reactions of families to children wtih Duchenne muscular dystrophy. *Gen Hosp Psychiatry.* 1979;1:262.

17. Brady MH. Lifelong care of the child with Duchenne muscular dystrophy. *Matern Child Nurs J.* 1979;4:227.

18. Gardner-Medwin D. Objectives in the management of Duchenne muscular dystrophy. *Isr J Med Sci.* 1977;13:229.

19. Maresh MM. Linear body proportions. *Am J Dis Child.* 1959;98:27.

20. Ziter FA, Allsop KG. The diagnosis and management of childhood muscular dystrophy. *Rocky Mountain Med J.* 1975;72:329.

21. Zatz M, Betti RTB, Frota-Pessoa O. Treatment of Duchenne muscular dystrophy with growth hormone inhibitors. *Am J Med Genet.* 1986;24:549–566.

22. DeSilva S, Drachman DB, Mellitis D, Kuncl RW. Prednisone treatment in Duchenne muscular dystrophy. *Arch Neurol.* 1987;44:818–822.

23. Jones DA, Round JM, Edwards RHT, Grindwood SR, Tofts PS. Size and composition of the calf and quadriceps muscles in Duchenne muscular dystrophy. *J Neurol Sci.* 1983;60:307–322.

24. Call G, Ziter FA. Failure to thrive in Duchenne muscular dystrophy. *J Pediatr.* 1985;106:939–941.

25. Tomkins JK, Collins SP. In vitro studies of protein metabolism in marine and human dystrophy. In: Ridman AD, Tomkins JK, eds. *Muscle, Nerve and Brain Degeneration.* Amsterdam: Exerpta Medica; 1978.

26. Dubowitz V. Muscle disorders in childhood. In: *Major Problems in Clinical Pediatrics.* London, England: WB Saunders Co; 1978;16.

27. Siegal IM. *The Clinical Management of Muscle Disease.* Philadelphia, Pa: JB Lippincott Co; 1977.

28. Allsop KG, Ziter FA. Loss of strength and functional decline in Duchenne's dystrophy. *Arch Neurol.* 1981;38:406.

29. Ziter FA, Allsop KG, Tyler FH. Assessment of muscle strength in Duchenne muscular dystrophy. *Neurology.* 1977;27:981.

30. Johnson EW, Kennedy JH. Comprehensive management of Duchenne muscular dystrophy. *Arch Phys Med Rehabil.* 1971;110.

31. Vignos PF. Respiratory function and pulmonary infection in Duchenne muscular dystrophy. *Isr J Med Sci.* 1977;13:207.

32. Walton JN, Gardner-Medwin D. Progressive muscular dystrophy and the myotonic disorders. In: Walton JN, ed. *Disorders of Voluntary Muscle.* Edinburgh, Scotland: Churchill-Livingstone; 1974.

33. Pryor HB, Thelander JE. Growth deviations in handicapped children: An anthropometric study. *Clin Pediatr.* 1967;6:501.

34. Vignos PJ, Spencer GE, Archibald KC. Management of progressive muscular dystrophy in childhood. *JAMA.* 1963;184:89.

35. Horton WA, Hall JG, Scott CI, Pyeritz RE, Rimoin DK. Growth curves for height for diastrophic dysplasia, spondyloepiphyseal dysplasia congenita and pseudoachondroplasia. *Am J Dis Child.* 1982;136:316.

36. Edmonds CJ, Smith T, Griffiths RD, Mackenzie J, Edwards RHT. Total body potassium and water, and exchangeable sodium in muscular dystrophy. *Clin Sci.* 1985;68:379–385.

37. Haymond MW, Strobel KE, De Vivo DC. Muscle wasting and carbohydrate homeostasis in Duchenne muscular dystrophy. *Neurology.* 1978;28:1978.

38. Jelliffe EF, Gurney M. Definition of the problem. In: Roche AF, Falkner F, eds. *Nutrition and Malnutrition: Identification and Measurement.* New York, NY: Plenum Press; 1974.

39. Parizbova J. Interrelationships between body size, body composition and function. In: Roche AF, Falkner F, eds. *Nutrition and Malnutrition: Identification and Measurement.* New York, NY: Plenum Press; 1974.

40. Flewellen EH. Ponderal index: Quantifying obesity. *JAMA.* 1979;241:884.

41. Edwards RHT, Round JM, Jackson MJ, Griffiths RD, Lilburn MF. Weight reduction in boys with muscular dystrophy. *Dev Med Child Neurol.* 1984;26:384–390.

42. Roche AF. Growth assessment of handicapped children. *Dietetic Currents*. 1979;6:25.

43. Hepper NGG, Black LF, Fowler WS. Relationships of lung volume to height and armspan in normal subjects and patients with spinal deformity. *Am Rev Respir Dis*. 1965;91:536.

44. Gleason C. *Nutritional Assessment of Boys with Duchenne Muscular Dystrophy*. Seattle: University of Washington; 1982. Thesis.

45. Rimoin DL, Horton WA. Medical progress: Short stature: II. *J Pediatr*. 1978;92:697.

46. Fomon SJ. *Nutritional Disorders of Children: Prevention, Screening and Followup*. Rockville, Md: US Department of Health, Education and Welfare; 1977.

47. Hamill PVV, Drizd TA, Johnson CL, Reed RB, Roche AF, Moore WM. Physical growth: National Center for Health Statistics percentiles. *Am J Clin Nutr*. 1979;32:607–629.

48. Frisancho AR. Triceps skinfold and upper arm muscle size norms for assessment of nutritional status. *Am J Clin Nutr*. 1974;27:1052.

49. Roche AF, Siervogel RM, Chumlea WC, Webb P. Grading body fatness from limited anthropometric data. *Am J Clin Nutr*. 1981;34:2831.

50. Frisancho AR. New norms of upper limb fat and muscle areas for assessment of nutritional status. *Am J Clin Nutr*. 1981;34:2540.

51. Kalisz K, Ekvall S. Energy requirements of the developmentally disabled child. In: Palmer S, Ekvall S, eds. *Pediatric Nutrition in Developmental Disorders*. Springfield, Ill: Charles C Thomas Publisher; 1978.

52. Berg K, Isaksson B. Body composition and nutrition of school children with cerebral palsy. *Acta Paediatr Scand*. 1979;205:41.

53. Garn SM, Weir HF. Assessing the nutritional status of the mentally retarded. *Am J Clin Nutr*. 1971;24:853.

54. Pipes P, Holm V. Weight control of children with Prader-Willi syndrome. *J Am Diet Assoc*. 1973;62:520.

55. Grogan C, Ekvall S. The effect of nutrient intake and physical activity on the body composition of myelomeningocele patients as determined by K40, urinary creatinine, and anthropometric measurements. In: *Federal Proceedings Abstracts*. Chicago, Ill: Federation of American Societies for Experimental Biology; 1977.

56. Food and Nutrition Board. *Recommended Dietary Allowances*. 9th ed. Washington, DC: National Academy of Sciences; 1980.

57. Cully WJ, Middleton TO. Caloric requirements of mentally retarded children with and without motor dysfunction. *J Pediatr*. 1969;75:380.

58. Eddy TA, Nicholson AL, Wheeler CC. Energy expenditures and dietary intake in cerebral palsy. *Dev Med Child Neurol*. 1965;7:377.

59. Swaiman KF, Wright FS. *Pediatric Neuromuscular Diseases*. St. Louis, Mo: CV Mosby Co; 1979.

60. Scott OM, Goddard C, Dubowitz V. Quantitation of muscle function in children: A prospective study in Duchenne muscular dystrophy. *Muscle Nerve*. 1982;5:291.

Chapter 5

Multiple Sclerosis

Donna L. Frankel

Multiple sclerosis (MS) is a chronic neurologic disorder that produces a wide variety of types and levels of disability. It has been recognized as a separate clinical entity by the medical community since the mid-1800s, but its etiology remains elusive, despite much study. Neither prevention nor cure is available. The diagnosis is one of exclusion and the actual course of the disease is not easily predictable, until there are several years of natural history for the person with MS. This combination of factors has resulted in problems for all persons involved in the management of this disease. For the clients, there is the frustration of delayed diagnosis, new uncertainties about the future, and fear of progressive disability, without the potential for benefit from standard medical treatments. For family and friends, there are the problems of dealing with the changes in a loved one, which may result in a change of roles for all in the immediate community. For physicians, there is the problem of a limited armamentarium to fight disease progression, with the too frequent response of turning the person with MS away from the office. For other health care providers, there is uncertainty about the disease course and the best ways to avert complications, as well as limited direction from physicians in working with these persons. The result can be an excessively pessimistic approach to management of the disorder. Yet, this pessimism is totally unfounded, because much can be done to assist a person with MS in leading a successful life, in spite of the disease. Health care providers must support persons with MS as they learn to cope with the inconsistencies of this disease and apply the known principles of medicine, rehabilitation, exercise, nutrition, and mental health to prevent and/or delay the onset of disability and complications. To accomplish this, health care providers must be knowledgeable about the disease and work toward maintaining an attitude of optimism in the approach to this disease. They must be able to be allies to persons with

MS, passing knowledge on to them and supporting their efforts to regain some feeling of control in their lives by striving to live in a healthy manner.

Good nutritional status is crucial to health. Thus, the registered dietitian and nutritionist have an important role to play in providing the long-term support that persons with MS need. In fact, the importance of this role is amplified, because of the combination of circumstances that come together with MS. Persons with MS frequently seek alternative means of treatment in response to the limitations of the standard medical community. Special diets and manipulation of individual nutrients provide one source of alternative treatments. Obviously, these can have an impact on the nutritional status of the person with MS, as well as his or her life style. Likewise, medications, the presence of disability, and/or adherence to other alternative treatments may have an impact on nutritional status.

This chapter is divided into four major sections. In the first section background information is provided on the disease of MS. The second section deals with some of the theories regarding the etiology of MS. The third section is a review of accepted, experimental, and alternative treatments of MS. In the fourth section an attempt is made to generalize this information to persons with chronic, variably progressive disabilities. The focus in all sections is on the nutritional implications.

DISEASE CHARACTERISTICS

MS is a disease of the central nervous system. The peripheral nervous system seems to be spared. At the anatomical level it was initially identified as scarring of the myelin tissue in the central nervous system on autopsy findings. Since that time it has been shown that there is an inflammation of the myelin, which may or may not proceed to permanent scarring.

Myelin is a substance that surrounds individual nerve fibers, acting as an insulator and speeding up conduction of nerve impulses. With sufficient disruption of the integrity of the myelin, the nerve impulse is either slowed or totally blocked, so that there is a loss of effective conduction of nerve impulses.

Epidemiology

The onset of MS generally occurs in persons between 20 and 50 years old. The highest prevalence rates are found in whites of Anglo-Saxon or Scandinavian origin. The prevalence is greatest in the northern latitudes of the temperate climate zone. It affects women more frequently than men.

Diagnosis

There are no specific objective tests for the diagnosis of MS. The major hallmark of the diagnosis is that there are two or more transient neurologic deficits occurring over time, indicating abnormalities in more than one area of the central nervous system. Thus, the diagnosis cannot be made with certainty at the time of the first attack. When this diagnosis is considered, testing is done to rule out other possible causes and to look for objective information that supports the clinical impression. The specific tests most commonly done include the following:

1. Oligoclonal bands in the cerebrospinal fluid. These are nonspecific proteins that are frequently elevated in persons with MS.
2. Evoked potentials, including study of visual, auditory, and/or somatosensory nerve tracts. A peripheral stimulus is given and the latency of the cortical response measured. A prolonged latency means that there is a problem in nerve conduction that delays the response. An absence of response means that nerve conduction is entirely blocked somewhere along the specific tract being studied. These tests are believed to be especially helpful in looking for evidence of a second lesion in a person who has only one clinically documentable abnormality but in whom MS is suspected.
3. Computed tomographic scan of the brain. Large areas of scarring (plaques) will show up.
4. Magnetic resonance imaging of the brain and/or spinal cord. This has proven to be very sensitive in the identification of plaques. In fact, it is so sensitive that plaques are found in totally asymptomatic persons. Hopes that this would be a specific diagnostic test for MS have not materialized because the plaques may come and go so that they may not be present at the time of testing.[1] Additionally, magnetic resonance imaging has demonstrated plaquelike abnormalities in some other disorders, so it is not a disease-specific test.

Thus, there is an inability to make a diagnosis of MS quickly, even when someone has a striking physiological impairment. It is important to do sufficient tests to rule out other pathologic processes. Once this is done, one must watch over time to see what evolves. The above tests will frequently be included in the initial workup, but they do not always give conclusive results.

Until one has reasonable certainty that the problem is MS, there is reluctance to give a specific diagnosis, to the extent that many physicians do not even mention that there is a high suspicion of MS. There have been many attemps to provide categories for the diagnosis of MS, such as possible, probable, or definite MS, in an effort to allow better subject identification for the purpose of scientific study and earlier, clearer diagnostic information for affected persons in the clinical setting. To date, there is a lack of consensus on the specifics of such categorization. This compounds the problem of early definitive diagnosis for the clinician in daily practice.[2]

In addition to the uncertainty of diagnosis, there are other undesirable ramifications that cause a definite reluctance in diagnosing someone with MS. The public (and many professionals) generally think of MS as a progressive, crippling disease. Persons with this diagnosis find barriers to getting employment, health and life insurance, long-term mortgages, and so on, because of the uncertainties of prognosis. In general, persons with MS, however, are troubled by the delay in diagnosis and think that this is done because physicians think that "it is all in their (the clients') heads" and that there is nothing really wrong with them. Health care providers must help persons with MS to realize the other reasons for reluctance to give the diagnosis prematurely and must let these persons know that there probably is a physiological reason for their symptoms even though the specific cause has not been identified. Physicians must become more comfortable with stating that MS is suspected and with outlining the plans for confirming or excluding the diagnosis.

Clinical Course

For many persons, MS is a relatively benign disease. Those with definite disability from MS often manage their disease well and lead healthy, productive, fulfilling lives. Thus, general pessimism is not the correct attitude in approaching these persons. Instead, health care providers must develop an attitude of supportive concern, helping persons with MS learn how to accept and live with the disease, optimizing their functional potential and preventing complications.

The two major clinical patterns that MS follows are listed below:

1. The exacerbating remitting course is characterized by intermittent episodes of neurologic impairment. Episodes may be entirely reversible and cause no permanent neurologic deficits. It is a benign course. The episode may be only partially reversible, leaving the person with some permanent disability, the level of which builds with each attack. This has a slowly progressive course. The frequency of attacks tends to decrease as disease duration increases.
2. The progressive course has no clear bouts of exacerbation and remissions but rather a progressive development of neurologic impair-

ments and associated disability. In a small number of these persons, the rate of progression will be quite rapid, with a poor prognosis.

Impairments

The physiological impairment that strikes a given person with MS is dependent on where the lesion occurs. Lesions are often silent, demonstrating no observable effect on function. Impairment results when the lesion causes blockage of the transmission of impulses in areas of the central nervous system that are critical to physiological integrity. There are four major types of impairment that can result from scarring:

1. impaired muscle strength with weakness or paralysis and/or alterations in muscle tone, especially spasticity
2. impaired sensation, with anesthesia, dysesthesia, hypoesthesia, and/ or hyperesthesia of the basic senses of light touch, position, vibration, and pain
3. impaired vision
4. impaired coordination

Management of Symptoms and Associated Functional Disability

These physiological impairments can impact the function of the person with MS in numerous ways, all of which may impact the nutritional requirements and/or nutritional status of the person. Functional problems are often aggravated by a warm environment or emotional stress. The duration of any specific functional impairment is variable, depending on whether or not and to what extent remissions occur.

Fatigue

Fatigue is a very pervasive and frustrating problem in persons with MS. The frustrations arise because it becomes physically impossible to function at the normal level of physical activity, despite the mental interest in doing so. At the same time, there is no obvious way for others to recognize the fatigue, so family, friends, employers, disability evaluators, and health care providers all find it hard to recognize that a true physiological impairment of function exists, rather than malingering. Thus, the person with MS becomes defensive and stressed, which serves to exaggerate the fatigue. Additionally, the person with MS may begin to doubt his or her own integrity and wonder if he or she is malingering or not, with further emotional toll. Fatigue may cause the loss of employment, break up of a marriage, and/or avoidance of medical care. This poor outcome is often the result of a lack of understanding of the problem, rather than just the physiological deficits produced by the fatigue.

Fatigue is now recognized by the Social Security Administration as a cause of disability in persons with MS, although it is still problematic to document its presence in sufficiently objective ways for a person to get disability support solely on the basis of fatigue.

When fatigue is a problem, nutritional implications develop because of the effect of the fatigue on the person's activity level. There may be a significant decrease in level of energy expenditure, with the potential for the development of obesity, unless caloric intake is lowered.

If the fatigued person is to remain independent in self-care, it becomes necessary to save and conserve energy. The most frequent ways of doing this are through rescheduling tasks during the day and decreasing personal energy expenditure. Thus, there may be a dependence on convenience foods. Instruction in the application of energy conservation principles to the tasks of food preparation and clean-up may be beneficial. Adaptive devices may help with these tasks. If the fatigue is excessive, there may be dependence on others for food shopping, preparation, and clean-up. The affected person must then learn how to work with family or friends who are providing the assistance or how to effectively manage a hired assistant with these responsibilities. Even having sufficient energy to eat a full meal at one sitting may become problematic. Thus, it may be necessary to adjust the meal schedule to optimize the energy level at the time of meals. Assistance with feeding may be necessary. Occasionally, consistency of food must be changed to reduce energy demands of feeding. Fatigue, as a single symptom, does not usually result in total inability to achieve adequate nutrition through oral feedings.

There are three pharmaceutical approaches to the management of fatigue.

1. The consumption of caffeine-containing beverages is frequently recommended. Generally, it is advised that these items be taken at, or just prior to, times in the day when fatigue is problematic.
2. Central nervous system stimulants are effective in some patients. Pemoline (Cylert) has fewer side effects than methylphenidate (Ritalin). The use of such drugs may be accompanied by loss of appetite.
3. Amantadine hydrochloride (Symmetrel) is presently being studied (and recommended clinically by some physicians) for control of fatigue. It is a medication with a recognized role in the management

of symptoms of Parkinson's disease and prophylaxis after exposure to influenza A virus. Interest in this medication developed after report of remission of fatigue in a few persons with MS taking it for antiviral purposes was noted. Nausea is a frequent side effect.

It is important to understand that there is no scientific proof that any of these pharmaceutical agents are clinically useful in the management of fatigue. In particular, management of fatigue in MS is not an approved use by the Food and Drug Administration of the prescription drugs mentioned here. Therefore, use of these agents should be done only under close supervision of a physician.

Mobility

There is a wide variability in the mobility dysfunction seen with MS. Factors contributing to impaired mobility include muscular weakness or paralysis, spasticity, and/or tremor that result in difficulty controlling movements and sensory impairments. The majority of persons with MS remain ambulatory during their lifetime, although it may be necessary to use assistive devices, such as canes, crutches, or walkers. Bracing of the lower extremities may be necessary for safe ambulation and/or lower extremity joint protection. Medications (Table 5-1) may provide some benefit in controlling spasticity or tremor. When there is severe weakness, total paraplegia, significant loss of balance, or alteration of muscle tone it may be necessary to use a wheelchair for mobility. There are a variety of chairs available from standard manual wheelchairs to electric scooters. The type

Table 5-1 Common Medications for Symptom Control

Symptom	Desired Effect	Medication
Spasticity	Decrease muscle tone	Baclofen
		Diazepam
Tremor	Improve motor control	Propranolol
		Clonazepam
Dysesthetic pain	Relieve/decrease pain	Tricyclic antidepressants*
		Carbamazepine
Neurogenic bladder	Decrease urgency	Oxybutynin*
		Propantheline*
		Imipramine*
		Flavoxate*
	Improve emptying	Bethanechol
Depression	Improve mood	Tricyclic antidepressants*

*Dry mouth is a significant side effect.

must be tailored to the physiological problems of the individual, with consideration of the social and financial support available and the environment within which the person functions. Persons in a wheelchair may be independent or dependent, depending on the level of disability.

The nutritional implications of changes in mobility are multiple. There will most likely be an alteration in energy expenditure. Ambulation with assistive devices, especially bracing, generally results in increased energy requirements for a given distance of movement. Some persons respond to this by decreased activity, with a decrease or no change in energy expenditure. Others respond by continuing at the same level of activity, with an increase in energy expenditure. Likewise, when one is dependent on a manual wheelchair for mobility, the effect on energy expenditure is variable, depending on the level of activity. However, when one becomes dependent on a power chair for mobility, there is generally a significant decrease in energy expenditure, despite the level of activity, because electricity has replaced human power for that mobility.

Shopping habits and activity in the kitchen may alter with changes in mobility as reviewed in the section on fatigue above. Additionally, architectural modifications may be needed for accessibility to promote or maintain independence.

Activities of Daily Living

There is a wide variability in the level of self-care capacity in persons with MS. This must be assessed in each person to fully understand the impact of the disease, because activities of daily living may be impacted by any or a combination of the neurologic impairments found in MS. As with the problems of fatigue and mobility discussed above, there will be a wide variation in the way dysfunction in activities of daily living may impact the person's nutritional status and requirements. Of particular concern are changes in upper extremity function that result in loss of ability to manage independently in the kitchen, including food preparation, self-feeding, and clean-up. The problems encountered and adjustments needed were reviewed in the section on fatigue.

Neurogenic Bladder

Urinary frequency and/or incontinence are frequently seen in persons with MS. Because of the erroneous but widespread belief that this dysfunction is just a part of the disease that one has to live with, many persons do not even see it as a problem to raise, unless asked specifically about it. Even then, it may not become obvious that there is a problem until physical examination or review of laboratory tests has been completed. The most common problem seen as a result of neurogenic bladder is severe restriction of fluid intake to prevent the problems of urinary frequency and incontinence. Persons may lead lives of near or total seclusion to avoid the social embarrassment of urinary incontinence. Thus, nutritional consequences generally fall into two major categories.

Fluid restriction, in and of itself, can be a serious source of dietary imbalance, putting unnecessary stress on the body to maintain normal or adapted biochemical and physiological function. There will be a dry mouth, which may lead to decreased solid food intake, loss of appetite, and problems with swallowing. Persons may compensate by sucking on hard candy to stimulate saliva production, resulting in increased consumption of sweets and increased problems with dental caries. Orthostatic hypotension may occur, resulting in increased risk for falls and serious injury in the independently mobile person. Intake of specific nutrients may be curtailed, because of a sudden decrease in the intake of a specific fluid high in some nutrient without compensatory correction of the diet to add the nutrient in another way (eg, a decrease in calcium consumption with cessation of drinking milk or decrease in vitamin C intake with a cessation of drinking fortified fruit juices and fruit drinks). Urine volume will be decreased, resulting in an increased solute load in the urine and thus increased potential for renal or bladder stone formation.

When frequent incontinence is not controlled, there is increased risk for perineal and, in women, vaginal infections. There is also increased risk for serious skin breakdown because of the irritating effects of continual moisture on the skin and infections. With uncontrolled urinary incontinence, there is generally a decrease in activity outside the home. In persons who try to maintain an active life, the basic cost of living may be increased because of the cost of adult incontinence supplies. Men may choose to use an external collection device or indwelling catheter to control the undesirable consequences of incontinence. Improper use of these devices can result in perineal infections and skin breakdown or urinary retention. Women may choose an indwelling catheter for the same reason. (There are currently two external collection devices for women on the market, but they are quite expensive, and successful applications are very limited to date.) With indwelling catheters, a large fluid intake (3 to 4 L/d) is helpful in avoiding the problems of infection and bladder stones that may develop. Regular medical follow-up for early recognition of altered physiological function and/or infections is needed to prevent long-term loss of renal function. Some persons manage with an intermittent catheterization program. In such instances there is generally a need to limit fluid intake to some degree. Persons may have undergone operative procedures to compensate for urinary bladder dysfunction. These may have an affect on

electrolyte balance. Specific effects, adjustments, and type of medical follow-up vary with the type of bladder management being used. Because of
the variable course of MS, methods of bladder management may change
over time. Thus information on management of the bladder should be
obtained on each individual being counseled, and information should be
updated periodically.

Fortunately, much can be done to control urinary frequency and incontinence. It may require that the person be referred to a knowledgeable
specialist for assessment and management. Referral to an MS clinic or
incontinence clinic will generally mean that the individual can have access
to a variety of specialists, with a multidisciplinary assessment. Appropriate
management is based on the etiology of the problem, which can vary from
urinary tract infections to mobility problems to impaired neural connections
to the bladder. If such specialized services are not available, the problem
can be discussed with the referring or primary care physician and referral
recommended to a urologist or physiatrist if it seems that the managing
physician feels that little can be done to improve the situation.

Neurogenic Bowel

MS can affect the control of bowel function. Fecal incontinence occurs
when the lower gut is not emptied adequately and regularly and there is
uncontrolled reflex rectal emptying. This can be managed through a regular
bowel program (Table 5-2). The main problems with fecal incontinence
are the social limitations that this places on a person, thus promoting
isolation and all its associated problems. For the dependent person there
is also an increased burden on the personal caregiver because of the need
for frequent changes in clothes and/or linens. Skin problems may develop
because of the frequent irritation from soiling. As with urinary incontinence, there is increased risk for perineal and, in women, vaginal infections
associated with incontinence of stool.

Constipation is the other major bowel problem seen in persons with
MS. When a person complains of constipation, it is important to investigate
further because bowel habits and what is considered normal are highly
variable. Constipation is considered to be medically disconcerting when a
person fails to routinely evacuate the bowels without laxatives or enemas
or manual disimpaction at least every 2 to 3 days. Because this topic is
believed to be private and/or unpleasant, clients generally do not discuss
it unless asked specifically, with attention by the examiner to all the details.
Frequently the constipation is a result of lack of awareness of the need to
have regular bowel habits, so that it is just ignored until it can be put off
no longer. The severe fluid restriction imposed by persons to control urinary frequency is the other major cause of constipation in persons with

Table 5-2 Components of a Routine Bowel Program

1. Regular time for evacuation of the bowel. The client should agree to try to have a bowel movement at a regular time. (Generally, every other day is adequate, but frequency may vary from daily to every 3 days or twice per week.) The ideal time is 15 to 20 minutes after a meal, to take advantage of the gastrocolic reflex, which is an internal trigger to empty the rectum when the stomach is full.
2. Adequate stool bulk. If bulk is insufficient, stools will be small and difficult to move through the intestines. Bulk can be increased by the addition of fiber to the diet. The amount of fiber, therefore, is titrated by the stool bulk. Generally, one tablespoon of Metamucil powder in water or juice, once to three times a day, is sufficient to provide adequate bulk. (This particular brand seems to work most effectively.) Results are less reliable with natural dietary fiber in most persons because of failure to consume the same foods with sufficient daily regularity to get a consistent fiber load. When stool bulk is excessive, the frequency of the bowel program should be increased and no fiber supplements are needed.
3. Appropriate stool consistency. This is controlled by the amount of fluid in the gut. Adequate fluid intake is necessary (at least 2 L/d, unless otherwise contraindicated). When fluid intake is good, and stools continue to be too hard, stool softeners should be added; docusate sodium, 100 mg, orally once to three times a day, with dosage titrated to stool consistency, should be adequate.
4. If unable to achieve regular bowel movements with a routine schedule and stimulation of the gastrocolic reflex, it may be necessary to add digital stimulation of the anal sphincter and/or a suppository (glycerine or bisacodyl USP) to the program.

MS. Frequently, an increase in fluid intake to 2 to 3 quarts per day will resolve the constipation problem. Unfortunately, this intervention also generally results in excessive urinary frequency and/or fecal incontinence. Thus, solving one problem may result in one or two new problems to manage.

Infrequent bowel evacuation, however, must be addressed. The major approach is through ensuring adequate fluid intake and an appropriate regular bowel program. (see Table 5-2) Without proper management there is an increased risk of fecal impaction. At its best this is an uncomfortable problem to resolve, and at its worst it can result in bowel rupture, which has a high morbidity and mortality, even with immediate surgical intervention.

Dysphagia

Swallowing problems are not encountered frequently in persons with MS, but when they are present they need careful assessment and management. The primary problems seem to be at the level of airway protection, with reports of choking. Asymptomatic aspiration may manifest itself by recurrent episodes of pneumonia. Persons may report intolerance of liquids or solids or both, so the assessment and management must be individualized. Where choking and/or recurrent aspiration are problems, it may be necessary to try to control endogenous secretions as well as manipulate food intake. Control of salival pooling may require frequent expectoration or suctioning. Medications with anticholinergic side effects (see Table 5-1), some of which are used frequently in persons with MS for management of urinary frequency or depression, may be helpful in decreasing the total amount of saliva produced. These persons are at risk for cachexia from avoidance of food intake and aspiration pneumonia from foodstuffs getting into the respiratory passages. The best approach is multidisciplinary assessment and management to identify the specific problem and work on acceptable compensatory strategies. Some large medical centers have special clinics devoted to assessment and management of swallowing problems. Professionals dealing with swallowing problems in their daily practice include physiatrists, otolaryngologists, oral surgeons, speech pathologists, and occupational therapists. If swallowing cannot be improved, enteral tube feedings may be required to prevent slow dehydration and/or starvation.

Skin Breakdown

The major factors contributing to skin problems in the person with MS include impaired sensation, impaired mobility, and soiling from urinary or fecal incontinence. The loss of protective sensation, however, is the most significant of these factors. Persons with normal sensation feel discomfort or pain when there is injury. When the integrity of their skin is at risk, there is subconscious movement, by reflex action, to relieve pressure before injury occurs. When there is paralysis, the person still feels the pain and will make a conscious effort to move. When the person feels no pain, regular shifts in position (pressure release) must become a routine habit of daily life or skin breakdown will occur. Additionally, daily skin inspection is necessary to note any potential areas of irritation or infection before breakdown occurs. When decubiti develop, optimal nutritional intake is an important component of the healing process. Nutritional needs are generally increased when a decubitus ulcer is present because of the loss of tissue and exudation of fluid from the open area.

Speech Impediments

Both dysarthria and dysphonia may be seen with MS. If these problems occur to the extent that intelligibility of speech is impaired, one must look to providing an adaptive means of communication. It may be necessary to schedule extra time for nutritional assessment and counseling to allow the person to communicate fully and freely. Impaired communication skills may result in social isolation, loss of employment, and increased dependence.

Cognitive Dysfunction

Because MS is a disorder of the central nervous system, it may cause problems in mental function as well as other more physical manifestations of disability. This fact has not been well accepted in the MS community but is real. Cognitive impairments may be quite subtle in the majority of persons, requiring formal neuropsychometric testing for identification and objective quantification. When such subtle problems exist, persons are often relieved to learn that they are not crazy but have a definite organic problem, despite initial reluctance to have this problem fully addressed and assessed.

The concerns for the dietitian in working with persons with cognitive impairments are centered on the areas of validity of dietary history and ability to follow through with plans of activity. Thus, the dietitian needs to be alert to the possibility of such problems and encourage formal evaluation if it seems that cognitive impairment is interfering with the goals of counseling. When the person has recognized deficits, the dietitian should learn what these are and apply available compensatory strategies in the counseling routine. This may include memory aids, if the client is reliable in using them independently, or gathering information from and instruction of personal caregivers as well as the client. Follow-up and monitoring for compliance and problems are essential.

Pain

The alteration in sensation may result in the presence of painful dysesthesias. This generally affects only limited parts of the body. Additionally, some persons with spasticity report the presence of very painful sensations with the spasticity. There is no simple way to resolve this set of symptoms. The most conservative approach is to try mental diversion. Persons should be encouraged to try to keep active and social. When trying to sleep, visualization and relaxation techniques can be helpful in controlling the discomfort for some persons. Another conservative approach to management is counterstimulation, such as pressure from support panty hose when the problem is in the legs. A transcutaneous electrical nerve stimulator can be an effective source of counterstimulation. Medications may be tried, but these are generally not very effective. Both antidepressants and antiseizure medications may be used in the management of the pain. Antispasticity medications to decrease the spasticity may relieve the discomfort associated with muscle spasms.

Altered Emotional State

Persons with MS, just like anyone else, may have mood alterations. In some cases, this may be the result of the disease process itself. In other cases, it is the result of the effects of the disease/disability on the person's life. Depression and anxiety are the major mood alterations that become problematic for persons with MS. These conditions can often be effectively managed through supportive discussions with peers or health care professionals, such as the dietitian, who are actually seeing the person for some other reason. Other times, professional treatment is needed. The dietitian may be the professional to recognize a serious mood alteration. If so, it should be brought to the attention of the referring physician so that formal assessment and treatment can be pursued. It may be necessary to delay dietary interventions until the mood problem is addressed and managed. Mood alterations may have an impact on compliance with treatment and management, usually in a negative manner.

THEORIES REGARDING THE ETIOLOGY OF MS

The cause of the inflammation in MS remains elusive, but it appears to be related to an aberration of the immune response of the body, such that there is an attack on one's own myelin. The major etiologic theories propose that there is a genetic component, probably some aberrancy of the immune system, and an environmental component, possibly a (or several) viral infection(s).[3,4] It seems that the environmental factor is most important in the first 15 years of life, so there is evidence to support a long latency period between the exposure to the cause of the disease and the clinical manifestations. Another factor seems to be alteration of the blood–brain barrier, which produces random vascular lesions at the level of arterioles, capillaries, and venules.[4,5]

Standard scientific opinion does not support nutrition as being an etiologic agent in the development of MS. However, there are some scientists and physicians who strongly believe that the key to MS lies with nutrition. Thus, it is important that dietitians and nutritionists working with persons with MS have some basic knowledge of this information.

The interest in diet as a contributory factor in the etiology of MS developed through studies of the geographical variability of the disease. A major proponent for a dietary etiology (and dietary treatment) is Dr. Roy Swank of Portland, Oregon. His recent text, *The Multiple Sclerosis Diet Book,* summarizes his long experience with MS, including studies of etiology and recommendations of a low-fat diet for treatment.[5] Some of the points that are stressed include:

- The increase in fat consumption in the U.S. diet, as a percentage of total calories, in this century has been accompanied by an increase in the percentage of saturated fats as well. During this time period, the incidence of MS in the U.S. has also increased.
- On a world-wide scale, two diet zones, high-fat versus low-fat, have been identified, which correlate to some extent with the incidence of MS.
- The correlation of the incidence of MS within Switzerland and Norway, with local dietary variations. MS is seen to a greater extent in areas where saturated fat intake is the highest.

With this background in mind, Swank has proposed that an abnormality in the metabolism of animal fats (saturated fatty acids in particular) leads to microemboli from an abnormal aggregation of blood cells at the microcirculatory level of the brain, resulting in a loss of integrity of the blood–brain barrier. As this barrier breaks down, toxic substances in the plasma leak into the brain, resulting in inflammation and destruction of the myelin sheath.

Evidence to support a role of disturbed fat metabolism in the etiology of MS has been reported by others as well. Examples from the recent literature include a report of a significant reduction in the linoleic acid content of white blood cells and platelets in persons with MS[6] and a report of a higher level of anti-oleic acid conjugate antibodies in sera of persons with MS than in sera of persons with other neurologic illnesses and normal control subjects.[7]

Mertin and Meade did a critical review of the information available to support the theories regarding a role of fatty acid metabolism in MS in 1977.[8] Their review attempts to demonstrate that the theory of a role of fatty acid metabolism in the pathogenesis of MS does not conflict with the major accepted theories of the etiology of MS. As a result of their review, they posed the thought-provoking question: "Could a metabolic alteration, genetically determined but of low penetrance and revealed only under the modifying effects of different diets and hormonal influences, prepare the CNS for the attack of a pathogenic agent at a distinct time in the life of the prospective MS patient?"[8]

Other indications to support a systemic metabolic abnormality abound. A few examples from the recent literature include demonstration of altered platelet aggregation with addition of specific agents to serum,[9] identification of serum factors that inhibit the growth of glial cells in the brain,[10] and alteration in the binding of zinc in red blood cell membranes.[11]

As one would expect, with all the unknowns about MS, numerous other possible nutritional influences have been investigated, including suggestions of specific foods as having a causative or preventive effect. Consideration has also been given to the possibility of specific nutrient deficiencies and food-borne toxins. However, there is little scientific support for nutrition as a specific etiologic factor in the development of MS at this time.

TREATMENT OF MS

Research on treatment is aimed at two forms of attack: (1) preventing the autoimmune response, which would prevent the disease, and (2) controlling the inflammation of the myelin so that irreversible scarring can be prevented. The major therapeutic regimens, including specific diet therapy and manipulations of specific nutrients, are reviewed by Sibley,[12] with inclusion of a description, rationale, evaluation, risks/costs, and conclusion for each regimen, including diets.

The only currently acceptable treatment of MS is the use of a short course of high-dose corticosteroids (or adrenocorticotropic hormone, which causes the body to produce large amounts of corticosteroids) in the face of an acute exacerbation. This therapy has been shown to reduce the morbidity of exacerbations in some persons with MS. Because it is a short course of therapy, side effects are minimal. There has been no evidence of a beneficial effect from long-term corticosteroid use, which is associated with serious side effects, including osteoporosis, fluid retention, and obesity.

Multiple clinical trials are under way with other immunosuppressant drugs and immunomodulators. In addition to medications, hyperbaric oxygen therapy and plasmapheresis are being investigated because of possible immunomodulator effects. Because the benefits are yet unproven and the treatments are costly (some with known serious side effects, others for which little is known about the long-term side effects), persons should be educated about the importance of using these potential treatments in controlled clinical trials only. Support for this concept can be included in nutrition counseling sessions, with an understanding of the frustration that results when the client feels that possible benefits are being withheld. The key to maintaining optimism is to recall for the client that the disability is frequently reversible as part of the natural course of the disease. Persons with MS have recovered from total blindness and total quadriplegia without specific treatment. Good supportive care is needed to prevent secondary complications, so that full function can return with such recoveries. The risk of harm from unproven therapy is real. Harm could result to the person for whom the clinical course may have been complete remission without active treatment. This would truly be a tragedy.

Persons with MS may wish to take any of these or other treatments out of sheer desperation, if for no other reason. It is suggested that they write or call the National Multiple Sclerosis Society* to get accurate information about treatments, including scientific support for efficacy and the location of specific clinical therapy trials. With the exception of drugs that have been used extensively with other diseases, there is little known about the nutritional effects and/or interactions related to these treatments so caution and keen observation are warranted.

Many persons with MS will be on some form of medication (see Table 5-1). There is little or no information about interactions with nutritional status for most of these drugs; however, most have some gastrointestinal side effects in a variable percentage of persons taking any of these medications. This is an area in desperate need of research.

Other forms of treatment to help control the symptoms and prevent complications include participation in a maintenance or therapeutic physical exercise program, proper care of skin and joints in areas with reduced mobility and/or sensation, and use of adaptive aids, equipment, and bracing to optimize function. Thus, persons should be encouraged to seek a team approach to care, just as is done with other clients in rehabilitation.

Nutritional Factors As Possible Therapeutic Agents

Nutritional therapy is a highly controversial area in the management of persons with MS. Most "therapeutic diets" and "therapeutic nutritional supplements" are based solely on anecdotal experience. None has been scientifically proven to have a beneficial effect in the control of MS. Yet, many persons with MS will choose to follow a specific diet or program of supplementation because they perceive greater benefit from trying some type of active treatment than doing nothing. Health care providers need to be aware of these alternative treatments and help clients assess them in terms of potential for benefit, potential for physical harm, and social and economic costs.

---

*205 East 42nd Street, New York, NY 10017 (212) 986-3240.

Unproven Therapeutic Diets

Multiple forms of diet therapy have been attempted in the efforts to control this disease process.

The therapeutic diet warranting the most serious consideration is that of the low fat diet, with or without supplementation of polyunsaturated fatty acids, advocated by Swank and Dugan.[5] Swank has personally followed subjects clinically for up to 36 years on this diet and reports that persons with MS who adhered strictly to his diet, with a saturated fat intake of less than 20 g/d, demonstrated less morbidity and mortality over time than those with higher levels of saturated fat intake. There was an increased intake of polyunsaturated fatty acids associated with the lower saturated fat intake, so the specific dietary factor of possible benefit is unclear. As critics of this theory note, however, this diet has not been rigorously tested in a double-blind controlled study and thus remains unproven. An additional criticism is the fact that the diet is found to be most effective when started early in the disease process, when there are no or few clinical signs of disease. Thus, it is debated whether these persons actually have MS in the first place. It remains to be seen if this diet can be successfully incorporated into a double-blind study for true scientific validation. Fortunately, this diet is actually quite similar to diets recommended for prevention of atherosclerosis; thus it presents little nutritional risk and may be healthier than the usual diet pattern of most persons.

Because of the concern about the etiologic relationship between a disturbance of the immune system and MS, allergen-free diets have been recommended. These diets have taken various forms. On a very general basis, elimination diets have been advocated, withholding foods commonly known to produce allergic reactions. This approach has not been tested formally. More specific therapeutic diets of this type have included the use of a gluten-free diet, in which limited formal studies have shown no benefit and there is a real risk of inadequate protein intake. A diet free from sucrose, tobacco, and propylene glycol has been recommended, based on the clinical experience of a limited number of persons with MS. Another hypothesis is that methanol, produced by metabolism of pectin and exaggerated with the concomitant ingestion of fructose, leads to autoimmunity to the myelin through formaldehyde production. Unripe fruits, fruit juices, and pectin-containing fruits and vegetables are eliminated from this diet. Because of a belief that menadione (Vitamin K_3) promotes the formation of sphingomyelin, this is added to the diet. Thus, there is a pectin and fructose-restricted diet, supplemented in menadione. This has only been evaluated in an uncontrolled series of persons with MS, without conclusive results. There was a high dropout rate.

The Evers diet advocates the use of unprocessed (raw) foods only, supplemented with germinated wheat. Some raw vegetables, especially leafy greens and stalks, are forbidden, in addition to salt, sugar, and condiments. Among the raw foods allowed are eggs, milk, and ham. Naturally processed wine, brandy, and honey are allowed. This diet is believed to be ineffective. Following it could be quite costly, as well as placing the person at risk for food-borne infections from the raw eggs, milk, and ham. Deletion of these items from the normal diet would increase the risk for protein deficiency.

The MacDougal diet combines the low fat diet with a gluten-free diet and supplementation with vitamins and minerals. This diet was based on MacDougal's personal experience with MS, including a complete and lasting remission. It has not been tested. Unnecessary supplements may be costly, and there is the risk of inadequate dietary protein intake, as found with the gluten-free diet.

Unproven Therapeutic Manipulation of Nutrients

In addition to diet therapy, manipulations of vitamins and minerals in various forms and dosages have been tried. There is no scientific proof of benefit to date. There is the risk of nutrient imbalance and excesses, in addition to the potential for increased dietary costs with this approach.

There is some evidence to suggest that supplementation of the diet with polyunsaturated fatty acids may reduce the rate and severity of exacerbations. Interest has been stimulated by knowledge of the biochemical role of polyunsaturated fatty acids in synthesis of other fatty acids and myelin, scattered reports of low linoleic acid levels in the serum of persons with MS, and a possible immunosuppressive effect of large doses of polyunsaturated fatty acids. A modest effect of slowing progression and reducing severity and duration of exacerbations has been demonstrated in some of the studies, but further investigation is still needed since efficacy has not yet been proven. Suppplements are found to be distasteful to some subjects, and some subjects have developed diarrhea. There is some cost increase with this supplementation. The long-term effects of these high levels of polyunsaturated fatty acids are not entirely clear, but recently there have been concerns voiced, especially regarding risk of premature aging and induction of cancers.

Although the incidence of MS is high in the northern latitudes, there is virtually no MS found in Eskimos. Because the Eskimo diet is high in fish oils, trials of fish oil supplementation have been undertaken. As in the case of polyunsaturated fatty acid supplementation, there are conflicting reports of efficacy, so further scientific study is warranted. Cost is modest. There is a residual fishy taste that is unpleasant.

Dietary supplementation with long-chain fatty acids from beef spinal cord has been tried without benefit. The underlying assumption was that a specific deficiency of these fatty acids caused MS. The concentration of these fatty acids rapidly increase in the brain during the normal process of myelination in infancy.

Because of claims that aloe vera juice has anti-inflammatory activity, consumption by persons with MS has been documented, with individual reports of recovery from exacerbations. This has not been studied in a double-blind controlled manner. Side effects of mild diarrhea and skin hypersensitivity have been noted.

Based on reports of impaired digestive tract function, supplementation with various and sundry enzymes at mealtime has been advocated. This is costly and without proven benefit.

Galactose is important in the formation of cerebroside, a component of myelin. Thus, it has been tried in persons with MS, both orally and intravenously. Only one, very limited study has been done. Dietary deficiency of galactose is essentially nonexistent. This treatment has not been proven to be effective.

Other Unproven Treatments

Unorthodox treatments abound to tempt the person with MS into false hopes and expensive, frequently risky activities. These run the gamut of injections of snake venom to replacing all mercury-based dental fillings with a "nonallergenic" amalgam to frequent cleansing enemas. Much time, energy, and money are wasted in these pursuits. Some can affect nutritional status because of effects on food intake or specific disturbances of metabolic processes. Dietitians have the potential to maintain professional contact with persons during such ventures and should be alert for possible nutritional problems (and medical problems) from such treatments. Generally, information about any of these treatments is available from the National Multiple Sclerosis Society. Health should be promoted in any way possible in spite of a client's insistence in continuing risky, expensive unproven therapies. Information and advice can be provided without being judgmental.

NUTRITION SUPPORT FOR PERSONS WITH CHRONIC ILLNESSES FOR WHICH THERE IS NO CURE

Some of the key features of MS, particularly the uncertainties and the excessive pessimism in the approach to management, are found in other disorders as well. Among the neurologic disorders, conditions such as Parkinson's disease, amyotrophic lateral sclerosis, and Huntington's chorea are just a few examples. Similar problems are faced by persons with many forms of cancer, collagen vascular disorders, progressive failure of specific organ systems, and, most recently, acquired immunodeficiency syndrome. In some cases, the certainty of early morbidity and mortality is much greater than with MS. Health care providers can become frustrated when faced with a progressive disorder that cannot be cured or controlled. This frustration is easily perceived and may result in avoidance of health care providers. Therapeutic advice from others, who promise cures and miraculous recoveries, will result in the expenditure of economic resources on unproven treatments, often with significant, but unacknowledged, risk to health. The difference in the two approaches, and the reason that health care providers lose out is called hope. The charlatans and quacks include hope in their messages. In efforts to totally inform clients and provide only medically necessary services, health care providers have lost many of the people most in need of support and caring. All members of the health care team must work together to reverse this trend; acknowledge the importance of caring, support, and hope; and learn how to provide them.[13]

Dietitians and nutritionists have a pivotal position that can be crucial to keeping persons with chronic illness linked to the medical community. As the rich history of numerous types of nutritional interventions in the efforts to control MS demonstrates, when nothing is known about a disease, or there is no treatment, persons naturally turn to diet as one means of achieving some form of control over their destiny. A new era is beginning in which the level of technical sophistication has been reached that allows very specific study of intermediary metabolism. This is resulting in an overwhelming amount of information that needs to be interpreted. Scientists are developing a new appreciation for the complexity of the living organism, which will evolve into a better understanding of the vast amount of individual variation that seems to have limited prior efforts at successful study and application of dietary and nutritional interventions. There is a need for new statistical methods to apply to these studies because of the high degree of individual variation. Thus, there is hope that the scientific basis of nutritional intervention may develop in a more effective way in the future.

In the interim, however, health care providers must be able to offer these persons hope and some feeling of control over their lives. Although there may be no specific nutritional therapy, the presence of a chronic disease has the potential to alter nutritional status and requirements. This is especially true when the disease is accompanied by functional impairments, be they physical, psychosocial, or vocational. Thus, these persons are at an increased nutritional risk and stand to benefit from learning about nutrition and undergoing individual assessment and counseling to meet their needs through diet. Second, because of the presence of a chronic disease there is less reserve in the body to tolerate other imbalances. When these can be controlled or prevented, health will improve in spite of the chronic disorder. Thus, good general nutritional habits, following the standard recommendations of nutritional thought, are beneficial to overall well-being in spite of the presence of chronic disease. Third, the functional disability accompanying a physiological impairment from a chronic disease can be aggravated by other factors, some of which can be well controlled through manipulation of the diet and regular exercise. Excessive weight makes mobility much more difficult in the person with muscle weakness, paralysis, or spasticity. Protein and/or calorie deficiencies increase the potential for skin breakdown in persons with impaired sensation and/or impaired mobility. Thus, the dietitian can offer real potential for physical and/or emotional improvement, even without the potential for cure, through effective nutrition counseling. The last point is that when these persons seek alternative treatments, they run the risk of harm to themselves. The problems of inadequate diets, which are often touted as cures, are well known. With a close relationship with a dietitian, a person pursuing an alternative treatment can be coached to look at the specifics of the treatment and learn of the potential risks. Possibly, the person will be able to make some alterations that reduce the risk without decreasing the potential for benefit. An example that comes to mind is a woman with MS who reports that she feels great when on a macrobiotic diet, and plans to resume it now that she is having an exacerbation. She was aware of many diets for MS and in particular mentioned that she had read Swank's book. She did not want to pursue Swank's diet because too many foods were included that were prohibited on the macrobiotic diet despite the fact that it provided a more nutritionally balanced intake. The one common factor of the two diets, the drastic reduction in the consumption of animal fats, was pointed out to her. With that knowledge in mind, she reconsidered the reduction of saturated fats in her diet rather than the macrobiotic diet. Additionally, she agreed to regular observation for nutritional deficiencies if she chooses to follow the macrobiotic diet. Thus, through the provision of knowledge alone there is less risk to this woman in her pursuit of self-control over her disease. Supportive education rather than condemnation can improve the lives of those who are otherwise left without hope.

REFERENCES

1. Paty DW. Multiple sclerosis: Assessment of disease progression and effects of treatment. *Can J Neurol Sci.* 1987;14:518–520.

2. Kurtzke JF. Multiple sclerosis: What's in a name? *Neurology.* 1988;38:309–316.

3. Ford HC. Multiple sclerosis: A survey of alternative hypotheses concerning aetiology, pathogenesis and predisposing factors. *Med Hypotheses.* 1987;24:201–207.

4. Poser CM. Pathogenesis of multiple sclerosis: A critical reappraisal. *Acta Neuropathol.* 1986;71:1–10.

5. Swank RL, Dugan BB. *The Multiple Sclerosis Diet Book: A Low-Fat Diet for the Treatment of M.S.* Garden City, NY: Doubleday & Co.; 1987.

6. Fisher M, Johnson MH, Natale AM, Levine PH. Linoleic acid levels in white blood cells, platelets, and serum of multiple sclerosis patients. *Acta Neurol Scand.* 1987;76:241–245.

7. Maneta-Peyret L, Daverat P, Geffard M, et al. Natural seric anti-fatty acid antibodies in multiple sclerosis. *Neurosci Lett.* 1987;80:235–239.

8. Mertin J, Meade CJ. Relevance of fatty acids in multiple sclerosis. *Br Med Bull.* 1977;33:67–71.

9. Prosiegel M, Neu I, Mehiber L. Encephalitogenic peptide and platelet aggregation in multiple sclerosis. *Acta Neurol Scand.* 1986;73:141–144.

10. Ferraro D, Salemi G, Cestelli A, et al. Inhibition of glial proliferation in vitro by serum from patients with multiple sclerosis. *Acta Neurol Scand.* 1987;76:237–240.

11. Ho S-Y, Catalanotto FA, Lisak RB, Dore-Duffy P. Zinc in multiple sclerosis: II. Correlation with disease activity and elevated plasma membrane-bound zinc in erythrocytes from patients with multiple sclerosis. *Ann Neurol.* 1986;20:712–715.

12. Sibley WA. *Therapeutic Claims in Multiple Sclerosis.* 2nd ed. New York, NY: Demos Publications; 1988.

13. Uretsky SD. It beats the truth. *Am J Hosp Pharm.* 1987;44:2373–2374.

BIBLIOGRAPHY

Matthews WB, Acheson ED, Batchelor JR, Weller RO. *McAlpine's Multiple Sclerosis.* New York, NY: Churchill-Livingstone; 1985.

Rosner LJ, Ross S. *Multiple Sclerosis: New Hope and Practical Advice for People with MS and Their Families.* Englewood Cliffs, NJ: Prentice-Hall; 1987.

Schapiro RT. *Symptom Management in Multiple Sclerosis.* New York, NY: Demos Publications; 1987.

Scheinberg C. *Multiple Sclerosis: A Guide for Patients and Their Families.* New York, NY: Raven Press; 1983.

Sibley WA. *Therapeutic Claims in Multiple Sclerosis.* 2nd ed. New York, NY: Demos Publications; 1988.

Waksman BH, Reingold SC, Reynolds WE. *Research on Multiple Sclerosis.* 3rd ed. New York, NY: Demos Publications; 1987.

Wolf JK, ed. *Mastering Multiple Sclerosis, A Handbook for MSers and Families.* Rutland, Vt: Academy Books; 1984.

Chapter 6

The Disabled Child

Margaret J. Morris, Daniel H. Ingram, Margaret Howison,
Carol Kaltreider, and Charles A. Nichter

Nutrition is a complex, dynamic, multisystemic process involving ingestion, absorption, and metabolism of food substances within an environmental context. Most often, this proceeds uneventfully with subsequent normal growth and development of the infant or child. However, change in this process can be drastic when the child has a significant disability. The eventual result is compromised nutrition with enormous family stress overwhelming everyone in the home.

Such an array of nutritional difficulties can be understood by viewing nutrition and feeding as a changing network of pathways involving oral-motor activity, health status, and psychosocial factors, as well as calories, minerals, vitamins, and cultural regulations. As an example, appropriate oral-motor skills require appropriate head, trunk, and hip positioning. Hypotonicity, hypertonicity, abnormal primitive reflexes, and a dislocated hip undermine the normal and pleasurable process of holding and feeding a baby. Frequent vomiting, choking, or aspiration pneumonia scare a parent and worry the primary care physician as well. Tongue thrust, drooling, or poor lip closure do not enhance caloric intake; rather, they create concerns related to texture, oral techniques, fluid volume intake, and possibly dehydration. Therapy with phenytoin (Dilantin) and gum hypertrophy can make normal feeding difficult, slow, or even unattainable.

Eating is social and developmental. To hold, fondle, or breast feed are the beginnings of a lifelong relationship between the infant and the parents. Similarly, feeding is an issue of behavior. With the developmentally delayed child, parents may experience anxiety because their infant son or daughter is not able to sit well in the high chair during meal time. Dysfunction in planning and executing movement patterns (sensory integration) may make self-feeding very difficult or impossible.

To tackle the entirety of the problem, the feeding program at the Elizabethtown Hospital and Rehabilitation Center of the Milton S. Hershey

Medical Center employs a transdisciplinary team approach. Since 1980, the primary purpose of this feeding clinic has been to work with children who exhibit severe feeding difficulties and who have not progressed well in community-based programs.

The feeding clinic employs a core team of professionals that includes an occupational therapist, a dietitian, a developmental pediatrician, and a nurse clinician. A unique transdisciplinary model is used that allows all of the professionals to evaluate and treat the patient during the scheduled visit. This provides a thoroughness in medical care that is very difficult to duplicate in the more traditional interdisciplinary approach. It should also be emphasized that during this 1-hour session, the parents are included as an integral part of the team and are involved in all problem solving and decision making relative to the development and implementation of an appropriate program for their child.

A beneficial outgrowth of this transdisciplinary approach has been to enhance the understanding and knowledge base of the team members with regard to the role and expertise of their fellow practitioners. Each team member learns from his or her fellow team members while teaching the parents and the child. A graphic representation of this transdisciplinary approach and shared therapeutic expertise is presented in Figure 6-1. As can be seen, team members can and do become involved in an area not traditionally considered to be his or her area of expertise.

Because the presenting problems are often complex and multidimensional, additional disciplines are often involved in the evaluation and treatment of the children and their families. Professionals representing disciplines such as developmental and/or behavioral psychology, pediatric surgery, social services, adaptive seating, and speech/language pathology are frequent participants in the feeding clinic.

In order to ensure an efficient, consistent, and comprehensive program and that the 1-hour clinic visit is conducted in a smooth and efficient manner, a specific set of goals has been developed for the initial visit and each succeeding visit. The following checklist is used by the team on the initial clinic visit:

1. Observe the parent or primary caregiver feed the child with food that is brought from the home.
2. Obtain a complete medical and developmental history.
3. Make height and weight measurements to establish baseline data and growth parameters.
4. Obtain a dietary assessment of the child based on a 3-day diet history kept by the family or a 24-hour recall.
5. Demonstrate appropriate positioning and feeding techniques with immediate training of the parent and a practice session.

FEEDING TEAM APPROACH

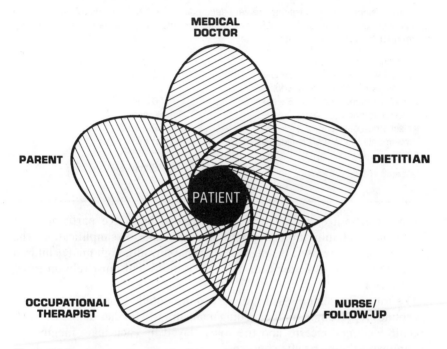

Figure 6-1 Feeding team approach. *Source:* Reprinted with permission of Elizabethtown Hospital and Rehabilitation Center, Elizabethtown, PA.

---

6. Develop, in writing, an individualized program of feeding techniques and nutrition intervention to be used in the home.
7. Determine if additional disciplines need to be involved and discuss them with the parents.
8. Schedule a follow-up clinic visit.
9. Each discipline present records notes into the child's medical chart.

While the above goals may change slightly because of the addition of other professionals, the above checklist is a basic framework of what is accomplished during each succeeding clinic visit. It should also be pointed out that "brainstorming" sessions with the parents are a routine part of each clinic session to ensure that program recommendations are realistic and can be carried out by the family and that progress is being made.

Historically, approximately one third of the feeding clinic clients will require a 6-week hospital admission for more intensive and comprehensive rehabilitation services (Table 6-1). As with the outpatient population,

Table 6-1 Nutritional Staffing Standards for Neurodevelopmental Clients during 6-Week Rehabilitation

Neurodevelopmental admissions are very demanding of a dietitian's time. As an inpatient at Elizabethtown Hospital and Rehabilitation Center for 6 weeks, the average client is typically charged for the following nutrition services:

1 nutrition consult	65 min.
2 meal rounds/week × 6 weeks	60 min.
1 progress note/week × 6 weeks	60 min.
3 modified menus/week × 6 weeks	90 min.
1 miniconference	60 min.
1 discharge conference	60 min.
2 treatments that are education sessions	30 min.
	425 min.
	or 7 hours

parents are both encouraged and expected to be active participants in their child's rehabilitation program. (For the sake of simplification, the term *parent* will be used throughout this chapter, although many children are seen who are in foster care or in institutions and must rely on those caregivers.)

The following sections will provide a more detailed look at the specific disciplines represented on the feeding team and will further delineate some specific feeding concerns and the roles played by each team member in dealing with these specific concerns.

NUTRITION INTERVENTION

As a core member of the feeding team, the dietitian is responsible for evaluating growth parameters, making nutritional assessments, teaching appropriate dietary alterations, and recording data for the medical records. These tasks, in and of themselves, are typical roles for a dietitian. However, the nature of the types of clients seen and the process of team interaction are unique.

Dietitians assessing the nutritional status of children with developmental disabilities must first understand normal pediatric stages in eating. Chronologically, a child may be 3 years old but cognitively more like a 6-month old. Most likely, the means by which one can achieve good nutritional status will have to be adjusted to accommodate the cognitive deficit. Normal developmental stages in eating are described in Table 6-2.

No matter what setting a dietitian is working in (ie, ambulatory versus inpatient), one of the most important aspects of evaluating a child with a developmental disability is simply observing his or her unique eating pattern. A dietitian's training in recognizing portion sizes, understanding caloric needs, and familiarity with counting calories can provide invaluable information on how much is being consumed within a given time frame. The feeding clinic setting is especially helpful in obtaining accurate data because families are asked to bring food from home to feed their child. This allows one to observe how nutritionally aware the parents are and to see visually if the lunch box from home complies with the feeding clinic instruction on textures, nutrient-rich foods, and portion sizes.

Within the feeding clinic setting, approximately 50% of the mothers are able to complete a 3-day food diary for their children. If this is unavailable, a 24-hour recall is attempted. Either system is initially evaluated for the following:

- calories consumed
- fluids consumed
- variety of foods used in a given day
- snacking (too much? too little?)
- cooking skills of the caregiver
- length of time feeding a meal

Children with developmental disabilities fluctuate widely in energy levels. Children with low muscle tone types of disabilities (eg, Down syndrome or Prader-Willi syndrome) will commonly reach growth potential with approximately one half the normal recommended daily allowances (RDA) levels. Palmer and Ekvall have found that in cerebral palsy, children aged 5 to 11 need 13.9 kcal/cm in mild to moderate cases; with greater restriction of movement, 11.1 kcal/cm is adequate. Children with athetosis problems may require enormous calorie levels in order to reach ideal body weight.[1] The most simple and effective way to tell if one is achieving the appropriate goal is by frequent monitoring of weight and adjustment of calories (and other nutrients) appropriately. For children who are sustaining themselves with marginal kilocalories, a multivitamin/mineral supplement is recommended.

Most of the children seen in the feeding clinic are underweight. Typically, the first recommendations made are simple, inexpensive diet alterations for increasing caloric density. If these suggestions are ineffective in obtaining better growth, use of an enteral supplement is frequently recommended at the second or third visit.

One extremely pervasive problem with this population tends to be fluid consumption. Most children with developmental disabilities fall short of

Table 6-2 Developmental Stages in Eating

Age	Oral-Motor Skills	Position for Feeding	Type of Food
1 month	Suckle–swallow, root, bite reflexes, and hyperactive gags	Held in arms at angle of less than 45°; supine with head elevated; side-lying	Takes 2–4 oz of breast milk or formula per feeding; six or more feedings per day
3 months	Suckle–swallow; retains oral reflexes	Supportive semi-sitting, 45° to 90°	Takes 7 or 8 oz of liquid per feeding; four to six feedings per day
5 months	Disappearance of suckle–swallow; phasic bite and release pattern of jaw; participates actively when spoon fed	Same	Takes 28–36 oz of liquid/day; begin feeding 2 tbsp cereal two to three times per day
6 months	True suck, coordinated swallow	Same	Liquid; begin feeding 2 tbsp cereal plus 2 tbsp fruit or vegetable two to three times per day
7 months	Tongue moves food side to side; good lip closure over spoon	Fed in sitting position with back at 90°; will need restrainer, pillows, tray	Liquid; begin adding pureed meat into program; needs 3 meals of solids to feel satiated
8 months	Rotary chewing; less pronounced gagging	Same	Three meals pureed or junior texture; intake of liquids will decrease as solids increase
9 months	Feeds self a cracker; holds own bottle	Fed in sitting position with seat back at 90°; seat belt needed for safety	Cut table foods into ½-inch bites (can feed self larger pieces of food that get soft in the mouth: graham crackers, saltines, biscuit)

Age			
10 months	Drinks from cup with assistance; may start to finger feed	Same	Same
11 months	Finger feeds; begins with spoon, palmar grasp	Same	Use a cup with meals; may advance to cow's milk if child is eating meats and whole grains well
15 months	Holds cup with two hands; feeds self with spoon, spilling some	Same	Eliminate all bottles; can eat approximately 2-tbsp size portions of meat, egg, cereals, vegetables, and fruit per meal; needs $\frac{1}{2}$ cup milk (or $1\frac{1}{2}$ oz cheese) four times per day
18 months	Takes filled spoon to mouth, turns at mouth and spills	Fed sitting unsupported at table or at small child's table and chair	Same
2 years	Fills and takes spoon to mouth without turning over	Same	Will begin to take 3-tbsp size portions occasionally
3 years	Combined feeding with fingers, spoon, and fork; holds cup with one hand; chews with mouth closed	Same	Begins to need $\frac{3}{4}$ cup milk four times per day
4 years	Drinks with straw, uses fork, gets drink of water without help	Same	Begins to take $\frac{1}{4}$ cup size portions at meal times
5 years	Eating and talking combined	Same	Same
6 years	Spreads with knife, assists to set table	Same	Begins to take $\frac{1}{2}$ cup size portions

Source: Reprinted with permission of Elizabethtown Hospital and Rehabilitation Center, Elizabethtown, PA.

the traditionally recommended 1.5 mL/1 kcal. In some cases, their bodies may have adjusted without bowel or kidney problems. Unfortunately, however, severe constipation tends to be a major problem for many of these clients. Because thin liquids are typically difficult for them to consume in adequate volume, this can be a difficult problem to resolve. Typically, the feeding clinic emphasizes use of additional fiber-rich fruits and vegetables for these cases until fluid intake is sufficient to incorporate more whole grains.

Collecting anthropometric data on children with developmental disabilities is an essential part of assessment. The National Center for Health Statistics (NCHS) growth charts continue to be a consistently helpful tool in evaluating changes in height and weight. Because children with developmental disabilities frequently are short in stature, a comparison of weight against height is the most accurate method of reading appropriate growth. Obtaining a length measurement can be very difficult if the client has scoliosis or limb contractures. However, with two staff members helping and a recumbent length board, a reasonable approximation can be made.

Additional data collection of triceps skin fold thickness will help in evaluation of muscle mass. Kaliszk and Ekvall have found that an overabundance of fat tissue may provide a false visual impression of adequate musculature.[2] Fee and co-workers find triceps skin folds are more helpful in monitoring obesity than monitoring malnutrition.[3] Skin fold measurements are taken at various stages over a period of time so that the client's progress can be evaluated. Preferably, the measurement is made by the same evaluator using the same methods and equipment in order to help standardize the technique.

Many investigators allude to the prevalence of poor nutrition in children with developmental disabilities. At our facility, we consider failure-to-thrive cases to be clients who have a weight that is two standard deviations below height measurement on the NCHS growth chart. The majority of the feeding clinic patients fall within this category. Any person staying at or below this level for 6 months, in spite of therapeutic feeding, coupled with medical and nutritional intervention, is viewed as being at serious nutritional risk. For many of these cases, the feeding team will recommend more invasive procedures. Parents are under stress and often adverse to the idea of Nissen fundoplication procedures and gastrostomy tubes.[4] Careful attention to the feelings of the parents is needed in guiding these families to opt for improved nutrition by these means. Our feeding team emphasizes that in spite of a gastrostomy tube we will continue to try to help a child to improve in oral-motor ability. A gastrostomy tube rarely is synonymous with no oral activity. With improved energy and better health, some children may show improved feeding skills. Unfortunately, the other side of this problem is that some children who are very marginal feeders presurgically will have less motivation to eat when nourished with a gastrostomy tube. One must be very honest with families in stressing the pros and cons of this decision.

Clearly, at times, there may be a need to recommend gastrostomy tubes early in a client's care. An inability to swallow one's own saliva, frequent aspiration, pneumonia, gastroesophageal reflux, dehydration, extended use of a nasogastric tube, and excessive time spent in eating are all of major concern and possible "red flags" in recommending early surgery.

Unfortunately, many children with developmental disabilities have multiple problems. For example, it is common for us to see a child with cerebral palsy, failure-to-thrive, severe constipation, improper seating, and uncontrolled seizures. Clearly, not all problems can be resolved in an hour's clinic visit. It is most helpful to ask the parents in these cases, "What do you want us to achieve today?" The parents' answer to this question will help a great deal in knowing how much the family understands about the child's condition. From this level of understanding, one can teach and expand the parents' skills.

Each clinic visit is tailored to the needs of the client. At times, practical nutritional advice is the most needed component of a particular session. At other times, a client's primary need is better supplied by other professionals. However, it is the consistent recording of nutritional parameters by which a patient's progress is being most frequently measured. A dietitian's expertise in recording pertinent data on calories, fluids, textures consumed, length of time spent in eating, and anthropometric data (Table 6-3) can serve as a valuable component of the feeding team process.

PSYCHOSOCIAL MANAGEMENT OF FEEDING PROBLEMS

The psychologist's role on the feeding team is both general and specific. It is the psychologist who assesses the parents in terms of their needs (both felt and expressed), their understanding of their child, and the expectations for their child. When a behavioral component exists as part of the feeding difficulty, the psychologist assists the parents in establishing specific goals and techniques for resolving the behavioral issues. This section will primarily address the family and their role in the feeding program.

Family Assessment

In working with these families, a prime area of importance and initial consideration is the role the parents play in the child's feeding difficulties.

Table 6-3 Neurodevelopmental Nutritional Assessment

The Elizabethtown Hospital and Rehabilitation Center

Managed by the University Hospital of The Milton S. Hershey Medical Center

Elizabethtown, PA 17022
(717) 367-1161

PATIENT NAME: _____

PATIENT NUMBER: _____

DIAGNOSIS: _____

NUTRITIONIST'S NOTE

	Age	Date	"	cm	%	lb	kg	%
					Height			Weight
Previous Visit:								
Today:								

H.C. _____ H.C.% _____ Ht. Age _____

Wt. Age _____ Wt. vs. Ht. _____

Estimated Ideal Body Wt. _____ % Ideal Body Wt. _____

Diet History Obtained By: (Check One) _____

3-Day Recorded Intake _____ 24-Hour Recall _____ Unable to Obtain

Estimated Intake: P.O. _____ % P.G. _____ %

Total Calories _____ _____

Total Fluids _____ _____

Cal/Kg _____ Cal/Cm _____

Length of P.O. Feeding Time: _____ min/meal _____ hrs/day

Diet Used:

_____

Overall Impression of Diet: _____

_____

Bowel Pattern: _____

Diet Recommended: _____

_____

Multivitamin Recommended: _____ Yes _____ No

Comments:

Source: Reprinted with permission of Elizabethtown Hospital and Rehabilitation Center, Elizabethtown, PA.

It is important to keep in mind that children are a product of their homes and their environments. First, if one is to help the child, one must understand the parents in order to determine their role in the feeding difficulty. Our second task is to educate them about needed changes. Restructure of the home environment, both during meal and nonmeal times, may be necessary.

This assessment of the parents is done by our team using a model similar to Kubler-Ross' grief cycles. In this model, five stages of grief have been delineated, starting with denial/isolation and moving through anger, bargaining, depression, and, finally, acceptance. According to Kubler-Ross, parents pass through these predictable stages of grief before finally reaching the acceptance stage. Although Kubler-Ross used these stages to describe the stages a person goes through in dealing with death, it is our experience that parents of developmentally disabled children often pass through stages similar to these in dealing with their child's disabling conditions. By assessing the stage the parent is in relative to both the disabling condition and/or the feeding difficulties, it is then possible to design a program that takes into account the parents' and the child's needs. If one is not sensitive to the emotional needs, both felt and expressed, of the parents, then the success of any feeding program is likely to be minimal. It is also important to recognize that all parents move through these stages at different rates and, again, the team working with the parents must be sensitive to the pace the parents exhibit. It often becomes necessary to "walk a fine line" between moving the parents and children too fast or too slowly through these stages.

In summary, the parents' level of acceptance of their child's condition plays a large role in determining the child's passage through the various stages of a feeding program. The parents' willingness to accept the program and their commitment to the feeding program will ultimately determine the long-term success or failure of the program itself.

Family As Team Members

One of the key factors that affect the success of the parents' involvement is the importance of having a team of professionals who are comfortable and flexible enough to engage in a give-and-take situation. Ideas must be shared freely and openly with staff members and parents. The recognition by professionals that parents often know their children better than anyone else on the team helps in developing a sense of trust by all parties and leads to optimum follow-through on the parents' part.

Once the parental and child assessment is completed, a feeding program can be developed and initiated. In developing a feeding program, it has been our experience at the feeding clinic that family members (parents/older siblings) should be included as an integral part of the team process as well as in the development of the feeding plan. By doing this, the family becomes actively involved in the feeding program and, thus, will generally exhibit a stronger commitment to the program, the team members, and the team process. It is therefore essential during team brainstorming sessions that the suggestions and ideas of the parents be acknowledged and incorporated into the feeding plan.

A second reason for family involvement in developing a comprehensive, successful feeding program is the need to determine the various aspects of feeding and mealtimes that are specific to each individual family. If these family-specific issues are not explored and incorporated into the program, then, again, the success of the program is likely to be compromised. There are numerous logistical, cultural, and systemic issues to be considered when developing a feeding program. The initial consideration is to assess the type of life style that is indigenous to each particular family. Such questions include

1. Is this a family that has a specific mealtime routine?
2. Is this a family that eats on the run?
3. Are there certain mealtime rituals established in the home?
4. Are there specific food preferences that are culturally based?
5. What are the mealtime expectations of the parents relative to the children's behavior?
6. What is the physical layout of the house and where are the meals primarily consumed?
7. What are the parents' attitudes toward snacks?
8. Do both parents work?
9. Is this a single parent?

These are but a few questions that need to be answered about the family and mealtimes. Obviously, these questions are best answered by the family members themselves. This ensures that any feeding plan will fit the life style and expectations of the family relative to mealtimes and eating. By exploring these questions, one can also determine whether the life style of the family is a contributing factor for the child's feeding problem. By exploring these questions, areas of difficulty can then be discussed with the family and they can assist in making necessary adjustments relative to mealtimes and their child.

Assessment of Child's Developmental Levels

As noted previously, most children with feeding difficulties also exhibit either handicapping conditions or developmental delays, which often cause difficulties beyond feeding. Also, in many cases, there is a strong behavioral component to the feeding difficulties. In light of this, it is essential to schedule a complete developmental assessment of the child in order to determine cognitive, speech/language (receptive and expressive), motor (fine and gross), social, and self-help levels. By doing this, one can provide objective information to the parents about their child's development and can use this information in the development of behavioral strategies and techniques for use as an integral part of the feeding program.

The child's developmental levels will affect any behavioral programming that may be necessary. In developing behavioral strategies, the child must have the cognitive abilities necessary to comply for behavioral modification. If the cognitive readiness is not present owing to developmental delays, then other alternatives (eg, medical intervention) may be required. When using behavior modification techniques, the family must be well educated in basic behavior theory, basic reinforcement/punishment systems, and the strong need for consistency on their part if the behavioral aspect of the feeding difficulty is to be ameliorated.

It is the experience of our team that positive reinforcement systems are generally the most successful, although, in particularly difficult cases adversive conditioning or punishment systems are used. These negative systems are used only as part of an inpatient admission and under specific direction and control of the feeding team. Generally, the parents, the team, and the child have a better feeling about the program when negative systems can be avoided.

OCCUPATIONAL THERAPY INTERVENTION

The occupational therapist assesses the oral-motor skills of the child. Some feeding teams may have a speech pathologist or physical therapist who fulfills the role. Because of the complexity of referrals, the scope of the evaluation has been limited, in most cases, to the actual process of taking in food. Self-feeding needs are referred to another resource, such as local outpatient programs, school, or inpatient treatment program.

The parent is asked to feed the child as it is done at home. This affords the feeding team the opportunity to see the feeding skills of both the feeder and the child as well as the interaction between the two. The occupational therapist will continue to assess the child's abilities while the parent and other team members address pertinent issues affecting the feeding process.

Before a successful assessment can be done, the child must be able to trust the evaluator. Sensitivity to the child's subtle methods of communicating is important. Sometimes the family will be able to help. Other times, the family may seem unaware that the child is trying to communicate.

Oral-motor patterns are assessed. These may be divided into three areas: abnormal, primitive, and higher level.

Abnormal or pathologic movement patterns are never seen in a normal developing infant. They come from the release of abnormal reflex patterns associated with central nervous system damage. They are usually associated with abnormalities of muscle tone and subsequent abnormal movement patterns. The child may be hypotonic, or floppy, with very low muscle tone and have little ability to move. He or she may be hypertonic, or stiff, with high muscle tone at rest or when movement is initiated and have little ability to control and grade motion. Abnormal movement patterns interfere with the development of the normal feeding process. They may be compensations for poor positioning and stability.

Primitive oral patterns occur normally in the first 4 to 6 months of an infant's development. They are gradually integrated and replaced by other more advanced movement patterns. The neurologically impaired child or child with mental retardation may retain primitive patterns. A 3- or 4-year-old child or, in fact, a 20-year-old may maintain the skills of a 3- to 4-month-old infant.

Higher developmental movement patterns occur in the last one half of the first year and are further refined in the first 2 or 3 years of life. These are selected for speech sounds.

The abnormal and primitive oral patterns influence the feeding process. To plan an intervention program, both patterns are further assessed by breaking them down into components of movement.

Many of the abnormal or pathologic movement patterns seem to be compensations for immature movements that were prevented from disappearing or integrating into the system because of high, low, or fluctuating muscle tone. The original normal immature pattern is called a normal block in development. When these persist in the neck and shoulders, normal development is not allowed and abnormal compensations are seen.

At 1 to 3 months, neck hyperextension is normal. If the head does not come forward and the chin down, abnormal oral characteristics may be seen. These may include tongue thrust, lip, cheek, and tongue retraction, jaw thrust, and strong jaw closure.

Neck asymmetry, the turning of the head to the side, and subsequent neck hyperextension are normal from 3 to 4 months. If the head does not come forward and to the midline with the chin down, strong asymmetrical lateral deviation of the jaw may occur in addition to the abnormal patterns indicated above.

Shoulder-humeral tightness is normal at 1 to 3 months of age. If the shoulders continue to be elevated, tightness in the upper chest will limit respiration and the suck-swallow process. The head assumes the two neck block positions, and subsequent abnormal patterns are seen.

Scapular adduction is normal at various stages as the infant develops. If the scapula causes the arms to pull back, the child cannot bring the hands to the mouth to prepare or desensitize the mouth for texture. Shoulder elevation and the two neck blocks may occur, causing abnormal oral movements.

A functional, symmetrical, and stable position will dramatically help to control the abnormal oral movements. The child must be upright with hips rolled under so that he or she is on the ischial tuberosities and not on the coccyx or tailbone. Hips are maintained with a seat belt fastened tight enough for only two adult fingers to slide under. The head is in the midline and forward. The neck is elongated to allow a chin tuck. The trunk is straight. Shoulders are forward and down with hands in lap or on a lap-board. Hips and knees should be flexed to 90°.

A custom-fitted chair is important to ensure a functional, symmetrical, and stable position. If this is not available, many seating devices may be temporarily adapted to meet the child's needs. Rolled-up towels and blankets, small pillows, and even a stuffed animal may be strategically placed to provide the necessary support.

Many infants may need to be fed in a seat if two hands are needed to facilitate the feeding process. Some infants and children may not tolerate a seat because their systems are very sensitive and/or there are behavior issues. A compromise in placement may be made, but the position must be the same.

The primitive oral movements of suck, swallow, biting, and chewing are assessed when the child is in an appropriate position. These develop from gross movement patterns of the jaw, lips, cheeks, and tongue and initially are seen in infants younger than 6 months of age. They eventually become the most refined movements in the body.

Abnormal sucking is one of the most common problems seen. It may be weak, disorganized, or not stimulated. The normal neonate has a true suck of rhythmical raising and lowering of the tongue and jaw as a unit. The lips are tight around the nipple.

A sucking pattern develops as the infant begins to develop extension and loses some of the newborn flexion. The parts of the mouth begin to separate as seen by an extension/retraction or in/out pattern of the tongue as it curls under the nipple.

Gradual separation of the jaw, tongue, and lips is seen as postural tone develops. The infant has the up and down tongue movements of the true suck. When the jaw can stabilize itself without the child biting on the cup rim, the lips separate to sip in the liquid or clean the spoon.

A nutrient suck has a one suck per second pattern. The child must coordinate suck, swallow, and breathing in a coordinated way. A nonnutrient suck has two sucks per second and is not coordinated with swallowing and breathing. Some infants suck on a pacifier but become disorganized or frightened when a nutrient suck is needed.

A swallow is initially chained to the suck–swallow reflex in which the infant depends on the suck to trigger the swallow. An independent swallow develops at 2 to 3 months. It includes the movement of the tongue, lips, and cheeks necessary to form a bolus from food or liquid in the front of the mouth and propel it into the pharyngeal area for swallowing. The child must be able to handle and organize lumps and solid foods without gagging from food on the back of the tongue.

A thin liquid or food may be difficult for a child to handle. Thickening of either with baby cereal, dehydrated baby food, or other thickening agents may assist in forming a bolus.

A child who cannot handle his or her own secretions may not be a candidate for oral feeding. It may be necessary to continue tube feeding while working on oral stimulation to swallow.

Biting and chewing are the more volitional aspects of feeding. Many children are referred to the feeding clinic because they reportedly do not chew. Assessment often shows that the child also has a poor suck. Chewing food may be a more obvious outward sign to those around the child. The steps leading to it may not have been as important to the family.

The rhythmical bite and release pattern of the phasic bite reflex is often confused with chewing. It is a series of jaw openings and closings that occurs when the teeth and gums are stimulated. It is normal up to 6 months of age.

Munching is the earliest form of chewing. Although the jaw moves up and down, the tongue stays in the center and does not separate to move to the side to transfer food.

Chewing involves the tongue and jaw: the up and down and side to side movement of the tongue as it moves food between the teeth and the unstereotyped vertical, diagonal rotary, and circular rotary movements of the jaw as it breaks up and pulverizes solid pieces of food in preparation for swallowing.

Primitive oral patterns become more integrated into the child's system when food texture is introduced. The mouth is challenged to use new patterns of movement. The type and nature of the food or liquid are dependent on the desired movement and the child's ability to perform.

After the child's abnormal and primitive oral patterns have been assessed, an oral program may be initiated. If oral feeding is viewed as a realistic goal by the team, the family will participate in hands-on feeding using therapeutic techniques.

MEDICAL STABILITY

Nutrition and feeding are a perplexing and changing maze of interacting systems involving the child, family, home, and sociocultural mores. This complex, physiologically efficient activity called feeding can be enormously disrupted in the case of a disabling condition. What can ensue is a decline in the child's health, leading to additional, potentially overwhelming stresses and difficulties.

As part of the feeding team, the pediatrician has many systems (including respiratory, gastrointestinal, musculoskeletal, neurologic, and psychosocial) to assess. Rather than generalize across such areas, the focus will be on two clinically important topics: seizure medication and gastroesophageal reflux.

Seizure Medication

In examining nutrition in its entirety, questions arise concerning drug–nutrient interactions. Specifically, what are the medications being used, what are they to do, and how will they affect nutrients and their assimilation?

Seizure medications are intended to curtail, minimize, or stop the frequency and severity of seizures. Such drugs are known as anticonvulsants and include such examples as phenobarbital, phenytoin, carbamazepine, valproic acid, ethosuximide, diazepam, and primidone. They are effective; 60% to 95% are seizure free for prolonged periods as the result of anticonvulsant therapy.[5] Such efficacy is achieved because of several factors involving dosage, frequency of administration, drug pharmacokinetics, and monitoring. It is with these same factors that anticonvulsants interface with nutrition.

Dosage refers to a specified amount of medication according to the weight of the child. As an example, valproic acid is begun at 10 to 15 mg/kg/d. The amount of drug is particularly important because of its association with potential side effects.[6] Some anticonvulsants, such as valproic acid and ethosuximide, can irritate the gastric lining, especially at the higher doses. They can also create sleepiness or mild incoordination, which, in turn, can interfere with and intensify the oral-motor dysfunctions in the marginal or problematic feeder. Decreased appetite, lethargy, and vomiting can be seen with higher doses of valproic acid. Increased drooling is a subtle side effect of the benzodiazepines, diazepam, or clonazepam.

It can be reassuring, however, that such side effects can be minimized. When starting the medication, a low dose should be chosen, with increases at systematic intervals. Gastric irritation can be alleviated by dividing the daily dose into two, three, or four increments. It may also be beneficial to give the medicines when the stomach is filled with fluid or food.

Frequency of administration involves the number of times the medicine is given. It can be scheduled once daily, twice daily, or more. Although straightforward to some degree, practical issues need to be strongly considered. Recalling the relationship of medication and feeding (ie, a full stomach), one may ask what is the taste of the medication and what is the route of its administration? As an example, if the medication has a bitter or sweet aftertaste, is given orally, and is disguised in food, this can decrease the pleasure of eating and, in turn, establish strong negative feelings for meals and the concomitant socialization. Gastrostomy feedings obviate this problem but create new questions and concerns. During what part of the feeding should the drug be given—beginning, middle, or end? Can the medication be mixed with the formula beforehand? What about the rate of formula flow? In one study, Holtz and associates documented that mixing medications, one of which was phenytoin, with formulas can negatively affect the pharmacology of the drug.[7] Relative to the rate of flow of the gastrostomy feeding, this may affect absorption, particularly if the rate is a rapid one. Bolus feedings can create loose stools or significant diarrhea. Similarly, a dumping syndrome picture can be observed with inadequate drug absorption when the gastrostomy tube is not secure on the abdominal wall.

Solutions do exist with individualized problem solving. A liquid form for most of the major anticonvulsants is available. Sometimes, the chewable tablets are minimally flavored and could be considered with applesauce or pudding if the child can tolerate such an oral approach. For gastrostomy tube feedings, one should first have a well-secured tube, not one that is wandering farther into the stomach. Second, the drug should not be mixed in the formula, bottle, or bag but rather given in the middle of a 30- to

45-minute feeding. Most formulas are well tolerated, but care should be given when employing calorie-dense formulas in young infants and children. Rapid transit and diarrhea can be observed with subsequent difficulties with drug absorption and appropriate serum levels.

Drug pharmacokinetics refers to the drug's action in the body and involves absorption, distribution, biotransformation, elimination, and drug interaction.[8] From gastric pH, antacids, and stomach emptying to protein-bound anticonvulsants, liver toxicity, vitamins, and fat stores, one can begin to see the enormity of the topic of anticonvulsant pharmacokinetics. Therefore, as an example of this complexity, rickets, and specifically the vitamin deficiency form, will be reviewed.

Rickets is a disturbance in bone mineralization with four basic causes. Along with vitamin D deficiency, there is renal tubular insufficiency, chronic renal failure, and hypophosphatasia. The exact pathogenesis for vitamin D deficiency associated with anticonvulsants is debated.[9] For example, vitamin D intake, sunlight exposure, physical activity, anticonvulsant dose, and duration of therapy are important variables.[10] Similarly, there is some evidence to suggest altered vitamin D metabolism or a decline in calcium and phosphate excretion.[11] The clinical manifestations are varied with thickening of ankles, knees, and wrists; beading of the ribs; bone pain; muscle weakness; frontal bossing; and delayed dentition. With the aid of clinical and radiographic features, a diagnosis is made and treatment initiated. Management consists of daily administration of a vitamin D supplement with a range from 1000 to 10,000 IU/d for several weeks.[12] Calcium supplementation may be helpful and, therefore, can be added to the regimen.

Monitoring entails obtaining a blood sample, documenting the serum concentration, and comparing that value with a normative range. These numbers serve as guidelines, not as absolutes, since many factors contribute to their final interpretation.[13] As an example, the child may receive the liquid or tablet, yet with his or her oral difficulties much of the medication is not ingested but rather rolls to the side of the mouth or onto a bib. A low blood level is obtained typically with the decision to then increase the medication. If the child thereafter has a "good day," he or she ingests the higher dose with possible toxic side effects, oscillating levels, and even increased seizure activity. This, in turn, begets another dosing increase.

The key to resolving any management issues is communication. The parent or caregiver needs to be involved in the decision-making process.[14] The physician should ask, but, if not questioned, the parents should offer the detailed information. There should not only be a description of the feeding session but also a required demonstration, including drug administration. When concerns arise and solutions are sought, a health care consumer attitude and a child advocacy approach on the parent's part are needed. Medical information needs to be discussed and reviewed. Mutual dialogue on facts, fears, and misgivings is a necessity in order to develop and maintain child and parent understanding and agreement. Without compliance, medicine and nutrition exist in a vacuum without clinical value or efficacy.

Gastroesophageal Reflux

Gastroesophageal reflux refers to an abnormal retrograde flow of gastric content into the esophagus because of a dysfunctional lower esophageal sphincter,[15] which is a functional, valvelike area between the stomach and esophagus. In addition to description of the disorder one needs an appreciation of its depth and scope, specifically its epidemiology, pathogenesis, diagnosis, and treatment.

Although it is difficult to document the exact frequency of gastroesophageal reflux, Carre estimated the incidence to be 2 per 1000.[16] Reviewing varied studies relative to severely disabled children, the frequency increases to a range from 110 to 270 per 1000.[17] Translated differently, the rate of gastroesophageal reflux is 50 times, and as high as 100 times, more frequent in this special population when compared with the general pediatric population.

As far as pathogenesis, the cause is not singular but rather multiple. Many dynamic factors contribute to the difficulties in the activity of the lower esophageal sphincter.[18] Three major interacting areas involve anatomical, musculoskeletal, and neurologic variables. The lower esophageal sphincter should lie between the thorax and abdomen at the level of the diaphragm. If this location is not achieved within the first 3 months, or a hiatal hernia has subsequently developed, abnormal pressures occur with subsequent lower esophageal sphincter dysfunction and reflux. Inadequate positioning can negatively impact on oral-motor skills, salivation, peristalsis, and esophageal clearing of foods, eventually leading to reflux. Neurologically, sucking, swallowing, chewing, and gastrointestinal motility involve the activity of several cranial nerves, the brain, spinal cord, and local electrical circuits involving neurotransmitters. When developmental delay is significant, difficulties can arise along these complex neuronal pathways, thus leading to lower esophageal sphincter dysfunction.

Various food substances in drugs can affect the lower esophageal sphincter pressure.[19] For example, chocolate, citrus juices, fatty meals, and caffeine can decrease the pressure. Similarly, theophylline and ethanol can decrease its pressure, whereas cholinergic agonists such as bethanechol or dopamine antagonists such as metaclopramide can increase its pressure.

In the diagnosis of gastroesophageal reflux the symptoms and radiographic investigations are the critical components. Children with this problem often vomit, cough, and seem irritable after a meal. They suffer from frequent colds, asthma, ear infections, and pneumonias. Clinically, they demonstrate failure to thrive with slow growth changes, particularly in weight. Radiographically, the barium swallow and milk scan can often be quite helpful, with a positive result in 60% to 85% of the cases.[20] However, in a few cases, a pH probe study may be required to further clarify reflux or another type of problem.[21]

Once diagnosed, treatment follows a pathway from medical management to surgical intervention. Positioning, dietary modifications, and drugs are the major steps in the care of gastroesophageal reflux. Infants and children may benefit from being in the prone position at a 30° angle following a feeding.[22] Small, frequent, and thickened feedings are employed while avoiding citrus juices, fatty foods, and chocolate. Standard antacids and cimetidine are chosen first, followed by bethanechol or metaclopramide.[26] Care should be taken in using bethanechol in children with reactive airway disease or cardiac disease since it can exacerbate the cardiopulmonary symptoms. Similarly, with all medications, there is a potential for negative side effects as well as drug interactions.

To perform surgery is a complex issue involving the client's health, present oral-motor skills, progressive gastroesophageal complications (ie, esophagitis, anemia, and stricture), surgical risks, and parental understanding.[24] Children with developmental disabilities frequently do not demonstrate major improvement during medical management and, as a result, require a surgical procedure (a Nissen fundoplication).[25] Complications are often varied with minimal or mild frequency.[26] There can be minor dysfunctions involving bloating, slow feeding, or retching, with more serious difficulties involving periesophageal herniation, prolapse, or obstruction. However, it should be noted that 90% to 95% of the children who undergo antireflux surgery have quite positive outcomes.[27]

To summarize medical stability, numerous physiological aspects need to be considered when examining feeding and nutrition. Two illustrations include medication, especially anticonvulsants, and gastroesophageal reflux. While focusing on all medical items is important, it is still only a portion of the entire clinical picture.

It is critical to maintain team process. This involves several individual members, particularly the child and the parents, sharing, exchanging, and even negotiating on several ideas in order to establish an appropriate management plan, as well as laying the foundation onto which a sensitive, caring relationship is built and maintained.

THE NURSE CLINICIAN'S ROLE

In the feeding clinic visit, there are multiple players as well as several complex agendas. The nurse clinician serves two important functions within that context—as a translator and as an implementor. The nurse clinician communicates health care information to the various team members and serves as a teacher and guide for the parents and caregivers. The following discussion deals specifically with the role of the nurse clinician in the management of a client with a gastrostomy tube.

Our clients typically return to the feeding clinic 6 weeks postoperatively. The pediatric surgeon has performed a Nissen fundoplication, tightening the lower esophageal sphincter, which corrects the gastroesophageal reflux, and inserted a mushroom gastrostomy tube. The gastrostomy site and abdominal incision are cleansed three times daily with half-strength hydrogen peroxide and normal saline. A $1\frac{1}{2} \times 1\frac{1}{2}$-inch square of stomahesive is applied around the gastrostomy site to protect the sensitive skin while healing takes place. The stomahesive is changed every other day. A regular disposable nipple has been placed on the gastrostomy tube to prevent the gastrostomy tube from sliding into the stomach and obstructing the duodenum or into the esophagus and interfering with swallowing. The child is fed by mouth as early as the first postoperative day.

The nurse clinician examines the abdominal incision and gastrostomy tube site to see if they are well healed and if there is any granulation tissue forming around the gastrostomy site. When granulation tissue is present there is often minimal leakage. The nurse clinician instructs the parent how to use the silver nitrate stick on the granulation tissue around the gastrostomy site, explaining that this must be repeated daily until the granulation tissue is gone and the area around the gastrostomy site is flat.

When the incision is healed, the child can begin tub baths. During the daily tub bath, the nipple on the gastrostomy tube should be turned inside out and washed thoroughly with soap and water. The gastrostomy site should also be washed gently with soap and water during the bath. The half-strength hydrogen peroxide and normal saline can be discontinued.

If the skin around the gastrostomy site does not become irritated, the stomahesive may be discontinued. A 2×2-inch gauze dressing may be used under the nipple around the gastrostomy site until the drainage stops. Drainage can be expected while using the silver nitrate stick. This dressing must be changed daily. The position of the nipple on the gastrostomy tube is checked by the nurse clinician. If the nipple is not kept close enough to the end of the gastrostomy tube, the balloon will not be snug against the inside of the stomach wall, and this can cause an increase in leakage.

If the mushroom gastrostomy tube is still in place (sometimes mushroom gastrostomy tubes clog or become accidentally pulled out), the pediatric surgeon removes the mushroom gastrostomy tube and replaces it with a Foley gastrostomy tube. The nurse clinician teaches the parents how to change the Foley gastrostomy tube, using a gastrostomy tube doll, as follows:

1. Assemble the equipment needed for the gastrostomy tube change: a disposable nipple, scissors, the proper size gastrostomy tube, two 5-mL Luer-Lok tip syringes, 5 mL tap water, lubricant or water, a plastic bag, and an orange stick or a hemostat.
2. Cut three small holes near the base of the nipple; this allows air to circulate on the skin around the gastrostomy site.
3. With the orange stick or the hemostat, slip the gastrostomy tube through the nipple so the base of the nipple will rest against the skin after the gastrostomy tube is inserted. *Do not cut the end of the nipple.*
4. Fill one 5-mL Luer-Lok syringe with 5 mL of tap water and attach the syringe to the smaller part of the gastrostomy tube.
5. Push the barrel of the syringe to inflate the balloon to check for any defect in the balloon.
6. Deflate the balloon by pulling back on the barrel of the syringe. Leave the syringe attached to the gastrostomy tube.
7. Attach the second 5-mL Luer-Lok syringe to the gastrostomy tube in the doll. Check to make sure the clamp has been removed from the gastrostomy tube.
8. Pull back on the barrel of the syringe to deflate the balloon on the gastrostomy tube. You should obtain 3 to 5 mL of water. Some of the water may have leaked out during the period of time the gastrostomy tube was in place.
9. Pull on the gastrostomy tube to remove it from the doll and place it into the plastic bag.
10. Lubricate the end of the new gastrostomy tube and insert the gastrostomy tube gently into the doll's gastrostomy stoma about 2 inches.
11. Inflate the balloon with 5 mL of tap water and pull gently on the gastrostomy tube until the balloon is snugged up against the stomach wall.
12. Gently push the nipple down until the base of the nipple is snug on the abdomen. This prevents the gastrostomy tube from sliding into

the stomach and obstructing the duodenum or into the esophagus and interfering with swallowing.

13. Gently instill 10 mL of tap water with a catheter tip syringe and aspirate the water. The gastrostomy tube should irrigate freely.
14. Place the clamp on the new gastrostomy tube.
15. Have the parents demonstrate with the gastrostomy doll that they understand the procedure and can change their child's gastrostomy tube.

On return for the next feeding clinic appointment, the parent changes the child's gastrostomy tube with the supervision of the nurse clinician. The nurse clinician should remember to praise the parents for a job well done. They are under much stress caring for the developmentally disabled child, and the gastrostomy change is one additional procedure to add to their long list of procedures to do for the child. While the gastrostomy tube provides a route for added nutrition and fluids, it also takes special care and extra time in an already busy schedule. The parents have been taught the tube feeding procedure for the gastrostomy tube before the child was discharged from the hospital following the Nissen fundoplication, and it will not be included here.

Questions about gastrostomy tube feedings are answered during the feeding clinic visit. The nurse clinician works through any problems the parents are having with the gastrostomy tube feedings and/or care. The gastrostomy tube must be changed every 6 to 8 weeks.

The feeding clinic is working to increase the types of textures the child will tolerate as well as his or her ability to tolerate an increased volume of liquids by mouth. The gastrostomy tube is used to supplement caloric and fluid intake, thus providing adequate nutrition for the child's growth and development.

If the child needs to continue the gastrostomy tube feedings for an extended period of time, the nurse clinician presents the option and advantages of a gastrostomy button to the parents. The gastrostomy button is a gastrostomy device that offers a superior solution for long-term gastrostomy feeding. The gastrostomy button eliminates many of the common problems, complications, and constraints associated with the gastrostomy tube. The gastrostomy button is a skin-level, silicone device for children and adults. It has an antireflux valve that helps prevent gastric back-flow and minimizes leakage through the lumen of the gastrostomy button. There is also a safety plug that provides extra security through increased holding power, in addition to the antireflux valve. The radiopaque silicone dome helps prevent external migration and eliminates the risk of balloon leakage or breakage. The all-silicone construction provides for complete biocompatibility. A continuous feeding tube with a 90° adaptor and a straight bolus feeding tube are color coded for reordering convenience.

These tubes can be used with other standard gravity or pump feeding sets. The gastrostomy button comes in three sizes with four shaft lengths. The most commonly used size at the feeding clinic is the 24 Fr with a 2.4 cm shaft. With the gastrostomy button there is no long tube to get caught in clothing or equipment. It also requires fewer replacements. One gastrostomy button may last 6 months to 2 years, whereas a gastrostomy tube requires replacement every 6 to 8 weeks.

The children in the feeding clinic who have received the gastrostomy button experience dramatic decreases in problems associated with a standard gastrostomy tube. Parents report a decrease in leakage, irritation, and granulation tissue around the gastrostomy site. There is also a decrease in irritation of the lining of the stomach, which often causes retching, gagging, and excessive gas.

The nurse clinician shows the parents pictures of the gastrostomy button and feeding tube and explains the procedure for gastrostomy button insertion. The child's gastrostomy tube is changed one size larger every week until a size 26 Fr gastrostomy tube has been inserted. This enlarges the gastrostomy stoma to facilitate insertion of the gastrostomy button with minimal trauma for the child. The pediatric surgeon removes the gastrostomy tube and applies topical lidocaine jelly 2% to reduce any possibility of discomfort during the procedure. The correct length of the shaft is determined with a stoma measuring device, the dome of the gastrostomy button is stretched with the obturator and inserted into the gastrostomy stoma, the obturator is removed, and the gastrostomy button is in place.

The nurse clinician demonstrates a feeding with the child's formula. If it is not time for a feeding, the demonstration is given with 1 or 2 ounces of water.

Frequently, only one parent is at the feeding clinic or a caregiver needs to obtain permission from parents to have the gastrostomy button inserted. These parents are provided with literature to take home. The nurse clinician calls in about a week for their decision. If they have decided to have the gastrostomy button inserted, an appointment is scheduled and the nurse clinician reviews the process of progressing the size of the tube to the 26 Fr gastrostomy tube. Opportunity is also given during this conversation for parents to ask any questions they might have at this time. One third of our patients have a gastrostomy tube at some time, and one fourth of the long-term gastrostomy tube feeders receive a gastrostomy button.

Marginal feeders who do not have a gastrostomy tube or gastrostomy button typically suffer with constipation. If constipation is severe, a radiograph of the abdomen is ordered. If the lower intestinal tract is distended with fecal material, a bowel program is ordered. The nurse clinician in-structs the parents how to carry out a bowel program and how to give an enema if they are not familiar with this procedure.

A bowel program commonly used at the feeding clinic is 50 mL of milk and 50 mL of molasses mixed together, warmed to a comfortable temper-ature (when tested on one's wrist), and given in the same manner as a soapsuds enema would be given. The milk and molasses enema should be given after the evening meal for three successive evenings. Eating, whether it be by mouth, gastrostomy tube, or gastrostomy button, stimulates the intestinal tract, thus producing better results with the enema. A glycerin suppository is given after the fourth, fifth, and sixth evening meals. If the results are good with the suppositories, the suppository is continued each evening. If the results are poor, a soapsuds enema is given the sixth evening, 1 hour after the glycerin suppository has been given. The nurse clinician will call the parents in 1 week to check on the progress and give further instructions.

Many children are admitted for an intensive feeding program and/or for therapy. These developmentally disabled children have spent many months in hospitals, and their parents are reluctant to have their child admitted to another hospital. The nurse clinician explains that the rehabilitation hospital is not like a general hospital, and the parents may stay with their child. The nurse clinician takes the family on a tour of the facility where they see the clients dressed in their own clothing and busy at school, occupational therapy, physical therapy, speech, or in the developmentally disabled playroom with the specially trained play therapist.

During the time the nurse clinician spends one on one with the parents, questions the parents were reluctant to ask while with the feeding team are addressed. If the answers are not clear the nurse clinician can refer questions to other team members or to the social worker and get the answers before the family leaves the clinic. When the nurse clinician is alone with the family, there is time to reinforce suggestions made by the feeding team on handling the child, the importance of oral stimulation before feedings, ways to add calories without a big increase in volume, and proper positioning of the child in the adaptive seat and feeder seat. Praising the parents for doing a good job with the general care of the child as well as for their ability to meet the child's special needs aids in giving parents courage to meet the new challenges they have been presented with at the feeding clinic.

Additional functions of the nurse clinician include obtaining specialized equipment; facilitating orders for laboratory and radiology tests and for medications; scheduling consultations for adaptive seating, orthopaedics, speech, and pediatric surgery; assisting with positioning the child for feeding; assisting with the feeding; and obtaining any necessary equipment and supplies for the parents to take home until they are able to obtain them from their supplier.

Telephone calls are made by the nurse clinician to confirm appointments and monitor the progress the parents are making with the child's home program since their clinic visit. The parents are given the nurse clinician's work telephone number so they can call if they are having difficulty obtaining necessary equipment or supplies and/or carrying out the home program they were given in the feeding clinic. The home program is discussed in the feeding clinic and written out for the parents to take home.

The nurse clinician takes preadmission pictures with the child positioned properly for feedings. This picture is attached to the preadmission form, which aids the staff nurses in implementing the feeding program on the day of admission. The nurse clinician takes pictures for slide presentations and videotapes for parents as well as caregivers in group homes, institutions, and schools.

CONCLUSION

Children with developmental disabilities are truly unique and special. Instead of activities of daily living being automatic, easily learned, or enjoyable, they are slow, tedious, or almost impossible to achieve. Concerning feeding and disabilities, the two overall rehabilitative goals are that of functionality and independence. These, however, need to be examined and managed in the context of the particular issues as well as the special child, parents, family expectations, and cultural biases.

The way to achieve functional independence and improvement thereof is a team process. This is not unidisciplinary, multidisciplinary, or interdisciplinary; rather, it is transdisciplinary. Each team member shares professional boundaries while maintaining respective areas of expertise. As mentioned previously, two absolute and critical team players include the child and the parents. For compliance and follow-through and for health care efficiency and efficacy, they need to be involved throughout the decision-making process.

To reach a better nutritional status or to improve feeding, one must address the child in totality. This includes positioning before, during, and after the meal. It requires appropriate oral techniques. There need to be a family assessment, developmental evaluation, and psychosocial services. Medical and nursing factors entail appropriate understanding and communication to all involved in the care of the child. Health care in general, and feeding in particular, can be accomplished optimally through a comprehensive, caring, transdisciplinary team process.

REFERENCES

1. Palmer S, Ekvall S. *Pediatric Nutrition in Developmental Disorders.* Springfield, Ill: Charles C Thomas Publisher; 1978:42–49.

2. Kaliszk K, Ekvall S. A nutritional interview for clients with developmental disorders. *Am Assoc Ment Defic.* 1984;22:279–288.

3. Fee MA, Charney EB, Robertson WW. Nutritional assessment of the young child with cerebral palsy. *Infants Young Child.* 1988;1:33–40.

4. Gisel EG, Patrick J. Identification of children with cerebral palsy unable to maintain a normal nutritional state. *Lancet.* 1988;1:283–286.

5. Delgado-Escueta AV, Treumain DM, Walsh GO. The treatable epilepsies. *N Engl J Med.* 1983;308:1508–1514.

6. Eadie MJ. Anticonvulsant drugs: An update. *Drugs.* 1984;328–363.

7. Holtz L, Milton J, Struek J. Compatibility of medication with enteral feedings. *J Parenter Enter Nutr.* 1987;11:183–186.

8. Dodson WE. Antiepileptic drug utilization in pediatric patients. *Epilepsia.* 1984;25:5132–5139.

9. Christiansen C, Rodero P, Tjehlesen L. Pathophysiology behind anticonvulsant osteomalacia. *Acta Neurol Scand.* 1983;94:21–28.

10. Hahn TJ. Drug-induced disorders of vitamin D and medical metabolism. *Clin Endocrinol Metab.* 1980;9:107–129.

11. Kruse K. On the pathogenesis of anticonvulsant–drug-induced alterations of calcium metabolism. *Eur J Pediatr.* 1982;138:202–205.

12. Hunt PA, et al. Bone diseases induced by anticonvulsant therapy and treatment with calcitriol. *Am J Dis Child.* 1986;140:715–718.

13. Troupin AS. The measurement of anticonvulsant agent levels. *Ann Intern Med.* 1984;100:854–858.

14. Nichter CA. Seizures: A developmental perspective. *Top Early Child Spec Ed.* 1987;6:75–91.

15. Herbst JJ. Gastroesophageal reflux. *J Pediatr.* 1981;98:859–870.

16. Carre IJ. The natural history of the partial thoracic stomach in children. *Arch Dis Childh.* 1959;34:344.

17. Sondheimer JM, Morris BA. Gastroesophageal reflux among severely retarded children. *J Pediatr.* 1979;94:710–714.

18. Weihrauch TR. Gastroesophageal reflux: Pathogenesis and clinical implications. *Eur J Pediatr.* 1985;144:215–218.

19. Nelson HA. Gastroesophageal reflux and pulmonary disease. *J Allergy Clin Immunol.* 1984;73:547–556.

20. Arasu TS, et al. Gastroesophageal reflux in infants and children: Comparative accuracy of diagnostic methods. *J Pediatr.* 1980;96:798–803.

21. Vanderplas Y, Sacre-Smits L. Continuous 24-hour esophageal pH monitoring in 285 asymptomatic infants 0–15 months old. *J Pediatr Gastroenterol Nutr.* 1987;6:220–224.

22. Orenstein SR, Magill HL, Brooks P. Thickening of infant feedings for therapy of gastroesophageal reflux. *J Pediatr.* 1987;110:181–186.

23. Jennett TC, Siegel M. Hiatal hernia and gastroesophageal reflux. *J Pediatr Gastroenterol Nutr.* 1984;3:340–345.

24. Fonkalsrud EW, et al. Surgical treatment of the gastroesophageal reflux syndrome in infants and children. *Am J Surg.* 1987;154:11–18.

25. Wilkinson JD, Dudgeon DL, Sondheimer JM. A comparison of medical and surgical treatment of gastroesophageal reflux in severely retarded children. *J Pediatr.* 1981;99:202–205.

26. Chang JH, et al. Surgical management of gastroesophageal reflux in severely mentally retarded children. *J Ment Defic Res.* 1987;31:1–7.

27. Spitz L, Kertans J. Results and complications of surgery for gastroesophageal reflux. *Arch Dis Child.* 1985;60:743–747.

BIBLIOGRAPHY

American Dietetics Association Position Paper. *Nutrition in Comprehensive Program Planning for Persons with Developmental Disabilities.* 1987:1068–1069.

Cramp I. *Nutrition and Feeding of the Handicapped Child.* Boston, Mass: Little, Brown & Co; 1987.

Illingworth RS, Lister J. The critical sensitive period with special reference to certain feeding problems in infants and children. *J Pediatr.* 1964;65:839–848.

Kubler-Ross E. *On Death and Dying.* New York: Macmillan Publishing Co, Inc; 1969.

Lucas B. Children with developmental disorders: Nutrition issues. *Dietitians Pediatr Practice.* 1988;11(2):1–2.

Morris SE, Klein MD., *Pre-Feeding Skills: A Comprehensive Resource for Feeding Development.* Tucson, Ariz: Therapy Skill Builders; 1987.

Rice B. Nutritional problems of developmentally disabled children. *Pediatr Nurs.* 1981;7:15–18.

Slaton DS, ed. *Development of Movement in Infancy.* Chapel Hill, NC: Division of Physical Therapy; 1981.

Appendix 6-A

Pre- and Post-Admission Scale for Neurodevelopmental Patients

Name _____

Date of Birth _____

Guardians _____

Diagnosis _____ _____

_____ Medical No. _____

Pre-Admission Comments: _____

_____

_____

_____

Post-Discharge Comments: _____

_____

_____

_____

The following items indicate a multiplicity of difficulties impacting on feeding patients. Each patient is to be monitored in Feeding Clinic for Pre-Admission status. The second evaluation is to occur in Feeding Clinic post discharge to help measure the impact an admission and intensive therapy has had on a patient and guardians. Please read instructions carefully:

Pre-Admission Date: _____   Post-Admission Date: _____

NEEDS LIST

Please mark an X in the appropriate column. An X in the Needs Monitoring Column implies a deficiency in a given area.

Not Applicable	Needs Monitoring		Not Applicable	Needs Monitoring
_____	_____	Adaptive seating	_____	_____
_____	_____	Poor dental occlusion	_____	_____
_____	_____	Poor dental health	_____	_____
_____	_____	Vision problems	_____	_____

_____	_____	Hearing problems	_____	_____
_____	_____	Respiration	_____	_____
_____	_____	Aspiration	_____	_____
_____	_____	Family education	_____	_____
_____	_____	Medication (seizure, antispasmodic, other)	_____	_____
_____	_____	Nutrient poor intake	_____	_____

PROBLEM LIST

To measure the degree to which a problem area has been solved mark an X in the appropriate column. Unless otherwise indicated. 0—Not applicable, 1—Mild Problem, 2—Moderate, Problem 3—Severe Problem

MOTOR PROBLEMS	Pre-Admission	Post-Admission
Head control (Circle appropriate number)	0–1–2–3	0–1–2–3
Muscle tone (high–low–mixed)	0–1–2–3	0–1–2–3
Self-feeding 0—Feeds self 100% with fingers/utensils/cup 1—50% or more 2—50% or less 3—No self-feeding	0–1–2–3	0–1–2–3
Suck 0—Sucks well from bottle or cup 1—Abnormal suck less than 50% when drinks from cup 2—Abnormal suck more than 50% when drinks on cup to/from mouth 3—No ability to initiate suck	0–1–2–3	0–1–2–3
Swallow 0—Swallows thin liquids and table foods 1—Swallows thickened liquids 2—Swallows only thickened pureed foods 3—No ability to swallow liquids or solids	0–1–2–3	0–1–2–3
After swallow Vomiting and gagging	0–1–2–3	0–1–2–3
Biting 0—Bites through hard cookie 1—Bites through soft cookie 2—Stabilizes jaw but does not bite through soft cookie 3—No ability to swallow liquids or solids	0–1–2–3	0–1–2–3
Chewing 0—Tongue rapidly transfers food from side to side 1—Tongue moves food to side when food placed between molars 2—Voluntary up and down jaw and tongue movement 3—Involuntary phasic bite response only	0–1–2–3	0–1–2–3

Total = _____   Total = _____   % Change _____

MEDICAL-NURSING PROBLEMS

Failure to thrive   0–1–2–3   0–1–2–3
   (0—not applicable) (1—3 months) (2—6 months)
   (3—more than 6 months)

Mode of feeding   0–1–2–3   0–1–2–3
   (0—100% oral) (1—75% oral) (2—50% oral) (3—0 oral)

Dehydration   0–1–2–3   0–1–2–3
   0—1 qt. or more of liquid/day
   1—3 cups/liquid/day
   2—2 cups/liquid/day
   3—1 cup or less of liquid/day

Constipation—diarrhea   0–1–2–3   0–1–2–3
   0—Soft stool
   1—Diarrhea
   2—Hard stool, good volume
   3—Hard stool, pellet size

Texture problems (Not applicable)   0–1–2–3   0–1–2–3
   0—Taking age-appropriate texture
   1—Soft
   2—Chopped
   3—Pureed

Length of feeding time for a meal   0–1–2–3   0–1–2–3
   (0—20 min.) (1—30 min.) (2—45 min.) (3—60 min.)

                    Total = _____   Total = _____   % Change _____

NEUROPSYCHOLOGY

Attention span   0–1–2–3   0–1–2–3

Behavior involvement
   Refusal to eat   0–1–2–3   0–1–2–3
   Crying during meals   0–1–2–3   0–1–2–3
   Other behavior problems interfering with feeding   0–1–2–3   0–1–2–3
Mental retardation   0–1–2–3   0–1–2–3

                    Total = _____   Total = _____   % Change _____

Source: Reprinted with permission of Elizabethtown Hospital and Rehabilitation Center, Elizabethtown, Pa.

Chapter 7

Dysphagia

Janel Schmitz

Dysphagia is defined as inability or difficulty in swallowing and is most commonly associated with neurologic or structural damage. However, it may also be caused by medical problems such as scleroderma. It is not of itself a disease but a symptom of a pathologic state such as multiple sclerosis or a cerebrovascular accident. Dysphagia can occur in anyone from the newborn to the elderly.[1] It may result in the client's inability to eat a piece of tough meat or drink a cup of coffee. It can also result in malnutrition, dehydration, aspiration pneumonia, and even death if it is untreated. Clients may be very aware or totally unaware of a swallowing problem.

The majority of persons swallow 600 or more times per day without conscious effort. For an estimated 6 to 10 million Americans, swallowing is a much more difficult, even impossible task. The incidence of dysphagia appears to be on the rise as the population in the United States ages.[2]

Not long ago, dysphagia was considered untreatable. In recent years diagnostic, as well as therapeutic, techniques have been developed for those who suffer with dysphagia. With proper therapy, many persons may be able to eat safely without worry. Others may simply need to take precautions. There are also those who may face a lifetime of not being able to eat again.

Because of the nutritional implications, it is essential that the dietitian's expertise be included in the dysphagia treatment plan. The dietitian has a basic understanding of the anatomy and physiology of the swallow, as well as knowledge of the indicators of dysphagia. The alert dietitian's initial nutrition assessment may be the first time dysphagia is recognized.

FEEDING THERAPY VERSUS DYSPHAGIA THERAPY

Feeding therapy focuses on how a person gets food to the mouth, where it is placed in the mouth, the manipulation of food in the mouth, the chewing of a bolus of different consistencies, the re-collecting of the bolus into a cohesive mass prior to the initiation of the swallow, and organizing the tongue movement to move the bolus toward the back of the mouth.[1]

Dysphagia therapy overlaps feeding therapy in that it is also concerned with where to place the food, tongue strength, and propulsion of the food backward in the mouth. By contrast, dysphagia therapy includes the stimulation of the swallow reflex and follows the bolus, liquid or solid, until it enters the esophagus.

ANATOMY OF THE SWALLOW

It takes 29 muscles and six cranial nerves working together to perform a successful swallow.[2] The anatomic areas involved include the oral cavity, pharynx, larynx, and esophagus.

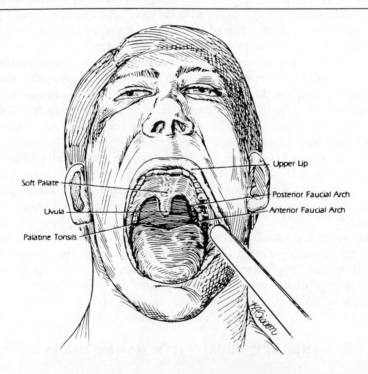

Figure 7-1 Frontal view of the oral cavity, showing anterior and posterior faucial arches. *Source:* Reprinted from *Evaluation and Treatment of Swallowing Disorders* (p 12) by J Logemann with permission of College-Hill Press Inc, © 1983.

The teeth, mandible, maxilla, soft palate, hard palate, uvula, lips, faucial arches, and pockets along the sides and in front of the mouth are structures of concern in the oral cavity (Figure 7-1).

Anatomic landmarks involved in the pharyngeal area of the swallow are the pharyngeal constrictors, including superior, medial, and inferior constrictors; pterygoid plates on the sphenoid bone; soft palate; base of the tongue; mandible; hyoid bone; thyroid and cricoid cartilages; and pyriform sinuses, which end at the cricopharyngeus muscle. The cricopharyngeus muscle is the most inferior structure of the pharynx and serves as the valve at the top of the esophagus (Figure 7-2). The larynx, which lies at the base of the tongue, is the primary protective mechanism that prevents food from entering the airway during swallowing. Side pockets known as valleculae are formed by the meeting of the tongue and epiglottis. The valleculae are common areas that cause difficulty for dysphagia clients (Figure 7-3).

The proper functioning of the esophagus is essential for successful swallow. The swallow is completed when food enters the stomach.[1]

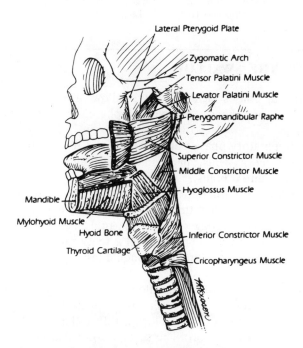

Figure 7-2 Lateral view of the pharyngeal constrictors (superior, medial, and inferior) and their anterior attachments. *Source:* Reprinted from *Evaluation and Treatment of Swallowing Disorders* (p 13) by J Logemann with permission of College-Hill Press Inc, © 1983.

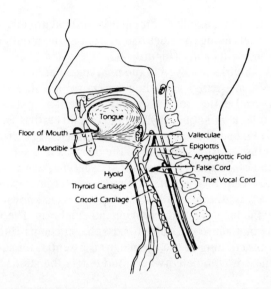

Figure 7-3 Midsagittal section of the head and neck. *Source:* Reprinted from *Evaluation and Treatment of Swallowing Disorders* (p 12) by J Logemann with permission of College-Hill Press Inc, © 1983.

PHASES OF THE SWALLOW

There are four phases included in a swallow. These are the oral preparatory phase, oral phase, pharyngeal phase, and esophageal phase (Figure 7-4).

The oral preparatory phase begins when food reaches the lips and includes the chewing of solids, manipulation of liquids and solids, and the forming of foods into a bolus.

The oral phase starts when the tongue begins to move the bolus toward the back of the mouth. When the food reaches the anterior faucial pillars, the swallowing reflex is triggered and the oral phase of the swallow is completed. Without a trigger, pharyngeal activity cannot occur. The oral phase is considered to be voluntary. It should last less than 1 second from start to finish.

The pharyngeal phase of the swallow is involuntary. There are four events that must occur during the pharyngeal phase for a successful swallow. Following the trigger of the swallowing reflex, the nasal cavity is closed off by the velopharyngeal port. The second event that occurs is the peristalsis of the pharynx, which is the function of the pharyngeal constrictors. The squeezing action of these muscles carries the bolus to the top of the cricopharyngeal sphincter, which is the opening at the top of the esophagus.

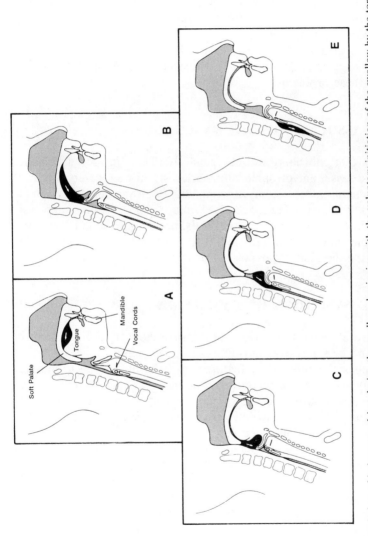

Figure 7-4 Lateral view of bolus propulsion during the swallow, beginning with the voluntary initiation of the swallow by the tongue (**A**); the triggering of the swallowing reflex (**B**); the bolus passage through the pharynx (**C**); the entry of the bolus through the cricopharyngeal sphincter into the cervical esophagus (**D**); and the completion of the pharyngeal stage of the swallow when the entire bolus is in the cervical esophagus (**E**). *Source:* Reprinted from *Evaluation and Treatment of Swallowing Disorders* (pp 22–23) by J Logemann with permission of College-Hill Press Inc, © 1983.

Third, there are three sphincters within the larynx that protect the larynx. These sphincters include the epiglottic and aryepiglottic folds, the false vocal folds, and the true vocal folds. Finally, the cricopharyngeal sphincter relaxes and allows the bolus to pass from the pharynx into the esophagus. The pharyngeal phase should take 1 second or less during the normal swallow. There should be very little food left in the pharynx when the pharyngeal phase is completed.

The esophageal phase last 8 to 20 seconds. This phase is not studied during a dysphagia evaluation because dysphagia therapy is ineffective in dealing with these problems.

DISEASES ASSOCIATED WITH DYSPHAGIA

Conditions that contribute to neurogenic dysphagia include achalasia, Alzheimer's disease, amyotrophic lateral sclerosis, anoxia, cerebral palsy, cerebrovascular accidents, demyelinating disease, dysautonomia, spinal cord injury, encephalitis, Huntington's chorea, meningitis, muscular dystrophy, Parkinson's syndrome, poliomyelitis, previous head and neck surgery, syringomyelia, trauma, and tumors. A diagnosis of any of these should alert the dietitian of possible dysphagia.[3]

SIGNS AND SYMPTOMS OF DYSPHAGIA

During the oral preparatory phase, the dietitian should note any difficulty in chewing and/or solids or liquids falling from the mouth.

The oral phase includes many features. A facial droop due to muscle weakness may allow food to be pocketed on the weak side. Drooling may indicate poor lip closure or a loss of sensation. A client complaining of food sticking in the mouth may have inadequate saliva to moisten foods, which hinders manipulation of a bolus.

Symptoms in the pharyngeal phase may include nasal regurgitation, resulting from inadequate closing of the velopharyngeal port. Foamy phlegm may occur as a result of the cilia in the respiratory tract attempting to clear away foreign material. The person may cough either before, during, or after a swallow. The dietitian should note if the person's voice changes after a swallow to sound wet, breathy, or hoarse since this indicates inadequate clearing of food. A weak cough may indicate that a person who is a questionable oral eater is at even greater risk. If the person is experiencing swallowing incoordination, which often occurs simultaneously with inappropriate breathing, the chance of aspiration is increased. Complaints of food sticking in the throat are extremely accurate in diagnosing dysphagia. The person can be asked to point to the anatomic area in which the sticking is occurring and, often, examination shows that food is pooling in the area indicated. Also, aspiration during the pharyngeal phase is an obvious sign of dysphagia.

Esophageal dysphagia is characterized by the person having more difficulty with solids. Common symptoms include hiccups, regurgitation, and food sticking, which is usually accompanied by pain.

SILENT ASPIRATION

Silent aspiration occurs when either liquids or solids enter the larynx with no outward indication from the person, such as coughing or complaints of food sticking. The clinician is unable to detect this condition in a clinical evaluation. Silent aspiration may occur because of decreased sensitivity in the laryngeal area or because the person has a weak cough. The first sign of aspiration may appear 2 to 12 hours after a meal and may be identified by increased temperature, rapid respirations, rapid pulse, cough, blood-tinged or frothy sputum, or wheezing.[4]*

DYSPHAGIA TEAM MEMBERS

It is essential to have a multidisciplinary approach when planning and implementing treatment for the person with dysphagia. Each team member contributes a special area of expertise. The goals of the dysphagia team are to (1) maintain or improve the client's nutritional status, (2) prevent aspiration, and (3) re-teach swallowing techniques. It is also the function of the dysphagia team to educate other health care providers about the risks and symptoms of dysphagia and to give advice as to treatment options.

A team typically consists of a physician, speech/language pathologist, occupational therapist, dietitian, nurse, and radiologist. The physician, speech/language pathologist, and occupational therapist offer expertise in the anatomy and physiology of the swallow and may perform therapy to improve swallowing techniques. The dietitian provides recommendations on nutrient and hydration needs and offers expertise on different diet textures needed, as indicated by the examination and therapy results. The

---

Source: Section on silent aspiration is reprinted from *RN* (1978;41:8), Copyright © 1978, Medical Economics Co Inc.

nurse carries out recommendations on a daily basis made by other team members. The nurse's observations of how well the person does between therapy situations is invaluable. The radiologist is considered a team member because he or she performs the videofluoroscopy swallowing evaluations. It is essential that the radiologist understand the objectives of the evaluation by the dysphagia therapist.[1]

EVALUATIONS

The clinician begins assessing the client with a clinical evaluation. In facilities with a dysphagia treatment program, the clinician responsible for evaluation is the speech/language pathologist or occupational therapist. If these services are unavailable, the dietitian may perform a basic clinical evaluation. If indicated, a dysphagia therapist then proceeds with video-fluoroscopy of the client.

The Clinical Evaluation

The clinician should observe the following in a client. When possible, the client should verbalize answers to the clinician's questions.

1. Does the person have good head control? The head should face forward and not be thrown backward. Aspiration is more likely to occur when the head is extended back in this fashion.
2. Can the person open his or her mouth voluntarily? The person may feel uncomfortable with eating and thus refuse to open the mouth. Also, inability to open the mouth may indicate that the person is unable to follow commands or has weak oral musculature or apraxia.
3. Can the person bring his or her lips together and close the mouth? Successful feeding is dependent on lip closure.
4. Can the person move his or her tongue in all planes? Weak tongue movement may lead to pocketing of the food and poor bolus control.
5. Can the person hold the bolus in the mouth? Control of the bolus is essential. When there is poor control, food may fall into the pharyngeal area without a trigger occurring, therefore leaving an unprotected airway.
6. Can the person form and hold material in a collective bolus? Without formation of a bolus, small amounts of food may be left in the mouth, causing future aspiration if the food falls into the pharynx when the patient is not actively swallowing.

7. Can the person lateralize material to both sides of the mouth? Manipulation of food in the mouth is essential to form a bolus.
8. Can the person mash food with the tongue to palate? This is a good indicator of tongue strength and mobility.
9. Does the person cough before initiation of the swallow? If the person is coughing before a swallow is initiated, it may indicate food is falling into the pharynx without a trigger. Without a trigger, the protective mechanisms of the larynx are not activated, thus leaving the airway open.
10. Is the person able to initiate a swallow on command? It is desirable that the person be able to swallow on command in order to be a safe oral eater.
11. Does the food stick to the palate? A lack of saliva or a lack of tongue mobility can cause this to happen.
12. Is there nasal regurgitation? This occurs when the velopharyngeal port does not close properly.
13. Does the person cough during the swallow? The cough may occur because the larynx does not close off properly. Or, the person may be unable to clear all the food from the pharyngeal area on one swallow and food then falls into the larynx. Food may also accumulate in the valleculae, and as it builds higher, it can fall over the epiglottis into an open airway.
14. Does the person complain of material sticking in the throat? Clients may be very accurate in identifying the anatomic area in which dysphagia is occurring. In one study of 750 patients, the client's diagnosis of the anatomic location of difficulty was correct in 99.2% of the cases.[1]
15. Is the vocal quality "gurgly" after the swallow? This occurs when food is not cleared, causing an accumulation of food on the vocal folds.
16. Does the person cough 2 to 3 seconds after swallowing? This may be observed when residual or pooled food falls into the airway after a swallow.
17. Does the person cough after three to four swallows? This may indicate that food is building up in the pyriform and vallecular sinuses with each swallow, gradually falling into the airway.
18. What material does the person seem to cough on more often? Is it solid or liquid, hot or cold? Are the liquids thin or thick? The answers to these questions will indicate the diet textures that are the most dangerous for the patient.
19. How long does the person's swallow take? If it takes longer than 10 seconds from the initiation of the oral preparatory phase to the end

of the pharyngeal phase, it is unlikely the person will be able to be totally maintained by oral nutrition.[1]

20. How long does the person take to eat a meal? If it takes longer than 45 minutes per meal, it is unlikely that the person will maintain adequate nutrition and hydration by oral feedings alone.
21. Does the person seem to be fearful of eating? Often persons with dysphagia will have an unexplained fear of eating, especially silent aspirators.
22. Has the person experienced any weight loss recently? It is common for the person with dysphagia to decrease food and liquid intake for fear of choking.
23. Is there a history of unexplained pneumonia in the medical records? The person may be a recurring aspirator who was not previously identified.

The person's swallowing reflex may be assessed by placing the fingers along the thyroid notch while the person swallows (Figure 7-5). The larynx will rise if the person is able to swallow. Sometimes a swallow can be stimulated by gently pushing up the person's larynx with the fingers or having the person flex his or her head forward.

The dietitian should note whether the person's cough reflex is a strong or weak one. Coughing is a protective mechanism that can clear food and fluids from the airway.

The gag reflex may also be tested by placing a tongue depressor toward the back of the tongue. Absence of a gag reflex is not necessarily an indicator that the person may be an unsafe oral eater. A person with a hyperactive gag reflex may have great difficulty eating.

Listen to the person's speech. Aphasia or dysarthria is likely to be accompanied by weakness of facial and throat muscles and impaired lip, tongue, and pharynx control. A hypernasal, slurred, hoarse, or breathy voice may also indicate muscle weakness.

A weak tongue will be unable to move a bolus effectively. The client's tongue strength can be assessed by having the person press the tongue against a tongue blade and push. While the person presses the tongue against one side of the mouth and then the other, the clinician feels through the client's cheek. The client then is directed to move the tongue out of the mouth and around in all planes.

Throughout the evaluation, the dietitian observes the client's orientation and/or neglect that is occurring. Disoriented persons may actually forget they have food in their mouths. Persons who are easily distracted may need to eat alone with supervision in order to be safe. Persons with impaired

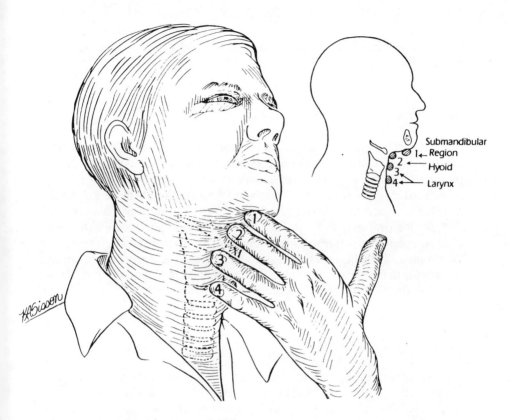

Figure 7-5 Hand placement for the swallow: **1,** submandibular area; **2,** hyoid region; **3** and **4,** larynx. *Source:* Reprinted from *Evaluation and Treatment of Swallowing Disorders* (p 121) by J Logemann with permission of College-Hill Press Inc, © 1983.

sensation on one side of the mouth who are unaware of it may have food collecting in the side of the mouth and falling into the airway later in the day, causing choking or aspiration. Does the person have a good memory? Would the person be able to follow special feeding instructions such as a double swallow or special head positions? Does the person act impulsively? Doing so may cause him or her to eat or drink too quickly, causing choking.

Once the previous questions are answered and if it appears to be safe, then the person is asked to swallow a small amount of water given by pipette and to chew a few ice chips. If a person has difficulty with these actions, the chances of being a safe oral eater are not good.[5]

Although the clinical evaluation can be performed thoroughly, research indicates that even the most experienced dysphagia therapists can fail to identify 40% of the persons who aspirate during a clinical evaluation.[1] Thus, it is often necessary to perform a videofluoroscopic swallow evaluation.

Videofluoroscopic Swallow Evaluation

In order to visualize the details of a person's swallow, a videofluoroscopic swallowing evaluation (also known as a modified barium swallow) can be performed. In this test, a trained technician has the person swallow a small amount of thin barium, a small amount of a thicker substance known as Esophotrast, and a cookie covered with a small amount of Esophotrast. The client's oral preparatory, oral, and pharyngeal phases are recorded. Oral and pharyngeal transit time and motility problems in these phases are determined. The clinician then extrapolates from the results of this study the appropriate diet prescription. The dysphagia specialist can also determine appropriate swallowing therapy.[1]

THERAPY TECHNIQUES

Dysphagia therapists work with a client to determine the safest position for swallowing. The head may be held forward or to one side or the other. The client may also learn to double swallow. Instructions may include alternating solid and liquid substances.

Thermal stimulation may be indicated for persons who have a delayed swallow. A cold laryngeal mirror is placed on the anterior faucial pillars. In therapy, done on a consistent basis, the trigger is sometimes quickened. Swallowing therapy can teach techniques to improve pharyngeal transit time. Coughing after a swallow to clear the throat can also be taught.[1]

DIETARY INDICATIONS

Dietary manipulation is part of the treatment. The clinician considers the proper liquid as well as solid consistency. Solids may be modified to include stiff gelled, gelled, strained, pureed, and ground foods of soft and regular consistencies (Table 7-1).

Stiff gelled foods are made by adding unflavored gelatin to strained baby food to form a gelled mixture. This may be indicated for persons who have poor oral control as a result of weak tongue movements. Use of this con-

Table 7-1 Dysphagia Diet Solid Consistencies

Level I: Stiff gelled
Level II: Gelled
Level III: Strained
Level IV: Pureed
Level V: Soft with ground meats
Level VI: Soft without ground meats
Level VII: Regular

---

sistency is used only in dysphagia therapy, and other nourishment is provided by alternative methods during this phase.

Gelled foods consist of puddings and gelatins. More tongue strength is required to form a bolus when using these foods. Enteral feedings are also necessary if this is the only diet texture to be given.

Strained foods are used once tongue strength has improved. If these foods are well tolerated, pureed or blended table foods can be added. Pureed foods have more consistency and are drier than strained foods. These consistencies can be used when the chewing mechanism is weakened. The person must be able to clear food from the sides and front of the mouth, as well as form a bolus with the tongue to be successful at this stage.

A soft diet with or without ground meats can be used if the chewing mechanism is intact. Once this is improved, a regular diet can be ordered.

Liquid consistencies often cause the greatest problem for persons with dysphagia (Table 7-2). Thin liquids can splash into the pharyngeal area without a swallow being triggered, thus falling into an open airway. To avoid this problem, liquids can be thickened with a variety of products, including strained foods, rice cereal, potato flakes, and cornstarch. There are special products available that thicken liquids without altering the taste. They include Thick-It from Milani Foods and Frutex from Crescent Foods.* Thick liquids allow the tongue to more easily form and control a bolus. Liquids should gradually be thinned to the person's tolerance.

The dietitian may notice that a person coughs when drinking hot thin liquids but not when drinking cold thin liquids. Cold foods trigger a swallow more easily than hot foods. Simply restricting the use of hot beverages and soups may make it safe for the person to swallow thin liquids.

Some foods are contraindicated for persons with dysphagia. These foods include foods with two textures, rice, and possibly bread. Foods with two

---

*Milani Foods, 2525 Armitage Avenue, Melrose Park, IL 60160, and Crescent Foods, P.O. Box 3985, Seattle, WA 98134.

Table 7-2 Dysphagia Diet Liquid Consistencies

Level I:	Thick liquids only.
Level II:	Moderately thick liquids. These include juice with some thickening agent, tomato juice, or apricot nectar.
Level III:	Thin liquids. There may be an additional restriction as to liquid temperature.

textures such as soup with noodles or vegetables or gelatin with fruit make it difficult for the person with dysphagia to control the bolus in the oral phase. While concentrating on chewing a vegetable in the soup, the liquid may splash into the pharyngeal area without a swallow being initiated. Rice is not recommended because it is difficult to form into a bolus. If there is inadequate saliva, bread may be difficult for the person because it becomes formed into a large, dry bolus, making it difficult to swallow.[6]

If a person requires a special diet or fluid consistency because of dysphagia, it is necessary to keep accurate fluid intake records as well as food records. It is common for persons with dysphagia to avoid eating or drinking adequate amounts because of the difficulty they have doing so. Persons in rehabilitation settings often eat in a dayroom/community dining area. Some persons may be embarrassed at food falling from their mouths so they restrict their intake. Allowing the person to eat alone may be necessary to improve intake.

CURRENT DIETETIC PRACTICES

According to a recent survey of 40 rehabilitation dietitians, the most common problems seen in persons with dysphagia are

1. Low tolerance to thick liquids
2. Inability to chew and swallow meats or protein foods
3. Dehydration
4. Inadequate nutrient intake
5. Depression and frustration
6. Confusion/impulsiveness, which causes the person to be unaware of potentially dangerous actions
7. Providing variety to the diet
8. Poor understanding by the person and family as to why dietary restrictions are necessary
9. Constipation.

The survey indicated that dietitians recommend enteral feedings if a client is unable to meet 75% of nutrient needs and 90% of fluid needs over a period of 3 to 5 days and it appears unlikely that intake will improve soon.[7] If it takes a person longer than 45 minutes to consume a meal, enteral feedings are considered. Therapy and rest schedules often keep the person in a rehabilitation setting very busy; therefore it is difficult to supplement the diet with high-calorie snacks. If a person comes to the rehabilitation setting with a significant weight loss from the acute care setting and is unable to eat enough for weight gain, it may be necessary to provide enteral feedings to regain good nutritional status.

If a client is receiving enteral feedings and gradually progressing to oral foods, enteral feedings are decreased in order to stimulate appetite. Enteral feedings are given at night to encourage oral feeding during the day. Accurate calorie counts are essential.

The survey also indicated that dietitians recommend discontinuing enteral feedings when 80% to 90% of the person's calorie needs and 100% of fluid needs can be met by oral feedings. It is recommended that a gastrostomy tube be kept in place for a period of time in case a setback is experienced.

CLIENT AND FAMILY EDUCATION

It is essential that staff counsel with family members regarding diet modifications. Without reassurance and information, the family may bring in food or give the person inappropriate and potentially dangerous foods or liquids. It is especially difficult for a person to go home having restrictions such as thick liquids only or pureed foods. There is generally poor compliance over a long period of time by both the client and the family.

Food has many roles and meanings. To take away the pleasure of joining in family celebrations and mealtimes can be devastating. Diet changes mean a tremendous change in life style because eating and dining out are common forms of entertainment in American society. It is essential that the client and family be prepared for the difficulties that may occur.

OTHER ROLES OF THE DIETITIAN

It is the dietitian's responsibility to perform the initial nutrition assessment of the client. The assessment includes the client's weight history, laboratory values, anthropometrics, tolerance to diet, as well as acceptance of the diet. Eating habits prior to hospital admission must be assessed. Dysphagia does not affect calorie or protein needs. Calorie and protein requirements that are appropriate for any accompanying disease states should be used.

The dietitian monitors ongoing nutritional status and participates in staffing meetings. Weekly chart notes are completed; a client may require charting more frequently during periods of rapid change.

The dietitian observes clients during meals and recommends appropriate diet progression, with consultation from the dysphagia therapist and physician.

Weight changes are monitored and the causes determined. The dietitian performs calorie counts and monitors fluid intake and output.

It is vital that dietary and nursing staff members understand the importance of the correct diet and liquid consistencies for each client. Nurses must be aware of liquid consistency to accompany medications. The dietitian is a key person in this education process.

The dietitian also teaches and counsels the client and caregivers regarding diet and food preparation methods. If a client is transferred to another hospital or long-term care facility, explicit instructions must be sent with him or her. In facilities without an active dysphagia treatment program, orders such as "thick liquids only" may not be understood so explanations should be sent.

The dietitian participates in scheduled dysphagia team meetings and also provides inservice education on nutritional care for dietary and nursing staff members, as well as in outreach programs to local long-term and acute care facilities.

CONCLUSION

The dietitian plays a vital role in the treatment of the client with dysphagia. It is essential that the dietitian understand not only the dietary indications of the client but also the anatomy, physiology, and treatment process of dysphagia. It is recommended that there be a section in the facility's diet manual for a dysphagia diet, explaining the proper liquid and solid consistencies. The dietitian must become an essential team member by understanding the entire spectrum of dysphagia from anatomy to diet texture.

REFERENCES

1. Logemann J. *Evaluation and Treatment of Swallowing Disorders.* San Diego, Calif: College-Hill Press; 1983.

2. Simmons K. Medical news and perspectives. *JAMA.* 1986; 255:3209.

3. Roueche JR. *Dysphagia, An Assessment and Management Program for the Adult.* Minneapolis, Minn: Sister Kenny Institute; 1980:17.

4. Miller DL. Aspiration: Foiling a silent killer. *RN.* 1978; 41(8):37.

5. Loustau A, Lee K. Dealing with the dangers of dysphagia. *Nursing '85.* 1985; 15(2):50.

6. Medcenter One Diet Manual. *The Dysphagia Diet.* Medcenter One, P.O. Box 640, Bismarck, ND 58502.

7. Schmitz J. *The Dietitian's Role in the Dysphagia Team.* Unpublished manuscript.

Chapter 8

Spinal Cord Injury

Randi Yarmeisch O'Brien

Advances in emergency and acute care medicine have improved the survival rate of persons with spinal cord injury (SCI), thus expanding the field of rehabilitation medicine and those specializing in the treatment of SCI. Rehabilitation of the person with SCI is designed to restore the client to the best functional capacity to promote independent living. This is a complex process aimed at the prevention and treatment of medical complications associated with SCI combined with extensive physical, occupational, and psychological therapies. The team approach to the treatment of these clients is crucial. This team often comprises the physician (physiatrist), registered nurse, physical therapist, occupational therapist, speech therapist, psychologist, orthotist, social worker, vocational counselor, and registered dietitian.

The importance of the registered dietitian as a team member is well recognized in most rehabilitation facilities. However, little information is available regarding nutritional assessment in SCI. The objective of this chapter is to provide guidance for the practicing rehabilitation nutritionist responsible for the nutritional management of the person with SCI. In this chapter, the focus is on the SCI, assuming a minimum of 3 months after injury in order to rule out metabolic complications associated with the acute or stressed state.

DEMOGRAPHIC INFORMATION

SCI is a catastrophic tragedy that occurs most often in young adults. Sixty-one percent of the SCI cases occur at the ages between 16 and 30 years old, with the average age at injury being 29.7 years.[1] Eighty-two percent of SCI patients are male, most likely because of their involvement in high-risk activities.[1] There are 73.9% of SCI patients who are white and 16% who are black. The proportion of whites with SCI is lower than the national racial proportions, which indicates that the incidence rate of SCI is higher among blacks.[1]

SCI may result from a vaiety of occurrences, but the most common cause is motor vehicle accidents. Forty-seven percent of reported SCI cases are due to motor vehicle accidents, 20.8% from falls, 14.2% from sports-related injuries, 14.6% from acts of violence, and 2.7% from other sources.[1]

A diagrammatic representation of spinal anatomy and classification of spinal injury is illustrated in Figure 8-1.

COMMON TERMS RELATED TO SCI

In order to promote common understanding, it is necessary to define selected technical terms:

Cervical: pertaining to the neck; specifically, the vertebrae in the neck of that part of the spinal cord.

Complete lesion: a lesion in which no motor or sensory function occurs below the area of spinal cord destruction at the site of the injury.

Condom catheter: a condom with an attached tube worn over the penis to collect urine.

Extent of lesion: the degree of neurologic function that remains below the area of injury. See complete and incomplete lesions.

Functional level: the level of motor function that allows the person with a SCI to perform various activities.

Heterotopic bone formation: calcium deposit around the joints due to SCI causing decreased range of motion.

Incomplete lesion: a lesion in which some motor and/or sensory function is evident below the area of injury.

Indwelling catheter: a tube inserted in the bladder for continuous urinary drainage.

Intermittent catheterization: the process of catheter insertion into the bladder for bladder emptying on a regularly scheduled basis within a 24-hour period.

Lumbar: the area below the thoracic segment of the spinal cord.

Paraplegia: loss of neurologic function below the area of the cervical spinal cord, often resulting in paralysis of the lower portion of the body.

C2 through C4: These persons have no movement of the upper extremities, although there is some control of the neck muscles. The C2 client requires ventilatory support, while the C4 client usually does not.

C5: The C5 clients have use of their biceps, can feed themselves with the aid of special equipment and perform simple activities of daily living such as grooming.

C6: The clients have use of their wrists. They can be independent in grooming and bathing, driving and preparing a simple meal.

C7: In addition to the above activities, C7 clients can straighten their arms. Some clients are capable of total independence and can live alone with some adaptations in their homes.

T1 through T6: The T1 client has all cervical segments intact and has normal hands. He or she should be capable of independent living in a wheelchair accessible environment. A client with a T6 injury has much better breathing due to control of chest muscles.

T12: The T12 client has complete trunk control, with good abdominal muscles. Sitting balance is good. Ambulation may be possible with long leg braces, though very difficult.

L4: The L4 client has use of the hip flexors and quadriceps. He or she can extend his or her knees and raise his or her feet. There is still some paralysis in the back of the legs, but ambulation is possible with the assistance of short leg braces.

Spinal reflex activity regulating autonomic processes such as bladder and bowel function is usually present in persons with lesions at T12 or above but is usually absent at L1 or below.

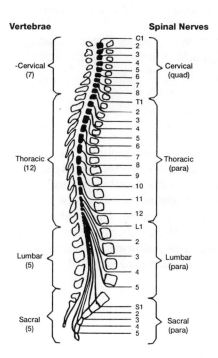

Figure 8-1 Vertebrae and spinal nerves from peripheral nerve injuries. *Source:* Reprinted from *Peripheral Nerve Injuries: Principles of Diagnosis* by W Haymaker and B Woodhall with permission of WB Saunders Company, © 1953. Legend: *Source:* Adapted from *Spinal Cord Injury: The Facts and Figures* (p 26) by SL Stover and PR Fine (Eds) with permission of the authors, © 1986.

Postural hypotension: a decrease in blood pressure on sitting or standing secondary to decreased blood volume induced by immobilization and decreased venous tone.

Quadriplegia: loss of neurologic function in the area of the cervical spinal cord, often results in paralysis from the neck down.

Range of motion: a measure of the joint's mobility.

Sacral: the area of the spinal cord below the lumbar level.

Thoracic: the area of the spinal cord between the cervical and lumbar areas.

Tilt table: a table with a footplate that is mechanically inclined to the vertical position to allow the person with SCI to acclimate himself or herself to standing.

Vertebrae: pertaining to any one of the 33 bones of the spinal column, including 7 cervical, 12 thoracic, 5 lumbar, 5 sacral, and 4 coccygeal.

NUTRITIONAL ASSESSMENT

Nutritional assessment of the person with SCI is a multifaceted process including nutrition history, anthropometric measurements, feeding assessment, estimation of nutrient needs, and assessment of biochemical data. Extensive data including specific defined guidelines for assessing the nutritional status of the person with SCI are not available. The rehabilitation nutritionist is often forced to rely on professional experience and clinical judgment to assess these clients' needs. The following guidelines were extrapolated from current literature and personal experience.

Nutrition History

Obtaining a complete and accurate nutrition history from a client with SCI may be difficult owing to impaired written or oral communication abilities. The nutritionist must be resourceful and use family members to obtain food intake information. Nutrition information specific to persons with SCI necessary for the development of an appropriate nutrition care plan include the following[2]:

- date and level of injury
- presence and history of decubiti
- presence and type of catheterization
- frequency of urinary tract infection

- frequency and duration of muscle tremors
- preinjury height and weight
- recent weight changes
- use of assistive feeding devices
- degree of ability to self-feed
- symptoms of swallowing difficulties
- activity level (including type of wheelchair, ie, manual or motor)
- medications used
- food allergies or intolerances
- information regarding the purchase and preparation of food at home

Anthropometric Measurements

Anthropometrics include the measurement of body weight, triceps skin fold, arm circumference, and arm muscle circumference. Body weight can be measured with a sling or wheelchair scale. Consecutive weights should be measured under consistent circumstances (the same time each day using the same scale and wheelchair). Weights should be obtained frequently to best monitor weight changes. Usually, a significant weight loss occurs during the acute phase followed by excessive weight gain in the chronic phase.[2] Even when body weight has been stabilized, the distribution of body weight will change. Muscle mass will decrease and an increase in fat deposition will occur.[2]

Methods for anthropometric measurements have been modified for clients with decreased mobility although reference standards do not exist. Interpretation of anthropometric data for the person with SCI is therefore quite difficult. It is also difficult to obtain measurements on these clients because of their limited mobility. Arm circumference measurements on persons with SCI tend to be lower than standards due to muscle atrophy, resulting in inaccurate assessments.

Measurement of body weight and percentage weight change is the most useful anthropometric measurement for accurate nutritional assessment. Lack of standard references for other anthropometric meaurements for this population makes it difficult to efficiently use these data for accurate interpretation of nutritional status.

Feeding Assessment

The nutritionist must assess the client's feeding, chewing, and swallowing abilities. Decreased motor function commonly interferes with self-feeding and may require a modified diet to facilitate independence and ensure adequate intake. Clients with reduced oral-motor function may benefit from a diet of textured foods that minimize chewing. Swallowing dysfunction, or dysphagia, is a most complex disorder requiring individual treatment based on the etiology of the swallowing dysfunction (see Chapter 7).

Feeding, chewing, and swallowing disorders are best evaluated and treated by a team approach. This team often comprises the physiatrist, nurse, occupational and/or speech therapist, and registered dietitian. The dietitian's role has been recognized as assessment of ongoing nutritional status, evaluation of nutrient intake, provision of appropriately textured nutrient-dense foods, and counseling.[2]

Calculation of Ideal Body Weight

The person with injury to the spinal cord is at risk for obesity due to immobilization and decreased energy expenditure. Maintenance of ideal body weight slightly below the average healthy adult is recommended to facilitate transfers and enhance self-care activities. Peiffer recommends assessing ideal body weight at 10 to 15 pounds below the values in the Metropolitan Life Insurance tables for paraplegics and at 15 to 20 pounds below these values for quadriplegics.[3]

Another method, practiced at the Rusk Institute of Rehabilitation Medicine, consists of a 5% to 10% reduction from ideal weight for paraplegics and a 10% to 15% reduction from ideal body weight for quadriplegics. Ideal body weight is calculated for females as 100 pounds for the first 5 feet of height with 5 pounds for each additional inch and for males as 106 pounds for the first 5 feet of height with 6 pounds for each additional inch of height (Table 8-1).[4]

Adequate muscle mass must be obtained. To the extent possible, weight change should occur gradually along with whatever physical activity possible to ensure loss of body fat rather than muscle.

Assessment of Kilocalorie Requirements

The Harris-Benedict equation is used to determine basal energy expenditures (BEE).[5]

Males: BEE = 66 + 13.7 (W) + 5 (H) − 6.8 (A) × Activity factor
Females: BEE = 655 + 9.6 (W) + 1.7 (H) − 4.7 (A) × Activity factor

where W = weight in kilograms, H = height in centimeters, and A = age in years.

Table 8-1 Calculation of Ideal Body Weight

Build	Female	Male
Medium	Allow 100 pounds for first 5 feet of height, plus 5 pounds for each additional inch.	Allow 106 pounds for first 5 feet of height, plus 6 pounds for each additional inch.
Small	Subtract 10%.	Subtract 10%.
Large	Add 10%.	Add 10%.
Paraplegic	Subtract 5% to 10%.	Subtract 5% to 10%.
Quadriplegic	Subtract 10% to 15%.	Subtract 10% to 15%.

For the person with SCI, an activity factor of 1.2 or 1.3 is used depending on the individual degree of activity and/or the extent of the physical therapy program. The nutritionist must use his or her best clinical judgment. An injury factor is not incorporated into this equation since in the chronic phase the person is usually medically stable. In cases of stress or infection, an injury factor may need to be incorporated. It is important to note that these calculations are only estimates of energy needs. Monitoring actual weight and modifying intake to account for changes is the best approach.

Assessment of Protein Requirements

Adequate protein intake is essential for the person with SCI to prevent decubitus ulcer formation, infection, and negative nitrogen balance. The average healthy adult requires 0.8 g of protein per kilogram of body weight. The person with SCI with infections and decubitus ulcers may require 1.0 to 1.5 g of protein per kilogram of body weight.[6] Adequate energy must be provided in order to ensure the proper use of the protein being provided. A nitrogen–calorie ratio of 1:150 should prevent the oxidation of amino acids for energy needs.[7] In cases of multiple infections, severe decubitus ulcer formations, and negative nitrogen balance, a ratio of 1:100 may be indicated. These needs may best be met by the provision of palatable high-protein supplements between meals.

Assessment of Vitamin and Mineral Requirements

Adequate vitamins and minerals must be provided to maintain health. The person with SCI may be at risk for vitamin or mineral deficiencies owing to a decreased appetite with a subsequent decreased oral intake often secondary to depression and/or fatigue. A standard daily multivitamin plus minerals is frequently recommended to prevent deficiencies. In the stressed client, therapeutic doses may be desirable. Supplemental vitamin C and zinc may be indicated when severe decubitus ulcers are present to promote wound healing.[8]

Assessment of Fluid Requirements

The rationale for high fluid intakes for persons with SCI is twofold. A high fluid intake of 2500 to 3000 mL is recommended for the prevention and treatment of infection and urinary calculi.[6] Also, a high-fiber diet needed along with proper bowel training and management necessitates a high fluid intake to prevent constipation or impaction.

Assessment of Laboratory Data

Routine laboratory assessment is crucial to determine ongoing nutritional status. Consistent monitoring will enable the nutritionist to intervene during the course of rehabilitation and prevent a decline in nutritional status. Due to the extended average length of stay of this population, and the need for cost containment, inexpensive and easily accessible laboratory data are used. Careful monitoring of serum albumin, total iron-binding capacity, serum calcium, hemoglobin, and hematocrit is routine practice.

Serum Albumin

The serum albumin concentration is routinely used in nutritional assessment as an indicator of visceral protein status. However, its use is limited for assessing current status due to its long half-life of 21 days. Since the person with SCI is often hospitalized for extensive periods, the serum albumin value may be monitored weekly to assess an improvement or decline in nutritional status. The literature suggests a high elimination rate of albumin in SCI, although conclusive evidence has yet to be provided.[3]

A serum albumin value greater than 3.5 mg/dL indicates that the person is at low nutritional risk; 3.0 to 3.4 mg/dL, at moderate nutritional risk; and below 3.0 mg/dL, at severe nutritional risk.[9] The serum albumin level will be decreased when decubitus ulcers are present, warranting a high protein intake to promote wound healing, improve visceral protein status, and replete protein lost through the exudate.

Serum Transferrin

Serum transferrin is a more sensitive indicator of visceral protein status because of its shorter half-life of 8 to 10 days. Transferrin can be derived from the total iron-binding capacity by using the formula $0.8 \times$ TIBC $-$ $43 =$ transferrin. The accuracy of this equation has been under scrutiny and it has been recommended that each institution develop a formula based on the laboratory methods used at the individual facility.[9] Serum transferrin values may be defined as follows: 200 to 300 mg/dL as normal, 150 to 200 mg/dL as mild depletion, 100 to 150 mg/dL as moderately depleted, and below 100 mg/dL as severely depleted.[9]

Hemoglobin/Hematocrit

Hemoglobin and hematocrit are routinely monitored since anemia is a frequent sequelae of SCI.[3] If the hemoglobin and hematocrit are decreased, mean corpuscular volume is reviewed to determine if the anemia is microcytic, macrocytic, or normocytic. Common nutritional anemias include folate or vitamin B_{12} deficiencies, which present as macrocytic anemia, and iron deficiency, which presents as microcytic anemia.

Serum Calcium

The nutritionist routinely reviews the serum calcium levels for both hypocalcemia and hypercalcemia. Fifty percent of total plasma calcium is ionized, while the remainder is protein bound, primarily to albumin. Decreased serum calcium levels seen with decreased serum albumin levels may not reflect a true hypocalcemia in terms of altered calcium metabolism. Instead, this picture is most likely to indicate a decline in calcium due to decreased albumin. A useful tool for reassessing a "pseudohypocalcemia" is that, generally, for every 1.0 g of albumin below 4.0 g, calcium will be lowered by 0.8 mg.[10]

Hypercalcemia is often noted in the male adolescent with SCI due to immobilization. Calcium supplementation or restriction is not recommended for this condition, and a more detailed explanation of this phenomenon is included in the section on immobilization hypercalcemia.

Medications

It is not uncommon for the SCI patient to be taking a variety of medications simultaneously. The most common medications are listed in Table 8-2.[11] A brief description of possible side effects that may require nutritional intervention is included.

Table 8-2 Common Medications and Their Nutritional Implications for the Person with SCI

Medication	Usual Dose	Classification	Comments
Methenamine mandelate (Mandelamine)	1 g, qid	Urinary antiseptic	Functions best in acid urine; may be beneficial to supplement with vitamin C; push fluids; may cause nausea, gastrointestinal distress
Vitamin C	500 mg	Vitamin supplement	Essential for wound healing; acidification of urine
Multivitamin/Mineral	1 tablet bid	Nutrient supplement	For supplementation of a decreased oral intake
Docusate sodium (Colace)	100 mg, tid	Stool softener	May cause diarrhea
Senna concentrate (Senokot)	2 tablets at bedtime	Stool softener	May cause nausea, vomiting, gastrointestinal distress
Glycerine	1 suppository	Suppository	No nutritional implications
Baclofen (Lioresal)	20 mg, qid	Muscle relaxant	Gastrointestinal distress rare; hepatotoxicity
Diazepam (Valium)	5 mg, qid	Antianxiety, muscle relaxant	Dizziness, drowsiness, fatigue, depression
Oxybutynin (Ditropan)	5 mg, tid	Smooth muscle relaxant	No nutritional implications
Phenoxybenzamine (Dibenzyline)	10 mg, tid	Peripheral vasodilator	Nausea, vomiting, diarrhea, gastrointestinal irritation
Acetaminophen (Tylenol)	1–2 tablets	Analgesic, antipyretic	No nutritional implications
Diphenhydramine (Benadryl)	50 mg at bedtime	Antihistamine	Gastrointestinal distress, constipation
Amitriptyline (Elavil)	25 mg, tid	Antidepressant	Dry mouth, nausea, vomiting, constipation, diarrhea, anorexia
Fluphenazine (Prolixin)	1 mg, tid	Antipsychotic	Dry mouth, constipation; do not take with megadose of vitamin C
Phenytoin (Dilantin)	100 mg, tid	Anticonvulsant	May cause folic acid and vitamin D depletion

Source: Adapted with permission from *Bulletin of the New York Academy of Medicine* (1986; 62[2]:176), Copyright © 1987, New York Academy of Medicine.

COMPLICATIONS ASSOCIATED WITH SPINAL CORD INJURY

Neurogenic Bladder

Renal failure secondary to obstructive uropathy was a common fatal complication of SCI until the advent of intermittent catheterization. Bladder physiology may be disrupted by SCI with resultant problems of urinary reflux, urinary retention, urinary incontinence, and stone formation. High residual urine will predispose the person with SCI to recurrent urinary tract infections and stone formation. This is a major cause of morbidity and mortality among SCI patients.

Management includes emptying the bladder of urine, which contains bacteria as well as solutes that may precipitate and form stones. Pharmacologic manipulation of the sympathetic and parasympathetic nervous system and/or intermittent catheterization are the treatments of choice. A high fluid intake is essential for dilution of the urine to reduce bacteria and solute concentration. A high fluid intake of 2000 to 3000 mL/d should be incorporated into the nutrition care plan.[7]

Neurogenic Bowel

Neurogenic bowel is frequently associated with SCI. Anal sphincter tone may be altered when the lesion involves the S2 to S4 level. Gastrointestinal complications associated with neurogenic bowel may be twofold: decreased peristalsis and/or altered sphincter tone. Programmed evacuation of the bowel is required for proper bowel maintenance. This is accomplished with laxatives (bulk, stool softeners, stimulants), digital stimulation, a high fiber diet, and adequate fluid.[12]

The role of the nutritionist during bowel training is to recommend a diet high in fiber, including whole grains, bran products, and fresh fruits and vegetables to provide bulk in a sluggish bowel.[6] A subsequent high fluid intake must also be provided to prevent impaction.

Constipation is frequently seen and may lead to fecal impaction. Diarrhea may also occur in fecal impaction as the liquid stool bypasses the impacted bolus.

Pressure Sores

The person with SCI is at high risk for the development of decubitus ulcers caused by immobilization, lack of pressure sensation, decreased circulation, and poor nutritional status. A person who has significant weight loss is especially prone to skin breakdown because of inadequate padding of subcutaneous tissue covering bony prominences.[13] In contrast, the obese client is equally prone to pressure sore formation because of decreased maneuverability and prolonged contact with surfaces and to moisture collection between folds of skin.[13]

Proper skin care provided by the nursing staff is crucial to the prevention and treatment of pressure sores. Early nutritional intervention is of utmost importance to prevent ulcer formation and promote wound healing. The nutritionist must play an aggressive role in the treatment of skin breakdown. First, adequate protein must be provided to prevent protein malnutrition and delayed wound healing. A high protein intake is often indicated to maintain positive nitrogen balance and replete high protein losses that may occur through large decubitus ulcers.[14]

Vitamin C supplementation may be beneficial because of its role in the hydroxylation of proline and collagen production.[8] If appetite is decreased and inadequate vitamin C intake is suspected, supplementation of 100 to 200 mg may be beneficial.[8] Zinc supplementation may also be helpful to promote wound healing. A daily dose of 15 to 20 mg of zinc should be adequate.[8]

Immobilization Hypercalcemia

Immobilization hypercalcemia is a metabolic complication frequently seen in children and adolescents with SCI.[15] It is characterized by an elevated serum calcium level, normal serum phosphorus level, and a normal or slightly elevated alkaline phosphate level. The urinary calcium concentration increases at approximately the fourth week after injury, peaks at 16 weeks, may remain high for 1 year, and normalizes by 1½ years.[16] Several disorders must first be ruled out, including hyperparathyroidism, chronic renal failure, metastatic cancer, multiple myeloma, adrenal insufficiency, and thiazide diuretic use. The symptoms associated with immobilization hypercalcemia include anorexia, abdominal cramps, nausea and vomiting, constipation, headache, lethargy, polydipsia, polyuria, and dehydration.[15]

Once immobilization occurs, bone resorption increases, resulting in disuse osteopenia and hypercalciuria. In adolescence, when bone turnover is greatly enhanced, the kidneys are unable to handle the calcium excess, excretion is reduced, and hypercalcemia occurs.

A low calcium diet is ineffective and is not recommended since the hypercalcemia results from increased bone resorption as opposed to increased calcium absorption from the gut.[7] Adequate hydration is the best treatment to prevent and/or correct dehydration and electrolyte imbalances.

Depression

The SCI client is most likely to experience some form of depression during the course of rehabilitation. The severity or duration of the depressed state is unpredictable. The nutritionist, as well as all members of the health care team, must be alert to the signs and symptoms of depression among persons with SCI. Severe depression will most certainly affect oral intake and, ultimately, nutritional status.

Persons with SCI often enter the rehabilitation unit with weight loss and protein depletion secondary to the hypermetabolism associated with trauma/ stress. Most likely, the reality of the disability does not become apparent until they are medically stable and engage in a rehabilitation program. The nutritionist is faced with a difficult task: to ensure the adequate calorie, protein, and fluid intake for maintenance or repletion of nutritional status when the client is depressed and uninterested in food.

The nutritionist must be patient, sensitive, and yet persistent. It will be most beneficial for the nutritionist to consult with the social worker and/ or psychologist involved in the case to best understand how to deal with a particular client for positive results.

CONCLUSION

The nutritionist is an integral member of the rehabilitation team caring for SCI clients and must play an aggressive role in the treatment of these persons. A timely and thorough nutritional assessment must be performed on the client's admission to the rehabilitation unit to provide nutritional intervention as soon as possible. Early detection of nutritional needs and/ or deficiencies is essential for optimal rehabilitation. Ongoing monitoring is important to maintain good health and avoid or reduce complication.

REFERENCES

1. Stover SL, Fine PR, eds. *Spinal Cord Injury: The Facts and Figures.* Birmingham: University of Alabama at Birmingham; 1986.

2. Gines DJ, Holliday ME, Erwin K. Nutritional assessment during rehabilitation of the spinal cord injury patient. *Top Clin Nutr.* 1987;2(4):41.

3. Peiffer SC, Blust P, Florante J, Leyson J. Nutritional assessment of the spinal cord injured patient. *J Am Diet Assoc.* 1981;78:501.

4. The American Diabetes Association and the American Dietetic Association. *A Guide for Professionals: The Effective Application of "Exchange Lists for Meal Planning."* 1977.

5. Blackburn GL, et al. Nutritional and metabolic assessment of the hospitalized patient. *J Parenter Enter Nutr.* 1987;1(1):14.

6. Lagger L. Spinal cord injury: Nutritional management. *J Neurosurg Nurs.* 1983;15(5):311.

7. Curtin HC, Harvey RF, Jellinek HM. Role of the clinical nutritionist as a member of a rehabilitation team. *Nutr Support Serv.* 1982;2(1):27.

8. Myers SA, Karamatsu J. Nutritional care of the patient with pressure sores. *Nutr Support Serv.* 1983;3(7):48.

9. Grant A, DeHoog S. *Nutritional Assessment and Support.* Seattle, Wash: Anne Grant and Susan DeHoog; 1985.

10. Tilkian SM, Conover MB, Tilkian AG. *Clinical Implications of Laboratory Tests.* St. Louis, Mo: CV Mosby Co; 1979.

11. Ragnarsson KT. Spinal cord injury: Old problems: New approaches. *Bull NY Acad Med.* 1986;62:176.

12. Drayton-Hargrove S, Reddy MA. Rehabilitation and long-term management of the spinal cord injured adult. *Nurs Clin North Am.* 1986;21:605–606.

13. Antypas PG. Management of pressure sores. *Curr Prob Surg.* 1980;17:229.

14. Lee BY. *Chronic Ulcers of the Skin.* New York, NY: McGraw-Hill Book Co; 1985.

15. Maynard FM, Imai K. Immobilization hypercalcemia following spinal cord injury. *Arch Phys Med Rehabil.* 1986;67:41.

16. Stewart AF, et al. Calcium homeostasis in immobilization: An example of resorptive hypercalciuria. *N Engl J Med.* 1982;306:1138.

SUGGESTED READING

Barboriak JJ, et al. Nutrition in spinal cord injury patients. *J Am Paraplegia Soc.* 1983;6:32–36.

Basson MD, Burney RE. Defective wound healing in patients with paraplegia and quadriplegia. *Surg Gynecol Obstet.* 1982;155:9–12.

Bildstein C, Laamid S. Nutritional management of a patient with brain damage and spinal cord injury. *Arch Phys Med Rehabil.* 1983;64:382–383.

Bloch RF, Basbaum M, eds. *Management of Spinal Cord Injuries.* Baltimore, Md: Williams & Wilkins Co; 1986.

Claus-Walker J, Halstead LS. Metabolic and endocrine changes in spinal cord injury: IV. Compound neurologic dysfunctions. *Arch Phys Med Rehabil.* 1982;63:632–638.

Cox SAR, et al. Energy expenditure after spinal cord injury: An evaluation of stable rehabilitation patients. *J Trauma.* 1985;25:419–423.

Freed MM. Traumatic and congenital lesions of the spinal cord. In: Kottke FJ, Stillwell GK, Lehmann JF, eds. *Krusen's Handbook of Physical Medicine and Rehabilitation.* Philadelphia, Pa: WB Saunders Co; 1982.

Greenway RM, Houser HB, Lindan O, Weir DR. Long term changes in gross body composition of paraplegic and quadriplegic patients. *Paraplegia.* 1969;7:301–318.

Grundy D, Russel J. ABC of spinal cord injury: Urological management. *Br Med J.* 1986;292:249–253.

Kermani SR, Siddiqui M, Zain S, Kazi ZK. Biochemical studies on pressure-sore healing in paraplegics. *Paraplegia.* 1970;8:36–41.

Lee BY, et al. Assessment of nutritional and metabolic status of paraplegics. *J Rehabil Res Dev.* 1985;22:11–17.

Maynard FM, Imai K. Immobilization hypercalcemia in spinal cord injury. *Arch Phys Med Rehabil.* 1977;58:16–24.

Mirahmadi MK, et al. Nutritional evaluation of hemodialysis patients with and without spinal cord injury. *J Am Paraplegia Soc.* 1983;6:36–40.

Newmark SR, Sublett D, Black J, Geller, R. Nutritional assessment in a rehabilitation unit. *Arch Phys Med Rehabil.* 1982;62:279–282.

Powers DE, Moore AO. *Food Medication Interactions.* Tempe, Ariz: Food Medication Interactions Publishing; 1983.

Schneider FJ. Traumatic spinal cord injury. In: Umphred DA, Jewell MJ, eds. *Neurological Rehabilitation.* St. Louis, Mo: CV Mosby Co; 1985.

Chapter 9

Traumatic Brain Injury

Sharon Yankelson

Head injury kills more Americans younger than age 34 than all other causes of death combined. Head injury resulting in traumatic brain injury (TBI) is the "silent epidemic" affecting 700,000 Americans yearly. A large percentage of persons per year sustain severe enough physical and cognitive deficits to prevent return to normal function, and a smaller percentage of persons suffer minor head injuries with social and behavioral problems that may exist unreported.

The number of persons surviving TBI has increased dramatically over the past 10 to 15 years due mainly to the advancement of medicine in the fields of emergency, intensive, and acute care. Consequently the number of persons requiring rehabilitation has increased along with the need for registered dietitians skilled in the area of TBI. Initially, involvement of dietitians was minimal, even at the acute stage of recovery, but with the realization that aggressive nutrition support was necessary for survival and with the advent of the nutrition support team, dietitians were able to provide appropriate and timely nutrition intervention. With a better understanding of each client's response to trauma and stress and the corresponding need for adequate calories and protein, the rehabilitation process can begin almost immediately by using appropriate feeding to prevent massive tissue catabolism, skin breakdown, infection, and other complications.

As these persons recover, they progress from acute care settings to a rehabilitation center. Many dietitians are now dealing with clients who present with an extremely diverse set of problems. One client may still be in coma and, although medically stable, may require close monitoring of nutritional status and frequent changes in tube feedings due to infection, the effects of medication changes, or constipation. Another client may be ambulatory and have severe cognitive and memory deficits, requiring individual nutrition counseling and diet manipulation due to extremely abnormal lipid values.

The dietitian must now draw on new skills of nutrition in rehabilitation to be an effective member of the health care team and face the challenge of adapting to a new and often difficult situation. Facilities that have coma stimulation programs including the dietitian focus on the possibility that with the right amount and type of stimulation persons can be brought out of coma. In working with the cognitively impaired patient, the dietitian becomes a therapist who must be cognizant of the client's level of understanding and participation, based on an entire team's evaluation. How is the dietitian to fulfill this role successfully?

CONSEQUENCES OF BRAIN INJURY THAT AFFECT NUTRITIONAL STATUS

An understanding of some of the consequences of TBI that have a bearing on nutritional status is a prerequisite to dealing successfully with a person with a head injury. Depending on how and where the brain is injured, a person may suffer a wide variety of injuries that lead to multiple deficits and handicaps. Even though some persons may appear, to the naked eye, to have suffered only physical damage as a consequence of the accident, one must be sensitive to the less obvious deficits such as loss of memory, motivation, or motor planning skills in order to provide the most appropriate treatment.

Almost 70% of persons with a TBI suffer from some form of dysphagia, which is defined as difficulty with chewing and swallowing. They may be totally devoid of the ability to handle food orally, or they may have progressed to tolerating only soft solids, while liquids continue to be administered via a tube (see Appendix B for procedures for preparation of dysphagia diets). Often the treatment of dysphagia is further complicated by damage to the person's olfactory nerves and taste buds so that the person rejects any attempt at feeding, due to an intolerance of all foods. The risk of aspiration can be increased by the client's lack of understanding of his or her feeding program owing to memory loss or expressive or receptive aphasia.

Memory and language play a major role in successful nutrition counseling; deficits in either can be a barrier that is a challenge to overcome. Loss of short-term memory may inhibit new learning or require that the same materials be presented repeatedly in a variety of ways. This situation is best illustrated when the dietitian is teaching a client the basic four food groups. With severe memory loss, many clients do not remember the items of a meal just eaten and, therefore, their ability to group and categorize foods is minimal. To help the client overcome this barrier, the dietitian may discuss the food with the client at the actual meal, review the menu in a timely manner, and also present the client with replicas (Dairy Council cut-outs or Nasco food models) of the meal at the subsequent therapy session. With short-term memory loss, long-term memory may still be intact, which often misleads the therapist to think that the client is capable of understanding, retaining, and implementing new information. However, the client may learn to use the long-term memory as a compensatory technique. For example, a food service manager who has suffered a TBI can easily recall general concepts about the restaurant she managed premorbidly. The client can describe a menu vividly, quote a recipe for a specialty item, or give very general job requirements for a cook. When pressed, however, to recall and repeat this information accurately and with the appropriate sequencing, as in the method of preparation in a recipe, she cannot and immediately reverts back to her initial strategy. In subsequent therapy sessions, she has no recollection of the content of the previous session.

Persons with TBI may exhibit one or more language deficits together with any of the other deficits. Expressive aphasia (the inability to express oneself even though one knows what one wants to say) and receptive aphasia (the inability to comprehend spoken language) are often seen in the head-injured client. A one-to-one interview with a client in this case may result in a highly explosive situation because of the person's frustration with the lack of ability to communicate. Anomia (a language defect in word finding and an inability to name objects on confrontation) may make it impossible to determine the client's knowledge of basic facts.

Damage to the hypothalamus may eliminate the satiety control mechanism in the brain. Persons with this type of brain injury manifest extremely bizarre eating behaviors that do not respond to any of the traditional methods of behavior modification. Persons with hyperphagia may have pica, may forage in trash receptacles, and may spend the majority of their day trying to steal, hoard, and eat whatever they can find. The situation is exacerbated by a loss of memory so that learning of new strategies to change this maladaptive behavior is often impossible. These clients frequently deny that these behaviors occur or that they may severely affect their social and vocational potential, and without this acknowledgment, change cannot occur.

When there is damage to the frontal lobe, which controls emotions, the therapist can be presented with clients who are extremely labile and who are lacking in motivation and a sense of responsibility. The clients may deny that they have any deficits and may refuse therapies, believing that they are ready to move back into the community. These clients may be very unwilling and uncooperative, regarding nutritional intervention and counseling as unnecessary. On the other hand, the dietitian may see persons who respond well to nutritional intervention while in a structured and supervised setting but have very poor carryover when alone, owing to their inability or unwillingness to take responsibility for their own life. These clients hold the dietitian and the food service department responsible for their nutritional status and believe that their weight or diet is not a personal problem.

The physical consequences of TBI are much easier to observe but no less difficult to treat. TBI may cause total paralysis of the body, or the person may have hemiplegia (paralysis of one side of the body). The person may have hemiparesis (muscle weakness on one side of the body affecting one or both of the extremities). Spasticity, causing an increase in skeletal muscle activity, may interfere with many procedures, such as obtaining an accurate height, or cause frequent emesis totally unrelated to type or amount of tube or oral feeding. Range of motion can be greatly inhibited, which would affect muscle tone, body strength, and overall endurance, all significant factors in improving and maintaining good nutritional status.

When persons with TBI suffer physical damage, the effects of physical damage may impact on their ability to perform basic daily living skills. For clients who need assistance to propel a wheelchair, and who are dependent on someone to prepare all their meals and possibly to feed them too, progress toward independent living is impeded. Often these clients eat only convenience foods with few fresh fruits and vegetables and may develop vitamin and mineral deficiencies. They are often obese owing to the high fat content of their diet and the lack of exercise and they may become severely depressed because of their dependency on others and only find solace in eating excessively. These consequences may further affect their overall rehabilitation potential.

EVALUATION OF THE PERSON WITH TRAUMATIC BRAIN INJURY

Knowledge of the deficits of the person with brain injury allows the dietitian to perform a thorough evaluation. In the rehabilitation setting, nutritional evaluation is an ongoing process. Changes in status can occur owing to a myriad of causes, which can be physical, emotional, or behavioral. Persons who suffer a major weight loss may be in relatively good physical condition but because of an increased awareness of their own deficits and a feeling of lack of control over their own life, they may choose to refuse to eat. A medication such as a corticosteroid may cause a sudden and excessive weight gain. Persons with dysphagia may progress to a soft diet with thick liquids and become dehydrated because of an insufficient fluid intake. In addition to these changes caused by external factors, changes occur as a result of spontaneous recovery, which may continue for 2 to 3 years after trauma.

The initial evaluation of the client should include the admitting diagnosis, height, weight (premorbid weight and changes that occurred post injury), laboratory data, current medications, and all pertinent drug–nutrient interactions, levels of activity, identification of feeding problems, and a one-to-one interview if appropriate. The opportunity to meet with the family or guardian is useful since premorbid information helps the dietitian to establish realistic goals. To attempt to change a client's life style to something totally different to what it was premorbidly is usually unsuccessful. The dietitian's role is to adapt current guidelines to the client's level of acceptance and familiarity.

Nutrition History

In an interview with a client who is relatively articulate and intelligible, the skilled dietitian can obtain relevant information about the client's premorbid history and present difficulties. Diet history, level of nutrition education, and skills in using food preparation and eating utensils can be identified.

The assessment of feeding skills is performed jointly by the dietitian, the occupational therapist, and the speech pathologist since each is attuned to a particular area of concern. The dietitian uses both observation at mealtimes and questioning of the client and family and also relies heavily on nursing staff and direct care workers for input. The format of the interview in terms of time frame, setting, and materials used is adapted to meet the individual person's needs. The dietitian may need to draw on the skills of the other disciplines in order to conduct a successful interview. With a client who suffers from expressive aphasia, the speech pathologists recommend the use of visual aids such as food models or newspaper advertisements to help the client identify foods he or she generally eats. For the client who is easily distracted and cannot stay on topic, the cognitive rehabilitation therapist recommends presenting only one concept at a time and keeping the interview short. Information on the client's reading and math skills help the dietitian to gear the interview to the client's educational level. If the interview cannot be conducted during the initial evaluation period, it may occur later when behavior, cognition, orientation, or awareness has improved. Sometimes a family member can assist with the interview since he or she may be able to prompt, interpret signals, and contribute information. This strategy can be counterproductive, when, for example, the family member discloses confidential information to the dietitian in front of the client or when the family member contradicts the client or interrupts the discussion. Rapport between the dietitian and the client may be seriously hampered by these events.

Anthropometric Evaluation

In the area of anthropometrics, the current standards generally cannot be applied directly to the head-injured population. Because the data are based on normal, healthy populations, the dietitian must adapt, adjust, and use experience and judgment to determine the range of acceptability. For the person with hyperphagia who is 100% above ideal body weight, a goal of reaching this weight is unrealistic and counterproductive. The dietitian can begin with a realistic goal, then adjust the target weight to meet the person's changing needs. Similarly, estimates of caloric requirements must be based on individual circumstances. Consider a 13-year-old boy who is 120% of his ideal body weight. Based on his age, sex, and injury status he requires more than 1800 calories per day. However, because he is in a wheelchair and cannot take part in any physical activity, his caloric needs are reduced to prevent rapid weight gain. In addition, the client may have severe behavioral problems including disruptive screaming episodes and constant complaints of hunger. Because of his dysphagia, he cannot be given the usual low calorie supplements such as raw fruits and vegetables so the calories are increased to allow for small servings of soft foods.

Obtaining anthropometric measurements is often difficult with the head-injured population. Persons who are comatose may have severe spasticity and high muscle tone, which causes the lower extremities to be contracted and the spine curved. A height measurement may be more accurate if taken when the person is more relaxed due to medication or physical therapy. Height can be measured in a supine position on a recumbent length board. When the person cannot be stretched out completely, height measurement can be done in segments with a steel tape. The measurements are taken, in a supine position, from the top of the back of the head to the base of the neck, holding the head as upright as possible. The person is then measured from the base of the neck to the waist, from the side of the waist to the knee and from the back of the knee to the heel. All these measurements are then totaled to give a relatively accurate height.

Bed, wheelchair, and upright scales are basic requirements in rehabilitation facilities. Bed scales are ideal for comatose clients and clients who are critically ill. The client is lifted gently by staff and lowered onto a canvas sling on the bed that is attached to a hoist. Once the person is lying securely in the sling, the hoist is raised off the bed and a weight can be read on the attached dial. Digital wheelchair scales are suitable for both persons who are nonambulatory and for clients who have severe ataxia (very poor balance and tremors), allowing for uncontrolled movement by the client. The scale has a large platform attached to it onto which the chair is wheeled, and after the client is weighed the weight of the wheelchair is subtracted. Consistency in weighing procedures is vital to good nutritional care. An increase in accuracy can be obtained if the person is always weighed on the same scale and at the same time of day each time. The person should be wearing minimum clothing. Staff must be sure to free the client and the wheelchair of any extra equipment that may be being carried with them.

THE TREATMENT PLAN

The treatment plan includes three major components: the status of the client on admission, the goals established (short and long term), and the strategies to be used to reach these goals. Goal setting must be realistic and is based on all the individual needs of the client. Using the standards available for the normal population and typical protocols, the dietitian adjusts these to reflect the client's premorbid treatment, present status, cognitive level, and recommendations of the team. Depending on the level of cognition, there may be more than one goal for the same nutritional problem. For example, for the client with hyperlipidemia, the diet may be changed to reduce cholesterol and fat and perhaps nutrition counseling could be added to increase the person's knowledge of diet and disease. For the underweight person on tube feedings, one goal could be to increase weight and a second goal could be to progress the client to partial or total oral feedings.

The strategies used vary according to the type of nutritional intervention necessary, as well as to the individual client needs. For the comatose person, on tube feedings, the goal may be to begin the process of oral feeding immediately when the person begins to respond to stimuli and exhibits a swallow reflex. For the client who is cognitively alert, many more goals and strategies can be used depending on the person's long-term prognosis and the team's discharge plans.

The advantages of the team approach are most evident in the situation when each discipline can identify the person's deficits and difficulties and the team can develop a transdisciplinary plan that keeps the client's needs as top priority. The dietitian may be involved in co-leading therapies with other team members as in an eating disorders program where a psychologist or cognitive rehabilitation therapist works with the dietitian to focus on changing behaviors while teaching the client the skills needed to control his or her own weight. A dietitian may also work with the speech pathologist or occupational therapist in an awareness program that teaches skills needed for community re-entry.

The dietitian is involved in developing and implementing feeding programs or advising other therapists of the person's particular nutritional needs with reference to physical activity, daily schedule, or dietary restrictions. Close communication with the physician becomes an integral part of the process.

Once the treatment plan is implemented, the dietitian must monitor the client on a regular basis and make changes in goals and strategies as needed. In a long-term rehabilitation setting, the frequency of monitoring may vary from daily, as with a medically unstable person, to every 2 weeks when weights and laboratory data are updated and a report is written about the client's overall progress.

There is a lack of educational materials designed for use with the person with a head injury. Existing nutrition materials can be adapted to the needs of the person with TBI. Plastic food models, food pictures, and simple games are used to teach the basic four food groups, the six exchanges, and simple menu planning. For the client with minimal short-term memory retention, visual stimulation can be more effective than the written word. For the client with a very low level of cognition, food names and categories can be reinforced through picture bingo and matching games. The dietitian can also simulate a cafeteria line with food models and teach the client sequencing, motor planning, and how to make choices. Materials developed for elementary and secondary school nutrition education can be adapted by modifying the language and using the lessons in a small group setting. Nutrition information in magazines and newsletters may also be useful.

Activities such as cooking, food preparation, label reading, visits to the grocery store, and daily menu writing prove to be very successful. Clients may be enrolled in a daily class geared to teaching skills for independent living where they would plan, prepare, and eat a meal, or they may make weekly trips to the grocery store to purchase the items for the class. They could be enrolled in a community re-entry program and spend every day working on home and personal management skills as a means to earn eligibility for placement in the community. Younger persons respond well to nutrition information that is taught through craft activities such as cutting out and gluing pictures of food onto paper, painting and coloring in pictures, and making food models.

Role-playing is a useful technique with clients with TBI. When one is teaching social skills such as dining out, buying groceries, or refusing inappropriate food, the therapist can confront clients far more successfully than in a traditional setting. Often the clients themselves express their feelings and opinions far more freely, feeling comfortable with the objectivity of the session.

THE FAMILY

The family dynamics play a major part in the rehabilitation process. The dietitian should be sensitive to the ever-evolving changes that occur within the family as the members come to terms with the reality of the head injury and its impact on their loved one. The diversity of family responses is as wide as the range of individual injuries.

Parents or spouses may regard continued tube feeding as a sign of regression and put pressure on the nurses and physicians to allow the person to eat orally prematurely. The dietitian can educate the family about the benefits and necessity of continued tube feedings, assuring them that optimal nutritional status is vital to successful rehabilitation and that if tube feeding is withdrawn too soon then overall progress can be delayed or stopped. When the family understands that the goal of the dietitian is also to advance the client to oral feedings, they become much more supportive of the plan.

With the cognitively alert, ambulatory client, who has hyperthalamic damage and is a compulsive eater, understanding the family's feelings about the behavior and their way of dealing with it is vitally important. The family dynamics themselves may create enormous pressure for the client, who then behaves in an even more bizarre fashion in the family's presence. Family members may offer the person a reward if he or she promises not to steal food, warning the person that failure to do so would severely disappoint everyone involved. Sometimes family members believe that when a person loses weight the behavior will disappear and they refuse to recognize that the brain damage is permanent and that the behavior must be modified if progress is to be made. Family involvement in the eating disorder program contributes enormously to success. Training in food preparation and feeding techniques for the families of persons with dysphagia allows for greater family involvement. Clients and families have the opportunity to socialize together away from the hospital and also to try and evaluate their ability to deal with the modified nutritional needs. Family education and involvement are part of the rehabilitation team goal and should begin as soon as possible and follow through into discharge planning.

CONCLUSION

Successful rehabilitation of a person with TBI requires timely and continued nutritional intervention. The dietitian is challenged to assist a wide spectrum of clients ranging from a comatose person to someone who is alert and ambulatory but has severe memory, physical, or behavioral deficits.

The dietitian integrates a client's nutritional skills with counseling and educational skills, supplemented by other therapists within the field of rehabilitation, and functions as an essential part of the team. As more head injury rehabilitation facilities recognize the need for specialized nutritional intervention, dietitians will be in greater demand. The nutritional status of the client must be evaluated, supported, and monitored by the dietitian.

BIBLIOGRAPHY

Bistrian B. Nutritional support of the long-term care patient: II. Nutritional assessment of the elderly. *J Nutr Support Serv.* 1988;8:17–21

Chernoff R, Forlaw L, Long J III. Enteral feeding of the critically ill patient: Study Kit. 6. Chicago: American Diabetes Association: 1985.

Childs A. Naltrexone in organic bulimia: A preliminary report. *J Brain Injury.* 1987;1:49–55.

Chumley WC. When the Standards Don't Fit: Assessing the Non-Normal Client. Taped Presentation, Chicago: American Dietetic Association Annual Meeting; October 1988.

Clifton G, Robertson S, et al. Enteral hyperalimentation in head injury. *J Neurosurg.* 1985;62:186–192

Filskov SB, Boll TJ. *Handbook of Clinical Neuropsychology.* New York, NY: John Wiley & Sons, Inc; 1981.

Foster K. The role of behavior management programs in the rehabilitation process. *J Cogn Rehabil.* 1988;January/February:16–19.

Heilman KM, Valenstein E. *Clinical Neuropsychology.* New York, NY: Oxford University Press; 1979.

Logemann JA. *Evaluation and Treatment of Swallowing Disorders.* San Diego, Calif: College-Hill Press; 1983.

Rapp RP, Young B, et al. The favorable effect of early parenteral feeding on survival in head-injured patients. *J Neurosurg.* 1983;58:906–912.

Reitan RM, Wolfson D. *Neuroanatomy and Neuropathology: A Clinical Guide for Neuropsychologists.* Tucson, Ariz: Neuropsychology Press; 1985.

Russell R. Nutritional support of the long-term care patient: I. Nutritional requirements of the elderly. *J Nutr Support Serv.* 1988;8:12–16.

Chapter 10

Elderly and Brain-Damaged Persons

*Madeline Uddo-Crane, Lynda Suhrer Roussel, William Drew Gouvier,
and Fredda Blanchard-Fields*

NUTRITIONAL ASSESSMENT

The aim of nutritional assessment is to identify persons who are malnourished, as well as those who are at risk of becoming malnourished. Nutritional assessment of elderly and brain-damaged persons is vital to their management, but concomitants of these conditions often make nutritional assessment of these groups difficult. Standard methods of assessing nutritional status include dietary, biochemical, anthropometric, and immunologic assessment.[1] The neurologic aspects related to selected methods of assessment, along with special considerations and contraindications when used with the populations of interest, will be described briefly.

Dietary Assessment

The general objective of dietary assessments is to evaluate a person's typical pattern of food consumption.[2] Types of dietary assessments include 24-hour recalls, food frequency records or questionnaires, food purchase records, dietary histories, and food intake records. These methods require that the client give an account of his or her dietary intake from memory.[3] This technique is of suspect validity among clients with memory impairment, which is a common problem among brain-damaged and elderly populations. Such persons are likely to have better recall for events from their remote past than for the past day and are thus prone to confabulate when evaluated by the standard 24-hour recall method.[4] Even in clients whose memory functions are better preserved, problems with confusion and temporal orientation are likely to lead to inaccurate reports, since persons may not be sure if they are recalling meal choices from yesterday or today for example.[2,5]

Anthropometric Assessment

Anthropometric techniques rely on physical measurements such as height, weight, skin fold thickness, and arm circumference to assess nutritional status. When using these methods with elderly and brain-damaged clients, several problems arise as a result of physical changes inherent in these populations. For example, measurement of height can be rendered invalid when a client's stature is affected by age-related height decreases, paralysis, orthostatic instability, or even simple difficulty in following the command to "stand up straight and tall."[6,7] Likewise, measurement of muscle mass in clients with neurologic disorders may not be valid measures of nutritional status either. This is because denervated muscle tissue wastes away from disuse, independent of dietary intake. In general, the degree of wasting is proportionally related to the degree of neurologic denervation; thus wasting may be widespread throughout the body or a local change, depending on the type of neurologic lesion.[8]

Special Conditions

Special problems in assessing nutritional status of neurologically impaired persons exist. These unique aspects must be taken into account when assessing this group. For example, paralysis or paresis of facial muscles or limbs may follow a cerebrovascular accident (CVA), neurologic disease, or head injury. Such deficits may make self-feeding quite difficult for the client and require the assistance of other rehabilitation professionals (eg, occupational therapists or physical therapists) to evaluate the need for assistive devices, adapted utensils, and/or additional therapy exercises to restore functional abilities. Other common concomitants of brain damage that may create feeding problems include dysphagia, or inability to swallow; visual neglect, which may result in one ignoring food on one side of the plate; aphasia, which may render one incapable of expressing his or her dietary needs or preferences; and apraxia or incoordination, which may leave one unable to perform the requisite movements necessary for eating.[9-11] Again, consultation with other rehabilitation professionals is desirable to thoroughly evaluate such problems and work out a satisfactory treatment intervention. For example, the speech pathologist may be able to assist in the evaluation and treatment of swallowing problems and may be able to offer recommendations to the dietitian about the consistency of foods and liquids the client can safely manage without aspiration. Likewise, the speech pathologist may be able to help develop nonverbal communication systems that allow aphasic clients to indicate their food choices. For clients with visual neglect, visual scanning training may correct this problem, but such training may take several weeks to conduct. In the meantime, clients with neglect might be coached to use a temporary compensation strategy involving incrementally rotating their plates in a clockwise direction after several bites, thus ensuring that they have the opportunity to view all the available food on the plate, even though all of it may never be in view at the same time.

DRUG–NUTRIENT INTERACTIONS

Drugs may have profound effects on nutrition. The elderly are particularly at risk for adverse drug–nutrient interactions because they are apt to take more drugs than other groups[12] and because elderly persons may react to drugs in unpredictable or paradoxical ways owing to age-related changes in drug distribution, absorption, elimination, and metabolism.[1,7] Additionally, elderly persons are at further risk for adverse drug–nutrient interactions because symptoms of nutritional deficits may be misdiagnosed as normal symptoms of aging (eg, decreased appetite, confusion, changes in hair and skin, fatigue).[13,14]

Adverse effects of drugs on nutrition may result in hyperphagia (increased appetite) or hypophagia (decreased appetite). However, drugs that typically increase appetite may in fact decrease appetite in elderly persons. As a result of such paradoxic effects of medication on the elderly, diligent monitoring is imperative. Medications that may increase appetite include psychotropics (eg, anxiolytics, antidepressants, antipsychotics) and antihistamines.[1,7,11,15]

Elderly persons may become malnourished as a result of hypophagia, secondary to certain drugs. For example, insulin, anti-inflammatory agents used to treat arthritis, cancer chemotherapy drugs, and opiate analgesics may cause nausea, vomiting, and anorexia.[7,11]

A major culprit of misdiagnosed cachexia, or wasting, in elderly persons is the cardiac glycoside digoxin.[16] Digoxin toxicity is life threatening and astonishingly common.[17] Digoxin levels must be ardently monitored by persons cognizant of the relationship between dose and body weight; that is, digoxin toxicity will result if levels are too high in relation to body weight.[5] Furthermore, "digitalis cachexia"[16] may be exacerbated by low potassium levels that may result from diuretic therapy.[17]

Adverse drug-nutrient interactions are multifaceted. Aside from causing an increase or decrease in appetite, many drugs that are likely to be used by elderly persons (eg, antacids, antibiotics, anti-inflammatory agents, cancer chemotherapy drugs, and laxatives) may interfere with vitamin and/or

204 NUTRITION MANAGEMENT IN REHABILITATION

nutrient absorption.[5,7,11] In addition, untoward effects of certain antibiotics, antidepressants, diuretics, chemotherapeutic agents, and antihistamines may cause dry mouth and/or may adversely affect gustation.[18] Such side effects may contribute to loss of pleasure derived from eating and hence increase chances of inadequate nutrient intake by the elderly client taking the medications.[1,11] Those concerned with the nutritional status of the elderly must be aware of the devastating iatrogenic nutritional deficiencies that may result from pharmacotherapy.

Among persons with neurologic disorders, epileptics and those with Parkinson's disease are particularly at risk for drug-induced nutritional deficiencies. Chronic use of anticonvulsant drugs (eg, primidone, phenobarbital, and phenytoin) may cause megaloblastic anemia as a result of attendant folate deficiencies. Additionally, anticonvulsants may induce a vitamin D deficiency resulting in osteomalacia, rickets, or hypocalcemia.[5,15,19,20]

During initial stages of treatment and when taken on an empty stomach, levodopa may cause loss of appetite, nausea, and vomiting in persons with Parkinson's disease.[21] A more therapeutically significant consideration in those clients taking levodopa is related to the interaction between levodopa and pyridoxine (vitamin B_6): pyridoxine may render levodopa ineffective in treating parkinsonism.[21] Additionally, there is evidence to suggest that levodopa therapy may lead to pyridoxine[22,23] and tryptophan[24] depletion. Because of possible adverse nutritional sequelae, monitoring of nutritional status of epileptics and persons with Parkinson's disease is essential.

NUTRITIONAL CONSIDERATIONS IN GERIATRICS

Acute diseases such as influenza, pneumonia, tuberculosis, poliomyelitis, and similar conditions were once leading causes of death.[25,26] Scientific discoveries such as immunization and antibiotics and environmental changes such as hygiene measures and improvements in nutrition have virtually eliminated death due to communicable diseases. Today, chronic disorders such as heart disease, cancer, and stroke represent the leading causes of death for older Americans.[27]

Two important points may be made about chronic diseases. First, symptoms of the disease may not emerge until many years after the onset of the disorder. Second, these diseases, although by definition not curable, are in many cases preventable through maintaining a healthy life style or by changes in the environment.[28] It is reasonable to suggest that nutritional status, as an important indicator of a person's life style, is directly related to the incidence of disease and of the well-being or overall health of a population.[29]

The current emphasis in nutrition for the older American is directed at preventing or decreasing the risk of chronic degenerative diseases and to changes in prevalent social expectations for older adults.[30,31] A comprehensive approach to health promotion should include individual, environmental, societal, and medical changes. Our approach focuses on an examination of the various factors affecting nutrition and their impact on health promotion in adults, particularly the elderly.

Factors Influencing Food Selection

The nutritional patterns of older persons are influenced by physiological, psychological, and social factors in addition to the general food supply. These factors present challenges to older adults living independently, to those caring for an aging parent, to physicians, and to dietitians who are involved in the promotion of health and well-being. Although advancing age does lead to changes in food intake and food preferences, it can be argued that older persons can adapt to such changes.

Taste and Smell

The choice of food is determined to a great extent by the chemical senses of taste and smell. With age, there is a steady decline in the number of frontal taste buds and in acuity of the chemical senses, particularly olfaction.[32] Changes in taste acuity are difficult to document. Confusion exists in part because of the multiple confounding factors that influence taste acuity, such as medication and illness.[33] For example, medications may contribute to loss of taste, nausea, dry mouth, and change in appetite.

Older adults often complain that foods taste bitter and sour. Most foods with bitter tastes have a strong olfactory component in their flavor. Consequently, an age-related decline in olfactory sensitivity might result in diminished capacity to discriminate between taste and smell.

Consequences of Physical Limitations

Impaired mobility, poor vision, or a tremor diminish the older person's ability to shop for and prepare his or her own meals. Poor eyesight can interfere with reading a nutrition label or preparing meals from a recipe or package directions. Physical limitations may result in loss of independence. Consequently, the older adult may become dependent on others for meal preparation or shopping or may rely on prepackaged foods, some of which have less-than-ideal nutritive value.[34,35]

Psychological Aspects of Food Selection

The diet of older adults reflects both traditional patterns and the availability of food items. Preferences are determined by a complex set of factors, including lifelong habits, attitudes, and assumptions about nutrition. Food patterns tend to vary with culture and geographic location.

Taste Preferences

It is widely accepted that older adults tend to prefer those foods familiar to their culture and geographic location.[36-38] For example, participants from congregate meal programs in central Missouri assigned favorable ratings to beef, potatoes, and chicken.[37] Least liked were those food items not readily available in the Midwest, such as pork and fish. A survey conducted in Italy indicated that persons aged 65 and over prefer meat, pasta, and soup.[39]

Ethnic Identity

Culture involves a set of values and customs that encompass a sense of identity. The need to retain some stability in one's sense of self becomes increasingly important in maintaining health and well-being in old age. Consideration of an older adult's ethnic heritage and taste preferences when planning meals proves to be an important contributor in adapting to change.[35-38,40]

Social Aspects of Food Selection

Eating is a social activity. Older adults experiencing changes in income and housing or loss of friends or spouse find their eating patterns change.

Economic Resources

Food choices are dependent on availability and economics. Unfortunately many older persons are living on reduced incomes, making it difficult to purchase food after rent and utilities are paid. It is important for the elderly with low incomes to try to use wisely the food money available, focusing on nutrient-dense foods.[35]

Ethnic elderly living independently and remaining in their neighborhoods often find that the Chinese grocery or Italian deli has been replaced by chain supermarkets that may not provide their favorite food. The specialty stores may have reopened at distant locations requiring transportation. Such constraints may contribute not only to a person's disinterest in food and subsequent changes in nutrient intake but also to a loss of self-esteem.

There is a great need for coordinated planning to provide services for the older population. Community projects to aid in food shopping might include free or inexpensive transportation.[35,40]

Dining Location

Evidence exists that nutrient density for residents of a nursing home may differ as a result of dining location. Welch and co-workers[41] found that the elderly who dine in their rooms consumed more milk than did residents dining in the dining hall, presumably because residents dining in their rooms had less frequent access to other beverages (eg, tea and coffee) and tended to consume food items placed in front of them. Residents eating in the dining hall consumed significantly greater amounts of vitamin E. It was found that nursing home personnel freely spread margarine on residents' bread and the residents appeared to be influenced by the company of others.

Perception of the Future

A person's perception of his or her personal future is a controlling agent in negotiating change in food habits. The need to maintain health becomes very significant when the future is perceived as positive (eg, new grandchildren, retirement). Conversely, perception of the future as negative (eg, cancer, loss of spouse) could result in nonadherence to a proper diet, poor self-esteem, and reduced concern for one's general health.[42]

The population most susceptible to change in behavior includes those persons living alone, those having recently lost a spouse, those with a perception of declining health, and those with low incomes. According to researchers, this population of older adults should be targeted for intervention strategies, such as health education programs.[31,36,43] Nutrition programs should be relative to the older person's special needs: fewer calories in view of reduced activity and metabolism but the same nutritional requirements recommended for younger adults and convenient, inexpensive nutritious meals.[40]

Nutrition Education

Nutrition education should focus on selection of foods that are both easy to prepare and high in nutritional quality. The older population desires foods that are convenient and also healthful. The general qualifications of an ideal food for the elderly are that it must be acceptable and readily available, inexpensive and processed from local ingredients, easy to prepare quickly, appetizing and amenable to easy mastication and digestion, able to be kept well even under poor storage conditions, able to be used in liquid form, and rich in proteins, minerals, essential elements, and calories.[40]

Information on food preferences can be used as a motivator for promoting nutrition education and by personnel in institutions and organizations who plan and prepare menus.[31,44] Nutrition education emphasizing food budgeting and health promotion along with quick and easy food preparation techniques would be most acceptable to the older consumer.

Nutrition education programs have been very successful in promoting health awareness.[45] Peer educators report that slides are most appropriate for holding the attention of the older audiences, whereas handheld charts may present problems for those with arthritic hands.[45] Nutrition quizzes concerning food labels and nutrient content of popular foods can serve as motivation for initiating meal planning sessions.

Dietitians, peer educators, as well as those caring for an aging parent, might dine with the elderly, directing conversations during the meal toward food. General comments made by the elderly about foods can be used to determine prevalent beliefs and attitudes toward nutrition.[46] These factors may be used as motivators for promoting positive behavior change.

NUTRITIONAL CONSIDERATIONS IN BRAIN-DAMAGED CLIENTS

Physiological Factors (See *Note*)

Problems with physical control of the arms, hands, head, and neck may result in feeding difficulties for the head-injured person.[47] For instance,

---

Note: Reprinted with permission from *Network: Dietetics in Physical Medicine and Rehabilitation* (1987;6[2]:1,4), Copyright © 1987, Nutrition and Rehabilitation Practice Group of the American Dietetic Association.

clients with lesions of the motor strip may partially, or completely, lose the use of the contralateral arm and hand, or lesions of the premotor cortex may interfere with the person's ability to perform the necessary sequence of arm, hand, head, and neck movements for self-feeding.[48]

Three other necessary physiological functions for eating are swallowing, sucking, and chewing. Various difficulties that are common in brain-damaged clients interfere with these three vital functions. For example, effective sucking requires breathing through the nose, and since many brain-damaged persons experience difficulty performing this function, sucking is reduced. Another common area of dysfunction is the tongue. Often brain-damaged persons are unable to perform the requisite tongue movements necessary for chewing and swallowing (eg, there may be lateral deviation and/or problems elevating the tongue). Other glossal problems include tongue thrust (a powerful and rhythmic extension of the tongue), retracted (contracted or shortened) tongue, and hypotonia (decrease of normal tonicity of tension).[49]

A hyperactive or hypoactive gag reflex is sometimes present in persons with head injuries. A hyperactive gag reflex may lead to vomiting during feeding and a hypoactive gag reflex may lead to choking. Hence, both conditions may seriously disrupt food consumption.[49] Aspiration pneumonia is a common consequence of a hypoactive gag reflex. Often a client may be able to swallow solid foods but will aspirate liquids. Videofluoroscopy may be indicated in the diagnosis of aspiration and other swallowing problems. Clients who are unable to safely swallow a liquid barium suspension may still be assessed by fluoroscopy, provided the barium suspension is set in gelatin, which many find easier to swallow.

Brain damage may lead to an inability to detect food temperature. Persons who manifest this dysfunction must be taught special techniques (eg, test the food with a thermometer; ask someone else to test it; look for steam) to avoid eating foods that are too hot to be eaten without burning oral tissues.[49]

The skin of brain-damaged persons may become hypersensitive to touch.[50] Aberrant feeding behavior may result when the hypersensitivity is of the facial and/or periodontal area. To avoid pain, these persons may wrap their lips over their teeth, which results in significant difficulty in sucking and chewing.

As a result of the aforementioned physiological difficulties (eg, problems with chewing and swallowing), the ingestion of solid foods may be contraindicated. Hence, solid foods may be pureed or finely chopped and mixed with baby food.[51] Such a monotonous and unappetizing diet may lead to decreased gustatory satisfaction, which may further complicate the existing nutritional problems. This problem might be countered by offering meals with foods of contrasting colors and flavors and by alternating food choices frequently.

The hypothalamus mediates feeding behavior of humans.[48,52] Therefore, hypothalamic lesions may cause aberrant hyperphagia (excessive intake of food) or aphagia (absence of eating).[52] Therefore, persons with hypothalamic lesions may experience profound appetite changes, which may require management through the use of stimulus control (keeping foods out of sight), portion control, and behavioral treatment targeting the deviant eating behavior.

It becomes evident that, owing to physiological problems, eating (a rudimentary behavior taken for granted by most) is potentially an exacting task for the brain-damaged person. The physiological complications are further exacerbated by common neuropsychological sequelae of brain damage (eg, depression, sustaining vigilance and concentration).

Psychological Factors*

Common sequelae of head injury are confusion and distractability.[53] The nature of the typical eating experience may intensify these symptoms. For example, the conventional table setting may be a source of distraction and confusion for the brain-damaged person.[51] That is, a table set with a patterned tablecloth, several eating utensils, and many different foods may overstimulate a brain-damaged person. He or she may begin playing with the utensils, reaching for the foods (overturning objects in the process), and creating chaos. Likewise, the presence of several other persons at the dinner table during meals may also contribute to the confusion. Therefore, it may be necessary to simplify and regulate the eating routine, such as reduce the place setting to essentials (a solid colored tablecloth or place mat set with only the plate and utensils needed for the food to be eaten at that time). Also, if the presence of several people during meals causes confusion, the client may require a quieter eating atmosphere. Furthermore, following a routine mealtime schedule (ie, having meals at the same time and in the same place every day) may help further reduce confusion and distraction.[54] Many head-injured clients experience problems with impulsivity and memory as well. These persons may rush their eating, and

---

*This section is reprinted with permission from *Network: Dietetics in Physical Medicine and Rehabilitation* (1987;6[3]:1–2,4), Copyright © 1987, Nutrition and Rehabilitation Practice Group of the American Dietetic Association.

stuff their mouths so full that they are unable to chew thoroughly or swallow carefully. In particular among clients with swallowing problems, this increases the risk of aspiration. Clients should be reminded to pace themselves slowly and then should be monitored and given ongoing reminders while eating if these problems arise.

Another common aftereffect of brain damage, reported particularly in clients with left hemisphere damage, is depression.[53] A common symptom of depression is an increase or decrease in appetite. Since depression may significantly worsen the aforementioned nutritional problems, treatment (ie, pharmacotherapy, psychotherapy, or a combination) should be considered.[55]

Many clients with neurogenic bladders become quite embarrassed by their frequent incontinence. It is not uncommon for these clients to impose fluid restrictions on themselves in order to manage this; however, this self-imposed treatment is counterproductive, since it leads to constipation, urinary tract infections, and electrolyte imbalances. A better strategy is to have a frank discussion with the client promoting increased fluid consumption along with scheduling more frequent opportunities to use the bathroom as a means to cope with incontinence. In addition, many head-injured young women may have a premorbid history of binge–purge bulimia and will continue to purge after the injury. One such case we encountered was of a client who was still quite confused and obtunded in the rehabilitation hospital and was losing weight on an 1800 calorie per day diet. A staff member or interested friend was instructed to sit with her for an hour after each meal, keeping her distracted with songs, games, and conversation until the immediate sense of fullness (her cue to purge) had passed. She began to regain her normal weight immediately thereafter.

It is feasible that because of the vast number of potential difficulties with eating the person will experience one or more quite aversive experiences associated with eating (eg, vomiting, gagging, choking).[47] Therefore, from a behavioral perspective, a person may become conditioned to avoid food. This is particularly common among clients maintained on chronic gastrostomy feedings. In such cases, it may be necessary for the therapist to employ behavioral techniques to extinguish this avoidance response by pairing food consumption with events and activities that are highly valued by the client, such as trips to a movie theater, to sporting events, or to a popular hamburger stand. Most head-injured clients remain somewhat disinhibited long after their acute rehabilitation. One significant consequence of this is that they often do not know when to stop doing whatever they are doing, whether this is talking, self-stimulation, or eating. In the case of eating, weight gain frequently is the result. It is important that clients not be given the opportunity to take food from others' plates, and their portions should be carefully controlled. Clients who insist on "seconds" should be given even smaller initial portions in order to compensate for this desire. Often it is preferable to keep the serving plates in the kitchen and out of the client's sight. As a part of the structure of mealtime, clients should be expected to sit and eat and not get up until done. Playing with food or leaving the table is a reason to take food away and not offer more until next mealtime. Although somewhat harsh, this helps to shape appropriate behavior.

One must remember, however, that the availability of social rewards (eg, friendships, outings, employment) is restricted for the head-injured client, and thus many turn to food as their primary source of solace and pleasure. Therefore, it is important that caregivers keep in mind the need to substitute alternative opportunities for pleasure and social rewards. Such alternate rewards are important even when food restriction is not an issue.

CONCLUSION

Several special assessment considerations and clinical implications are emphasized. First, because of the drug–nutrient interactions, prudent monitoring of pharmacotherapy with elderly and neurologically impaired clients is critical. As stated, drugs may cause a drastic increase or decrease in appetite. Furthermore, drugs prescribed to treat certain disorders common to elderly and brain-damaged persons may cause nutritional deficiencies. As a result of such drug–nutrient interactions, it is essential that a detailed drug history is included in assessment of these clients.

Second, because nutritional complications may be secondary to certain psychological, social, and/or economic concomitants of old age or brain damage (eg, poverty, seclusion, depression, confusion), assessment of these areas may be helpful in developing a plan for nutritional rehabilitation. Community nutrition services (eg, home-delivered and group meals) offer a solution to these nutritional problems while possibly providing a serendipitous remedy to their cause; that is, they offer participants an opportunity to socialize while receiving nutritional, inexpensive (or gratis) meals.[56] While such services may be generally beneficial to the populations of interest, confused clients may decompensate as a result of the commotion created by group meals or home visits.[57] Once again, the importance of assessment is underscored (ie, appropriateness for such programs should be determined during assessment).

An aim of community nutrition programs is to make meals more enjoyable for the participants, and it has been postulated that favorable nutritional outcomes are enhanced when meals are both enjoyable and consistent with premorbid eating habits.[58] That is, clients are more likely to comply with diets that are tasty, varied, easily prepared or obtained and are similar to foods that they are accustomed to eating. Hence, sociocultural factors should be considered an integral part of nutritional rehabilitation. In addition, ways of decreasing boredom and increasing culinary appeal of meals should be considered, such as food sharing programs in which each participant is responsible for cooking a meal on specified days. Such programs offer variety and minimal inconvenience to any one person while encouraging socialization and engagement. Maximum contrast among tastes and textures is also likely to help decrease nutritional boredom; clients should be encouraged to eat meals that mix sweet and sour, hot and cold, and crisp and soft foods. Also, meals of various colors and/or flavors may decrease monotony in the diets of those who, because of physiological disabilities, are unable to eat solid foods.[59]

An additional factor to consider during assessment is dentition. Intake and enjoyment of meals may decrease as a result of pain caused by poorly fitting dentures, inadequate oral hygiene, or diseases of the mouth.[58] Dentition should be assessed in order to address such dental-related nutritional complications.

The presence of motor deficits (eg, muscle weakness, paralysis, and/or incoordination) that may impede the person's ability to perform the necessary movements for eating should be assessed as well. In such cases, special eating utensils may assist the client in maintaining eating autonomy. For example, special knives, spoons, forks, plates, and drinking devices have been developed toward this end.[11] Assessment of such disabilities and matching the client to the proper device may be of great practical utility.

The assessment of elderly and brain-damaged clients is often an arduous task; nevertheless, it is an essential element of rehabilitation and/or health maintenance. Because of the unique aspects of the populations of interest, a uniform approach using a single method may be inadequate. Therefore, it is strongly recommended that an individualized, multitrait-multimethod approach to assessment be employed.[60] That is, several different methods of assessment should be employed to measure nutritional status and the type of assessments should be determined based on the client's capabilities and limitations. Such an approach would increase construct validity; hence one would be more confident that measurements were reflecting nutritional status, as opposed to other variables. Additionally, assessments should be conducted with the underlying aim of developing effective treatments (ie, nutritional assessments should be treatment valid).[61]

Although there are similarities between elderly and brain-damaged clients, it is imperative that the two populations be viewed as distinct. Subgroups of brain-damaged persons (eg, trauma victims, epileptics, and those with certain neurologic disease) are often in early stages of life and, regardless of age, brain damage is a distinct entity. It is essential that those working with these groups are aware of the unique physiological and psychological demands of each.

REFERENCES

1. Taylor KB, Anthony LE. *Clinical Nutrition.* New York, NY: McGraw-Hill Book Co; 1983.

2. Dwyer JT. Assessment of dietary intake. In: Shils ME, Young VR, eds. *Modern Nutrition in Health and Disease.* 7th ed. Philadelphia, Pa: Lea & Febiger; 1988.

3. Young CM, Trulson MF. Methodology for dietary studies in epidemiological surveys: Strengths and weaknesses of existing methods. *Am J Public Health.* 1960;50:803–814.

4. Nesheim RO. Current methods of assessing food intake. In: Selvey N, White PL, eds. *Nutrition in the 1980s: Constraints on Our Knowledge.* New York, NY: Alan R. Liss, Inc; 1981.

5. Roe DA. *Geriatric Nutrition.* Englewood Cliffs, NJ: Prentice-Hall, Inc; 1987.

6. Chernoff R, Lipschitz DA. Nutrition and aging. In: Shils ME, Young VR, eds. *Modern Nutrition in Health and Disease.* 7th ed. Philadelphia, Pa: Lea & Febiger; 1988.

7. Roe DA. Diet, nutrition and drug reactions. In: Shils ME, Young VR, eds. *Modern Nutrition in Health and Disease.* 7th ed. Philadelphia, Pa: Lea & Febiger; 1988.

8. Twomey PL, St. John JN. The neurologic patient. In: Rombeau JL, Caldwell MD, eds. *Clinical Nutrition: Enteral Nutrition.* Philadelphia, Pa: WB Saunders Co; 1984.

9. Howard RB, Herbold NH. *Nutrition in Clinical Care.* New York, NY: McGraw-Hill Book Co; 1982.

10. Kaplan PE, Cerrullo LJ. *Stroke Rehabilitation.* Boston, Mass: Butterworths Publishing Inc; 1986.

11. Williams SR. *Nutrition and Diet Therapy.* 5th ed. St. Louis, Mo: Times Mirror/Mosby College Publishing; 1985.

12. Gotz BE, Gotz VP. Drugs and the elderly. *Am J Nurs.* 1978;78:1347.

13. Bowman BB, Rosenberg IH. Assessment of the nutritional status of the elderly. *Am J Clin Nutr.* 1982;35:1142–1151.

14. Gupta KL, Dworkin B, Gambert SR. Common nutritional disorders in the elderly: Atypical manifestations. *Geriatrics* 1988;43:87–97.

15. Roe DA. *Drug Induced Nutritional Deficiencies.* Westport, Conn: AVI Publishing; 1976.

16. Banks T, Nayab A. Digitalis cachexia (letter). *N Engl J Med.* 1974;290:746.

17. Hoffman BF, Bigger JT Jr. Cardiovascular drugs. In: Gilman AG, Goodman LS, Rall TW, Murad F, eds. *The Pharmacological Basis of Therapeutics.* 7th ed. New York, NY: Macmillan Publishing Co, Inc; 1985.

18. Barley B. Drugs: Taste killers. *Am Health.* 1984;3(1):22.

19. Dreyfus PM. Nutritional management of neurological disorders. In: Selvey N, White PL, eds. *Nutrition in the 1980s: Constraints on Our Knowledge.* New York, NY: Alan R. Liss, Inc; 1981.

20. Rall TW, Schleifer LS. Drugs effective in the therapy of the epilepsies. In: Gilman AG, Goodman LS, Rall TW, Murad F, eds. *Pharamacological Basis of Therapeutics.* 7th ed. New York; NY: Macmillan Publishing Co, Inc; 1985.

21. Bianchine JR. Drugs for Parkinson's disease, spasticity and acute muscle spasms. In: Gilman AG, Goodman LS, Rall TW, Murad F, eds. *Pharmacological Basis of Therapeutics.* 7th ed. New York, NY: Macmillan Publishing Co, Inc; 1985.

22. Evered DF. L-dopa as a vitamin antagonist. *Lancet* 1971;1:914.

23. Friedman SA. Levodopa and pyridoxine deficient states. *JAMA.* 1970;214:1563.

24. Lehmann J. Levodopa and depression in parkinsonism. *Lancet.* 1971;1:140.

25. Fries JF. Aging, natural death, and the compression of morbidity. *N Engl J Med.* 1980;303:130–135.

26. Ordy JM. Nutrition as modulator of rate of aging, disease, and longevity. In: Ordy JM, Harman D, Alfin-Slater RB, eds. *Nutrition in Gerontology.* New York, NY: Raven Press; 1984;26:1–17.

27. Fredman L, Haynes SG. An epidemiologic profile of the elderly. In Phillips HT, Gaylord SA, eds. *Aging and Public Health.* New York, NY: Springer; 1985.

28. Gaylord SA. Biological aging: Public health implications. In Phillips HT, Gaylord SA, eds. *Aging and Public Health.* New York, NY: Springer; 1985.

29. Barrows CH, Kokkonen GC. Nutrition and aging: Human and animal laboratory studies. In: Ordy JM, Harman D, Alfin-Slater RB, eds. *Nutrition in Gerontology.* New York, NY: Raven Press; 1984;26:279–322.

30. Fries JF, Crapo LM. *Vitality and Aging: Implications of the Rectangular Curve.* San Francisco, Calif: WH Freeman Co; 1981.

31. Sorenson AW, Ford ML. Diet and health for senior citizens: Workshops by the health team. *Gerontologist.* 1981;21:257–262.

32. Fanelli JT, Kaufman M. Nutrition and older adults. In: Phillips HT, Gaylord SA, eds. *Aging and Public Health.* New York, NY: Springer; 1985.

33. Kohrs MB. Effectiveness of nutrition intervention programs for the elderly. In: Hutchinson ML, Munro HN, eds. *Nutrition and Aging.* Orlando, Fla: Academic Press; 1986:139–167.

34. Lipson LG, Bray GA. Energy. In: Chen LH, ed. *Nutritional Aspects of Aging.* Boca Raton, Fla: CRC Press; 1986;1:161–171.

35. Schlenker ED. *Nutrition in Aging.* St. Louis, Mo: Times Mirror/Mosby College Publishing; 1984.

36. Hendricks J, Calasanti TM. Social dimensions of nutrition. In: Chen LH, ed. *Nutritional Aspects of Aging.* Boca Raton, Fla: CRC Press; 1986;1:77–115.

37. Holt V, Nordstrom J, Kohrs MB. Food preferences of older adults. *J Nutr Elderly.* 1987;6:47–55.

38. Schiffman SS, Covey E. Changes in taste and smell with age: Nutritional aspects. In: Ordy JM, Harman D, Alfin-Slater RB, eds. *Nutrition in Gerontology.* New York, NY: Raven Press; 1984;26:43–64.

39. Fidanza AA. Nutritional status of the elderly: Nutritional knowledge, food preferences and life styles connected with the nutritional process. *Int J Vitam Nutr Res.* 1984;54:361–369.

40. Rao DB. Problems of nutrition in the aged. *J Am Geriat Soc.* 1973;21:362–367.

41. Welch PK, Endres JM, Rifkin DM. A comparison of the dietary intake of institutionalized elderly fed in two different settings. *J Nutr Elderly.* 1986;6:17–30.

42. Shifflett PA. Future time perspective, past experience, and negotiation of food use patterns among the aged. *Gerontologist.* 1987;27:611–615.

43. Shifflett PA, McIntosh WA. Food habits and future time: An exploratory study of age-appropriate food habits among the elderly. *Int J Aging Hum Dev.* 1986–1987;24:1–17.

44. Betts NM, Vivian VM. Factors related to the dietary adequacy of noninstitutionalized elderly. *J Nutr Elderly.* 1985;4:3–14.

45. Shannon BM, Smicklas-Wright H, Davis BW, Lewis C. A peer educator approach to nutrition for the elderly. *Gerontologist.* 1983;23:123–126.

46. Betts NM. A method to measure perceptions of food among the elderly. *J Nutr Elderly.* 1985;4:15–21.

47. Caldwell V. *Cerebral Palsy: Advances in Understanding and Care.* New York, NY: North River Press; 1956.

48. Kolb B, Whishaw I. *Fundamentals of Human Neuropsychology.* 2nd ed. New York, NY: WH Freeman & Co; 1985.

49. Farber SD. *Neurorehabilitation: A Multisensory Approach.* Philadelphia, Pa: WB Saunders Co; 1982.

50. Sinclair D. *Cutaneous Sensation.* London, England: Oxford University Press; 1967.

51. Berko FG, Berko MJ, Thompson SC. *Management of Brain Damaged Children.* Springfield, Ill: Charles C Thomas Publisher; 1970.

52. Carlson NR. *Physiology of Behavior.* Boston, Mass: Allyn & Bacon; 1981.

53. Lezak MD. *Neuropsychological Assessment.* 2nd ed. New York, NY: Oxford University Press; 1983.

54. Tobis J, Lowenthal M. *Evaluation and Management of the Brain Damaged Patient.* Springfield, Ill. Charles C Thomas Publisher; 1980.

55. Carson TP, Carson RC. The affective disorders. In: Adams HE, Sutker PB, eds. *Comprehensive Handbook of Psychopathology.* New York, NY: Plenum Press, 1984.

56. Williams JB, Munley A, Evans L. *Aging and Society: An Introduction to Social Gerontology.* New York, NY: Holt, Rinehart & Winston, Inc; 1980.

57. Gouvier WD, Uddo-Crane M. Feeding problems of head injured clients: Psychological factors. *Network Diet Phys Med Rehabil.* 1987;6(3):1–2,4.

58. Cape RDT. Geriatrics. In: Schneider HA, Anderson CE, Coursin DB, eds. *Nutritional Support of Medical Practice.* 2nd ed. Philadelphia, Pa: Harper & Row Publishers, Inc; 1983.

59. Uddo-Crane M, Gouvier WD. Feeding problems of head injured clients: Physiological factors. *Network Diet Phys Med Rehabil.* 1987;6(2):1,4.

60. Campbell DT, Fiske DW. Convergent and discriminant validation by the multitrait-multimethod matrix. *Psychol Bull.* 1959;56:81–105.

61. Nelson RO, Hayes SC. Some current dimensions of behavioral assessment. *Behav Assess.* 1979;1:1–16.

Chapter 11

Aging

Kathleen Wreford

In the 1980s there was a strong emergence of interest in the nutritional needs of the elderly population. Until recently, the elderly has been one of the most neglected groups with respect to investigations of nutritional status and establishment of nutritional requirements. This may have been in part because few people lived beyond 65 years of age in the past. For example, in 1870 only 3% of the population were age 65 or older. Currently about 11% of the population is older than 65 years of age, and it is projected that 20% of the population will be older than age 65 by the year 2030.[1] The elderly is the fastest growing population as a result of a decreased fertility along with a decreased mortality rate. Technical advances leading to better diagnosis and treatment of disease have contributed to longevity. While reaching age 65 in the past was the result of health and social programs, living beyond age 65 is now attributed to medical and surgical intervention such as cardiac surgery, dialysis, and use of hypertensive drugs, which enable the elderly to live longer but with impairments or disabilities.[2]

With increasing life expectancy, more persons are living beyond ages 75, 85, and even 90, some of whom comprise rehabilitation admissions. Whereas one might prejudge the necessity for rehabilitation of an 85-year-old and project disposition to a nursing home, it appears to be the norm rather than the exception for such a client to receive a full schedule of therapy and return to his or her home environment on discharge.

Elderly persons are the greatest consumers of health resources in the United States. They use 40% of acute care hospital days, purchase 25% of all prescription drugs, and consume more than 50% of the federal health care budget.[3]

Demographically, the elderly are heterogeneous. They vary in age, sex, marital status, education, job skills, work experience, social background, living situations, and health.[4] The diversity of the elderly population as well as the chronologic, genetic, physiological, and psychosocial factors that influence the aging process all contribute to a person's rehabilitation potential. Therefore, as each person ages differently under varying circumstances, each will have different needs, capabilities, and expectations.

Medical advances have led to rehabilitative treatment of the disabled elderly persons, who comprise three subgroups: (1) developmentally disabled persons surviving past middle age, (2) adults having suffered trauma at an earlier age (eg, post polio or spinal cord injury), and (3) adults whose disabilities are due to recent trauma (eg, falls or accidents) or diseases that became more prevalent or intense in the eighth stage of life or for whom medical or surgical intervention has been effective but with residual impairment.[2]

It is not unusual to note an elderly client with a primary diagnosis followed by a list of secondary diagnoses that either impact on nutritional status or may be affected by nutritional intervention. Examples include a person with a left cerebrovascular accident (CVA) having a history of hypertension, diabetes, and coronary artery disease or the person with a right hip fracture with chronic obstructive pulmonary disease, anemia, and hypertension.

Eighty-six percent of the elderly have at least one chronic disease. Most common conditions reported by the elderly have been arthritis, impaired hearing or vision or both, diabetes mellitus, chronic heart conditions, or some degree of mental failing. Fifty-six percent of those older than age 75 are limited in activities of daily living owing to chronic conditions.[5]

The difficulty of separating diseases related to aging from those resulting from disuse continues to be a challenge for investigators. Consider those persons whose condition may have been influenced by self-care or lack of it prior to the onset of a disability (life style/habits, ie, stress, smoking, alcohol abuse, misuse of medications, and dietary noncompliance) in conjunction with medical disorders that may have contributed to the disability (diabetes, hypertension, coronary artery disease) excluding noncontrollable factors such as heredity. Hence, care of the disabled elderly person is complex.

Dietitians are faced with the challenge to provide care that addresses the nutritional concerns affected by aging as well as those that are further compounded by disease and disability. Since there is a cumulative effect of these changes, it is important that health care professionals recognize the impact of both disability-related changes and age-related changes.

PHYSIOLOGICAL CHANGES

Before examining age-related factors that may alter nutritional status, it must be noted that such changes are not found equally in all elderly persons. Potential deficits that may be incurred as a result of the aging process (Table 11-1) are as follows: decreased sensory skills (vision, hearing, smell, taste, and touch) result in reduced enjoyment of eating and mealtime; altered digestive function (resulting from dentition, deglutition, stomach, and gastrointestinal disorders) may affect intake, digestion, absorption, and utilization of nutrients; physiological changes (decreases in bone mass, basal metabolic rate, and total body water and increases in adiposity, insulin resistance, and resistance to blood flow in the peripheral vessels) can alter the need for specific nutrients and may require dietary modifications as part of the treatment of the condition; and increased frailty or decreased short-term memory may affect the person's ability to acquire or prepare food.

Fenderson has pointed out the problems of older persons as they live progressively to their limits are essentially the same as those who are disabled earlier in life. Performance and opportunity may be compromised, social stigma may be experienced, physical restoration may be required, coping and communication skills need to be augmented, housing and transportation barriers must be overcome, and often the harsh economic realities of disability and aging must be confronted.[6]

SOCIOECONOMIC FACTORS

Other factors may exist and impact on nutritional status to an even greater extent. The effects of socioeconomic factors such as poverty/reduced income, social isolation, polypharmacy and alcohol abuse; the psychological conditions of depression or cognitive deficits/altered mental status; and disability all have the potential to alter food intake and/or nutrient absorption.

Elderly persons living on a fixed income, in poverty, or having reduced buying power may resort to subtle or even drastic changes in eating habits. Studies have demonstrated that elderly persons with low incomes consume less milk, meats, fruits, and vegetables, resulting in a lower intake of calcium, riboflavin, protein, iron, vitamin A, and vitamin C.

To an already restricted income, adding the expenses of higher medical bills, attendant care, special transportation, equipment, and home modifications as well as the need to allocate monies for medical necessities and household utilities drastically limits the food dollar. Elderly persons may need encouragement to select health-promoting food choices over empty calories, seek food stamps as a right and not a social stigma, and participate in income maintenance programs.

The elderly may also endure social isolation. Needing to feel useful, they may experience loneliness. Fear of dying and anxiety aroused by failing

Table 11-1 Physiological Effects of Aging

Physiological Changes	Implications and Intervention
Decreased visual acuity and peripheral vision Decreased focus or ability to dilate pupil to light changes	May restrict activity (eg, difficulty driving, fear of operating kitchen appliances). Inability to read dials, recipes, labels, prices; increased difficulty in food procurement and preparation. In an institution, provide well-lighted areas and prevent glare, which can aggravate vision; orange, red, and yellow colors are best recognized.
Decreased ability to hear higher-pitched tones	May self-impose restrictions on social activity (eg, eating out, asking store clerks questions). Speak directly to the person; allow for lip reading. Remove background noise as possible. Speak in lower tones at high volume.
Decreased touch sensitivity	Possible clumsy spills and accidents carrying food or during meals. Use textured versus smooth glasses, utensils, etc, which are easier to handle.
Decreased smell or taste sensation, decreased number of taste buds. Increased sour and bitter, with decreased salt and sweet sensations	Foods may lose appeal, have less flavor, or be less appetizing. Motivation to prepare food decreased. May attempt to use more salt or sugar to compensate for loss of taste. Add to this decreased appetite related to illness and effects of medications/depression or "diet" and intake may grow worse. Use alternative herbs and spices, food demonstrations, or special cooking sessions.
Dentition—loss of/missing teeth, ill-fitting dentures, decreased salivation, periodontal disease	Decreased ability to chew or swallow; decreased food appeal; dry mouth; may restrict variety and choose softer, low-fiber, high-calorie choices. Serve moist rather than dry foods, re-educate on improving taste/appearance of food, while avoiding excess calories.
Stomach—parietal cells produce less hydrochloric acid	Slight difficulty digesting food; possible bacterial contamination of gastric juice, known as bacterial overgrowth, requires antibiotic therapy; achlorhydria associated with lack of intrinsic factor may result in pernicious anemia. Use smaller, frequent meals; assess for macrocytic megaloblastic anemia, which may require vitamin B_{12} injections or iron supplements.
Intestine—decreased enzyme excretion, vascular insufficiency, lactose intolerance, decreased gastrointestinal motility	Potential for impaired absorption of calcium, iron, zinc, protein, fat, and fat-soluble vitamins. May have difficulties digesting dietary calcium or protein. Longer transit time may be mistaken for constipation. May have a need for increased protein of 1 g/kg/d versus recommended daily allowance of 0.8 g/kg/d.

Table 11-1 *continued*

Physiological Changes	Implications and Intervention
	Ensure calcium sources via diet or supplement. Encourage adequate fiber and fluids and avoidance of harsh laxatives.
Decreased bone density, loss of calcium from bone in jaw and skeleton	Tooth loss causes difficulty chewing; bone fractures lead to decreased mobility, which hinders procurement and preparation of food.
	Stress calcium in diet as protective, not curative. Caution against excess vitamin D intake; encourage calcium-rich foods in meals; refer for shopping assistance.
Reduced basal metabolic rate, lean body mass, and activity with increased body fat	Decreased calorie needs; vulnerability to obesity. Decreased activity may also result from retirement or chronic illness.
	Stress weight control and prevention of weight gain and avoidance of empty calories.
Insulin resistance with increased adiposity and decreased insulin response to dietary sugar	Decreased tolerance for concentrated sweets/calories; type II diabetes mellitus.
	Offer small, more frequent meals. Modify diet to avoid simple carbohydrates, limit fat and calories, and increase dietary fiber. Help client understand and accept diet rationale and implementation.
Increased resistance to blood flow in peripheral blood vessels	Diagnosis of hypertension, accompanied by sodium restriction and possibly medication.
	Discuss diet modifications, sources of sodium in food and over-the-counter medications, and use of alternative seasonings.
General increases in frailty; poor balance and muscle weakness	Difficulty purchasing and preparing food. Discuss labor-saving techniques. Refer to meal services and shopping assistance.
Loss of short-term memory	Potential for increased kitchen accidents, food poisoning, or skipping meals. Reinforce kitchen safety and proper food handling.

health and faculties can make them vulnerable to charlatans. Thus the food budget may be further sacrificed to purchase high-priced products, such as organic foods and various supplements. Frequent use of medications, both prescribed and available over the counter, create a potential for impaired appetite, decreased absorption or use of nutrients, or increased requirements for nutrients.

Housebound elderly persons have significantly lower intakes than active persons of the same age or those participating in congregate meal settings. Lack of socialization at mealtime or difficulty procuring and preparing food may contribute to apathy toward food preparation, decreased appetite, reliance on junk foods/snacks, seeking food as a comfort with resultant undesired weight gain, and, for some, reliance on alcohol with neglect of food in general.

Alcoholism is an underestimated, underrecognized, and frequently denied condition among elderly persons and has a serious negative effect on nutrient intake and utilization. Physicians and other health care professionals must be more aggressive in identifying and treating alcohol problems of elderly persons. The problem of the closet drinker may come to light if he or she becomes frail or poor and has to ask for help in obtaining alcohol.[7]

PSYCHOLOGICAL CONDITIONS

Depression, whether reactive or endogenous, may appear as symptoms of altered eating habits, anorexia, and weight loss and has been observed generally in the rehabilitation population. The elderly client may experience reactive depression as a result of feelings of rejection by the younger generation or as a sense of loss at the death of friends or of the realization of the effects of a newly acquired disability on his or her life. Endogenous depression is organically based and seen in conditions such as Alzheimer's disease, parkinsonism, closed head injury, central nervous system malignancies, and CVAs. Although drug intervention has been successful in relieving the level of depression, some antidepressants (eg, methylphenidate) have the side effect of appetite suppression, endangering the already anorectic person.[8]

Depression may be misdiagnosed as dementia, since the symptoms are similar. Dementia, a general mental deterioration due to organic or psychological factors, is often associated with organic brain syndrome. Organic brain syndrome denotes a group of disorders associated with loss of mental function due to a known pathology, exclusive of manic-depressive psychosis and other psychiatric illnesses. Alzheimer's disease and senile dementia are also classified under organic brain syndrome. Having various origins, organic brain syndrome may be related to myxedema and uremia, drug-induced encephalopathy, CVAs (related to atherosclerotic brain atrophy), brain cancer, and others. Organic brain syndrome related to nutritional causes are Korsakoff's disease (alcoholic thiamine deficiency); pellagra's psychosis (niacin deficiency); mental changes occurring with pernicious anemia (vitamin B_{12} deficiency); and nutritional dementia (folacin deficiency). In early stages, reversibility of nutrition-related syndromes may be possible, while later success may be diminished due to permanent brain damage.[9]

Conditions that alter mental status can significantly reduce a person's food/nutrient intake by affecting the ability to properly select a balanced diet, procure and prepare food, and safely eat the essential amounts of food, as well as diminishing the desire to eat. Aside from organic brain syndrome and dementia, other cognitive disorders may consist of disorientation, lethargy, and disorders of thought organization and motor planning as well as frank psychosis.[8]

Particularly common in persons with head injury and stroke are problems of orientation and level of consciousness. Confusion may be compounded by changes in the environment, since the person may experience several transfers between home, hospital, rehabilitation unit, or nursing home, in addition to room changes within a health facility.

Mental status may be affected by drug treatment for parkinsonism, hypertension, spasticity, and pain as well as therapy with anticholinergics, antipsychotics, sedatives, and some anticonvulsants. Potentially correctable problems could include electrolyte imbalances, vitamin deficiencies (vitamin C, thiamine, vitamin B_{12}, nicotinic and folic acid), as well as pseudodementia of depression and delirium tremens of alcohol withdrawal if recognized. Urgent medical conditions that alter mental status include serious systemic infections, central nervous system infections, abnormal thyroid function, Cushing's disease, hepatic stupor, uremia, congestive heart failure, and postoperative and post-traumatic psychosis.[8]

COMMON AGE-RELATED DISABILITIES

Disabilities most commonly treated in rehabilitation that impact on nutritional status are visuospatial perceptual deficits, motor disabilities, and dysphasia.

Visuospatial deficits are most common among persons with a right-sided CVA, also known as left hemiplegia. One of the many deficits a person may experience is hemianopsia or field cut. The person experiences a blindness of half field of vision in which he or she sees objects only on the right. In some cases this is accompanied by neglect, in which he or she ignores the weak, affected side. This explains the behavior of a person with a left hemiplegia consuming food only from the right side of the tray who then continues eating when the tray is rotated. The person recognizes what had been previously "hidden" food. Unless the client is made aware of this existing "blind spot" a poor nutrient intake may result. Visuospatial deficits will be discussed further in the section on CVAs.

Loss of mobility may lead to an inadequate intake by hindering the person's ability to access, prepare, and consume foods. Apparent barriers to intact feeding skills include myopathies, neuropathies, arthritis, hemiplegia, and tremors. The use of feeding devices may correct some disorders, but some persons will require assistance with feeding to avert nutrition deficits.

Decreased mobility of the disabled elderly client may further lower his or her energy requirements (already decreased with age), potentially leading to undesired weight gain and even obesity. The inherent medical complications of obesity, particularly hypertension, diabetes, and degenerative joint disease may arise, as well as exacerbation of problems associated with disability, such as arthritic pain. The obese person's primary physical disability may be complicated by hindering mechanical functions such as transfers and ambulation, delaying rehabilitation, and creating unnecessary bodily stresses on caregivers.

Immobility impacts directly on one's nutritional status. The desire to eat may be poor, with accompanying depression, and digestion and elimination may be diminished. Nitrogen and calcium metabolism may be affected. Significant negative nitrogen balance of an extensive amount has been noted after 1 week of immobilization. Intake of at least twice the recommended daily allowance of protein may be required in order to achieve positive nitrogen balance.[10] Excessive calcium withdrawal from bones has been reported to occur in hemiplegics as early as 2 weeks after the onset of a stroke.

Skin integrity may be challenged as pressure sores (decubitus ulcers) can develop on bony structures (ie, heels, toes, ankles, knees, hips, ribs, elbows, or on buttocks from prolonged compression). As a result of excess weight or lack of movement, increased pressure is exerted on areas of skin tissue covering the bone prominences, promoting tissue breakdown.

On the other hand, the person who is underweight has a thinner layer of subcutaneous fat to protect skin in pressure areas, for which an intake adequate in calories and high-quality protein is recommended. Inadequate protein intake or ingestion of poor-quality protein may result in edema, which increases the distance between cells and capillaries, leading to a diminished flow of nutrients and oxygen and removal of waste products. Adequate nutrient intake with emphasis on ingestion of sufficient vitamins A and C and folic acid (required for cell integrity and oxygen transport) is essential.[10]

Bowel and bladder incontinences acquired with some disabilities may affect one's nutritional intake/status. Cognitively oriented persons may reduce consumption of food or beverages to avoid the embarrassment of "accidents," especially during therapies. As a result, adequate hydration or nutritional intake may be at risk.

Brain impairment and disturbances in osmoregulatory mechanisms may render a person unable to respond to thirst, leading to decreased fluid intake. In some CVAs damage in the posterior pituitary area interferes with antidiuretic hormone production, causing excessive water excretion rather than reabsorption by the kidney, which can result in dehydration. Already at risk for inadequate hydration and electrolyte imbalance, when the effects of fever, vomiting, diarrhea, prescription drugs, and other medical conditions are added the person's situation can become precarious.

Dysphagia can inhibit food and fluid intake, posing a risk for inadequate nutrition and hydration. A result of impaired cranial nerve involvement, this swallowing disorder has been noted in 25% to 32% of all clients with CVAs[11] and has been reported in 59% of 240 elderly nursing home residents studied.[12] It may also occur in persons with brain tumors, head injury, and Alzheimer's and Parkinson's disease. Early detection and treatment are important in order to prevent nutritional debilitation, as well as to develop swallowing abilities within the limitations of the physical condition.

The elderly person's disabilities are frequently the result of a disease process. Incidence of cardiovascular disease, arteriosclerosis, hypertension, and vascular lesions of the central nervous system increases rapidly in the elderly population. Risks for CVAs increase in cases of arteriosclerosis or hypertension.[10,13]

Complications of diabetes mellitus, such as peripheral neuropathy, compromised skin integrity and infections (gangrene), and cardiovascular risks leading to peripheral vascular disease may result in disabilities of lower extremity amputation, paresis, or paralysis. The client may require strengthening skills following hip fractures or total hip replacements or may need treatment for the debilitating effects of arthritis. These conditions are frequently accompanied by various medical diagnoses that require nutrition intervention.

CEREBROVASCULAR ACCIDENTS

CVAs or strokes occur most frequently in persons between the ages of 50 to 80 years, with a rate two to three times higher in the 65-plus age group. The result of sudden alterations in blood supply to an area of the brain, CVAs produce a loss of central nervous system function in which motor control, sensation, and cognition may be markedly affected. Two major mechanisms by which CVAs occur are occlusion and hemorrhage.

Occlusive strokes are caused by an obstruction of a cerebral blood vessel due to thrombosis or embolism. A thrombus is a blood clot (consisting of platelets and fibrin) that occludes the cerebral blood vessel at the site of formation. While arteriosclerosis is reported to be one of the most common causes of thrombosis, additional risk factors include hypertension, diabetes, hyperlipidemia, obesity, and cigarette smoking.

An embolus is a formed clot. Risk factors consist of cardiac valvular disease, cardiac arrhythmia, and atherosclerotic plaque in the large vessels of the neck, particularly the internal carotid artery.

A hemorrhagic stroke is a blood vessel rupture that bleeds into surrounding brain tissue or the subarachnoid space. Hypertension is a major risk factor for this most serious form of stroke. Damage frequently occurs in the gray matter of the cerebral hemisphere known as the basal ganglia. Should a rupture occur in the brain stem or cerebellum the fatality risk increases.

The effects of stroke and subsequent recovery may vary depending on the area of the brain injured and degree of injury. However, similarities can exist regardless of the brain site affected. Persons may experience (1) weakness or paralysis on the side of the body opposite the lesion, most often referred to as hemiplegia; (2) possible blindness on the opposite outer halves of the visual fields of both eyes (homonymous hemianopsia); (3) some memory loss; (4) a slower ability to perform tasks; (5) fatigue more easily than before the stroke; (6) emotional lability (uncontrolled, but inappropriate, crying or laughter); and (7) depression, which has been documented in 30% to 50% of stroke survivors.[14] The changes may result in a decreased appetite, a loss of interest in eating, an inability to self-feed, or a longer mealtime, which if left unrecognized could lead to a deterioration of nutritional status.

Some persons may experience perseveration, the tendency to use an involuntary verbal or motor response that persists inappropriately. This can impede one's ability to extract information (eg, diet history, food preferences). Use of simple verbal commands and changing the subject can be helpful.

Incontinence of bowel and bladder may also be a concern. Treatment may consist of a bowel and/or bladder program and use of anticholinergics. Those clients whose bladder incontinence has been related to spasticity have responded well to tranquilizers (eg, dantrolene and baclofen).

Despite similarities of the effects of stroke, classic differences between the effects of right and left CVAs exist. While the right hemisphere of the brain controls spatial and visual perceptions, creativity, and nonverbal memory, the left hemisphere is usually responsible for speech, analytical capabilities, and verbal and auditory memory.[15] Each hemisphere consists of four lobes that are responsible for specific functions (Figure 11-1). An understanding of both the similar and different traits of stroke may be of

BRAIN FUNCTION AND STROKE EFFECTS

Frontal Lobe

Controls voluntary movements.
Houses motor area for speech,
known as Broca's area.
Impulses travel through spinal
cord to direct movement on the
opposite side of the body.
Anterior portion of lobe controls
emotional behavior and complex
intellectual abilities.

Parietal Lobe

Receives and interprets sensory
impulses from skin, muscles,
joints, and tendons on opposite
side of the body. Sensations processed: pain, heat, cold, pressure,
recognition of size, shape, and texture
of objects; location and
intensity of stimuli; awareness of
body parts.

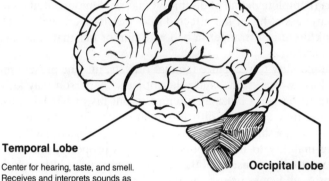

Temporal Lobe

Center for hearing, taste, and smell.
Receives and interprets sounds as
words.
Right handed - left temporal lobe is
            dominant,
Left handed - right temporal lobe is
            dominant (for speech
            interpretation)

Occipital Lobe

Receives and interprets visual stimuli.

In addition to side or hemisphere, site of stroke influences injury.

Site of Injury	Potential Effects on Function
Anterior Cerebral Artery	Contralateral hemiperesis: leg affected more than arm. No sensory loss, face unaffected.
Middle Cerebral Artery	Contralateral hemiparesis: arm affected more than leg. Sensory loss and facial involvement common; if dominant hemisphere—dysarthria, visual defects, and speech problems.
Posterior Cerebral Artery	Defective vision without sensory or motor impairment. Variable clinical symptoms if posterior circulation or vertibrobasilar arteries are involved, Common dysphagia, and severe dysarthria; hemi- or quadraparesis.

Figure 11-1 Brain function and stroke effects.

assistance in interacting more effectively with the person with a CVA in order to provide adequate nutritional care.

The person with a right-sided CVA has left hemiplegia. Spatial relations and perception are affected, and the person with left hemiplegia can have altered interpretations of sensory input. Deviations in spatial relations may be seen as overreaching the water glass and knocking it over; being unable to differentiate objects such as an orange versus a ball; or being unable to distinguish top from bottom, horizontal from vertical, or front from back. The environment may also appear tilted, which could affect balance during ambulation and transfer attempts.

Anosognosia (complete denial of disability) may be demonstrated by the person's unawareness of his or her affected side, or left-sided neglect. The client may think there is a stranger in bed with him or her that is actually his or her weaker half.

Agnosia, the inability to recognize familiar objects, may be present and can include colors, words, faces, and other objects. A person may know that clothes are to be worn but may attempt to put his or her leg into a sleeve. He or she may also have difficulty identifying pieces as part of a whole (eg, buttons on a shirt, pictures as part of a book, words on a menu).

Apraxia, the inability to use an object or words properly, may exist. The person may attempt to use a toothbrush as a hairbrush. Although the client can identify and state its use, he or she must still learn how to use it. This can mean retraining in the use of eating utensils.

The person with a right-sided CVA may be more impulsive and impatient, possibly foreswearing safety (attempts to leave bed or rise from wheelchair without much-needed assistance) and may be more difficult to teach. Verbal communication may be preferred, which should be simple, concrete, direct, and repetitious.

The person with a left-sided CVA has right hemiplegia and may experience right hemianopsia. This client may experience a great deal of anxiety, disorganization, and depression from excessive sensitivity to his or her many deficits but may also be more cautious and teachable. The right hemiplegic is more prone to impairments that affect communication, particularly aphasia. Three types of aphasia are common: (1) receptive or fluent, (2) expressive, and (3) global.

Receptive or fluent aphasia, caused by lesions in Wernicke's area of the temporal lobe, is a difficulty in interpreting speech, leaving the person unable to understand most of what is said to him or her (almost like listening to a foreign language). In turn, the patient's rapid speech, which for the most part does not make sense, appears to be foreign to the listener. The person, however, believes he or she is making perfect sense. Frustration results for both the client and the listener. Furthermore, the client cannot interpret or correct his or her own words or choices and develops a "word salad" combining bits of different words into one word or stringing phrases into uncomprehensible sentences, known as fluent aphasia.

Some strategies to improve communication with this client are to use simple words, common phrases, or short sentences; demonstrate and gesture while talking; write out instructions; and, most important, allow adequate time for the person to express himself or herself.

Expressive aphasia is caused by lesions in Broca's area located near the motor speech segment in the frontal lobe. The person with expressive aphasia is unable to say words he or she is thinking; speech tends to be choppy and telegraphic. Since speech perception is unaffected the person realizes his or her speech does not always make sense.

These persons respond best to questions requiring yes and no answers. Close-ended questions are asked to verify the client's understanding. Occasionally an open-ended question allows the person to practice speaking intelligibly.

Extensive lesions lead to global aphasia (a combination of receptive and expressive aphasia), which is the most severe and frustrating for the client and health care professional. Use of gestures and pointing may help as well as redundant wording. Patience is of utmost importance along with persistence.

The dominant auditory association/speech center area in the brain is generally located opposite the person's dominant hand. Therefore, while a right-handed person with a left-sided CVA experiences a communication disorder, the left-handed person with a left-sided CVA may not. Awareness of the person's dominant side and location of the CVA are clues to some effects the person may exhibit.

Dysarthria is related to weakness, paralysis, or incoordination of one or more muscles used to speak and can occur without aphasia. While speech is usually intelligible it may be slurred, monotone, high pitch, and of a hoarse, breathy voice quality. Dysarthria can be severe and language unintelligible, however, if the lesion occurs below the cerebral cortex (mid brain or mid brain stem). This person is more likely to have chewing and swallowing disorders. Symptoms that may interfere with eating abilities are weakness or paralysis of facial muscles, decreased or absent gag reflex, and inability to clear salivary secretions.

Dysphagia has been common in bilateral or brain stem CVAs but not entirely limited to this group. In the past this condition may have gone undetected as "silent aspirators" went unnoticed. Persons lacking a gag reflex appeared to swallow with no difficulty but actually particles of food trickled into the lungs. This circumstance creates the potential for aspiration pneumonia, which can be a fatal complication. The mechanisms, diagnosis, and treatment of dysphagia are reviewed in Chapter 7.

For all persons with a CVA who are able to eat, a major nutrition goal is to provide meals of an appropriate consistency that honor individual preferences as much as possible and meet nutritional requirements. Interviewing the client or caregiver (should communication/orientation hinder the process) for pertinent dietary information and routine follow-up is essential in achieving satisfaction and reaching goals.

Adequate nutrition, especially calories, protein, and fluid, is vital. Although CVAs have not been categorized among hypermetabolic conditions, it has been suggested that persons with a stroke may be as or more catabolic than persons undergoing elective abdominal surgery, such as a vagotomy or cholecystectomy. A "rule of thumb" proposes that persons with a stroke receive a minimum of 2000 calories per day beginning at least 72 hours following infarction.[16] However, further research is warranted.

Since actual protein and calorie requirements have not been established for the elderly person with a CVA, use of weekly weights may be beneficial in assessing and adjusting calorie recommendations. In practice, a 7% reduction in calculated basal metabolic rate (based on Dietrich's work with immobilized subjects)[10,17] has been a general guideline for estimation of the disabled person's energy needs, to which additional metabolic factors may be applied. While promoting adequacy of caloric requirements, prevention of undesired weight gain must be considered.

Careful attention to nutritional monitoring is imperative, including assessing the person's intake via daily nutrient intake records and/or meal observations. Fluid status via electrolyte indices, nursing intake and output records, and weights are barometers to the adequacy of the person's hydration.

Following stroke, nutrition intervention must also address those medical conditions (and predisposing risk factors) that may improve through diet modifications. Hypertension, diabetes mellitus, hyperlipidemia, and obesity may require care to prevent complications. Clients referred to major rehabilitation centers are now more complex, having dominant, rather than nondominant, coronary artery disease, renal disease, and severe diabetes mellitus.[18]

Along with nutritional support and intervention efforts, education of the client and/or family on these modifications is necessary in order to promote balance of these medical conditions and overall health. Since research has not yet demonstrated the degree of success dietary intervention plays in averting the recurrence of strokes, the dietitian's greatest impact may be on stroke prevention, altogether.

Efforts to prevent stroke remain controversial, and they range from conservative to aggressive. The aging process has been linked with rising plasma triglycerides, total cholesterol, and high-density lipoprotein-cholesterol (HDL-C) levels. Although high plasma cholesterol and low HDL-C concentrations are coronary artery disease risk factors for the elderly, they are not as significant as for younger subjects. Therefore the question arises whether improvement of serum lipids can actually prevent progression of atherosclerosis or cause its regression in the elderly population.

Kasim suggests that the current research data are inconclusive and that a common sense approach be taken. More attention should be given to appropriate diet for all older persons as well as evaluation of medication associated with hypercholesterolemia (eg, antihypertensives and antianginal drugs such as thiazides and β-blockers).[19]

More aggressively, Smith and co-workers cite evidence suggesting that hypercholesterolemia should be treated in elderly persons and propose that cholesterol reductions are likely to have the same positive effects on health in both old and young. Their conclusions are based on the results of several research projects: the Framingham Study and follow-up studies of 20 and 28 years later, the Cooperative Pooling Project, and the Lipid Research Clinics Prevalence Study.

The general consensus of these projects has been that total cholesterol is a significant predictive factor for coronary heart disease. Measures of blood cholesterol are recommended for use as a screening tool. For persons with screening values above 200 mg/dL, having a family history of premature cardiovascular disease or with other cardiovascular risk factors (uncontrolled hypertension or diabetes, obesity, physical inactivity, or smoking), a 12-hour fasting blood sample is drawn for a lipid profile to further evaluate. Framingham has demonstrated the low density lipoprotein/high density lipoprotein (LDL/HDL) ratio to be the best predictive measure for risk of coronary heart disease in those 50 to 80 years of age. An LDL/HDL ratio of 3.0 and LDL cholesterol value of less than 150 mg/dL are recommended for prevention of coronary heart disease.[20]

Smith and co-workers recommend the following dietary prescription:

- Weight loss goals that will help determine daily caloric level
- Percentages of caloric intake: 15% protein, 30% fat, and 55% carbohydrate as advocated by the Phase I American Heart Association diet
- Saturated fat restricted to no greater than 10%
- Sodium restriction, if indicated

- Meal and carbohydrate spacing for the person with glucose intolerance or diabetes

Should regular follow-ups demonstrate poor results, drug therapy may be initiated.[21]

Although lipid restrictions among the elderly in treatment of coronary heart disease remain debatable, reduced calorie and fat intake to avoid obesity is advocated, as well as recommendations to stop smoking. Cholesterol restrictions have been advised for the management of elderly persons with diabetes mellitus.[22]

PARKINSON'S DISEASE

Another neurologic disorder seen in aging persons is Parkinson's disease. Most persons are not admitted to a rehabilitation facility specifically for the treatment of Parkinson's disease but rather for other debilitating conditions related to or possibly independent of the disease. The incidence of this disorder is 130 per 100,000, and the mean age at onset is 60. Parkinson's disease is a degenerative condition of the basal ganglia of the brain in which insufficient amounts of the neurotransmitter dopamine are produced. Symptoms consist of bradykinesia (slowness of movement), tremors, rigidity, loss of facial expression, and abnormalities of the autonomic nervous system. Potential nutritional consequences may include difficult chewing, dysphagia, drooling, chronic constipation, and weight loss.

The drug treatment of choice, a combination of levodopa and a decarboxylase inhibitor, has potential side effects of nausea and vomiting. For this reason, drug prescription is generally delayed until symptoms of Parkinson's disease have progressed beyond the mild stage.

Dietary influences on the effectiveness of this particular drug treatment have been investigated in recent years. Drug therapy consists of two mechanisms: (1) Levodopa crosses the blood–brain barrier to convert to dopamine and (2) the decarboxylase prevents intestinal breakdown of the levodopa during digestion, thus promoting use of levodopa in smaller dosages. Studies of users responding poorly to levodopa have concluded that large amounts of neutral amino acids in the diet may compete with the levodopa for intestinal absorption and passage through the blood–brain barrier, resulting in lowered drug effectiveness and exacerbation of symptoms. On this basis, use of a low protein diet during the day, followed by an evening meal that provides at least the recommended daily allowance for protein, has been prescribed. Such diet manipulation has been reported to improve daytime mobility and reduce drug dosage in many of the persons evaluated.[23-25] Critics of these studies argue the following:

1. Research should have been performed as a double-blind design to account for influential emotional factors that can affect severity of disease symptoms.
2. Seventy-five to 80% of those with Parkinson's disease respond to levodopa treatment without diet intervention; therefore the majority was not represented.
3. The reports and diets used may have exaggerated potential drug–nutrient interactions of levodopa. Large amounts of pyridoxine have been known to interfere with levodopa action; however, the accompanying decarboxylase should negate the effects of pyridoxine.

Further research is needed, and it is suggested that practitioners exercise caution in manipulating the protein content of the diet. Should a lower protein diet prove beneficial, adequacy of all other nutrients must be ensured.[26]

MUSCULOSKELETAL DISEASE

Musculoskeletal disease and injuries commonly seen in elderly persons develop at various stages of life but may be more disabling with age. By themselves, most skeletal problems are likely to be accepted, but when they are combined with vision and hearing deficits that impede activities such as reading, watching television, or writing, they tend to become disabling.[27]

The musculoskeletal system consists of four structures: bone, ligaments, joints, and muscles. Although the aging process has been popularly accepted as the cause for changes in these structures, genetic and acquired factors determine the location of the disease process, occurrence, severity, and complications.

Diseases that usually develop early in life but may be seen as major causes of disability in the elderly include polymyositis, progressive systemic sclerosis, rheumatoid arthritis, ankylosing spondylitis, psoriatic arthropathy, and alveolar bone loss with periodontal disease.[28] Those occurring in middle to later life include osteoarthritis, pseudogout, osteoporosis, Paget's disease, infectious arthritis, and rheumatic polymyalgia.[29] It is important to recognize the debilitating effect of these diseases, which may impact on one's ability to maintain adequate nutritional status.

Osteoporosis has been defined as an "age-related disorder characterized by decreased bone mass and increased susceptibility to fractures in the absence of other recognizable causes of bone loss," which affects an estimated 15 to 20 million persons. Five million spontaneous fractures result in the United States annually. Related bone disorders of a major concern are spinal compression fractures occurring in 25% of women of 60 years of age or older; hip fractures occurring in 30% of women after age 65, and concomitant alveolar bone loss of the mandible occurring in persons age 45 years or older that leads to periodontal disease and significant tooth loss in later years,[30] potentially contributing to a decreased intake of food. Additionally, vertebral compression fractures result in a loss of height; changes in chest configuration may impair breathing; and changes in torso configuration may cause displacement of organs or intestinal distention. Death-related respiratory complications from bed rest and hospitalization occur in 12% to 20% of persons with hip fractures.[31]

Decline in cortical bone mass begins at age 35 and somewhat earlier for trabecular bone. The rate of loss is greater for females than males and is partially accelerated by the menopause. Paradoxically, the rate of loss appears to diminish after the age of 70. Other risk factors, in addition to age and sex, are sedentary life style/immobilization, small bone mass, fair skin, lactose intolerance, smoking, dieting in general, and treatment with anticonvulsants or corticosteroids.

Unfortunately, osteoporosis is not usually diagnosed until it is too late and there is no effective treatment. Therefore prevention is the goal.

Treatment of osteoporosis is under investigation, including means of determining an earlier diagnosis, using various pharmacologic applications and methods of reducing bone loss or replacing bone. Research into approaches for maintaining satisfactory calcium balance in order to prevent further bone loss in the person with osteoporosis includes increasing dietary calcium, use of calcium supplements, and estrogen replacement with or without additional calcium.

Riis and colleagues found estrogen replacement therapy alone to be effective in preventing both trabecular and cortical bone loss in postmenopausal women.[32] On the other hand, in a study of elderly women, Albenese demonstrated, via use of radiodensitometric measurements, that provision of dietary and supplemental calcium helped reduce bone loss. This suggested that following a previously low intake of dairy products, calcium supplementation may slow or even reverse bone loss without estrogen replacement.[30]

Evaluating clients for contributing risk factors as well as extreme dietary imbalances that affect calcium, such as high intakes of protein, phosphorus, oxalates, and phytates, may be beneficial. Certain diseases, surgical procedures, and drugs may be associated with the development of osteoporosis in as many as 20% to 40% of persons with hip fractures.[33]

High doses and prolonged use of adrenal corticosteroids, used in treatment of arthritis, inflammatory bowel disease, asthma, cancer, and other conditions, can increase bone destruction and suppress bone formation and may increase hypercalciuria. Drugs affecting calcium and vitamin D metabolism include isoniazid, heparin, aluminum-containing antacids, and anticonvulsants. Diseases that can cause disturbances in calcium balance include hyperthyroidism, disorders of the intestinal mucosa, and hyperparathyroidism.[34,35] Cancer of the prostate and Paget's disease have been linked to bone loss. Nutrition intervention plays a critical role in many of these situations. Provision of a daily calcium supplement can prevent development of "steroid osteoporosis" in persons receiving long-term treatment with glucocorticoid drugs.[36]

Current data suggest that once osteoporosis is evident, no known treatments, therapies, or supplements can reverse the condition, although estrogen therapy along with calcium supplementation may arrest its progress. Recommended treatment for postmenopausal women with osteoporosis includes increasing physical activity, ingestion of 1500 mg of calcium per day, and use of estrogen replacement therapy. Although estrogen replacement therapy has been shown to cease postmenopausal bone loss for as long as treatment exists, the resumption of menses and fear of cancer may discourage women from using it.[37] Since not all women experience osteoporotic fractures, an increase in calcium intake and physical activity may be adequate. Clients should be encouraged to seek medical advice and should be informed of the uncertainty of these recommendations. Promoting the consumption of a well-balanced diet, adequate in all nutrients including calcium, and physical activity within the limitations of the client's disability is a reasonable target.

Additionally, persons should be advised that other factors, such as home environment, poor vision, balance, or coordination, as well as the use of tranquilizers, all influence the tendency to fall, thus contributing to fracture risk.[38] Awareness of medical conditions that increase the potential of a fall is important, such as ischemic heart disease, cerebrovascular disease, uncontrolled diabetes mellitus, parkinsonism, and spinal stenosis. Installation of safety equipment, such as grab bars and hand rails, wearing sturdy shoes, and removal of throw rugs, are just a few practices the elderly may employ to lessen their risk of falling.

Unlike osteoporosis (loss of bone mass), osteomalacia is characterized by defects in bone mineralization and has generally been thought of as an uncommon adult disease. Bone mineralization is dependent on availability of calcium, phosphorus, and vitamin D. Causes of osteomalacia include inadequate dietary intake of vitamin D combined with absence of sunlight; intestinal disorders that alter absorption (total gastrectomy, sprue); abnormalities of urinary excretion (chronic renal disease, congenital abnormalities); and certain drugs (phenytoin). Osteomalacia is a reversible disease that can be treated by supplying adequate dietary intakes of calcium, phosphorus, and vitamin D.

Once a fracture is repaired or total hip replacement performed, the person begins therapy to regain strength and develop compensatory skills in daily function and ambulation. The person also is to avoid falls. Specific dietary goals include the following:

- Providing adequate calories and protein required for the increased metabolic demands of healing from fractures/surgery and the increased needs of therapy activity
- Examining the client's home eating habits, rehabilitation intake, and laboratory test results for potential nutritional risks and implementing means of repletion
- Addressing dietary modifications that aid in control of accompanying medical conditions (eg, diabetes, hypertension) that, if uncontrolled, can exacerbate other problems or delay healing
- Preventing excess weight imbalance (severe loss or gains) that may hinder the person's ability to ambulate or aggravate other medical conditions
- Educating the person or caregiver about the appropriate dietary modifications required to maintain control of medical conditions and promote general health while in house and after discharge

These principles also apply to dietary treatment of the amputee. However, in the case of an amputation, greater emphasis may be placed on achieving control of related medical conditions, since previously poor compliance in controlling these may have been a contributing factor to the development of the need for an amputation. Dietary intervention, along with other medical treatment of such conditions, aim at preventing further medical complications of the disease process (eg, additional amputations) related to infections, neuropathy, or muscle weakness (see Appendix C).

Obesity has been related to the development of many diseases, including maturity-onset diabetes, essential hypertension, and hypertensive heart disease. Its impact on reduced mobility of the disabled person and as a compounding factor on other disabilities has been discussed earlier. Although attempts to reduce weight have been met with limited success, best results have been achieved through the combined application of diet, exercise, and behavior modification. The support of caregivers has been beneficial in accomplishing results. So, too, success may be seen in newly diagnosed elderly persons with diabetes or cardiac disease with potentially life-threatening situations who may be more motivated to adhere to recommendations.

Cardiovascular disesases among the elderly include congestive heart failure, atherosclerotic heart disease, hypertensive heart disease, and peripheral vascular disease (related to diabetes or atherosclerosis).

Indications for sodium restrictions in the elderly are prevention and treatment of congestive heart failure and management of essential hypertension.[22,39] Depending on the severity of the ailment, varying degrees of sodium restrictions may be prescribed. Use of low sodium, low potassium seasonings (blends of herbs and spices) may be routinely offered to increase palatability, instead of a salt substitute, in order to avert the potential consequences of excess potassium on the aging kidney and heart.

The elderly most commonly experience diabetes as maturity-onset, Type II related to obesity and declining glucose tolerance associated with aging.[40] Type II diabetes may also be concomitantly linked with type IV hyperlipoproteinemia. Serious complications of uncontrolled diabetes include neuropathies, cutaneous infections, peripheral vascular disease, coronary artery disease, and retinal changes, as well as gastrointestinal stasis and malabsorption, many of which lead to disabling conditions. Therefore, diabetes control is essential to maintain status of the client's current condition and to avert further complications.

Goals for treatment of diabetes in the older person include provision of optimum nutrition for the aging process needs, achievement of appropriate blood glucose and lipid levels, and maintenance of a reasonable weight. Small weight losses of 13 to 24 pounds have resulted in improvement of glucose intolerance.[41]

Constipation among the elderly person may be the result of various causes: poor dentition, inadequate food intake, a previously low fiber intake, a low fluid intake, immobility, decreased intestinal muscle tone, failure to act on urges to defecate, laxative abuse, ingestion of constipating drugs, and bowel obstruction. Once obstruction is medically ruled out and causes of constipation are determined, dietary interventions to induce bowel regularity may be initiated, which consist of ingestion of a hot breakfast or a hot beverage the same time each morning, followed by a visit to the bathroom shortly thereafter; use of a moderately high fiber diet, being gradually implemented to avoid side effects (flatulence, abdominal bloating, or loose stools); and provision of adequate fluids.

Diverticulosis and diverticulitis are disorders of aging.[42] Conditions that aggravate diverticular disease such as constipation, diarrhea, and irregular defecation can be avoided by provision of a moderately high fiber diet, excluding lignin sources.

Gluten-sensitive enteropathy, celiac sprue syndrome, though usually occurring in younger persons, has been known to develop in persons of later years, especially women. Although typical symptoms consist of weight loss, diarrhea, steatorrhea, and indications of multiple nutritional deficiencies, clinical signs may vary. Once diagnosed, implementation of a gluten-free diet results in substantial improvement. Additionally, some persons may experience lactose intolerance during the period in which the disease is active and a lactose restriction may be necessary to prevent the occurrence of fermentative diarrhea. As recovery increases, lactose tolerance may gradually return. Common nutritional deficiencies found in cases of celiac sprue are folacin and vitamin D, and other problems may be observed.[22,43]

NUTRITION ASSESSMENT

The incidence of malnutrition among the rehabilitation population as well as the impact of nutritional support has been well documented through the studies of Newmark and co-workers. These researchers quantified possible explanations for the high occurrence of protein–calorie malnutrition on a rehabilitation unit to include chronic disease processes (eg, degenerative neurologic disease, chronic obstructive pulmonary disease); failure to recognize increased calorie and protein requirements of persons with kwashiorkor who are obese, including diabetics and nondiabetics; recent acute catabolic processes (eg, infections, bone fractures); depression causing poor dietary intake; and chewing and/or swallowing difficulties or inability to manage feeding oneself, resulting in poor intake.[44] All of these apply to the disabled elderly client.

The significance of nutrition in the incidence of disease related to morbidity and mortality has long been recognized. Nutritional status is a major component in the success of a person's response to medical treatment, trauma, and stress. Recently, Glenn and co-workers attempted to correlate nutritional parameters, particularly serum albumin and total lymphocyte count to outcome of rehabilitation. Although they could not directly link nutritional status to a person's strength and ability to perform, serum albumin levels were found to predict increased risk of time lost from therapy due to medical complications.[45] In the rehabilitation setting, time lost from therapy affects reimbursement dollars for services. One would speculate that poor nutritional status affects the person's rehabilitation potential.

Determining nutritional status of the disabled elderly client may represent a challenge. Many parameters (anthropometric, biochemical, he-

matologic, immunologic, and nutritional) used to determine nutrition status
do not have normal ranges for older persons or age-adjusted standards.[3,46]
Additionally, national nutrition standards for specific disabilities have not
been established. Although a complete nutritional profile may be ideal,
this can be burdensome and costly and may not be practical for many
rehabilitation units. In the era of limited medical dollars and decreased
staff, parameters used to identify persons at nutritional risk must be
realistic.

A simplified screening tool recommended by Roubenoff and associates
served to identify every malnourished client within their medical service.
Assessing weight loss, serum albumin, and total lymphocyte count and
identifying the presence of anorexia, dysphagia, or diarrhea led to identification of those persons requiring nutritional assessment and support.[47]

The initial evaluation should include the following:

1. Admission height and weight, usual weight, premorbid weight
   (if recently ill), recent weight changes, and duration of their
   occurrence
2. Current diet
3. Primary and secondary diagnoses
4. Laboratory indices: serum albumin, hemoglobin, hematocrit,
   total lymphocyte count, and electrolytes, as well as those appropriate to specific medical conditions
5. Prescribed medications
6. Physical and cognitive factors that may affect nutrient intake/
   nutritional status or education process: hearing, vision, men-
   tation/orientation, mobility, particularly the ability to chew,
   swallow, or self-feed
7. Existence of gastrointestinal problems that may be of nutritional concern: appetite, nausea, vomiting, flatulence, diarrhea, constipation, dehydration, and food allergies

The medical record, particularly physician admission notes, laboratory
reports, and nursing data base are an efficient means of obtaining most of
the above information. Records from the transferring facility provide supplemental data on factors that may have previously influenced the person's
nutritional status, such as medical complications or surgery; orders to give
nothing by mouth related to tests, intubation, or nausea; administration
of enteral or intravenous feedings that may have not been adequate; or
an unrecognized need for feeding assistance at the onset of a disability. In
short, those events that existed prior to the person's admission to the
rehabilitation setting pose an ongoing nutritional concern. Previously doc-

umented nutrition parameters also serve as a base of comparison with those found during rehabilitation.

An interview of the client and/or caregiver can verify collected information as well as elaborate on additional details, such as nutrition history and degree of past dietary compliance, food preferences, frequency of alcohol intake, and use of over-the-counter medications, as well as examination of psychosocial and economic factors that impact on nutritional status.

Obtaining a food intake record (usually for three consecutive days) and monitoring of intake and output records help to objectively define the adequacy of nutritional intake and hydration status. Food intake diaries may also call the staff's attention to the need for assistance or encouragement to eat.

Anthropometric measures, particularly height and weight, are readily accessible. Height can be a constant for determination of appropriate weight. Difficulties in estimation of height due to a client's inability to stand erect or unaided can be overcome by use of recumbent height or knee–heel height estimations.

With the disabled elderly, ideal body weight is not a goal but rather a guide. Weighing should be performed routinely and followed over time to assess weight changes as muscle or fat changes versus shifts in fluid compartments. Routine monitoring provides feedback regarding the appropriateness of the calorie level so adjustments can be made accordingly to achieve desired weight loss/gain.

Triceps skin fold and mid arm muscle circumference measurements are performed serially to demonstrate the effects of therapy in the client. The aging process contributes to changes in body composition, in particular decreased muscle mass, increased fat, and changes in skin compressibility and elasticity, which in addition to lack of age-adjusted standards may affect their reliability.

Many biochemical parameters are affected by an age-related decline in renal function, shifts in fluid balance, drug–drug or drug–nutrient interaction, or the long-term effects of chronic or multiple diseases.[3] When the impacts of these are considered, use of parameters such as albumin, transferrin, hemoglobin, and hematocrit are still practical components of nutrition assessment in the elderly.

Along with the chronic diseases that accompany aging, elderly persons demonstrate an increased use of medications, both prescription and over the counter. While single or multiple medications may be prescribed for one chronic condition, the occurrence of several illnesses in one person increases the number of drugs prescribed and complexity of potential interactions. As well, the elderly person's desire to improve health may promote use of over-the-counter remedies. Over-the-counter medications should not be neglected since they are frequently used by the elderly (particularly laxatives, antacids, and analgesics) and are not without nutritional consequences.

Drugs interfere with the nutritional status of older persons in four ways. They can suppress or stimulate appetite, alter nutrient digestion and absorption, alter metabolism and use of a nutrient, or alter excretion of a nutrient.[48] The aging process may also result in a delayed clearance of some drugs, so that their effects may linger. Likewise, the person's nutritional status or diet may influence the efficacy and toxicity of drug therapy.

Major adverse side effects of drugs on nutritional health of the elderly include obesity per hyperphasic effects; malnutrition related to anorexia, nausea, vomiting, and adverse reactions to food; and vitamin or mineral depletion caused by maldigestion, malabsorption, hyperexcretion, and impaired utilization. Drugs that significantly affect the control of diet-related disease must be considered.[22]

NUTRITIONAL REQUIREMENTS

No specific standards exist for determination of energy and protein requirements for the disabled elderly. Evidence suggests long-term disability and inactivity reduce the need for calories, but how much is uncertain.

The Harris-Benedict equation accounts for height, weight, age, and sex. After the basal metabolic rate is determined, the immobility factor of 7% may be deducted to adjust this rate. To that calculation, activity and injury factors may be applied, as the person's condition warrants, to project calorie needs. Determination of caloric needs for the amputee requires adjustment of appropriate body weight, using segmental weight for limb applications,[49] while accounting for metabolic demands and medical condition (see Appendix C). For the obese person, calculation of energy needs may be performed based on ideal weight in order to prevent further weight gain.

For the extremely underweight patient, use of actual weight as the base for calculation of energy needs is suggested. This conservative approach is recommended in determining energy requirements for the underweight elderly person who is particularly sensitive to the metabolic stress induced by caloric overload. Starvation has been associated with declines in body function (reduction in basal metabolic rate, cardiac output, renal concentrating ability, pulmonary capacity, and increased intestinal atrophy), in which provision of excess calories can create a metabolic stress on these systems.[50]

Therefore, the goal of nutritional support of this client is slow repletion. Calories should be provided gradually, to maintain the person's nutritional status. Once the client is stable, repletion may begin. As energy intake is increased, pulse, respiration, and body temperature should be monitored. If these should increase for no identifiable reason (such as sepsis), one should suspect overload and reduce calories to the last tolerated level.[50] Routine weekly weights aid in assessing the success of calorie recommendations and adjusting calorie levels provided.

Evidence regarding changes in protein requirements for the elderly is debatable. Some studies have suggested that protein needs do not decline with age. As caloric requirements decrease, the protein–calorie ratio increases and ingestion of high-quality protein is emphasized. Increased protein may not be beneficial and can result as a stress, particularly on the kidneys. While 0.8 g/kg/d is the recommended daily allowance for younger adults, a protein intake of 1.0 g/kg/d for adults age 75 and over has been recommended.[51] The elderly person usually will not require or tolerate protein intakes of greater than 2 g/kg/d. Maintenance of nutrition status requires a protein intake of 0.8 to 1.0 g/kg/d with 1.4 g/kg/d required for anabolic needs. High protein intakes require careful monitoring of levels of blood urea nitrogen and serum ammonia to prevent protein intoxication associated with hepatic failure, chronic renal failure, and cancer metastasis.[50,52]

Energy requirements of the elderly diminish owing to a decline in basal metabolism and reduced physical activity. As the calorie intake is reduced accordingly, adequacy of protein, vitamins, and minerals is the focus of concern. The Health and Nutrition Examination Survey (HANES) study has found that elderly persons fall short of meeting the full 1980 recommended daily allowances of any nutrient. Thus are the elderly eating poorly, or are the 1980 recommended daily allowances inappropriate to be applied to the elderly?[51]

The 1980 recommended daily allowances include the elderly in one group, age 51 and older, which assumes that the needs of a 51-year-old are the same as those of an 85-year-old. Much of the data on which these allowances are based has been extrapolated from studies of younger groups.[53] Furthermore, few studies have been performed on elderly persons age 75 years or older. Since recommended daily allowances are intended to meet the needs of healthy persons, they do not take into account the nutrition implications of age-related physiological changes, effects of acute and chronic degenerative diseases, drug- and alcohol-induced deficiencies, and physical trauma.

It has been suggested that vitamin A and folate levels in the 1980 recommended daily allowances may be set higher than necessary, while the levels for vitamins B_6, B_{12}, D, and calcium may be insufficient, owing to age-related changes in metabolism.[51]

Dietary surveys that included elderly persons found that they frequently had a reduced intake of water-soluble vitamins and the minerals calcium, iron, and magnesium. However, since results were based on biochemical indices whose normal ranges were established for younger populations, when compared with the 1980 recommended daily allowances the validity of the conclusions is debatable.[53]

Therefore, the recommended daily allowances may better serve as a guideline for potential deficiencies among elderly persons. Whereas one may exhibit an inadequate intake of specific nutrients, the impact of illness, drug–nutrient interactions, and/or age-related changes and disability on these nutrients is vital.[53] Diet adequacy and use of vitamin, mineral, and nutrient supplements must be evaluated on an individual basis.

Adequate hydration is of great importance in the elderly. Dehydration is possibly the single most common cause of confusion in the elderly hospitalized person and the most easily rectifiable. In the strictest sense, dehydration is depletion of pure water, leading to hypernatremia. Elderly persons are more susceptible to dehydration for two reasons: (1) progressive decreases in the functional capacity of kidneys along with an age-related decrease in total body water content and (2) an increase in the number of potential conditions that may restrict fluid intake or increase fluid output.

Factors that may contribute to a decreased fluid intake, resulting in volume depletion, are a decrease in thirst and taste sensations and impaired mobility that diminishes accessibility to hydration opportunities (eg, CVA, osteoarthritis, Alzheimer's disease). Increased fluid output may be the result of such circumstances as gastroenteritis, uncontrolled diabetes mellitus, diuretic therapy, and prolonged exposure to heat, which can lead to an acute state of dehydration.[54]

Decreased taste sensations have been known to result in decreased food intake and a simultaneous reduction in fluid ingestion. Impaired thirst or a reduced motivation to drink requires staff encouragement of the client to consume enough liquids. A beverage placed within the person's reach may not be taken. Fluid alert signs posted at the head of the bed and on the person's wheelchair help to remind all members of the health care team to offer liquid throughout the day.

Reduced mobility may affect the person's access to liquids. Three such chronic diseases that alter mobility are osteoarthritis, CVA, and Alzheimer's disease. Persons with a CVA may be unaware of a beverage if it is placed in their field of neglect. Cerebral degeneration, diminished cognition, or orientation may affect the ability to recognize the need to drink fluids. In addition, any disability that hinders mobility or diminishes cognitive function in the elderly may promote risk of dehydration.

The effects of poor fluid intake are further compounded by circumstances that cause increases in fluid output. Fluid losses (as well as electrolytes) of vomiting and diarrhea, increased urinary excretion related to uncontrolled diabetes and/or diuretic therapy, and heat exposure all place the elderly person at risk for dehydration.

Fluid intake must be enough to compensate for routine losses (through skin, lungs, kidneys, and bowel) and for unusual losses (fever, vomiting, diarrhea, or hemorrhage). Goals for fluid intake should be to provide at least 1 mL/calorie/d or 30 mL/kg/d.[3,54]

NUTRITION SUPPORT

The goals of nutritional support are twofold: (1) prevention or repletion of nutritional deficits and (2) implementation of diet modifications to promote health improvement.

Identifying individual food preferences and providing assistance with menu selections when necessary are intended as a means to promote client meal satisfaction, with an improved nutrient intake. They also demonstrate a personal interest in the client. Well-being may be enhanced by the recognition that individual needs are respected and attempts to meet them are made. For persons whose memory loss or confusion hinders obtaining information, conferring with family members/caregivers provides them with a source of comfort and satisfaction that no part of client care is ignored. Ancillary dietary staff are trained to recognize these functions as significant interactions that impact on the client's care and nutritional status.

Food and meals have been viewed as a source of comfort and one of the few areas of control a person has while in a hospital or rehabilitation facility. The client may not be able to dictate his or her diet prescription but has the right to select the food that he or she will eat. Practitioners have noted that clients eat better, enjoy meals more, and may display satisfaction with diet modifications if the foods resemble their previous home eating pattern.

Mealtimes may be affected by a busy therapy schedule, resulting in a rushed atmosphere and a poor nutrient intake. Disabled elderly clients require ample eating time, especially those having difficulties with vision, chewing, swallowing, and coordination or those who fatigue easily. More time allowed for meals can result in more food being eaten. Breakfast is encouraged since it appears to be the meal best eaten by elderly persons and most items are easy to chew and digest.

For those who achieve rapid satiety, offering small meals with in-between meal feedings/supplements, as much as daily therapies accommodate, may be beneficial. Informing other members of the health care team of the food needs of clients may result in improved intake. Occasionally, persons with extremely poor appetites may be enticed to eat foods brought from home by family or friend. Some diet prescription compromises may reduce problems of decreased appetite, poor intake, and resistance to hospital diet regimens.

Diet modifications must be skillfully implemented and tailored to the individual client. Factors to consider include the degree or type of diet restrictions in relation to age, disability, and quality of life, as well as level of the client's nutritional state; the severity of disability/disease and appropriate application of diet modifications; and the client's acceptance of and adherence to diet regimen.

In examining these factors, it is important to weigh the potential benefits of diet modifications in promotion of health versus the consequences to health should diet modifications be liberalized or absent from treatment. For instance, the noncompliant person with diabetes having a recent above-knee amputation may avert further complications with medical treatment, including diet and exercise, whereas the benefit of strict cholesterol restrictions prescribed for a severe CVA may be debated. As consumption of even small quantities of food may be difficult for the debilitated person, nutritional restoration may take precedence over some diet restrictions.

Some practitioners have found use of a liberalized geriatric diet beneficial in achieving the dietary guidelines recommended for Americans, while promoting client satisfaction and improved dietary intake. The objective is to minimize the negative effects of major food restrictions and promote the client's psychological well-being. This meal plan offers daily 1500 to 2000 calories; 3 to 4 g sodium; 65 to 70 g protein, including 4 to 6 ounces of meat and 6 mg iron; 2 cups of milk or the calcium equivalent; 64 ounces of fluid; and natural fiber. It is designed for the geriatric client who does not require strict diet modifications. However, it may be used as a base for tailoring special diet modifications as the client's health warrants, for example in cases of renal disease, ascites, severe hypertension, pulmonary disorders, and brittle diabetes.[55]

In addition to providing diet modifications as a means of nutrition intervention and health promotion, many facilities have devised guidelines to better meet the needs of elderly clients. In particular, foods are provided according to the diet prescription but modified for ease in mastication, swallowing, and digestion, as well as compensation for decreased dexterity (use of diced, bite-size, softer items and casseroles or smaller, more frequent, snack type meals to aid a decreased appetite).

When food and beverages cannot be taken by mouth because of severity of dysphagia, enteral nutrition support may be initiated. Nutrition support impacts strongly on the person's rehabilitation process. The overall goal is to replenish current deficits and/or to prevent the onset or progression of malnutrition by providing adequate calories and nutrients.

Route and delivery of enteral nutrition will be determined largely by the person's mental and physical status. An alert person having satisfactory pharyngeal reflexes to protect the airway from aspiration generally tolerates intragastric feeding. For those whom aspiration is a risk, owing to an altered state of consciousness or dysfunction of cranial nerves IX to XI, the choice of tube to access the gastrointestinal tract must be evaluated cautiously.[56-58]

If a nasogastric tube is used, it should be small in diameter to reduce disruption of the esophagogastric sphincter and positioned distal to the pylorus for feeding in the jejunum. Administration of the enteral feeding into the proximal small bowel provides three barriers of protection against aspiration: the upper esophageal sphincter, lower esophageal sphincter, and pylorus. Indications for use of a nasogastric tube to administer enteral nutrition are based on the need for short-term nutrition support (days or weeks) or when the duration of therapy is uncertain.

When long-term nutrition support is required, enteral alimentation is best delivered via jejunostomy or gastrostomy. Use of a jejunostomy may be considered for high-risk aspirators. Although feeding via the gastrostomy has been well tolerated by persons with strokes, it is not advised for use for persons at risk of aspiration, since a gastrostomy poses the threat of tracheobronchial aspiration.

Once the method of delivery is determined, enteral nutrition support affords the person an opportunity to develop swallowing skills (within limitations) without sacrificing nutritional status in the interim. It is a safe, effective, and economical method to provide adequate nourishment while promoting maintenance of the functional and structural integrity of the gastrointestinal mucosa. This is beneficial because a normal gut not only digests and absorbs nutrients but also provides a protective role in the detoxification and elimination of many parasites, viruses, bacteria, chemical toxins, and drugs that may be harmful to health.[58,59]

Although tube feeding access is determined by the client's condition, the rate of tube feeding administration may be influenced by the rehabilitation environment. Continuous enteral feedings are used most commonly in the acute care facility, which promotes tolerance and decreases the risk of aspiration. However, in the rehabilitation setting daily therapy treatments may be hindered by tube feeding equipment. Two methods have been used to promote increased mobility, better access to therapies, and possibly improved client well-being. Use of continuous-drip nocturnal feedings or bolus feedings (around the clock or patterned four times a day as meals and night feedings) has helped provide optimal therapy time, as well as provided the person daytime opportunities to practice feeding skills without interfering with appetite.

These enteral feeding methods may be more time-consuming for staff and require monitoring for possible signs of intolerance, such as diarrhea, nausea, and vomiting. However, as clients adjust to their enteral feeding schedule, improvement in therapy attendance and outcomes can be seen.

EDUCATION AND COUNSELING

Successful nutrition intervention and education must actively involve the client and caregivers (family, friends, housekeeper, etc) in the decision- and goal-making process. As is the case in all disciplines within rehabilitation, the goal of the dietitian is to facilitate the client in assuming responsibility for his or her own self-care.

For some elderly disabled, the mere act of eating may be difficult enough to achieve, let alone meeting the challenge of maintaining special diet modifications, obtaining foods, and preparing meals at home. In this case, the caregiver plays a key role in assuming nutritional care and diet implementation on discharge.

While the practitioner may find one elderly client extremely resistant to any diet modifications, another client may not be willing to deviate from previously prescribed dietary practices, even if they are unnecessary. Just as sensory and physiological effects of aging and occurrence of chronic illness vary among the elderly, so, too, are the willingness to learn and motivation to make changes. The national trend toward health promotion has included the elderly, who also are altering their diet and life style to improve their health.

A study entitled "Aging and Health Promotion: Market Research for Public Education," conducted by the Office of Disease Prevention and Health Promotion, National Institute on Aging and the National Cancer Institute in the Public Health Service and Administration on Aging, determined that although the elderly are very interested in maintaining and improving their health, knowledge about specific habits and their association with chronic diseases and conditions was limited. Six primary areas were identified as significantly related to conditions prevalent in the elderly and having the potential for change: (1) fitness/exercise, (2) nutrition, (3) safe and proper use of medicine, (4) accident prevention, (5) prevention services, and (6) smoking. Evidence that many persons could identify diet restrictions but could not describe components of a balanced diet suggests a need for simple, well-integrated information on selecting healthy meal plans rather than only what ingredients or foods to avoid. Other research indicated that when educated about health habits, older persons had higher levels of compliance and behavior change than other age groups, concluding that the elderly are an interested and motivated audience for health information.[60]

Particular concepts to incorporate in nutrition education for the elderly include appropriate means of weight control, practical methods to alleviate constipation, improvement of calcium intake via increased consumption of dairy products, ways to achieve a balanced diet, and tips to stretch the food dollar.[60,61] In one survey, 40% of respondents never examined food labels when shopping because of difficulty reading labels due to print size or package coloring, lack of time or interest, absence of labels on fresh foods, and difficulty in understanding information.[60] Education about food label use could benefit persons in managing their prescribed diet while selecting nutrient-rich, economical foods.

As a means of promoting self-care, successful diet counseling requires client motivation as well as encouragement and direction from the practitioner. Individualization of the client's regimen to accommodate his or her capabilities, eating habits, cultural and religious beliefs, as well as socioeconomic and mobility factors, assists in developing a realistic meal plan to promote compliance.

While the decreased nutrient intakes of the housebound elderly are well documented, it is suggested that economic factors have the greatest impact on food selections, meal pattern, and diet adequacy. Better acceptance of dietary modifications may be achieved by recommending consumption of inexpensive food, suggesting high-cost specialty foods only when absolutely necessary. Housebound elderly persons have been found to frequently use inexpensive, nutrient-dense foods such as milk, potatoes, and bread, and this should be encouraged.

The disabled elderly person may be vulnerable to dietary fads. A reasonable approach in this case is to discuss the merits and potential harm of fads in an objective, nonjudgmental, direct, and open-minded fashion. Judgmental responses could be counterproductive.[62]

Diet counseling involves more than offering a list of do's and don'ts, or providing a diet sheet before discharge. Such brevity de-emphasizes the importance of diet modifications on health improvement. The client needs facts about diseases and available techniques for their management to help him or her understand and assume responsibility for self-care. Realistic tasks that the client can manage alone, or with help of a caregiver, must be agreed on. Success depends on the person's ability to perform all tasks involved with varying degrees of complexity and alter the organization of his or her life.[63]

Orem theorizes that the client must be able to recognize that a new life style centers around three basic self-care requirements: (1) universal, (2) health deviation, and (3) developmental skills. Universal self-care consists of routine life functions of personal hygiene, eating, exercise, elimination, and sleeping. Health deviation self-care evolves from the occurrence of an injury, disease, or illness. Developmental skills are the physical, mental, socioeconomic, and emotional components required for a person to master tasks in the aforementioned two areas, as well as the ability to recognize a self-care deficit.[63,64] Backscheider identified four self-care capabilities as physical, mental, motivational/emotional, and orientation (Table 11-2).[63,65] Based on these theories, a University of Michigan group developed a model in which the client's ability to engage in nutrition self-care could be methodically assessed. A deficit in any one function may require alterations in education techniques or may influence the degree to which a person may be able to perform tasks.[63,66]

Physical capability includes the need for dexterity. Should this function be affected by disability (eg, stroke or arthritis), use of utensils to prepare food may be impaired. The person may require retraining or assistive devices; substitution of lightweight products (eg, skim milk powder instead of fluid milk); and "brown bag" meals prepared by home visit assistants.

Mental capabilities include application of learned skills, such as menu planning, to include diet modifications or reading literature to enhance knowledge of one's condition. Consider the widower who has never cooked and must now learn to do so along with developing compensatory skills for a disability or the client with a low reading level. Extensive training and support will be needed.

Motivational/emotional capabilities encompass the client's self-worth and self-image, as well as his or her willingness to engage in self-care, much of which influences the client's acceptance of the need for diet intervention and receptivity to nutrition education. Often a person's behavior and dietary changes are enhanced by the development of a support system (caregivers or persons responsible for meal preparation). Alternatively, a spouse, siblings, or friends may attempt to demonstrate their affection or compensate for the disability and possibly their own guilt feelings by offering excessive food, desserts, or snacks. If changes are to occur outside the health care facility, counseling and education must involve caregivers, particularly those who help the person shop, cook, and eat.

Table 11-2 Capabilities Essential to Nutrition Self-Care

Physical		Mental	
General Capability	Specific Capability	General Capability	Specific Capability
Diabetes			
Dexterity	Use of utensils to prepare food	Learned skills	Read food labels/count
			Cook
Movement and general energy (exercise)	Activity level consistent with food intake		Use diet exchange
	Relieve stress and tension		Classify foods
			Plan diet
	Control weight		Learn words for different forms of sugar
	Increase blood circulation	Functions of cerebral cortex	Amounts of food in diet, diet exchanges
	Use glucose effectively		Classify food substances
		Operative knowing	Discriminating and classifying clusters of events—keep daily record of insulin, food, and activity
			Decision making about diet for time period based on judgment
Hypertension/Congestive Heart Failure			
Exercise	Activity consistent with physical limitations and adequate nutrient intake not to induce fatigue	Learned skills	Cook without salt when edema and/or congestive failure present
Dexterity	Use of utensils to prepare food		Plan menu and diet without salt or distending foods
	Take own blood pressure		Read literature to enhance knowledge of condition
Respiration	Free of congestion and shortness of breath		Read labels on food items for sodium content
		Functions of cerebral cortex	Types and times for medications
			Amounts of sodium and potassium in diet

Table 11-2 continued

Motivational / Emotional		Orientations	
General Capability	Specific Capability	General Capability	Specific Capability
Diabetes			
Self-value (independent of others)	Ability to eat differently from group—special diet	Time and priority habit	Predictability of mealtimes
	Question how a dish is prepared if eating out		Organization of activities around meals
Self-Image and self-concern	Acceptance of need for therapeutic regimen (diet)	Acceptance of body functioning and self-care	As stimulus for ongoing nutrition/diet education
	Consistent attention to health (weight, exercise, diet)		
Emotional control	Consistency of adherence to diet regimen		
	Stick with usual portion sizes		
	Insulin reaction/ ketoacidosis		
Willingness to engage in care	Design appropriate diet regimen		
	Purchase special cookbook		
	Maintain normal weight		
Self-discipline	Selection of stress-relieving mechanisms— eating and drinking		
	Selection of foods— preference versus needs		
Hypertension/Congestive Heart Failure			
Self-value (independent of others)	Ability to eat differently from group—follow special diet controlled for calories, sodium, and/or cholesterol	Time and priority habit	Small, frequent, easily digested meals if dyspnea or angina is present
Self-image and self-control	Acceptance of need for special therapeutic diet regimen	Acceptance of body functioning and self-care	As stimulus for learning about condition and role of electrolytes
	Consistent attention to health (weight, exercise, diet)		Awareness of symptoms that trouble is imminent
Emotional control	Consistency of adherence to diet regimen		
	Fear of eating		

continues

Table 11-2 Capabilities Essential to Nutrition Self-Care

Physical		Mental	
General Capability	*Specific Capability*	*General Capability*	*Specific Capability*
		Operative knowing	Discriminate and classify specific events—swelling in appendages from fluid accumulation, difficulty breathing, elevated blood pressure
			Select foods by type and quantity to avoid stomach distention and pressure on diaphragm; minimum circulation needed for digestive absorption process
	Obesity/Weight Reduction		
Dexterity	Use of utensils to prepare food	Learned skills	Read labels for nutritional values versus empty calories
Exercise	Calorie expenditure greater than calorie intake		Use alternative methods of food preparation to frying—broil, bake, stew
Appetite	Food selections of high biologic value	Functions of cerebral cortex	Learn calorie values of foods
		Operative knowing	Decision making about setting reasonable goal for weight loss
			Avoid fad diets
	Kidney Disease/Renal Failure		
Dexterity	Use of utensils to prepare food	Learned skills	Read labels for protein, sodium, and potassium levels
Movement and general energy	Activity level consistent with calorie intake to keep tissue catabolism to minimum		Count calories; measure grams of protein, sodium, and fluid intake
General health	Free of anorexia, nausea, vomiting, mouth ulcers		Use foods in diet with high biologic value
		Functions of cerebral cortex	Discriminating and classifying clusters of events—normal blood levels and absence of clinical conditions improves appetite

Table 11-2 continued

Motivational/Emotional		Orientations	
General Capability	*Specific Capability*	*General Capability*	*Specific Capability*
Willingness to engage in care	Attend support groups; special diet instruction; purchase special cookbook		
Self-discipline	Selection of foods—preference versus need		

		Obesity/Weight Reduction	
Self-value (independent of others)	Better health	Time and priority habit	Predictability of mealtimes and sizes
	Willing to modify lifetime eating habits	Acceptance of body functioning and self-care	Organization of exercise program into daily regimen
	Longer life		
Self-image and self-concern	More pep		Involvement in behavior modification program as ongoing system to maintain weight reduction
Emotional control	Slimmer figure		
	Channel stress relief through activity other than eating		
Willingness to engage in care	Consistency of management		
	Engage peer support offered through various support groups		

		Kidney Disease/Renal Failure	
Self-value (independent of others)	Ability to eat differently from group—follow special diet controlled for protein, electrolytes, and fluid	Time and priority habit	Regularity of three meals and amount consumed to eliminate system overload
	Adherence to diet can make difference between independence and dependence		Regular periodic check of blood values
Self-image and self-concern	Clinical conditions cause gastrointestinal upsets, bad breath, ulcerations of mouth		
	Willingness to learn about condition and therapy		

continues

Table 11-2 continued

Physical		Mental	
General Capability	Specific Capability	General Capability	Specific Capability
		Operative knowing	Consuming a balanced intake in 3 meals promotes a sense of well-being and improved appetite
			Cheating on diet overloads system with nitrogen, potassium, sodium, and fluid

Source: Reprinted from *The Science and Art of Self Care* by J Riehl-Sisca with permission of Appleton & Lange, © 1985.

Orientation capabilities include time and priority and acceptance of body function and self-care. Predictability of mealtimes in diabetes treatment is important, along with the ability to recognize symptoms of hypoglycemic and hyperglycemic reactions.

Assessing the person's capabilities assists in determining the level of education that is realistic for his or her needs. Whereas one person may fully comprehend the diabetic exchange list and desire an exact regimen, another may do best with a simplified version that may encourage regular mealtimes, balanced meal choices, and avoidance of simple carbohydrate and high fat foods. Since the disabled elderly client may have several diet prescriptions, small, incremental changes may be best implemented. The person can incorporate new goals as each technique is mastered. Goals may include implementing regular mealtimes; choosing one high fiber food per day, then one per meal; or avoiding specific salty foods. Rinsing regular canned vegetables to reduce the sodium content instead of purchasing special high-priced items or including frozen prepared entrees supplemented with a piece of fruit and a beverage for some meals may achieve basic compliance and promote nutritional adequacy without being overly restrictive or difficult.

Nutrition education materials are designed to compensate for vision and hearing deficits. Larger print, preferably black on white, and nonglossy paper should be used. The dietitian should provide adequate lighting and make sure the client wears his or her glasses, if they are needed. Instructions should be spoken slowly in lower-pitched tones, using short sentences. If

Table 11-2 continued

Motivational/Emotional		Orientations	
General Capability	Specific Capability	General Capability	Specific Capability
Emotional control sufficient to make judgments and carry out action	Abnormally high potassium levels interfere with normal heart rhythm		
	Excess loss of sodium leads to dehydration		
Self-discipline	Selection of stress-relieving mechanism other than eating and drinking		
Willingness to engage in care	Selection of foods		
	Dialysis		
	Develop and follow diet regimen		

the person wears a hearing aid, the dietitian should verify that it is working, and should speak at the person's eye level to allow for lip reading should hearing be impaired.[67]

The setting for the discussion should be comfortable with reduced distractions and surrounding noises. Since some elderly persons may have a short attention span, frequent short visits may be focused on single concepts and review of previous information. Assistance with menu selection also serves to reinforce appropriate meal choices for use at home. Food models to depict portion size and type of food, food labels and containers to identify appropriate selections, and sample dietetic products to view and taste are helpful tools to improve comprehension.

When interacting with caregivers, one should note that many spouses, siblings, or caregivers may be older also and may experience as many effects of aging as their disabled counterparts. Therefore, consideration is given to their vision, hearing, and level of comprehension. Tips on label reading, dining out, and grocery shopping promote easier implementation after the client's discharge.

NUTRITION INTERVENTION AND THE HEALTH CARE TEAM

The health care team's impact on the disabled elderly client's nutrition intervention and education, as well as its acceptance, is significant. Time constraints of the person's hectic therapy schedule can affect his or her opportunity and ability to eat. Therapists' awareness of such problems can cause schedule rearrangement in order to promote adequate time for meals or the client's participation in feeding groups to improve needed skills.

Nurses may identify persons experiencing nutritional problems and refer them to the dietitian. Nurses offer one-on-one reinforcement of dietary modifications, following nutrition counseling provided by the dietitian.

Physical therapists may include intensive exercises and must recognize the potential for, as well as the signs of, hypoglycemia in the person with diabetes and be able to respond appropriately. Likewise, some group classes designed to educate the disabled elderly client on accident prevention, range of motion exercises, and the process of his or her particular disease may include dietary risk factors.

Occupational therapists assess the person's need for assistive feeding devices and special utensils. Evaluation of the client's kitchen skills may be performed in a cooking class, and recipes chosen for preparation can reinforce compliance.

Therapeutic recreation includes special dining activities and restaurant visits. Encouraging the client to select foods similar to his or her prescribed diet helps demonstrate that it is possible to eat out and follow the meal plan.

Social workers emphasize the importance of the person's nutritional care and diet intervention by including the dietitian in family conferences and instruction schedules. In preparation for discharge, the social worker may be more effective at linking the client with logistically accessible home assistance and congregate meal services and financial assistance resources, such as food stamps.

The health care team serves to treat the person as a whole, rather than as a fragment in each discipline. From the dietitian's perspective, effective interaction of the team members is vital in meshing the reality of nutrition education, its reinforcement, and its acceptance. The disabled elderly client has acquired nutrition information from many sources (eg, magazines, friends, or advertisements), some of which may be limited in validity. Mixed messages from various health care professionals can serve only to confuse the client's understanding of his or her diet plan and limit its acceptance. It may also cause confusion as to what information or professional is reliable. Education of, and communication between, health care team members promote consistency of the information provided, which will enhance understanding and acceptance of diet intervention, as well as assure the client's confidence in the team.

CHALLENGES AND FUTURE PROSPECTIVES

Addressing the nutritional concerns of the disabled elderly person has many challenges. Many variables are recognized that impact on the nutritional status of the elderly, and more have yet to be identified. Changes in normal nutrition requirements with aging and the impacts of disease and disability on the recommended daily allowances have not been elucidated.

The interrelationship among nutrients, health, disease, environment, socioeconomic status, climate, medications, and genetics all need further investigation.[3,52,53] The parameters used for nutrition assessment of the elderly disabled population require evaluation to promote valid interpretation. While the needs of the geriatric person are unique, research in the field is difficult because of poor subject cooperation and high incidence of chronic physical and psychologic illnesses.[68]

Dietitians must weigh the level of and need for diet intervention and seek to provide satisfactory nutrition support that considers the quality of life. To quote Professor George Morris Piersol, founder of rehabilitation at the University of Pennsylvania Medical School, "We have added years to life. Let us now add life to years."[2]

REFERENCES

1. Kane RL, Kane RA. Long-term care: Can our society meet the needs of its elderly? *Ann Rev Public Health.* 1980;227:53.

2. Brody SJ, Ruff GE, eds. *Aging and Rehabilitation—Advances in the State of the Art.* New York, NY: Springer Publishing Co; 1986.

3. Chernoff R. Aging and nutrition. *Nutr Today.* 1987;22(2):4–11.

4. Shanus E. Health status of older people: Cross-national implications. *Am J Public Health.* 1974;64:261–264.

5. Williams FT. The aging process: Biological and psychosocial considerations. In: Brody SJ, Ruff GE, eds. *Aging and Rehabilitation—Advances in the State of the Art.* New York, NY: Springer Publishing; 1986.

6. Fenderson DA. Aging, disability, and therapeutic optimism. In: Brody SJ, Ruff GE, eds. *Aging and Rehabilitation—Advances in the State of the Art.* New York, NY: Springer Publishing; 1986.

7. Winograd CH. Nutritional assessment of the elderly. *Geriatr Consult.* 1988; 6(6): 13–15.

8. Arego DE, Koch S. Malnutrition in the rehabilitation setting. *Nutr Today.* 1986; 21(4):28–32.

9. McGee-Harvey A, et al. *The Principles and Practice of Medicine.* 20th ed. Englewood Cliffs, NJ: Prentice-Hall, Inc; 1980.

10. Hargrave M. *Nutritional Care of the Physically Disabled.* Minneapolis, MN: Sister Kenny Institute; 1979.

11. Horner J, Massey EW. Silent aspiration following stroke. *Neurology.* 1988;38:317–319.

12. Trupe EH, Siebens H, Siebens AA. Prevalence of feeding and swallowing disorders in a nursing home. *Arch Phys Med Rehabil.* 1984;65:651.

13. Blumenthal HT. Aging: Biologic or pathologic? *Hosp Pract.* 1978; April:129.

14. Robinson RG, Price TK. Post-stroke depressive disorders: A follow-up study of 103 patients. *Stroke.* 1982;13(5):635–641.

15. Okamato GA. Cerebral vascular accidents. In: *Physical Medicine and Rehabilitation.* Philadelphia, Pa: WB Saunders Co; 1984.

16. Mountokalakis T, Dellos C. Protein catabolism following stroke (letter). *Arch Intern Med.* 1984;144:2285.

17. Deitrick JE, et al. Effects of immobilization upon various metabolic and physiologic functions of normal men. *Am J Med.* 1948;4:3–36.

18. Kaplan PE. Stroke and rehabilitation. In: Brody SJ, Ruff GE, eds. *Aging and Rehabilitation—Advances in the State of the Art.* New York, NY: Springer Publishing Co; 1986.

19. Kasim S. Cholesterol changes with aging: Their nature and significance. In: *Fitness and Aging.* Wayne State University seminar. *Geriatrics.* 1987;42(3):73–80.

20. Smith DA, Karmally W, Brown WV. Treating hyperlipidemia: Whether and when in the elderly. *Geriatrics.* 1987;42(6):33–44.

21. Smith DA, Karmally W, Brown WV. Treating hyperlipidemia: Making dietary control work in the elderly. *Geriatrics.* 1987;42(7):39–43.

22. Roe D. *Geriatric Nutrition.* Englewood Cliffs, NJ: Prentice-Hall, Inc; 1987.

23. Pincus JH, Barry K. Influence of dietary protein on motor fluctuations in Parkinson's disease. *Arch Neurol.* 1987;44:270.

24. Pincus JH, Barry K. Dietary method for reducing fluctuations in Parkinson's disease. *Yale J Biol Med.* 1987;60:133.

25. Nutt JG, et al. The "on-off" phenomenon of Parkinson's disease: Relationship to levodopa absorption and transport. *N Engl J Med.* 1984;310:483.

26. McKee G, ed. Protein restriction for parkinsonian patients. *Nutr MD.* 1987; 13(10):4–5.

27. Eckstein D. Common complaints of the elderly. *Hosp Pract.* 1976; April:67–74.

28. Brenenstock H, Fernanto KR. Arthritis in the elderly. *Med Clin North Am.* 1976; 60:459–1211.

29. Smith R. Bone disease in the elderly. *Proc R Soc Med.* 1976;69:925–926.

30. Albenese AA. Calcium nutrition throughout the life cycle. *Bibl Nutr Dieta.* 1983; 33:80–90.

31. Fuller E. Warding off osteoporosis. *Patient Care.* 1985; January:20.

32. Riis B, Thomsen K, Christiansen D. Does calcium supplementation prevent post-menopausal bone loss? A double-blind controlled study. *N Engl J Med.* 1987;316:173–177.

33. Riggs BL, Melton LJ III. Involutional osteoporosis. *N Engl J Med.* 1986;314:1676–1686.

34. Rivlin RS. Women's health: Osteoporosis. *Public Health Rep.* 1987; July/August (suppl):131–135.

35. Haussler MR. Vitamin D metabolism, drug interactions and therapeutic applications in humans. In: Hathcock JN, Con J, eds. *Nutrient and Drug Interactions.* New York, NY: Academic Press; 1978.

36. Reid IR, Ibbertson HK. Calcium supplementation in the prevention of steroid-induced osteoporosis. *Am J Clin Nutr.* 1986;44:287–290.

37. Gorden GS. Estrogen and bone. *Clin Orthop.* 1985;200:174.

38. Wardlaw G. The effects of diet and life-style on bone mass in women. *J Am Dent Assoc.* 1988;88:17–22.

39. Wintrobe MM, et al. *Harrison's Principles of Internal Medicine.* New York, NY: McGraw-Hill Book Co; 1970.

40. Ireland JT, Thompson WST, Williamson J. *Diabetes Today: A Handbook for the Clinical Team.* Aylesbury, England: HM&M Publishers; 1980.

41. Liu G, Coulston A, Lardenois C, et al. Demonstration of the clinical impact of small amounts of weight loss in treatment of NIDDM. *Diabetes.* 1983;32(suppl 1):79A.

42. Bouchier IAD. *Gastroenterology.* 2nd ed. London, England: Bailliere Tindall; 1977.

43. Hovdenak N. Prevalence and clinical picture of adult gluten-induced enteropathy in a Norwegian population. *Scand J Gastroenterol.* 1980;15:401–404.

44. Newmark SR, et al. Nutritional assessment in a rehabilitation unit. *Arch Phys Med Rehabil.* 1981;62:279–282.

45. Glenn MB, et al. Serum albumin as a predictor of course and outcome on a rehabilitation service. *Arch Phys Med Rehabil.* 1985;66:294–297.

46. Clark GS, Blackburn GL. Nutritional assessment and support of the elderly patient. *Am J Intravenous Ther Clin Nutr.* 1983;March:7–17.

47. Bistrian B. Nutritional support of the long-term care patient: II. Nutritional assessment of the elderly (alluded to Roubenoff R, et al. *Arch Intern Med.* August 1987;147:1462–1465). *J Nutr Support Serv.* 1988;8(10):17.

48. Roe D. Drug–nutrient interactions in the elderly. *Geriatrics.* 1986;41(3):57–74.

49. Brunstrom S. *Clinical Kinesiology.* Philadelphia, Pa: FA Davis Co; 1972.

50. Shuran M, Nelson RA. Updated nutritional assessment and support of the elderly. *Geriatrics.* 1986;41(7):48–70.

51. Russell RM. Nutritional support of the long-term care patient: I. Nutritional requirements of the elderly. *J Nutr Support Serv.* 1988;8(10):12–16.

52. Blackburn GL, Harvey KB. Nutritional assessment as a routine in clinical medicine. *Postgrad Med.* 1982;71:46–63.

53. Blumberg JB. Nutrient requirements for the healthy elderly. *Contemp Nutr.* 1986; 11(6).

54. Erkert JD. Dehydration in the elderly. *J Am Acad Phys Assist.* 1988;1:261–267.

55. Luros E. A rational approach to geriatric nutrition. Ross Timesaver, *Diet Currents.* 1981;8(6).

56. Olivares L, Segoria A, Revuelta R. Tube feeding and lethal aspiration in neurological patients: A review of 720 autopsy cases. *Stroke.* 1974;5:654.

57. Bernard M, et al. Incidence of aspiration pneumonia in enteral hyperalimentation. *J Parenter Enter Nutr.* 1982;6:588. Abstract.

58. Matthews L. Enteral nutrition in the geriatric stroke patient. *J Nutr Support Serv.* 1986; 6(11):22–23.

59. Schanker LS. On the mechanism of absorption of drugs from the gastrointestinal tract. *J Med Pharm Chem.* 1960;2:343.

60. Fanelli MT, Abernathy MM. A nutritional questionnaire for older adults. *Gerontologist.* 1986;26:192–197.

61. Abdellah FG. Public health aspects of rehabilitation of the aged. In: Brody SJ, Ruff GE, eds. *Aging and Rehabilitation—Advances in the State of the Art.* New York, NY: Springer Publishing Co; 1986.

62. Okamato GA. Nutrition. In: *Physical Medicine and Rehabilitation.* Philadelphia, Pa: WB Saunders Co; 1984.

63. Pletcher MS. Nutrition self-care: An adaptation and component of the therapeutic regimen. In: Sisca JR, ed. *Science and Art of Self-Care.* Norfolk, Conn: Appleton-Century-Crofts; 1985.

64. Orem DE. *Nursing: Concepts of Practice.* 2nd ed. New York NY: McGraw-Hill Book Co; 1980.

65. Backscheider J. Self-care requirements, self-care capabilities and nursing systems in the diabetic nurse management clinic. *Am J Public Health.* 1974;64:1138–1146.

66. Horn BJ, Swain MA. *Development of Criterion Measures of Nursing Care*: Volume 1, Final Report. Ann Arbor, Mich: University of Michigan, School of Public Health; 1977.

67. Pilberg S, Hosty K. Communication and the elderly. In: Lewis CB, ed. *Aging: The Health Care Challenge.* Philadelphia, Pa: FA Davis Co; 1985.

68. Calloway CW. Summary: What we know and what we need to find out. In: *Assessing Nutritional Status of the Elderly—State of the Art.* Report of the 3rd Ross Roundtable on Medical Issues; 1982.

Chapter 12

Arthritis

Patricia Giblin Wolman

Arthritis is used as a generic term in lay publications to identify several disorders grouped together because of common symptoms, not common etiology or treatment. Most popular books or articles make no distinction among types of arthritis when suggesting treatments or cures for "arthritis." The focus in this chapter is on osteoarthritis and rheumatoid arthritis with some discussion of gout and lupus erythematosus. Nutrition-related theories and therapies, both proven and unproven, as well as the effects of current arthritis treatments on nutritional status, are examined.

TYPES AND INCIDENCE

The most common form of arthritis is osteoarthritis. Approximately 16 million persons in the United States suffer from it. This degenerative disease, usually occurring in persons over 50 years of age, generally affects weight-bearing joints but may also affect fingers.

Rheumatoid arthritis may begin at any age but commonly starts between 20 and 45 years of age. Three to 4 million persons in the United States, most of them women, have rheumatoid arthritis. Both small and large joints are affected and inflammation is widespread.

Gout is an acute form of arthritis typically treated with drugs, although diet therapy can help to reduce symptoms and increase quality of life. Approximately 2 million persons in the United States, mostly male, have gout.

Systemic lupus erythematosus is a connective tissue disease with arthritis symptoms often seen in conjunction with glomerulonephritis or nephrotic syndrome. Almost all of the cases occur in females with onset in the third decade or earlier.

NUTRITION THERAPIES UNDER INVESTIGATION

Until recently arthritis sufferers were told that there was no nutrition treatment other than the maintenance of ideal body weight and a varied diet. Overweight persons with osteoarthritis and gout were told to lose weight and underweight rheumatoid arthritis victims were told to gain weight. All were instructed to eat a balanced diet, but no hope of change in their disease status was offered based on dietary intake. In 1984, the Arthritis Foundation acknowledged in its bulletin that there may be some nutrition therapies that merit further investigation.[1] In fact, there may be several different treatments depending on the type of arthritis, etiology, and symptoms.

Allergies

As early as 1914 food allergies were associated with arthritis. Sensitivity to food resulting in joint pain and swelling is often found in conjunction with such other allergic disorders as hay fever, asthma, and rhinitis.[2] Many investigators believe that in some sensitive persons, certain foods may be allergens causing or exacerbating rheumatoid arthritis.[3] Panush and Webster have defined differences in types of reactions to food (Table 12-1). Food allergic disorders and food sensitivity are defined as immune

Table 12-1 Terminology for Types of Reactions to Food

Term	Definition
Adverse reaction to food	Clinically abnormal response attributed to ingested food (additive or substance)
Food allergic disorder	Adverse reaction to food involving an allergic or immune response
Food sensitivity	Adverse reaction to food based on immunologic mechanisms (synonymous with food allergic disorder)
Food intolerance	Nonimmunologic, abnormal, physiological response to food (additive or substance)
Food idiosyncrasy	Abnormal response to food or additive unlike normal physiological or pharmacologic response (can resemble sensitivity reaction but without immune mechanism)
Food poisoning	Reaction to noxious constituent found naturally in a specific food or secondary to contamination by microorganisms or parasites

Source: Reprinted with permission from *Medical Clinics of North America* (1985;69[3]:533–546), Copyright © 1985, WB Saunders Company.

responses while adverse reaction to food, food intolerance, food idiosyncrasy, and food poisoning are not.

Case studies and limited clinical trials offer evidence that some clients may be sensitive to specific foods causing rheumatoid arthritis symptoms. The prevalence of food allergic disorders or food sensitivities is estimated to be between 5% and 10% of persons with rheumatoid arthritis. Milk, cheese, dairy products, meats, beef, corn, wheat, egg, chocolate, preserved foods, sodium nitrate, tartrazine, and coloring agents have been implicated as possible allergens.[4-6] Parke and Hughes reported a case study of a 38-year-old woman with rheumatoid arthritis on whom every form of drug therapy was tried with no reduction in symptoms. In fact, she had allergic reactions or side effects to the medications. When all dairy products were removed from her diet, she had decreased morning stiffness, less synovitis, and improvement in all clinical measures of rheumatoid arthritis. After 10 months on a diet devoid of dairy products, she was given a food challenge and her condition worsened within 24 hours. Clinical indicators of rheumatoid arthritis changed as well as subjective evaluations. She developed IgE antibodies to milk and cheese during the challenge.[7]

Hicklin and co-workers reported that 22 persons with rheumatoid arthritis, including 15 who tested positive for rheumatoid factors, had improvement of symptoms when exclusion diets identified the foods that caused their symptoms. When the identified foods were reintroduced, symptoms recurred. Adverse reactions to a mean of 2.5 foods were reported. Fourteen persons reacted to grains, eight to pits and nuts, seven to cheeses, five to eggs, and four to milk and/or beef. Chicken, fish, potato, onion, and liver were each reported to be associated with symptoms by one person.[8] Ratner and co-workers reported that seven females with rheumatoid arthritis who were lactose intolerant and seronegative had a reduction in symptoms when consuming a milk- and milk protein–free diet. They experienced recurrence of symptoms when milk or milk protein was reintroduced to their diets. Subjects who were not lactose intolerant or who were seropositive did not respond to the milk-free diet.[9] Darlington and colleagues observed significant reduction in morning stiffness and pain and lowered erythrocyte sedimentation rate, platelets, and C3 in nearly 50 persons with rheumatoid arthritis placed on elimination diets to identify food sensitivities. Persons with a family history of allergy responded better than those with no history.[10]

When Panush and colleagues studied 26 persons with rheumatoid arthritis on a 10-week, controlled, double-blind study of a no meat, no dairy products, no additives diet promoted in the popular press,[11,12] no differences between the control and experimental groups were observed in clinical, laboratory, or immunologic measures. However, two of the subjects had improvement in morning stiffness, swollen joints, grip strength, and other objective measures and remained on the diet after completion of the study. One seropositive female, with a history of allergy to dust, pollens, onions, and other sensitivities, remained improved for 9 months after the study by eliminating dairy products, ice cream, and chocolate. When any of these products were reintroduced, she experienced an increase in symptoms. A seropositive male subject with a history of food intolerance reported a decrease in rheumatoid arthritis symptoms on the experimental diet and an increase in symptoms when specific meats, spices, or alcoholic beverages were reintroduced into his diet.[12]

When Welsh and associates fed Old English rabbits cow's milk instead of water for 12 weeks, 36% of them developed rheumatoid-like lesions as opposed to only 4% of the control, water-drinking, rabbits. Welsh and associates hypothesize that immune complexes were deposited in the joints of the milk-drinking rabbits and that gut flora was altered, allowing arthritogenic bacteria to proliferate.[13]

Felder and co-workers gave pork under controlled conditions to six rheumatoid arthritis patients who had a history of allergy to many foods including pork. None of the six subjects had subjective or objective arthritic reactions to the ingestion of pork. They also surveyed 158 persons with rheumatoid arthritis to identify histories of food intolerance. The investigators concluded that rheumatoid arthritis and allergy are rarely related.[14] Although understanding of the mechanisms that may be involved in food allergy and rheumatoid arthritis symptoms in humans is only beginning, some sensitive clients do seem to benefit from exclusion of specific foods from their diets. Most have a family history of other allergies and are also allergic to such nonfood substances as cat hair, dust, or pollen. Foods that cause arthritis symptoms may also produce nasal and gastrointestinal symptoms. The offending foods appear to be specific to each client. Because food allergies appear to be specific to each person, a challenge of only one food may not be diagnostic. Even skin tests are of no help. The subjects must actually ingest the food, and intake and any symptoms must be recorded conscientiously over several weeks.

Elimination Diets

Although allergy may be associated with only 5% to 10% of rheumatoid arthritis cases, the potential benefits to those with histories of allergy may make the tedium of following an elimination diet worthwhile. The Rowe elimination diet excludes all fruits, cereals, milk and milk products, eggs, and wheat.[2] Denman and associates' elimination diet excludes meats, milk, dairy products, eggs, preserved foods, coloring matter, chocolate, and wheat except for whole grain bread or suggests placing clients on an elemental diet for 7 to 10 days with no solid food ingestion.[15] Foods are then added back to the diet one at a time and pain and joint swelling or disability are recorded.

A good deal of cooperation and perseverance is required of the client, dietitian, and physician. Subjectivity becomes a problem since the client is asked to define which specific foods, if any, are related to symptoms. Some investigators have pointed out that any improvement observed during an elimination diet may be due to incidental weight loss or placebo effect.[10] In spite of these problems, elimination diets are safe and noninvasive and should be considered for cooperative, allergy-prone clients.

Fasting

A liquids-only diet or 7- to 10-day fast has been used as a prelude to an elimination diet, the rationale being that any potential allergens would be excluded in preparation for the elimination diet. In many cases, fasting itself has been shown to relieve symptoms of rheumatoid arthritis. Skoldstam and colleagues found improvement in the erythrocyte sedimentation rate, walking time, and finger ring size and reduction in analgesic intake, pain, and stiffness in 16 persons with rheumatoid arthritis who fasted except for drinking fruit and vegetable juices.[16] Lithell and associates studied 10 persons with arthritis and psoriasis on a 2-week fast that included only vegetarian broths and drinks, herbal teas, and berry drinks. Eight of the subjects reported a lessening of symptoms during the fast.[17] Other studies have indicated statistically significant clinical improvement during short-term fasts.[5,18]

Several investigators have suggested that fasting may in some way alter immune function, resulting in a reduction in inflammation.[16,17,19] Short-term fasting, under medical supervision, appears to be safe and may even be beneficial for some clients with arthritis but should always be used with caution. Since fasting can precipitate a gouty attack, it should not be used as a treatment or as a part of a diagnostic procedure for persons with gout.

Omega-3 Fatty Acids

The use of omega-3 fatty acids, specifically eicosapentaenoic acid, is being investigated in the treatment of the inflammation associated with several forms of arthritis.[20] Prostaglandins are fatty acid derivatives. Series

1 prostaglandins are synthesized from linoleic acid and series 2 prostaglandins are synthesized from arachidonic acid. Eicosapentaenoic acid gives rise to series 3 prostaglandins,[21] which are less likely to cause inflammation than series 2 prostaglandins.[19] Ziff has suggested that a change in the fatty acid composition of the diet may be helpful in decreasing the inflammation associated with arthritis. A diet low in linoleic acid, a precursor of arachidonic acid, and high in eicosapentaenoic acid may inhibit production of series 2 prostaglandins and leukotriene B_4, both of which increase inflammation.[22] Laboratory animals with lupus erythematosus who were fed eicosapentaenoic acid lived longer than the control animals. The treatment was especially effective if started at the onset of their disease.[1] Substitution of polyunsaturated fatty acids with saturated fatty acids (eg, coconut oil) in the diets of laboratory animals also appears to reduce inflammation.[22]

Sperling and associates found that 12 persons with rheumatoid arthritis had statistically significant differences ($P < .036$) in joint pain index and the client's assessment of disease activity ($P < .0069$) after 6 weeks on a supplement of 20 g of Max-EPA (2.7 g of eicosapentaenoic acid and 1.8 g docosahexenoic acid) fish oil per day. However, there were no statistically significant changes in joint swelling, morning stiffness, grip strength, or erythrocyte sedimentation rate.[23] Kremer and colleagues gave 33 rheumatoid arthritis patients 15 Max-EPA capsules per day containing 2.7 g of eicosapentaenoic acid and 1.8 g docosahexenoic acid or an identical-appearing placebo for 36 weeks. Those ingesting the fish oil concentrate had delayed onset of fatigue ($P < .05$) and fewer tender joints ($P < .007$). Such measures as morning stiffness, grip strength, personal assessment of pain, physicians' assessment of pain, walking time, and joint swelling showed improvement, but the results were not statistically signficant.[24]

More controlled double-blind research needs to be conducted to elucidate the effectiveness of an increased omega-3 fatty acid intake in treating arthritis and to understand the roles of prostaglandins and leukotrienes in the promotion or inhibition of inflammation. In the meantime, encouraging greater intakes of high omega-3 fatty acid foods such as mackerel, salmon, bluefish, and sardines is harmless and may have some anti-inflammatory effects. Treatment with omega-3 fatty acid capsules is not recommended at this time because not enough is known about their physiological effects over the long term.

OTHER UNPROVEN THERAPIES

The popular literature abounds with treatments and purported cures for arthritis based on anecdotal evidence rather than controlled, double-blind studies. Some of these therapies (eg, no dairy products diets, fasting, and elimination diets) may have merit especially for those who have specific food sensitivities. Table 12-2 is a list of several popular nutrition regimens for arthritis with the rationale, if any, given by its proponent(s).

Vegetarian Diets

Several variations on vegetarian diets have been recommended for arthritis therapy over the past 20 years. Lithell and associates found that ten persons with arthritis and psoriasis improved during the fasting phase of the diet but that their conditions worsened somewhat while on a vegan diet. Nevertheless, the subjects reported that they felt better on the vegan diet than they had on their original diets but not as well as they had during the fasting phase.[17] In another study, Skoldstam measured the effectiveness of a 4-month vegan diet with no sugar, corn flour, salt, alcoholic beverages, coffee, or tea. The 20 subjects with rheumatoid arthritis showed improvement in ability to perform activities of daily living and reported less pain. However, such objective measures as grip strength, index of joint tenderness, number of joints involved, inflammation, erythrocyte sedimentation rate, concentration of C-reactive protein and C3 did not change in 60% of the patients.[43] Although some of the clients felt better, there was no apparent change in the disease process. Still, if clients experience less pain and can be more independent, the vegan diet or other vegetarian diets can be a harmless and generally beneficial regimen. Those following a vegan diet need to understand protein complementarity and may need to supplement vitamins B_{12} and D and calcium and zinc.

The same may be said about many of the other therapies for arthritis. Even if they are not helpful in treating the disease, they are at least innocuous. Exceptions include those therapies that promote toxic doses of vitamins and minerals; enemas; ingestion of raw milk, raw nuts or bone meal, excessive amounts of high cholesterol or high saturated fat foods; or elimination of entire food groups.[44]

Vitamin and Mineral Supplementation

Vitamin and mineral supplementation in excess of up to 3000 times the Recommended Dietary Allowances (RDA)[45] has been suggested for the amelioration or cure of arthritis in the popular press.[44] The vitamins and minerals and amounts recommended by various proponents are listed in Table 12-3. Although serum levels of vitamins A, C, B_6 (pyridoxine), B_1

Table 12-2 Unproven Nutrition Regimens for Arthritis

Regimen	Rationale	Reference
Vegetarian diet	Meat ingestion causes or aggravates arthritis	25
Vegetarian diet that prohibits cooked foods and processed foods; coffee enemas and nutritional supplements are included	Cleansing effect on body	26
Vegetarian diet that prohibits cooked or processed food and all grains except sprouted grains	Cleansing effect on body	27
Vegetarian diets with eggs (twice a week) and saltwater fish (once a week); fruits only in season and citrus fruits only two to three times a week	Cleansing effect on body	28
Vegetarian diet with refined carbohydrates, limited saturated fats, and reduced caffeine; 1 tbsp cod liver oil per day	Reduces incidence of arthritis in persons older than 40 years of age	29
No-dairy-products diet	Dairy products cause mucus formation and calcium deposition, which leads to arthritis	27, 30
Whole milk at room temperature taken 5 minutes before meals or on an empty stomach; butter is allowed but no margarine, skim milk, or buttermilk	Whole milk and butter lubricate joints and thus alleviate pain	31
No meats, dairy products, or additives	Arthritis is caused by allergy to meats, dairy products, additives, and other foods	11
Fish, brown rice, and vegetables allowed	All other foods cause allergic reaction resulting in arthritis	32
No corn, wheat, milk, coffee, tea, sugar, beef, pork, eggs, peanuts, cola drinks, oranges, apples, butter beans, tomatoes, or chocolate	Arthritis symptoms are a result of an allergic reaction to these foods	33
Fresh foods or foods canned in glass; unprocessed nuts; cereals boiled in spring water; wheat in baked, puffed, or boiled forms; baker's chocolate; sugar in spring water allowed	Other foods may cause arthritis symptoms; a food diary is suggested and other foods may be added one at a time if there is no reaction	34

Table 12-2 continued

Regimen	Rationale	Reference
Fasting	Cleanses the system and rests the body	25, 27, 35
Fast of 3 to 5 days before an elimination diet	Rids the body of toxins	33, 34, 36
Fast plus two enemas per day	Rids the body of toxins	28
Three-pronged treatment • fast and elimination diet • six-meal high protein, low carbohydrate diet • no nightshade foods (white potatoes, peppers [except black], eggplant, tomatoes)	Arthritis is caused by allergy, hypoglycemia, and solanine poisoning (nightshade foods are a source of solanine)	27
High protein, high fat diet including 2 to 4 eggs daily, at least 1 qt milk, 1/4 lb liver, brewer's yeast, generous portions of meat, fowl, and seafood		37
High unrefined carbohydrate and low animal fat diet with supplements		38
Apple cider vinegar and honey three times a day, 1 drop Lugol's iodine solution per day three times a week, diet high in unprocessed carbohydrates, very little meat, and fruits that grow in the climate in which one lives	Vinegar thins body fluids and makes tissues around joints more tender; honey relieves pain	39
No highly processed foods, liver, kidney, or margarine; no cooking in aluminum pans		40
Specific food ingestion; pecans, bananas, brewer's yeast, wheat germ, sour cherries, avocados, pokeweed berries	Certain foods are said to give relief from arthritis	25
Garlic		25, 41
Alfalfa		41
Wheat germ oil		28
Blackstrap molasses		42

Source: PG Wolman, "Management of Patients Using Unproven Regimens for Arthritis." Copyright The American Dietetic Association. Reprinted by permission from *Journal of the American Dietetic Association* (1987;87[9]:1211).

Table 12-3 Vitamin and Mineral Supplementation for Arthritis in the Popular Press

Nutrient	Amount	Reference	RDA (for age 51+) or Adequate and Safe Amount	Comments
Vitamin A	25,000 IU Not specified	37 32, 46, 47	5,000 IU	Chronic vitamin A toxicity may occur at levels of 25,000 IU/day over an extended period.[48]
Vitamin D	2,500 IU 200,000–600,000	37 49	200 IU or 5 mg	Potential toxicity in amounts several times the RDA for long periods.[45]
Vitamin E	200–400 IU 300–600 IU 2,000–20,000 IU Not specified	36 28, 37, 42 46 25, 32, 40	15 IU	Generally safe. Some scattered reports of toxicities at dosages between 400–1,000 IU.[45] Dosages of 400–800 mg probably not toxic.[48]
Vitamin C	750–1,500 mg 1,000 mg 1,500 mg 2,000 mg 4,000–100,000 mg Not specified	38 36 28 37 49 25, 31, 40, 46	60 mg	In pharmacologic doses has been shown to alleviate lower platelet and plasma vitamin C levels in aspirin-taking arthritics and to increase serum levels of IgA, IgM, and C3.[45,50] May cause gastrointestinal symptoms in doses greater than 4,000 mg. Large doses can interfere with copper absorption and increase uric acid excretion. May cause false-positive or false-negative urine glucose results and false-negative results for blood in stool.[48]
Thiamine	Not specified	46	1.2 mg	Serum thiamine levels are decreased in rheumatoid arthritis patients.[50] Elderly may use less efficiently.[45] Very little evidence of toxicity.[48]
Vitamin B_6	25–100 mg 500–1,000 mg 500–2,000 mg Not specified	25 36 46 40	2.2 mg	Intake found to be low in arthritics.[51] B_6 dependency has been produced in adults who took 200 mg for 33 days.[45] Supplementation interferes with metabolism of levodopa.[48]
Vitamin B_{12}	500 µg	36	3.0 µg	Long biological half-life.[45] Nontoxic; may give false-negative results for pernicious anemia due to high circulating blood levels of B_{12}.[48]

Nutrient	Dosage claimed	Ref.	Safe/RDA amount	Comments
Pantothenic acid	100–500 mg 400 mg 600 mg 1,000 mg Not specified	32 37 26 36 40, 41	4–7 mg	Blood pantothenic levels are decreased in rheumatoid arthritis.[50] Intake found to be low in arthritics.[51] Relatively nontoxic; some gastrointestinal disturbances seen at levels between 10,000 and 20,000 mg/d.[45]
Niacinamide	100–200 mg 1,500–4,000 mg	32 36	16 mg Niacin Equivalents	Reasonably safe in amounts up to 4,000 mg/d.[48]
Calcium	150–1,000 mg 500 mg 3,000 mg	36 32 37	800 mg	Intake found to be low in arthritics.[51] Actual needs may be higher than RDA in postmenopausal women.[52]
Magnesium	250 mg 200–300 mg Not specified	32 36 25	350 mg	Intake found to be low in arthritics.[51] High doses may be a problem if patient has impaired kidney function or takes large amounts of magnesium laxatives or antacids.[48]
Iron	Not specified	25, 32	10 mg	25–75 mg/day probably safe.[45] May be beneficial to those with some blood loss due to heavy aspirin use.[53]
Zinc	15–50 mg 50 mg Not specified	36 54 25, 32, 46, 47	15 mg	Intake found to be low in arthritics.[51] One study showed 220 mg three times a day to be beneficial.[55] Toxicity documented at 2,000 mg or more.[45] Excess zinc intake lowers blood copper levels.[48]
Copper	Not specified	32	2–3 mg	Intake of up to 10 mg probably safe.[45] Toxicity seen with ingestion of 20 g copper sulfate.[48]
Selenium	50–100 µg Not specified	36 46	50–200 µg	Considerable differences in amounts of selenium found in foods from different regions.[45] Harmful at levels greater than 2.5–3.0 mg.[48]
Manganese	Not specified	55		Toxicity seen in humans in form of airborne pollutant.[45,48]
Silicon	Not specified	32, 41, 55	2.5–5.0 mg	Need for silicon has not yet been demonstrated in humans. There is a decline in silicon content of arterial vessels in the skin of aging humans.[56]
Choline	500–1,000 mg	36	400–900 mg average intake	Toxicity has not been documented at levels up to 16 g/d for as long as 4 months.[57]
Inositol	Not specified	46		Average US intake is about 1,000 mg.[48]

Source: PG Wolman, "Management of Patients Using Unproven Regimens for Arthritis." Copyright The American Dietetic Association. Reprinted by permission from *Journal of the American Dietetic Association* (1987;87[9]:1211).

(thiamine,) and pantothenic acid have been reported to be below normal in persons with arthritis, supplementation does not appear to have a therapeutic effect on arthritis symptoms.[1,20,58–60]

Serum zinc and selenium have also been reported to be low in arthritis.[20,60,61] Simkin gave 24 persons with rheumatoid arthritis 220 mg of zinc sulfate three times a day for 12 weeks in a double-blind study. Those taking the zinc supplement reported less joint tenderness and swelling, less morning stiffness, and improved walking time than those taking the placebo.[55]

Low serum and plasma levels of selenium have been reported in persons with rheumatoid arthritis and juvenile arthritis. Selenium supplementation increases blood levels to normal values but does not appear to improve the clinical symptoms.[61]

The cause of the iron deficiency often associated with rheumatoid arthritis is not known. The anemia is not the hypochromic, microcytic type seen in iron deficiency but hypochromic, normocytic.[60] In addition, persons have normal or increased iron stores and iron supplementation does not help unless there has been blood loss.[20] Gastrointestinal bleeding in elderly persons with osteoarthritis taking large daily doses of aspirin may result in blood loss requiring iron supplementation.[5,62]

Low serum levels of vitamins and minerals are more likely due to the anorexia or undernutrition resulting from the discomfort of arthritis rather than a contributing cause.[60] Supplementation in the form of a multiple vitamin and mineral with no more than 100% of the RDA for any vitamin or mineral would be harmless and may help to improve nutrition status especially in those with poor appetite and limited food intake.

DRUG THERAPIES AND NUTRIENT INTERACTIONS

The major drugs prescribed for treatment of arthritis are salicylates, nonsteroidal anti-inflammatory agents, antimalarials, D-penicillamine, corticosteroids, immunosuppressive agents, and gold.[63,64] Most of the drugs cause some degree of gastrointestinal disturbance, loss of appetite, or taste changes; all of which result in a decrease in food intake (Table 12-4).[63,65] Drug–nutrient interactions occur between salicylates, D-penicillamine, methotrexate, corticosteroids, gold, and some vitamins and minerals (see Table 12-4).

Sahud and Cohen found that persons with rheumatoid arthritis taking more than 12 aspirins per day had lower platelet levels of vitamin C than normal or other subjects with rheumatoid arthritis not taking high daily doses of aspirin. Even though they found no relationship between platelet levels of vitamin C and severity of rheumatoid arthritis, Sahud and Cohen recommended vitamin C supplementation in persons with rheumatoid arthritis taking more than 12 aspirins per day.[66]

Bigaouette and colleagues claim that zinc, copper, cobalt, and magnesium are chelated by D-penicillamine and vitamin B_6 is deactivated by it.[64] Simkin hypothesized that the reason for D-penicillamine's effectiveness is its ability to increase the absorption of zinc.[55] Touger-Decker states that D-penicillamine is detrimental to zinc, copper, and iron status[63] (see Table 12-4).

Folate stores are reduced and folate metabolism hindered in methotrexate therapy.[64,65,67] Methotrexate dosage must be regulated to give relief from symptoms without the toxic effects of folate deficiency.[67]

Urinary excretion of calcium, zinc, and nitrogen may be increased during prednisone therapy.[64] Persons with arthritis receiving corticosteroid therapy may require supplementation. Robinson recommends a dietary intake of at least 1000 mg calcium and 400 IU of vitamin D per day to avoid the osteopenia observed during corticosteroid therapy. If those levels of dietary intake are unrealistic, he suggests a supplement of at least 50,000 IU of vitamin D two to three times per week and a daily calcium supplementation of at least 500 mg.[60] Further side effects, nutrition interactions, and dietary suggestions are given in Table 12-5 for many of the medications commonly prescribed for arthritis syndromes.

Salicylates and nonsteroidal anti-inflammatory drugs reduce pain, inflammation, and other symptoms of arthritis, but they do not retard disease progression as the antimalarials, D-penicillamine, and gold salts may.[63] Although any side effects of drug therapy on the nutrition status of the person with arthritis should be monitored carefully, and ameliorated immediately, it must be recognized that drugs are an integral part of arthritis therapy. Dietitians and nutritionists should be aware of the possibility that some clients may stop taking all medications while following a popular but as yet unproven nutrition therapy for arthritis.[44]

ASSESSMENT AND DIET MODIFICATIONS

A careful nutrition history is taken, including foods eaten and excluded, types and amounts of supplements taken, prescription and over-the-counter medications ingested, weight fluctuations, and ability to shop, prepare food, and self-feed.[44,63] Inadequate food intake may be the result of morning stiffness causing omission of the breakfast meal or of impairment of the dominant hand, wrist, elbow, or shoulder, making it difficult to shop for, prepare, or self-feed.[62,63]

Table 12-4 Medication Side Effects

Side Effects	Salicylates	NSAIDs*	Antimalarials	D-Penicillamine	Cortico-Steroids	Immuno-Suppressive Agents	Gold
Nutritional Status							
Anorexia			X	X		X	
Stomatitis		X		X	X	X	X
Nausea	X	X	X	X		X	
Vomiting	X	X	X	X		X	
Gastritis	X						
Duodenal ulcer		X					
Peptic ulcer	X				X		
Constipation		X					
Gastrointestinal hemorrhage	X	X				X	
Diarrhea		X†	X	X		X	
Altered taste				X			X
Metabolic Status							
Glucose intolerance					X		
Proteinuria				X			X
Negative nitrogen balance					X		

Altered serum potassium	X	X	
Edema	‡	X	
Depressed total lymphocyte count		X	X
Anergy		X	X
Increased blood urea nitrogen	X		
Anemia	X	X	
Decreased Vitamin–			
Mineral Status			
Ascorbic acid	X		
Folate	X		X§
Zinc	X	X	
Copper		X	
Calcium		X	X
Iron		X	X

*NSAIDs, nosteroidal anti-inflammatory drugs
†Meclofenamate only
‡May occur with pre-existing edema
§Methotrexate only

Source: R Touger-Decker, "Nutritional Considerations in Rheumatoid Arthritis." Copyright The American Dietetic Association. Reprinted by permission from *Journal of the American Dietetic Association* (1988;88[3]:327).

Table 12-5 Dietary Suggestions Associated with Drugs That Alter Nutrient Absorption

Drug (Use)	Nutritional Implications		Dietary Suggestions
	Gastrointestinal Side/Adverse Effects	Other Reactions	
Methotrexate (antineoplastic, antipsoriatic)	Abdominal distress Diarrhea Gastrointestinal ulceration and bleeding Nausea/vomiting	Folacin antagonist (irreversibly binds with dihydrofolate reductase) Malabsorption of folacin, vitamin B_{12}, and fat Hyperuricemia Loss of appetite Altered taste acuity Sore mouth and lips	Drug: Absorption may be decreased by milky meals. Diet therapy: May indicate increased intake of alkaline-ash foods and beverages and the ingestion of 2000 mL water per day to aid in excretion of uric acid. Avoid the use of alcoholic beverages. Caution patient against self-medication with over-the-counter preparations, especially the use of supplements containing p-aminobenzoic acid and folacin. Other: Alert physician if patient reports diarrhea, abdominal distress, bloody vomit, or black tarry stools.
Penicillamine (chelating agent, antiarthritic, antiurolithic, heavy metal antagonist)	Diarrhea Epigastric pain Nausea/vomiting	Inhibits pyridoxal-dependent enzymes Chelates copper, iron, and zinc Unpleasant taste Decreased taste acuity (salt, sweet) Loss of appetite	Rheumatoid arthritis—Drug: Take with water on an empty stomach at least 1 hour apart from any meals, food, milk, or snacks. Other: Diet therapy may include vitamin B_6 supplementation for persons with rheumatoid arthritis. Drug should be taken separate from iron and other mineral supplements.
Pyrimethamine (antimalarial)	Vomiting (dose related)	Inhibits dihydrofolate reductase (inhibitory potential greater on the intact microorganisms than on host)	Drug: Take with meals or snacks to minimize gastric irritation. Diet therapy: May indicate concomitant administration of preformed folic acid (folinic acid)

		to prevent anemia; caution against the use of *p*-aminobenzoic acid supplements.
Adrenal corticosteroids	Megaloblastic anemia (large doses) Loss of appetite (large doses) Excreted in breast milk Fluid and electrolyte disturbances Negative nitrogen balance Protein catabolism Lipolysis with possible redistribution of body fat Anti–vitamin D activity (inhibits calcium absorption) Appetite stimulation Weight gain Excreted in breast milk	Drug: Take with food or low-sodium snack to minimize gastric irritation. Diet therapy: May include the need for a sodium-restricted diet, a diet high in potassium and protein, and caloric restriction or weight monitoring (especially during long-term therapy). Adequate intake of vitamin D–containing foods may be indicated. Advise client that alcohol may enhance ulcerogenic potential of drug.
Aspirin (analgesic, antipyretic, anti-inflammatory)	Bloating Indigestion Nausea/vomiting Ulcerogenic potential Gastric pain or bleeding Heartburn Nausea/vomiting Increased vitamin C excretion and potassium depletion (large doses) Iron-deficiency anemia (long use or overuse) Salicylate excreted in breast milk	Drug: Take with 250 mL water (for rapid analgesia) or food to reduce gastric irritation. (Drug absorption may be delayed when aspirin is taken with food.) Swallow enteric tablets whole. Some buffered preparations contain sodium and may be contraindicated for persons on sodium-restricted diets. Diet therapy: May caution against concomitant intake with alcoholic beverages; may indicate the need for adequate fluid intake and emphasize the intake of foods rich in vitamin C. Vitamin C supplementation may be prescribed for vitamin C–depleted patients receiving large doses of the drug. Other: Drug should be cautiously used in clients prone to vitamin K deficiency. Drug-induced gastric bleeding may contribute to or aggravate iron-deficiency anemia.

continues

Table 12-5 continued

Drug (Use)	Nutritional Implications		Dietary Suggestions
	Gastrointestinal Side/Adverse Effects	Other Reactions	
Indomethacin (anti-inflammatory, analgesic)	Bloating Constipation (or diarrhea) Heartburn/indigestion Nausea/vomiting Stomach pain Ulcerogenic potential	Sodium and fluid retention Weight gain (mild) (edema) Excreted in breast milk	Drug: Even though food may slightly delay or reduce absorption, take drug after meals or with food to reduce gastric irritation. (An antacid may be prescribed.) Diet therapy: Inform client to avoid alcoholic beverages. Even though salt and fluid retention effects are less pronounced than with phenylbutazone, a sodium-restricted diet may be indicated. Other: Drug-induced gastric bleeding may contribute to or aggravate iron-deficiency anemia.
Sulfasalazine (anti-inflammatory)	Diarrhea Gastric distress Nausea/vomiting	Impaired folacin absorption Loss of appetite Excreted in breast milk	Drug: Take with 250 mL water or after meals or with food to minimize gastric irritation. Diet therapy: Ensure adequate fluid intake to maintain at least 1200 to 1500 mL urine output per day. Encourage the intake of foods high in folacin.

Phenylbutazone (anti-inflammatory)	Constipation (or diarrhea) Heartburn/indigestion Salt and fluid retention Weight gain (edema) Excreted in breast milk	Drug: Take with meals to minimize gastric irritation. Diet therapy: May indicate the need for a sodium-restricted diet. Instruct client to avoid alcoholic beverages.
Colchicine (antigout)	Diarrhea (may be severe) Nausea/vomiting Abdominal pain Malabsorption of sodium, potassium, fat, carotene, and vitamin B_{12} due to altered mucosal function Decreased lactase activity Loss of appetite	Drug: Take with water immediately before, with, or after meals to reduce gastric irritation. Diet therapy: May indicate increased intake of alkaline-ash foods or beverages and low-purine foods, no alcoholic beverages, and a high fluid intake of >2000 mL/d. Other: Gradual weight reduction may be suggested. Alert physician if person reports any gastrointestinal side effects.

Source: CH Smith and WR Bidlack, "Dietary Concerns Associated with the Use of Medications." Copyright The American Dietetic Association. Adapted by permission from *Journal of the American Dietetic Association* (1984; 84[8]:901).

Kowsari and co-workers studied 24 subjects with osteoarthritis and found their diets to be below two thirds of the RDA for magnesium, zinc, vitamin E, folacin, vitamin B_6, and pantothenic acid.[51] Certainly not all persons with arthritis have poor diets, but those who do need to be identified and treated, not because any nutrient inadequacy is the cause of the arthritis but for their general health and well-being.[19]

Dietary treatments for arthritis have been generally unsuccessful in the past, but such therapies as allergy diets, fasting, and high omega-3 fatty acid diets among others have promise and need further investigation under double-blind conditions. These studies are difficult to conduct, since the subjects almost always know when they are on the experimental diet. In addition, most arthritis sufferers experience spontaneous remissions and fluctuations in the severity of their symptoms, making it difficult to know what changes can be attributed to the diet treatment.[3,10,20] Also, relief from symptoms while following certain diets appears to be specific to some clients but not to others with apparently the same syndrome.[20] Therefore, diet therapy must be carefully individualized with particular attention to body weight, nutrient intake, food allergies or sensitivities, and possibly type of fatty acid intake.

Maintenance of Normal Weight

The mainstay of diet therapy for arthritis has been the achievement and maintenance of ideal body weight. Persons with osteoarthritis and gout have been told to reduce to ideal body weight because osteoarthritis and hyperuricemia have been correlated with overweight and obesity.[60] Weight loss has also been recommended for persons with rheumatoid arthritis who are at or below ideal body weight with the rationale that the low calorie diet could produce malnutrition and eventual immunosuppression, resulting in the alleviation of symptoms.[68]

Weight loss in cases of gout should be gradual since ketosis may increase the likelihood of an attack of gout. Although weight loss is recommended for overweight persons, the low purine diet is rarely used now because of the effectiveness of the medications available for treatment of gout. In clients with rheumatoid arthritis and lupus erythematosus anorexia and inanition are more common than increased body weight.[60]

Food Preparation and Eating Skills

Treatment of clients with various forms of arthritis centers on relieving their symptoms and minimizing the side effects of their treatment. Simple activities of daily living can become extremely painful and have devastating effects on nutritional status. Efforts should be made to maintain as much independence as possible. The use of a stool to sit on in the kitchen while preparing meals, the availability of utensils, and the use of blenders, food processors, electric can openers, and lightweight pots and pans may help a client continue to function as the major family food preparer. Suction cups on the bottom of stainless steel bowls, rubber aids for jar opening, and proper counter height can make food preparation safer and less painful. If meal preparation becomes too difficult, meals on wheels or homemaker services may be required to ensure adequate nutrition.[69]

Special eating utensils may be needed. A detachable plate guard will keep food from falling off the edges, and foam padding wrapped around utensil handles make them easier to grasp. Finger foods can also be helpful if they are easy to hold and do not fall apart.[63] A suction cup may be placed under the dinner plate to hold it firmly on the table. Terrycloth glass covers and flexible straws can make drinking easier and avoid spillage.[63,69] Assessment and training by an occupational therapist are useful complements to the nutrition intervention by the dietitian.

Meeting with a local arthritis group on a regular basis not only will provide innovative ideas for coping skills but will also give much needed emotional support to clients and their families. The groups listed below can help by providing information about local or regional chapters, meetings, and newsletters:

The Arthritis Foundation
1314 Spring Street, N.W.
Atlanta, GA 30309

Arthritis Health Professions Association
1314 Spring Street, N.W.
Atlanta, GA 30309

The American Lupus Society
23751 Madison Street
Torrance, CA 90505

L.E. Support Club (Lupus Erythematosus)
3103 Hartnell Blvd.
Isle of Palms, S.C. 29451

Lupus Foundation of America
1717 Massachusetts Avenue, N.W., Suite 203
Washington, DC 20036

Lupus Network
221 Ranch Drive
Bridgeport, CT 06606

National Lupus Erythematosus Foundation
5430 Van Nuys Blvd., Suite 206
Van Nuys, CA 91401

Some feeding aids suppliers are listed below.[70] Many others are available
at hospital and home health wholesale or retail distribution centers.

Research Products Corporation
1015 East Washington Avenue
Madison, WI 53701

Fred Sammon, Inc.
Box 321
Brookfield, IL 60513-0032

J.A. Preston Corporation
71 Fifth Avenue
New York, NY 10003

Cleo Living Aids
3957 Mayfield Road
Cleveland, OH 44121

REFERENCES

1. Panush RS. Controversial arthritis remedies. *Bull Rheum Dis*. 1984;34(5):1–10.

2. Zussman BM. Food hypersensitivity simulating rheumatoid arthritis. *South Med J*. 1966;59:935–939.

3. Darlington LG. Does food intolerance have any role in the aetiology and management of rheumatoid disease? *Ann Rheum Dis*. 1985;44:801–804.

4. Hadley SL. Diet and arthritis. *Minn Med*. 1987;70:533–534.

5. Kroker GF, Stroud RM, Marshall R, et al. Fasting and rheumatoid arthritis: A multicenter study. *Clin Etiol*. 1984;2(3):137–144.

6. Panush RS, Webster EM. Food allergies and other adverse reaction to foods. *Med Clin North Am*. 1985;69:533–546.

7. Parke AL, Hughes GRV. Rheumatoid arthritis and food: A case study. *Br Med J*. 1981;282:2027–2028.

8. Hicklin JA, McEwen LM, Morgan JE. The effect of diet on rheumatoid arthritis. Paper presented at the British Society for Allergy and Clinical Immunology, Guy's Hospital, London, December 1, 1979.

9. Ratner D, Eshel E, Schneeyour A, Teitler A. Does milk intolerance affect seronegative arthritis in lactase-deficient women? *Isr J Med Sci*. 1985;21:532–534.

10. Darlington LG, Ramsey NW, Mansfield JR. Placebo-controlled, blind study of dietary manipulation therapy in rheumatoid arthritis. *Lancet.* 1986;1:236–238.

11. Dong CH, Banks J. *New Hope for the Arthritic.* New York, NY: Thomas Y Crowell; 1975.

12. Panush RS, Carter RL, Katz P, Kowsari B, Longley S, Finnie S. Diet therapy for rheumatoid arthritis. *Arthritis Rheum.* 1983;26:462–469.

13. Welsh CJR, Hanglow AC, Conn P, Barber THW, Coombs RRA. Early rheumatoid-like synovial lesions in rabbits drinking cow's milk. *Int Arch Allergy Appl Immunol.* 1985;78:145–151.

14. Felder M, De Blecourt ACE, Wuthrich BW. Food allergy in patients with rheumatoid arthritis. *Clin Rheumatol.* 1987;6:181–185.

15. Denman AM, Mitchell B, Ansell B. Joint complaints and food allergic disorder. *Ann Allergy.* 1983;51:260–263.

16. Skoldstam L, Larson L, Lindstrom FD. Effects of fasting and lactovegetarian diet on rheumatoid arthritis. *Scand J Rheumatol.* 1979;8:249–255.

17. Lithell H, Bruce A, Gustafsson IB, et al. A fasting and vegetarian diet treatment trial on chronic inflammatory disorders. *Acta Derm Venereol.* 1983;63:397–403.

18. Uden AM, Trang L, Venizelos N, Palmblad J. Neutrophil functions and clinical performance after total fasting in patients with rheumatoid arthritis. *Ann Rheum Dis.* 1983;42:45–51.

19. McCrae F, Veerapen K, Dieppe P. Diet and arthritis. *Practitioner* 1986;230:359–361.

20. Bollet AJ. Nutrition and diet in rheumatic disorders. In: Shils ME, Young VR, eds. *Modern Nutrition in Health and Disease.* 7th ed. Philadelphia, Pa: Lea & Febiger; 1988.

21. Hamilton EMN, Gropper SAS. *The Biochemistry of Human Nutrition.* St. Paul, Minn: West Publishing Co; 1987.

22. Ziff M. Diet in the treatment of rheumatoid arthritis. *Arthritis Rheum.* 1983;20:457–461.

23. Sperling RI, Weinblatt M, Robin J, et al. Effects of dietary supplementation with marine fish oil on leukocyte lipid mediator generation and function in rheumatoid arthritis. *Arthritis Rheum.* 1987;30:988–997.

24. Kremer JM, Jubiz W, Michalek A, et al. Fish oil fatty acid supplementation in active rheumatoid arthritis. *Ann Intern Med.* 1987;106:497–502.

25. Bricklin M. *The Practical Encyclopedia of Natural Healing.* Emmaus, Pa: Rodale Press; 1983.

26. Hulke M. *The Encyclopedia of Alternative Medicine and Self-Help.* New York, NY: Schocken Press; 1979.

27. Kulvinskas V. *Planetary Healers Manual.* Woodstock Valley, Conn: Omangod Press; 1975.

28. Airola PO. *There Is a Cure for Arthritis.* West Nyack, NY: Parker Publishing Company; 1979.

29. Kordell L. *How to Keep Your Youthful Vitality After Forty.* New York, NY: GP Putnam & Sons; 1969.

30. Kulvinskas V, Tasca R. *Life in the 21st Century.* Woodstock Valley, Conn: Omangod Press; 1981.

31. Alexander DD. *Arthritis and Common Sense.* Hartford, Conn: Witkower Press; 1958.

32. Kunin RA. *Meganutrition.* New York, NY: Mosby/Times Mirror; 1981.

33. Eagle R. *Eating and Allergy*. Garden City, NY: Doubleday; 1981.

34. Mandell M, Scanlon LW. *Dr. Mandell's 5 Day Allergy Relief System*. New York, NY: Thomas Y Crowell; 1979.

35. Gross J. The fast way to rejuvenate body and spirit. *Vegetarian Times* 1984;June:32.

36. Fredericks C. *Arthritis: Don't Learn to Live With It*. New York, NY: Grosset & Dunlap; 1981.

37. Davis A. *Let's Get Well*. New York, NY: New American Library; 1972.

38. Cheraskin E, Ringdorf WM, Sisley EL. *The Vitamin C Connection*. New York, NY: Bantam Books; 1983.

39. Jarvis DC. *Arthritis and Folk Medicine*. New York, NY: Fawcett Crest; 1960.

40. Rothblatt HB, Pinorsky D, Brodsky M. *How to Stop the Pain of Arthritis*. Hollywood, Fla: Compact Periodicals; 1985.

41. Lindberg G, McFarland JL. *Take Charge of Your Health: The Complete Nutrition Book*. New York, NY: Harper & Row Publishers, 1982.

42. Frank BS, Miele P. *Dr. Frank's No-Aging Diet*. New York, NY: Dial Press; 1976.

43. Skoldstam L. Fasting and vegan diet and rheumatoid arthritis. *Scand J Rheumatol*. 1986;15:219–223.

44. Wolman PG. Management of patients using unproven regimens for arthritis. *J Am Diet Assoc*. 1987;87:1211–1214.

45. Food and Nutrition Board. *Recommended Dietary Allowances*. 9th rev ed. Washington, DC: National Academy of Sciences; 1980.

46. Pearson D, Shaw S. *Life Extension: A Practical Scientific Approach*. New York, NY: Warner Books; 1982.

47. Mazer E. Health fronts: Arthritis inflammation reduced with zinc and retinoic acid. *Prevention* 1984;July:4.

48. Marshall CW. *Vitamins and Minerals: Help or Harm*. Philadelphia, Pa: George F. Stickley Co; 1983.

49. Rodale JI. *The Complete Book of Vitamins*. Emmaus, Pa: Rodale Books; 1976.

50. McCarty DJ. *Arthritis and Allied Conditions*. 9th ed. Philadelphia, Pa: Lea & Febiger; 1979.

51. Kowsari B, Finnie SK, Carter RL, et al. Assessment of the diet of patients with rheumatoid arthritis and osteoarthritis. *J Am Diet Assoc*. 1983;82:657–659.

52. Osteoporosis. National Institutes of Health Consensus Development Conference Statement 5, No. 3, publication No. 1984–421–132:4652. Washington, DC: US Government Printing Office; 1984.

53. Katz WA. *Rheumatic Diseases: Diagnosis and Management*. Philadelphia, Pa: JB Lippincott Co; 1977.

54. Passwater RA, Cranton EM. *Trace Elements, Hair Analysis and Nutrition*. New Canaan, Conn: Keats Publishing Co; 1983.

55. Simkin PA. Oral zinc sulphate in rheumatoid arthritis. *Lancet*. 1976;2:539–542.

56. Carlisle EM. Silicon. In: *Nutrition Reviews' Present Knowledge in Nutrition*. 5th ed. Washington, DC: Nutrition Foundation; 1984.

57. Kuksis A, Mookerjea S. Choline. In: *Nutrition Reviews' Present Knowledge in Nutrition*. 5th ed. Washington, DC: Nutrition Foundation; 1984.

58. Freyberg, RH. Treatment of arthritis with vitamin and endocrine preparations. *JAMA*. 1942;119:1165–1171.

59. Oldroyd KG, Davis PT. Clinically significant vitamin C deficiency in rheumatoid arthritis. *Br J Rheumatol.* 1985;24:362–363.

60. Robinson WD. Nutrition and rheumatic diseases. In: Kelley WN, Harris ED Jr, Ruddy S, Sledge CB, eds. *Textbook of Rheumatology.* Philadelphia, Pa: WB Saunders Co; 1981.

61. Rheumatoid arthritis and selenium. *Nutr Rev.* 1988;46:284–286.

62. Kennedy JT, Krondl M. Evaluations of the dietary adequacy of elderly osteoarthritic individuals treated with acetylsalicylic acid. *J Can Diet Assoc.* 1987;47:232–238.

63. Touger-Decker R. Nutritional considerations in rheumatoid arthritis. *J Am Diet Assoc.* 1988;88:327–331.

64. Bigaouette J, Timchalk MA, Kremer J. Nutritional adequacy of diet and supplements in patients with rheumatoid arthritis who take medications. *J Am Diet Assoc.* 1987;87:1687–1688.

65. Hollingsworth JW. Rehabilitation and conservative management of joint disease in the elderly. In: Kay MMB, Galpin J, Makinodon T, eds. *Aging: Immunity and Arthritis Disease.* New York, NY; Raven Press; 1980.

66. Sahud MA, Cohen RJ. Effect of aspirin ingestion on ascorbic acid levels in rheumatoid arthritis. *Lancet.* 1971;1:937–938.

67. Morgan SL, Baggott JE, Altz-Smith M. Folate status of rheumatoid arthritis patients receiving long-term, low dose methotrexate therapy. *Arthritis Rheum.* 1987;30:1348–1356.

68. Coughlan RJ, Hazleman BL. Dietary manipulation in rheumatoid arthritis. *Lancet.* 1986;1:442. Letter to the Editor.

69. Rosenberg AL. *Living with Your Arthritis.* New York, NY: Arco Publishing Co, Inc; 1979.

70. Natow AB, Heslin J. *Nutritional Care of the Older Adult.* New York, NY: Macmillan Publishing Co; 1986.

Chapter 13

Information Power for the Dietitian

John R. Schweitzer

INFORMATION: WHO WIELDS THE WAND?

As a child, I enjoyed the classic Disney film *The Sorcerer's Apprentice*. In this animated fable, Mickey Mouse grabs the opportunity to try his hand at using the old master's magic. He forces the broom to carry water, one of his least favorite chores. Initially, he is delighted at the results, seeing the broom carrying bucket load after bucket load up from the well. However, he becomes alarmed when he cannot figure out how to stop them. Before the Sorcerer returns to save him, Mickey has been deluged by water and is powerless to stop the automated broom from dutifully bringing endless buckets of water. Once as an "apprentice" computer user, I experienced a similar sense of helplessness as the "magic" printer continued to print out rolls of continuous feed paper despite my efforts to control it.

In the 20th century we have developed the engines to grind out information in a seemingly endless and overwhelming flow, much like Mickey's broomstick servants. Our civilization has begun to replace the heavy, industrial machines with smart, lightweight information processors. These new machines have the potential to give us great power to use information in our work. As professionals we might pause to review what information is, how we want to use and respond to information, and, finally, how to plan for getting a handle on its power to help us do our work.

The purpose of this chapter is to suggest a long-range strategy for access, storage, and retrieval of information for the dietitian who is practicing in the clinical area of rehabilitation. Arguments are made that (1) information is evaluated based on its use to the user (ie, "user-defined") and (2) information is being generated at such a rapid pace that it is difficult to manage using traditional storage and retrieval methods. This chapter has been written to develop practical knowledge about collecting information through database approaches, storing information in a manner that is compatible with databases (both print and nonprint), and retrieval of this information for use by the dietitian in working with professional colleagues and clients. Sources of information that are discussed include national, regional and local databases, networks, and community resources. Examples of how each of these might provide information power to the dietitian are presented and methods for planning and implementing a personal, information handling system are outlined.

INFORMATION PROCESSING CONSIDERATIONS

At the adult level, "information is where you find it." Adults are goal oriented and seek answers to their questions about how to operate, manipulate, and control their environment. As persons mature into adult life, they perceive patterns of stimuli in their environment and build an internal, cognitive map of how their environment works.[1]

Indeed, the word "information" may be derived from "a formation within." Information taken alone has no weight or physical consistency. However, information applied to other humans or electromechanical devices can cause physical changes in the environment. We drive automobiles, start production lines in factories, pilot airplanes, and operate on patients in an effective manner only when we have adequate information.

Information (as contrasted to "noise") is sought by the person who "needs to know." *Noise* is defined as any stimulus that interferes with our receipt of information. Too much information for our capacity to process information can cause information to be lost or unavailable when needed or simply not processed due to distraction by other noise. Noise can become information if it has a pattern that we learn to recognize as meaningful.

As an example, recall yesterday's mail delivery. Did you flip through the various pieces of mail deciding which to open and which to set aside for later reading and perhaps which you would not open at all? Most of us are deluged with print messages that compete for our attention. Much of this is "junk mail," or "noise." Perhaps you have experienced a sense of irritation at having such mail delivered at all. If you were waiting for a check payment or a job acceptance letter, then the sense of irritation at having to deal with the "noise" might have been higher. To take this analogy one step farther, perhaps after discarding a "junk mail" announcement about a workshop, a colleague calls and asks you to save the registration coupon in the announcement so he can preregister. At that point, the "junk mail" may be redefined as useful information and may cause you to hunt for it in your wastebasket.

CONTROL OF INFORMATION

"Information overload" was a buzz word of the early 1970s and was often associated with a professional person's irritation and psychological stress. In the latter 1980s with the onslaught of the computer, we are beginning to glimpse the impact of information on our personal and professional lives.

Professional catalogues, brochures, and bulletins arrive in our mailboxes and on our desks at an alarming rate. Duplicating machines have allowed for cheap reproduction for parallel processing of multiple copies of this information within our organizations. Facsimile machines have accelerated the rate, capacity, and distance of information transmission. The impact of this technology and related-information tools, such as E-mail, has disarmed us of our ability to delay responses due to mailing and transmission time. We can no longer use the old hedge, "The check is in the mail." The sheer volume and immediacy of information in our society are truly revolutionary.

If one accepts the premise that information is user-defined, then perhaps we all need to have a survival strategy for information handling. Electronic media have become an affordable tool for this process. Storage and retrieval of end-user information is a process that is no longer the sole domain of computer science or data processing centers. We need to develop a plan for how we are going to cope with the overwhelming wave of information.

THEORETICAL PERSPECTIVES

Communication theory grew out of the post–World War II study of the psychosocial processes at work with the newer technology of telecommunication. The father of cybernetics, Norbert Weiner, has written, "To live effectively is to live with adequate information."[2] As professionals, judgments must be made a priori about what constitutes information (ie, that which is useful).

In evaluating information for its usefulness to a decision maker four criteria might be applied: (1) content, (2) availability (timeliness), (3) accuracy, and (4) completeness. Content-appropriate information is defined as printed or mediated information that has a match between the user's "need to know" or "shared codes" that are agreed on between members of the user's profession. Timely information is critical in modern, daily behavior. Instructions that come after the time at which they are required obviously are less useful in guiding our actions. Although they may have historical value, such messages do not allow us to predict or anticipate the outcomes of our behavior. Accuracy is defined simply as a correspondence between a message and observable facts. A distinction between accuracy and precision should be made. For example, a degree of precision may be required when interacting with a computer. Machine codes must have the precise number of digits and sequence in order for them to be "read" by the computer. Human speech seldom has the need for this level of precision; however, accuracy is imperative for communication to be functional. Finally, information must be complete. Many of us have been frustrated by having mail returned because of an incomplete address element.

The criterion of completeness is important to one of the steps of the storage/retrieval process as well as to the selection of information. For example, if I am writing a dissertation on a subject, I may wish to store an entire article. If I merely wish to know the results and an overview of a research study, I may only wish to index and store the abstract. In summary, to be useful, information must be content appropriate, timely, accurate, and complete.

These criteria should prove useful in determining whether one should incorporate information into one's professional information system and will lead to the next phase: developing a personal information handling system.[3]

AN INFORMATION PROCESSING MODEL

The steps of processing information have been formulated as:

Selection→Collection→Storage→Retrieval→Transmittal

If information meets established criteria, the selection process may be through another person, a printed article or text, a videotape or film, or, as computers become more generally available, the digitized format.

In collecting information, the professional should consider subsequent phases of the information processing model. For example, what are the space constraints? Will storage be local or remote? How often will the collection be accessed? Of increasing concern for the computer user is whether the information will be used by someone other than the primary user.

If others are going to require access to the local information system, the retrieval functions may need to have alternate methods of transmission. For example, the computer user may wish to consider a telephone modem for files transfer.

Facsimile machines may be used with or without a computer interface. Ethical considerations include confidentiality of client records, copyright laws regarding published information, and proper credits when applying another professional's information.[4]

PLANNING FOR INFORMATION PROCESSING

In developing a master plan for collecting, storing, and retrieving information, the professional should apply the criteria. If a message is not current enough to be accessed within a year's time, it should not be kept in the personal storage system. Archives have been developed for this purpose. Some business managers indicate that if a piece of correspondence or information does not get used quarterly, they move it to long-term storage, keeping only a reference or index of retired information. If this guideline is to be followed, the professional information consumer should consider how difficult the retrieval of the complete document might compare with the difficulty and expense of maintaining it in the immediate, working environment.

A DATABASE APPROACH

The creation of new information can proceed in the clinical context by medical research and development and clinical experience in the practice of nutrition and medicine. These professional functions have resulted in information being collected into knowledge bases. A physician or dietitian is trained in a professional, pre-service academic program to be an expert in a particular knowledge base. As experts enter the field, they add information to their knowledge in a pattern that may be coded using descriptive, professional terminology.

To a person not trained in this terminology, or who comes from a different experiential background, this language may appear to be "jargon." But to professionals within the field, this language is a form of a "shared code." A shared code allows a referent system that enables one professional to share experiences with another. This process operates in most fields and may provide the basis for building a professional information handling system. A first step in developing an information system for the individual dietitian might be to develop an index of terms that are used on a regular basis to describe functions or actions or objects (food items or nutrients) that can be used as "headers" or "descriptors" under which records of interest can be stored.

This intellectual indexing process is not new; Aristotle proposed it as a field of study called epistemology. He believed that the development of categories of things that are experienced was a step in the process of knowing about the world. The act of naming phenomena is a basic building block of science. Biology, as a field of science, grew out of a taxonomic or "naming" approach to cataloging living systems observed and recorded by naturalists. The coding and indexing of professional experiences are generally accepted as a basis for the personal, professional communications and may provide a useful way of building an organizational scheme for our library or information system. Dietitians may wish to proceed to the library to review the indexing schema used in such professional indexes as *Index Medicus* and the subject listing in the *Journal of the American Dietetic Association* before developing a personal storage/retrieval coding system. The advantages of this approach are that it allows the person to build a personal database that can be networked into the existing national and regional databases. In the past 5 years these databases have become increasingly accessible to individual professionals. With the advent of the microcomputer, software programs have been developed that will allow the person to build either a personal database or network with larger professional databases.

EXAMPLES OF DATABASE PROGRAMS

For dietitians who have access to a microcomputer for developing and using a database, there are numerous application software programs available to aid in the organization, storage, and retrieval functions. Four of these are briefly described: *dBase III* (Ashton-Tate), *Rbase:5000* (MicroRim), *File Express* (ShareWare), and *HyperCard* (Apple Computers, Inc). *dBase III* is an "applications" software package that operates on an IBM PC AT/XT or the newer OS-2 models. It is a powerful, professional-level database manager program. Developed for business-type applications, it will serve the professional dietitian in many ways. Some examples are establishing client records, diet and menu filing, report generation and writing, mail-merging (a process allowing a link between data records, such as address elements and a word processor–based letters), and searching assistance in finding files with "headers" that allow a second-generation file to be developed. For example, a dietitian may wish to view all records of clients who have been in for diet counseling or therapy who were referred for "osteoporosis." A more precise sorting and matching procedure can be performed in very helpful ways, providing the dietitian with a powerful analytic tool in addition to the benefit of having a sophisticated storage–retrieval system. One disadvantage of *dBase III* is cost (prices vary for educators and professional discounts but are in the range of $300). Another disadvantage is that *dBase III* (as with other programs) requires considerable learning and a basic level of "computer literacy." Those who have experience in using a computer for word processing or have used other applications software packages should be able to develop needed skills within a few sessions on the self-instructional package(s) available.

Rbase:5000 is a powerful business and research-oriented database manager applications package. *Rbase:5000*, like *dBase III*, is a "relational database" software language. This program was developed to provide both the programmer and the "power user" (a nonprogrammer with computer literacy) a management tool for handling ever-expanding data and records.

Rbase:5000 is compatible with any of the IBM XT or higher-level PC computers. Developed by a National Aeronautics and Space Administration contract to track and sort performance of the individual tiles on the space shuttles, this program was later reconfigured for the commercial software market and is a powerful tool for handling text files in alphanumeric formats. It can be used with other software programs, such as *WordPerfect* (Microsoft) and has many similar features to *dBase III*. It shares some of the same disadvantages as *dBase III* (ie, cost and learning time required to develop proficiency). However, as with *dBase III*, numerous "user-friendly" applications have been developed with this program (eg, *Clout* [MicroRim]) and are available through various magazines and catalogues.[5]

File Express (ShareWare) was developed by a programmer who has made it available to ShareWare users. ShareWare is a concept of the Association of ShareWare Professionals, a corporation that markets their programs in a co-op fashion. If the program is useful and is kept by the evaluator, they are given a suggested price for a "contribution." In this manner, software can be marketed more cheaply and without costly copyright safety systems. *File Express* is a simple-to-use database manager. It has less capacity for text (by file size and number of files) than either *Rbase:5000* or *dBase III*. It has limitations in reconfiguring of the files and organization once the user has defined the fields and component sections. However, it is an easy program to begin working in databases and requires fewer than two to three sessions to become proficient with its various features. It is inexpensive and is extremely useful for developing an electronic telephone address or mailout system.

The most recent development in relational database programs is Apple Computer's *HyperCard* system. A copy of *HyperCard* is sent out with each new MacIntosh microcomputer and can be thought of as both an operating system (like MS-DOS in IBM's system) and a powerful database tool. *HyperCard* allows the database user to merge text files (ie, print and numbers) with graphics (ie, pictures, diagrams, tables, and graphs) with unprecedented ease. The concept of this is based on an idea called *Hypertext,* which conceptually links print and pictorial data via a system of "links." These links can be continuously reformulated to allow for both new information and new ways of thinking about the data.

Hypertext could be a very useful tool for shared databases. An example might be in the interdisciplinary team approach to using information about a new diet or drug therapy. The comments of each team member could be entered into the database records and updated with secondary and tertiary responses by other team members. New statistical or pictorial information could be added to the database as made available by contributing team members.[6]

Examples of database applications programs are growing in number and complexity. One positive trend is in the direction of providing software and telecommunications connections among the different databases and the various user groups nationally and globally. The next section of this chapter introduces some examples of national databases that have been developed in the area of rehabilitation.

NATIONAL/REGIONAL DATABASES

The national database model developed from cross-referenced journal articles that were stored on magnetic tape for processing within a large-format computer data processing center. Journals selected are abstracted for the database by trained, medical librarians who also would assist in acquiring the entire article for the end-user. Abstracts, with required citations for acquisition of the full-text article, are keyed into the database via on-line terminals. Previously, this required an intermediate step of "batch card" data entry. The database vendor uses a large, main frame computer to "play back" the requested tapes. These usually are stored for retrieval and transmittal via a computer terminal or microcomputer with a telephone modem. A "modem" is a modulator-demodulator that transforms the digital, computer-generated signals into a standard telephone signal. A user would access such a system via a personal computer equipped with a modem and a long-distance telephone call. Reduced rates are available for longer searches. The user would be required to be computer literate and have researched the required codes, have a password and user ID number, and, finally, have enough knowledge of the subject (eg, nutrition and rehabilitation of the spinal cord–injured client) to use specific terms as vehicles for the search for desired information. The database most widely known and used by medical professionals is based on the *Index Medicus*. Vendors, such as *Dialog* or *BRS* (Bibliographic Retrieval Services) provide retrieval services to local libraries on a fee-for-services basis and are available for off-line searches at most modern municipal or university-based libraries. For the dietitian in the field who may not have direct access to a computer with a terminal, the best approach might be to conduct a database search with a trained librarian's assistance. The cost for a search using *BRS* or *Dialog* with 100 citations (printed "off-line") should be less than $50.[7] Increasingly, medical professionals are becoming more comfortable with computers and may wish to develop their own direct-access database systems.[8] The hardware costs for such a system have now come down below $1,000. Software support programs can be found for about $200.

NETWORKING INFORMATION POWER

Networks develop to provide experts with peer contacts who share information and its application to current problems in the field. Electronic mail (E-mail) and a related technology, electronic bulletin boards, have proven to be a way of using the computer to send-receive messages about practice-related problems, scheduling training and other professional development activities, comparing notes, and seeking consensus. E-mail simply provides you with two-way access to the computers in your and your colleague's office or home. You agree to leave your machine on (perhaps while occupied, much like a telephone answering machine) and connect your computer to a modem. Your electronic "pen pal" composes a message in either a word processing or ASCII-code file and then uses a software program to send the file to your computer via the telephone modem connection. You read your mail at your leisure when you return to your computer terminal. The receiver can either erase the message, store it on a disk, and/or print it out on paper.[9] The electronic bulletin board works like E-mail except there is a host computer that is programmed to "scroll" messages that participating members can "post" for a specified time. Typical uses of this are for position announcements, training and professional meetings, and sharing computer programs that can be "downloaded" or copied onto the members' computer.[10] Readers who want to use these media for networking information might be well-advised to set up protective passwords, particularly if sensitive information is to be shared.

GETTING STARTED WITH INFORMATION

Getting a "handle" on the power of information might begin with setting limits on what personal expectations the dietitian has for the system. It may be that lack of secretarial support prompts the need for an electronic telephone/address system. If a microcomputer is available, one could begin by acquiring an application program that will organize the information desired. A personal database can be developed almost as easily as typing a list of names, addresses, and phone numbers. The difference is that the screen can access any name(s) using the sorting power of the computer. If the professional needs to contact all colleagues who have specialized in a particular field such as infant feeding or dysphasic, post-traumatic brain injury nutrition, the computer can assist in organizing address elements within the database. A clinical dietitian may wish to retrieve the diet histories of all their elderly clients to determine progress or need for follow-up contacts. A database program can assist with bringing this information into focus. For the researcher/academic professional, an application program that will help access current research articles from clinical journals might be the best first step in gaining power over information. Two examples mentioned earlier are *Bibliographic Retrieval Services* (BRS) and *DIALOGUE.* As microcomputer storage medium become cheaper and more powerful (ie, "hard" disks and CD-ROM), electronic vendors such as these are marketing their search-support software for microcomputer operators rather than the large, mainframe computer searcher. (For a list of available databases, please refer to Appendix 13-A.)

Whatever phase the reader is entering with regard to information systems, the concepts developed in this chapter should prove useful in defining what type of information should be selected and how best to collect, store, retrieve, and transmit the needed information. As a final illustration, it is striking to reflect that the recent flurry of professional publications about the "cold fusion" physics experiments at the Univeristy of Utah were published worldwide within days using facsimile machines and computers. Researchers could not wait for the traditional journals to publish proofs or disproofs of the initial results. Just as the Gutenburg press spread scientific and technical knowledge throughout Europe in the 16th century, so may the new information age bring knowledge within the grasp of all.

REFERENCES

1. Lindsay PH, Norman DA. *Human Information Processing: An Introduction to Psychology.* 2nd ed. New York, NY: Academic Press; 1977.

2. Buckley W, ed. *Modern Systems Research for the Behavioral Scientist: A SourceBook.* 6th ed. Chicago, Ill: Aldine Publishing Company; 1977.

3. Hussain KM. *Development of Information Systems for Education.* Englewood Cliffs, NJ: Prentice-Hall, Inc; 1973.

4. Bohl M. *Information Processing.* 4th ed. Chicago, Ill: Science Research Associates, Inc; 1984.

5. Krasnoff B, Dickinson J. Project Database II. *PC Magazine.* 1986;5(12):103–227.

6. Conklin EJ. Hypertext: An introduction and survey. *Computer.* 1987; September: 17–41.

7. Dionne RJ. Science libraries at a crossroads. *Am Scientist.* 1988;76:268–272.

8. Randall M. Easy access: Let your terminal do the walking. *Disabled USA.* 1984; April: 14–17.

9. Smith K. E-Mail to anywhere. *PC World.* 1988;6(3):220–223.

10. Young T. Making the right connection. *Mainstream.* 1988;13(14):9–11.

Appendix 13-A

Information Resources in Rehabilitation

ABLEDATA
Adaptive Equipment Center
Newington Children's Hospital
181 East Cedar Street
Newington, CT 06111
1-800-344-5405

CONET
Cooperative Network for Rapid
 Dissemination of Information on
 Assistive Devices
Trace Research and Development
 Center
University of Wisconsin
Madison, WI 53705-2280
(608) 262-6966

IBM
National Support Center for
 Persons with Disabilities
P.O. Box 2150
Atlanta, GA 30055
(404) 238-3000

IBM/Special Needs Exchange
P.O. Box 434
Pawtucket, RI 02862
Note: free-text searching via
CompuServe 1-800-848-8990.

REHABDATA
National Rehabilitation
 Information Center
3455 Colesville Road, Suite 935
Silver Spring, MD 20910-3319
1-800-346-2742

ERIC
Educational Research Information
 Clearinghouse
030 Huntington Hall
Syracuse, NY 13244-2340
(315) 423-3640

Clearinghouse on the Handicapped
Dept. of Education
Room 3132
Switzer Bldg.
Washington, DC 20202-2319

U.S. Department of Commerce
National Technical Information
  Service (NTIS)
5285 Port Royal Road
Springfield, VA 22161
NTIS provides indexes to both
  print and electronic databases
  under contract to the federal
  government.

SCAN
Shared Communication and
  Assistance Network
American Association of
  University Affiliated Programs
  (AAUAP)
8605 Cameron Street, Suite 506
Silver Spring, MD 20910
(301) 588-8252
SCAN members can access
  databases and electronic bulletin
  boards in a "user-friendly"
  environment.

CompuServe
Information Service
P.O. Box 20212
5000 Arlington Centre Boulevard
Columbus, OH 43220
CompuServe is a consumer-
  oriented storage/retrieval vendor
  of a wide range of information
  services.

JRRD On-Line
Journal of Rehabilitation Research
  and Development
VA Rehabilitation of Database
Office of Technology Transfer
VA Prosthetics R&D Center
103 S. Gay Street
Baltimore, MD 21202
(301) 962-1800
For CompuServe users, key in
  "Go Rehab."

Chapter 14

Health Promotion

Norma F. Berry

The philosophies of the health promotion–disease prevention and wellness movements are consistent with the positive philosophy in which rehabilitation is rooted. In practice, however, health promotion–disease prevention and wellness often are not associated with the disabled person or with the rehabilitation process.[1] The purposes of this chapter are to assist readers to formulate ideas about how health promotion–disease prevention and wellness can be applied in the areas of rehabilitation, with specific consideration for the role of the dietitian, and to explore associations among health promotion, independent living, and quality of life for disabled persons. Key terms associated with health promotion–disease prevention and wellness are defined and briefly discussed at the outset to ensure congruency of understanding about them. These terms are *health; wellness; primary, secondary,* and *tertiary prevention;* and *health promotion.*

DEFINITION OF TERMS

A frequently quoted definition of *health* is stated in the preamble to the Constitution of the World Health Organization: "health is a state of complete physical, mental, and social well-being and not merely the absence of disease or infirmity."[2] During the past decade, our society has come to understand health as a multidimensional condition characterized by the existence of a positive state of physical, mental, and social well-being.[3]

Dunn, regarded by some as the father of the wellness movement, defined *wellness* in a similar manner: "high-level wellness is an integrated method of functioning which is oriented toward maximizing the potential of which the individual is capable . . . within the environment where he is functioning."[4] Ardell described wellness as a dynamic, ever-changing, fluctuating state of being that encompasses the dimensions of self-responsibility, nutritional awareness, stress awareness and management, physical fitness, and environmental sensitivity.[5] Another way to organize the major elements of a wellness-oriented life is along six dimensions: social, emotional, spiritual, physical, occupational, and intellectual.[6] Each dimension is viewed as a continuum that extends from health to disability or death.[7,8] From the wellness perspective, the goal is to achieve the highest possible level of health within the genetic and environmental limitations of the person. Although concurrent optimization of all dimensions of health or wellness suggests an ideal condition that may not actually be attainable, it is, nevertheless, possible for every person, regardless of disability, to choose to excel in some dimension(s).[1,7] According to Ardell, "It is possible to be 'well' at the same time that one has an illness. One can still accept life at its fullest and strive for its highest potential."[5] Furthermore, as Warms stated, "if health is maximization of one's potential along various dimensions, then disability poses no obstacle to maximizing one's potential."[9]

Using principles of epidemiology, Leavell and Clark conceptualized disease prevention as having three levels: primary, secondary, and tertiary.[10] *Primary prevention* refers to fostering health and preventing disease before it begins; it involves removing underlying causes of disorders or health problems. *Secondary prevention* suggests early intervention into existing illness and includes early detection of disease and prompt intervention to relieve discomfort and prevent disability and death. *Tertiary prevention* refers to minimizing disability from existing illness through treatment and rehabilitation efforts.

Although health promotion has been defined by many authors, recently it has been delineated to include both health and wellness concepts.

> *Health promotion* is the science and art of helping people change their lifestyle to move toward a state of optimal health. Optimal health is defined as a balance of physical, emotional, social, spiritual and intellectual health. Lifestyle change can be facilitated through a combination of efforts to enhance awareness, change behavior, and create environments that support good health practices. Of the three, supportive environments will probably have the greatest impact in producing lasting changes.[11]

Health promotion can be achieved through a wide range of programs that are designed to impact the health status of participants by helping them change their long-term life style practices. Health promotion programs generally begin with efforts to motivate clients to take responsibility for their own health, and they involve processes of expanding awareness through education about health risks, promoting behavior changes to reduce one's health risks, and providing a supportive environment for maintaining a change in lifestyle.[8]

RELATIONSHIPS: HEALTH PROMOTION–DISEASE PREVENTION AND REHABILITATION

These definitions suggest an ecologic view of health promotion–disease prevention and wellness that is compatible with the rehabilitation process.[1] Goals that are fundamental to planning rehabilitation care include prevention of further disability and restoration of maximal potential function to each client. Therefore, health promotion–disease prevention and rehabilitation appear to have several common features: both are directed by the concepts of helping persons help themselves and of enhancing independent functioning of each person served; both emphasize education about oneself; and both maintain a goal-oriented, self-initiated focus on personal growth and improvement.[12]

Efforts by the U.S. government toward health promotion and disease prevention, as described in the 1979 Surgeon General's report *Healthy People,* focus on primary prevention for the general, nondisabled population and strategies that maintain and promote health among persons already healthy.[3] No specific mention was made about prevention strategies for those who are disabled. More recently, in 1988, Congress authorized the Public Health Service to establish a Disabilities Prevention Program (DPP) within the Centers for Disease Control. Goals of the DPP include reducing the incidence or severity of primary and secondary disabilities and promoting independence, productivity, and integration into the community of persons with disabilities.[13] The World Health Organization policy, "Health for all by the year 2000," has resulted in a strategy of health for all in Europe. One of the targets of this strategy is "better opportunities for disabled persons," which is aimed at equalization of opportunities for disabled persons and their full participation.[14]

The usefulness and importance of integrating rehabilitation, health promotion–disease prevention, and wellness have been noted in recent literature. Brandon recommended that the content areas of health promotion and wellness that are especially applicable to persons with disabilities include principles of self-responsibility, nutritional awareness, physical fitness, and stress management.[1] Each of these areas can affect the physical, psychological, and social dimensions of health for well persons as well as for persons with disabilities. In a study of clients with spinal cord injuries, Warms found that although the health care services generally provided to those clients were related to disability, they also desired health promotion services that were not regularly obtained. Specifically, the clients desired services related to exercise, fitness, stress management, and nutrition counseling.[9] Nadolsky emphasized that rehabilitation is not synonymous with disability and suggested that both disabled and nondisabled persons who seek personal improvement or well-being services can benefit from programs that combine rehabilitation and wellness concepts.[12] Hodges observed that persons with disabilities are often more vulnerable to risk factors for ill health, disease, and secondary disabilities; therefore, the concepts of health promotion–disease prevention and wellness take on heightened need for them.[15] Brooks suggested that joining the forces of rehabilitation and health promotion programs could improve the potential for lasting life style changes among clients.[16] Major emphases of the recently established DPP are on both disability prevention and the promotion of healthy lifestyles.[13]

Health promotion–disease prevention programs for well persons and for disabled persons include similar principles and fundamentally are alike. Only the specifics of implementation may vary. Furthermore, some existing rehabilitation programs include health promotion–disease prevention features. For instance, the independent living movement for disabled persons emphasizes individual responsibility for self-care; a comprehensive concept of health that includes social-psychological, physical, and spiritual dimensions that are subject to individual choice-making; achievement of a person's highest potential; and the importance of social influences in health maintenance.[16] Life style management, which is characteristic of health promotion programs, also appears very similar to the self-care regimen followed by persons who have chronic disability.[16]

Quality of life (QOL), a goal of health promotion and preventive care as well as of rehabilitation, also has been conceptualized to be made up of the same factors for persons with disabilities and persons without disabilities. A consensus report from the project, "Quality of Life for Persons with Disabilities," expresses this conclusion[17]:

- QOL is essentially the same for persons with and without disabilities. Persons with disabilities want the same things for their lives, have the same needs, and want to fulfill social responsibilities in the same way other members of society do.
- QOL is largely a social phenomenon and primarily a product of interaction with others. This requires a "social ecological" definition of

QOL for the individual that incorporates the QOL of significant others in the setting.

- QOL is the product of individuals with disabilities meeting basic needs and fulfilling responsibilities in community settings (family, recreating, school, and work). Individuals who are able to meet basic needs while fulfilling responsibilities in ways that are satisfactory to themselves and to significant others in the setting are more likely to experience a high quality of life.
- QOL is a matter of consumer rather than professional definition. QOL issues should be defined by consumers and other citizens rather than by professionals in the field. Ultimately it is how the individual perceives and evaluates his or her own situation, rather than how others perceive it, that determines the QOL that he or she experiences.

It is true that persons with disabilities may view strategies of primary prevention that emphasize modifying individual behaviors and the environment as having failed, especially if their primary disability was preventable. For them, prevention means prevention of secondary disabilities, that is, secondary prevention. Clearly, disabled persons need good nutrition, proper exercise, immunizations, and environmental modifications; they should not smoke or consume excessive alcohol, and they need sufficient awareness to control these risks. At the same time, specific disabilities may make the measures needed to control preventable risks different from those needed by persons who are not disabled. Examples of such needs include appropriate exercise methods for clients with arthritis or progressive neuromuscular diseases; understanding of relationships between diet or exercise and certain drugs used for clients with epilepsy or chronic mental illness; recreational services and facilities for clients with mental retardation; public health informational materials for clients with cognitive deficits due to traumatic head injury; public spas and integrated fitness programs for persons with spinal cord injury; auditory street crossing signals for the blind; fully captioned public service announcements for the deaf; and education in human sexuality for persons with disabilities.[15]

HEALTH PROMOTION–DISEASE PREVENTION AND REHABILITATION IN THE WORKPLACE

Health promotion and preventive care have been cited as significant ways to reduce health care costs as well as improve quality of life. "Major emphasis on health promotion has the potential long-term benefits of extending longevity, enhancing quality of life, and reducing health care costs."[3] Many businesses and industries have recognized the validity of this concept and have initiated health promotion–disease prevention and wellness programs in the workplace.[8,18-20]

Strategies used by corporations to maximize the health of their workers, and thus improve cost management, may be viewed as applications of health promotion–disease prevention at two levels. The first level involves health maintenance and primary prevention; the second level includes measures to restore health and includes secondary and tertiary prevention. Employers use health promotion programs to reduce the risk of illness and injury among workers by helping them maintain or start healthy life styles or stop unhealthy life style behaviors. In the event that injury or illness does occur, the goal is to minimize the impact of the problem on employees' work productivity and personal life style.

While health promotion–disease prevention programs in corporate settings often have been designed for able-bodied workers, many programs currently implemented by employers for persons with disabilities are appropriately considered part of health promotion–disease prevention efforts. For instance, disability management, which may include such programs as return to work, transitional work programs, job accommodation, employee assistance plans, and industrial-based rehabilitation exemplify health restoration measures and secondary and tertiary prevention strategies.

Thus, health promotion–disease prevention can be viewed as a comprehensive framework applicable to a continuum of intervention; it is both proactive and systematic. Health promotion–disease prevention programs apply to all workers and facilitate the positive outcome of maintaining gainful employment for them.

Health promotion–disease prevention strategies also are responsive to the needs, philosophies, and goals of employers. Positive outcomes for employers may include cost savings from decreased absenteeism, injury, and sick leave; increased employee satisfaction; facilitation of individual responsibility for health and thus maximization of health of the employee population; enhanced corporate image; and improved recruitment.[19]

THE DIETITIAN'S ROLE IN HEALTH PROMOTION

What is the role of the dietitian in health promotion–disease prevention activities? Martin and associates investigated beliefs and behaviors of dietetic practitioners regarding health promotion and disease prevention,[21] and their findings indicated that health habits of the dietetic practitioners themselves were better than health practices of the general female population, an important finding since evidence indicates that personal habits influence counseling activities with clients.[22] While the dietitians agreed that the health behaviors identified in the study were important to the health of the average person, only a few of them gave routine attention to those practices in their professional practice, and generally they expressed lack of confidence in their ability to counsel clients about health behaviors other than weight control, high fat diets, elevated blood pressure, and exercise patterns. Confidence of the dietitians in their counseling skills was associated with the intensity of their efforts toward helping clients modify selected health risks. The dietitians strongly agreed that health promotion will be more important in the future.[21]

Dietitians' commitment to health promotion–disease prevention is highly significant in primary as well as secondary and tertiary health care in order that clients can be helped to achieve their highest possible level of health. Dietitians are prepared to assume the unique responsibility of translating nutrition information into practical, workable measures to promote health. They also have knowledge and skill in psychosocial and behavioral measures, which when supplemented with awareness and knowledge of health promotion–disease prevention concepts, provide them with important background to effectively review clients' life style practices and health habits and identify existing problems. Therefore, consideration of all the dimensions of health promotion–disease prevention should be a part of dietitians' initial and subsequent client assessments. Dietitians should keep abreast of psychological, emotional, and environmental factors that may put clients at health risk and address those factors as part of nutrition education and counseling. Although they may not have the skills necessary to effectively counsel clients in all areas of health promotion–disease prevention, dietitians should apply their expertise to the extent possible and make appropriate referrals when indicated.

The team approach to client care, which is central to the rehabilitation process, affords the dietitian many opportunities to promote the benefits of good nutrition to other health care professionals and to recommend healthful approaches they can use when incorporating food and eating practices in activities of daily living. For instance, when the occupational therapist is teaching clients to prepare food, the emphasis should be on nutritious foods. Items prepared could be a bowl of cooked whole-grain cereal cooked in a microwave oven, a fruit dessert made from a variety of fresh or canned fruit topped with yogurt, or a toasted sandwich filled with chicken or tuna salad. Whereas candies, other sweets, or high fat, highly salted foods may be used by some health care professionals to reinforce positive client responses, the dietitian could recommend that measures other than food be used as reinforcers. For instance, engagement in an appropriate form of physical activity, which often may be overlooked as an important way to be independent, could be used for positive reinforcement and would promote the physical and emotional well-being of the client at the same time.

CONCLUSION

Health promotion–disease prevention and rehabilitation have similar philosophies and social foundations. Programs in the two human service areas are compatible, mutually complementary, and, when integrated, can significantly enhance health care for persons with disabilities. Although they may not have been identified as such, many existing rehabilitation programs such as independent living for disabled persons and disability management in the workplace currently incorporate basic tenets of health promotion–disease prevention. A goal and a challenge to dietitians in rehabilitation settings is to expand and enhance their efforts in health promotion–disease prevention. Such efforts will facilitate achieving the goal of optimal functioning for persons with disabilities.

REFERENCES

1. Brandon J. Health promotion and wellness in rehabilitation services. *J Rehabil.* 1985;51(4):54.

2. *World Health Organization, What It Is, What It Does, How It Works.* Irvington-on-Hudson, NY: Columbia University Press; 1965.

3. *Healthy People. The Surgeon General's Report on Health Promotion and Disease Prevention.* Washington, DC: US Department of Health, Education, and Welfare publication 79-55071, 1979.

4. Dunn H. *High Level Wellness.* Arlington, Va: RW Beatty Co; 1961.

5. Ardell D. *High Level Wellness.* New York: Bantam Books; 1979.

6. Hettler W. Wellness: Encouraging lifetime pursuit of excellence. *Health Values: Achieving High Level Wellness.* 1984;8:13.

7. Richardson G, Berry N. Strength intervention: An approach to lifestyle modification. *Health Education* 1987;18(3):42.

8. O'Donnell M, Ainsworth T. *Health Promotion in the Workplace.* New York, NY: John Wiley & Sons; 1984.

9. Warms C. Health promotion services in post-rehabilitation spinal cord injury health care. *Rehabil Nurs.* 1987;12:304.

10. Leavell HR, Clark EG. *Preventive Medicine for the Doctor in His Community.* New York, NY: McGraw-Hill Book Co; 1965.

11. O'Donnell M. Definition of health promotion: III. Stressing the impact of culture. *Am J Health Promotion.* 1989;3(3):5.

12. Nadolsky J. Rehabilitation and wellness: In need of integration. *J Rehabil.* 1987; 53(2):5.

13. Seekins T, Smith N. Prevent secondary disabilities: Involve consumers. *The Rural Exchange.* 1989;2(3):1.

14. Hermanova HM. Disability indicators and WHO Programme: "Health for all by the Year 2000." *Rev Epidemiol Sante Publ.* 1987;35(3,4):236.

15. Hodges A. Health promotion and disease prevention for the disabled. *J Allied Health.* 1986;14:315.

16. Brooks N. Opportunities for health promotion: Including the chronically ill and disabled. *Soc Sci Med.* 1984;19:405.

17. Goode D. *The Proceedings of the National Conference on Quality of Life for Persons with Disabilities.* Valhalla, NY: The Mental Retardation Institute, New York Medical College; 1988.

18. Tate D. The healthy corporation: Disability management and health promotion practices at the workplace. *J Rehabil.* 1987;53(3):63.

19. Tate D, Habeck R, Schwartz G. Disability management: A comprehensive framework for prevention and rehabilitation in the workplace. *Rehabil Lit.* 1986;47:230.

20. Galvin D. Health promotion, disability management, and rehabilitation in the workplace. *Rehabil Lit.* 1986;47:219.

21. Martin J, Holcomb JD, Mullen P. Health promotion and disease prevention beliefs and behaviors of dietetic practitioners. *J Am Diet Assoc.* 1987;87:609.

22. Wells K, Lewis C, Leake B, Ware J. Do physicians preach what they practice? *JAMA.* 1984;252:2846.

Appendix A

Rehabilitation-Related Organizations (Lay and Professional)

ASSOCIATIONS

Rehabilitation

A Chance to Grow
5034 Oliver Avenue, N.
Minneapolis, MN 55430
(612) 521-2266

American Academy of Physical
  Medicine and Rehabilitation
122 S. Michigan Avenue,
  Suite 1300
Chicago, IL 60603
(312) 922-9366

American Association for
  Rehabilitation Therapy
P.O. Box 93
North Little Rock, AR 72116

American Board of Rehabilitation
  Medicine
130 S. Michigan Avenue,
  Suite 1310
Chicago, IL 60603
(312) 922-9368

American Congress of
  Rehabilitation Medicine
130 S. Michigan Avenue,
  Suite 1310
Chicago, IL 60603
(312) 922-9368

American Dietetic Association
216 West Jackson Boulevard,
  Suite 800
Chicago, IL 60606-6995
(312) 899-0040
(Dietetics in Physical Medicine
  and Rehabilitation Practice
  Group)

American Kinesiotherapy
  Association
c/o David Ser
259-08, 148 Road
Rosedale, NY 11422
(718) 276-0721

American Rehabilitation
  Counseling Association
5999 Stevenson Avenue
Alexandria, VA 22304
(703) 823-9800

Association of Academic
  Physiatrists
8000 Five Mile Road, Suite 340
Cincinnati, OH 45230
(513) 232-8833

Association of Medical
  Rehabilitation Directors and
  Coordinators
87 Elm Street
Framingham, MA 01701
(617) 877-0517

Association of Rehabilitation
  Nurses (Nursing)
2506 Grosse Point Road
Evanston, IL 60201
(312) 475-1000

Commission on Accreditation of
  Rehabilitation Facilities
2500 N. Pantano Road
Tucson, AZ 85715
(602) 886-8575

Commission on Rehabilitation
  Counselor Certification
1156 Shore Drive, Suite 350
Arlington Heights, IL 60004

Council of State Administrators of
  Vocational Rehabilitation
1055 Thomas Jefferson Street,
  N.W., Suite 401
P.O. Box 3776
Washington, DC 20007
(202) 638-4634

Hospitalized Veterans Writing
  Project
5920 Nall, Room 117
Mission, KS 66202
(913) 432-1214

International Center for the
  Disabled (ICD)
340 E. 24th Street
New York, NY 10010
(212) 679-0100

International Federation of
  Physical Medicine and
  Rehabilitation
1000 N. 92nd Street
Medical College of Wisconsin
Wauwatosa, WI 53226
(414) 259-1414

International Rehabilitation
  Medicine Association
Dept. of Physical Medicine
1333 Moursund Avenue,
  Room A-221
Houston, TX 77030
(713) 799-5090

National Association of
  Rehabilitation Agencies
1411 K Street, N.W., Suite 400
Washington, DC 20005
(202) 347-4350

National Association of
  Rehabilitation Facilities
P.O. Box 17675
Washington, DC 20041
(703) 556-8848

National Association of
  Rehabilitation Instructors
c/o National Rehabilitation
  Association
633 S. Washington Street
Alexandria, VA 22314
(703) 836-0850

National Association of
  Rehabilitation Professionals in
  the Private Sector
P.O. Box 218
Blue Jay, CA 92317
(714) 336-1531

National Council on
  Rehabilitation Education
c/o Jennifer Maddux
2921 Ermine Way
Farmers Branch, TX 75234
(214) 241-4747

National Institute for
  Rehabilitation Engineering
P.O. Box 841
Butler, NJ 07405
(201) 838-2500

National Rehabilitation
  Information Center
4407 Eighth Street, N.E.
Washington, DC 20017
(202) 635-5826

Rehabilitation Commission:
  Federation Employment &
  Guidance Service
114 Fifth Avenue
New York, NY 10011
(212) 741-7110

Rehabilitation Information Round
  Table
c/o Phyllis Quinn
American Physical Therapy
  Association
1111 N. Fairfax Street
Alexandria, VA 22314
(703) 684-2782

Rehabilitation International
22 E. 21st Street
New York, NY 10010
(212) 420-1500

RESNA: Association for the
  Advancement of Rehabilitation
  Technology
1101 Connecticut Avenue, N.W.,
  Suite 700
Washington, DC 20036
(202) 857-1199

Section for Rehabilitation
  Hospitals and Programs
c/o American Hospital
  Association
840 N. Lakeshore Drive
Chicago, IL 60611
(312) 280-6671

Vocational Evaluation and Work
  Adjustment Association
c/o June E. Ruff
P.O. Box 31
Anderson, IN 46015
(317) 642-0201

World Rehabilitation
400 E. 34th Street
New York, NY 10016
(212) 340-6062

Arthritis

Arthritis Foundation
1314 Spring Street, N.W.
Atlanta, GA 30309
(404) 872-7100

Association for People with
  Arthritis
P.O. Box 954
Six Commercial Street
Hicksville, NY 11802
(800) 323-2243

Cardiovascular/Pulmonary

American Association of
 Cardiovascular and Pulmonary
 Rehabilitation
53 Park Place
New York, NY 10007
(212) 766-4300

Cerebral Palsy

American Academy for Cerebral
 Palsy & Developmental
 Medicine
2315 Westwood Avenue
P.O. Box 11086
Richmond, VA 23230
(804) 355-0147

United Cerebral Palsy
 Associations
66 E. 34th Street
New York, NY 10016
(212) 481-6300

United Cerebral Palsy Research
 and Educational Foundation
66 E. 34th Street
New York, NY 10016
(212) 481-6437

Cleft Palate

American Association for Cleft
 Palate
Administrative Office
331 Salk Hall
Pittsburgh, PA 15261
(412) 681-9620

Geriatrics

American Association for
 Geriatric Physiatry
P.O. Box 376-A
Greenbelt, MD 20770
(301) 220-0952

American Geriatrics Society
770 Lexington Avenue, Suite 400
New York, NY 10021
(212) 308-1414

American Society for Geriatric
 Dentistry
211 E. Chicago Avenue,
 Suite 1616
Chicago, IL 60611
(312) 440-2661

National Geriatrics Society
212 W. Wisconsin Avenue,
 3rd Floor
Milwaukee, WI 53203
(414) 272-4130

Society of Geriatric
 Ophthalmology
2912 W. Tuscon
Canton, OH 44708
(216) 456-0047

Head Injury

A Chance to Grow
5034 Oliver Avenue, North
Minneapolis, MN 55430
(612) 521-2266

National Head Injury Foundation
333 Turnpike Road
Southborough, MA 01772
(617) 485-9950

Multiple Sclerosis

National Multiple Sclerosis Society
205 E. 42nd Street
New York, NY 10017
(212) 986-3240

Muscular Dystrophy

Muscular Dystrophy Association
810 Seventh Avenue
New York, NY 10016
(212) 586-0808

Prader-Willi Syndrome

Prader-Willi Syndrome
   Association
5515 Malibu Drive
Edina, MN 55436
(612) 933-0113

Spinal Cord Injury

American Association of Spinal
   Cord Injury Nurses
432 Park Avenue, South,
   4th Floor
New York, NY 10016
(212) 686-6770

National Spinal Cord Injury
   Association
600 E. Cummings Park, Suite 2000
Woburn, MA 01801
(617) 935-2722

Visual/Hearing Disability

American Deafness and
   Rehabilitation Association
Box 55369
Little Rock, AR 55369
(501) 663-4617

Association for Education &
   Rehabilitation of the Blind &
   Visually Impaired
206 N. Washington Street,
   Suite 320
Alexandria, VA 22314
(703) 548-1884

Rehabilitation of Deaf-Blind
   Adults
111 Middle Neck Road
Sands Point, NY 11050
(516) 944-8900

Rehabilitation Center for the
   Visually Impaired
770 Centre St.
Newton, MA 02158
(617) 969-6200

RELATED PUBLICATIONS

Department of Health, Education,
   and Welfare
Office for Handicapped
   Individuals
Washington, DC 20201
Programs for the Handicapped
   (monthly)

Helen Keller National Center for
   Deaf-Blind Youth and Adults
111 Middle Neck Road
Sands Point, NY 11050
Nat-Cent News (quarterly)

Job Development Laboratory
The George Washington
  University
Rehabilitation Research and
  Training Center (RT-9)
2300 I St., N.W., Room 420
Washington, DC 20037
Intercom (quarterly)

National Center for Law and the
  Handicapped
1235 North Eddy Street
South Bend, IN 46617
Amicus (bimonthly)

National Congress of
  Organizations of the Physically
  Handicapped
7611 Oakland Avenue
Minneapolis, MN 55423
COPH Bulletin (quarterly)

National Technical Institute for
  the Deaf
1 Lomb Memorial Drive
Rochester, NY 14623
Focus (quarterly)

President's Committee on
  Employment of the
  Handicapped
Washington, DC 20201
Disabled USA (monthly)

Sensory Aids Foundation
399 Sherman Avenue
Palo Alto, CA 94306
(quarterly reports)

Telesensory Systems
3408 Hillview Avenue
Palo Alto, CA 94304
TSI Newsletter

Appendix B

Procedures for Preparation of Dysphagia Diets

Sharon Yankelson

GENERAL RULES

1. Label each container of pureed food with the following:
   a. Name
   b. Date prepared
   c. Type of food
2. Refrigerate all foods after they have been pureed.
3. Put foods in size cup specified on special diets.
4. Since water will dilute the flavor of foods, use water only when other liquids are not appropriate or if directions call for water.
5. In place of water use:
   a. Liquid drained from canned fruits and vegetables
   b. Fruit juices, nectars
   c. Gravies
   d. Milk
   e. Syrup
   f. Tomato or barbecue sauce

Canned Foods

1. Drain food thoroughly—save liquid.
2. Puree food by itself.
3. Thin with reserved liquid *or*
4. Thicken with appropriate thickening agent according to menu directions.

301

Cookies, Graham Crackers, and Cakes

1. Puree to fine crumbs.
2. Remove pieces that do not puree to fine crumbs.
3. Use only fine crumbs in preparing food.
4. Combine with food as indicated in menu.

Meats and Fish

1. Puree meat until smooth.
2. Add gravy, tomato sauce, barbecue sauce, etc. to moisten and form desired consistency (use approximately 1 oz of liquid per serving of meat).
3. To thin, use milk or a small amount of water.
4. Bread and/or cheese may be added to obtain desired thickness.

Food Combinations

1. When combining smooth foods (eg, Jell-O and pudding or pureed fruit and pudding), do not puree either of the two. Fold the fruit into the pudding or the pudding into the Jell-O.
2. Items such as fruit and ice cream: puree the most liquid first (fruit).
3. Drain excess liquid from the pureed food.
4. Then, add the food used to thicken, such as ice cream, and puree.

Powdered (Dehydrated) Baby Food

1. Add to foods of a similar nature to thicken, such as green beans with pureed canned green beans, etc.
2. Do not add water immediately.
3. Add water only if after mixing the dehydrated and pureed food the mixture is too thick.

Note: When adding cheese to vegetables, meat, etc, these items should be hot so the cheese will melt.

List of Thickeners

1. Potato pearls (dehydrated)
2. Bread
3. Dehydrated baby food

Unsuitable Foods to Puree

1. Refrozen broccoli
2. Sausage
3. Carrots
4. Zucchini
5. Turkey ham
6. Fish
7. Chicken pattie

RECIPES

Debbie's Slushy

1/4 lb frozen fruit
1/2 packet Alba 77
2 tbsp. nonfat dry milk
1/4 cup water

Combine all ingredients in food processor or blender. Blend until all fruit is very fine. Makes one 16-oz cup. Recipe may be doubled and kept frozen. Microwave as needed.

Milkshake

6 oz ice cream
8 oz milk

Combine in blender and mix until smooth. Makes one 16-oz cup.
Chocolate: use chocolate ice cream or chocolate milk
Vanilla: use vanilla ice cream, milk, and 1/4 tsp. vanilla extract
Strawberry: use strawberry ice cream or 1/4 tsp. strawberry flavoring

Smoothie

8 oz flavored yogurt
1 peeled banana (or 1 cup drained canned fruit)
5 $\frac{1}{2}$ oz apple juice
1 cup crushed ice

Combine all ingredients in blender. Mix until ice and fruit are smooth. Makes one 16-oz cup.

Low-Cal Slushy

4 ice-tray cubes of ice
1 tsp Crystal Lite drink powder

Ice must be very frozen, so that it will chip off. Place 1 ice cube at a time in food processor and blend until all ice is in chips, add Crytal Lite just to flavor ice. Makes 1 cup.

Milk Gel

1 qt whole milk
1 ½ tbsp gelatin, unflavored Knox or equivalent
3 tbsp + ½ tsp dry powder milk
1 ½ tsp granulated sugar
¼ tsp maple or vanilla flavoring

Heat ½ of the milk in steamer or double boiler until hot but not boiling (approx. 170°). Stir gelatin into ¼ amount of cold milk. Strain into hot milk mixture. Stir well to dissolve gelatin. Blend remaining cold milk, dry milk powder and flavoring on #2 speed for 5 seconds. Strain into gelatin–milk mixture. Stir well. Chill until firm. Whip, using wire whip, only until all lumps are removed. Volume increases approximately 25% with whipping. Makes 3 ounces whipped gel per serving. Nutritional content: 4.25 g protein, 110 mg calcium, 60 calories per 3 ounces.

Gel Juice

Apple
1 tbsp unflavored gelatin
3 cups apple juice

Orange
1 tbsp unflavored gelatin
1 ¼ tbsp sugar
3 cups orange juice

Pineapple
1 tbsp unflavored gelatin
1 tbsp sugar
1 ½ cups apple juice
1 ½ cups pineapple juice

Cranberry
1 tbsp unflavored gelatin
3 cups cranberry juice

Soak gelatin in 1 cup juice. Heat in steamer or double boiler about 2 minutes or until gelatin is dissolved. Add sugar. Add remainder of chilled fruit juice. Refrigerate to set. Whip with wire whip. Serving size: 4 ounces.

Weight According to Type of Amputation

Type of Amputation (Percent Loss)

Sex/ Height	Ref. Weight Range*	Single below Knee (6%)	Single at Knee (9%)	Single above Knee (15%)	Double below Knee (12%)	Double at Knee (18%)	Double above Knee (30%)	Single Arm (6.5%)	Single Arm below Elbow (3.6%)
Males									
5'2"	128–150	120–141	116–137	109–128	113–132	105–123	90–105	120–140	123–145
5'3"	130–153	122–144	118–139	111–130	114–135	107–125	91–107	122–143	125–146
5'4"	132–156	124–147	120–142	112–133	116–137	108–128	92–109	124–146	127–151
5'5"	134–160	126–150	122–146	114–136	118–141	110–131	94–112	125–150	129–154
5'6"	136–164	128–154	124–149	116–139	120–144	112–134	95–115	127–154	131–158
5'7"	138–168	130–158	126–153	117–143	121–148	113–138	97–118	129–157	133–162
5'8"	140–172	132–162	127–157	119–146	123–151	115–141	98–120	131–161	135–166
5'9"	142–176	133–165	129–160	121–150	125–155	116–144	99–123	133–165	137–170
5'10"	144–180	135–169	131–164	122–153	127–158	118–148	101–126	135–169	139–174
5'11"	146–184	137–173	133–167	124–156	128–162	120–151	102–129	137–172	141–177
6'0"	149–188	140–177	136–171	127–160	131–165	122–154	104–132	140–176	144–181
6'1"	152–192	143–180	138–175	129–163	134–169	125–157	106–134	143–180	147–185
6'2"	155–197	146–185	141–179	132–167	136–173	127–162	109–138	145–184	150–190

Height									
6'3"	158–202	149–190	144–184	134–172	139–178	130–166	111–141	148–189	153–195
6'4"	162–207	152–195	147–188	138–176	142–182	133–170	113–145	152–194	157–200
Females									
4'10"	102–131	96–123	93–119	87–111	90–115	84–107	71–92	95–123	98–127
4'11"	103–134	97–126	94–122	88–114	91–118	84–110	72–94	96–125	99–130
5'0"	104–137	98–129	95–125	88–116	92–121	85–112	73–96	97–127	100–133
5'1"	106–140	100–132	96–127	90–119	93–123	87–115	74–98	99–130	102–136
5'2"	108–142	102–134	98–130	92–122	95–126	89–117	76–100	101–133	104–138
5'3"	111–147	104–138	101–134	94–125	98–129	91–121	78–103	104–137	107–142
5'4"	114–151	107–142	104–137	97–128	100–133	93–124	80–106	107–142	110–146
5'5"	117–155	110–146	106–141	99–132	103–136	96–127	82–109	110–146	113–150
5'6"	120–159	113–149	109–141	102–135	106–140	98–130	84–111	113–150	116–154
5'7"	123–163	116–153	112–148	105–139	108–143	101–134	86–114	116–154	119–158
5'8"	126–167	118–157	115–152	107–142	111–147	103–137	88–117	119–156	122–162
5'9"	129–170	121–160	117–155	110–145	114–150	106–139	90–119	121–160	125–165
5'10"	132–173	124–163	120–157	112–147	116–152	108–142	92–121	124–163	128–168
5'11"	135–176	127–165	123–160	115–150	119–155	111–144	95–123	127–166	130–170
6'0"	138–179	130–168	126–163	117–152	121–158	113–147	97–125	130–169	133–173

*Reference: Weight range from Metropolitan Life Insurance Company, 1983. The figures represent weights from age 25–29, based on lowest mortality. Weight in pounds according to frame (indoor clothing weighing 5 lb. for men, 3 lb. for women; shoes with 1-inch heels).

Source: Reprinted with permission of Shree Chatterjee, Moss Rehabilitation Hospital, Philadelphia, PA.

Index

Sucking problem
  brain-damaged person and, 193
  disabled child and, 123-24
Swallowing problems. See Dysphagia
Swank, R. L., 99, 102, 106

T

Taste
  aging and, 227
  elderly and, 189
Taylor, R. L., 49
Team approach
  aging and, 239-40
  dysphagia and, 147-48
  feeding program and, 110, 119-20,
    121-25, 129-30, 130-35
  health promotion and, 291
  nutrition intervention and, 37
  SCI and, 159, 164
  social barriers and client and, 4
  TBI and, 181-82
  team composition and, 2
Telephone calls, nurse clinician and, 135
Temper tantrums, 49
Traumatic brain injury (TBI). See Brain
  injury (traumatic , TBI)
Tube feeding. See also Enteral feeding
  cerebral palsy and, 12-13, 40
  disabled child and, 116-17, 126-27,
    130-33
  TBI and, 183

U

Urinary incontinence. See Incontinence
Urinary tract infection, SCI and, 169
University of Michigan, 233

V

Vaginal infection, 93
Vegetarian diets, 251
Videofluoroscopic evaluation
  brain damage and, 193
  dysphagia and, 148, 152
Vitamin D., 17, 39, 127

osteomalacia and, 220
Vitamin and mineral supplementation,
  arthritis analysis and, 251-56
Vocational career services, Prader-Willi
  syndrome and, 60-61
Vomiting
  cerebral palsy and
    anticonvulsants and, 18
    feeding problems and, 11, 12

W

Warms, C., 288
Warren, J. L, 54
Webster, E. M., 246
Weight. See also Obesity
  aging and, 206, 208, 225
    CVI and, 215
    arthritis and, 264
  brain-damaged client and, purging
    and, 195
  cerebral palsy and, 21, 23, 30-31
  disabled child feeding program and, 113
  dysphagia and, 156
  muscular dystrophy and, 70, 72-74,
    75-76
  Prader-Willi syndrome and, 49-50, 51,
    56, 57
  SCI and, 163, 164
  TBI and, 180-81, 182
    loss of, 178-79, 183
Weiner, Norbert, 273
Weinstein, M. L., 22
Welch, P. K., 191
Wellness (defined), 285-86
Welsh, C. J. R., 248
Willi, H., 47
Wodarski, L. A., 50
Workplace, health promotion-disease
  prevention and, 289-90
World Health Organization (WHO), 285, 287
  definitions and, 2-3

Z

Ziff, M., 250
Zipf, W. B., 48

About the Editor

Deon J. Gines, RD, LDN, PhD, is an associate professor of nutrition and dietetics at Louisiana Tech University, Ruston, Louisiana. She is a consultant at the University Rehabilitation Center, which provides support for severely disabled students. Dr. Gines' teaching and research areas include rehabilitation and developmental disabilities.